EAST LOTHIAN

The Author

Malcolm Fife read geography at the University of Edinburgh and after graduating with a Master of Arts degree worked for Borders Regional Council, where he produced information packs for schools on the history and geography of the region. He later joined Edinburgh City Council, in the park-patrol section, and in this capacity also wrote a wide variety of information sheets and leaflets about the history and features of the city's parks. During his twenty years with the city council he also contributed to the very popular book, *Edinburgh's Green Heritage*. He has a strong connection with East Lothian: his mother owned a holiday cottage in the conservation village of Dirleton for many years and he has happy memories of summer days spent walking in the local countryside and on Yellowcraig beach. Fife is an accomplished photographer, specialising in industrial and maritime subjects, and has worked for major photographic libraries, book and magazine publishers and postcard companies. He is also a prolific author: his shorter work has appeared in the *Scots Magazine* and he has had books published on a wide variety of subjects, including Edinburgh's historic Nor loch, Calton jail and (another speciality) Scotland's aerodromes, several of which are located in East Lothian.

EAST LOTHIAN

Exploring a County

Malcolm Fife

Fort Publishing Ltd

First published in 2021 by Fort Publishing Ltd, Old Belmont House,
12 Robsland Avenue, Ayr, KA7 2RW

Typeset by 3btype.com
Cover design by Mark Blackadder
Front-cover photograph: Bass Rock, courtesy of Alamy.com
Back-cover photograph: Deciduous woodland in late autumn, East Linton.
Prestonkirk parish church is on the left, while in the background North Berwick
Law looms large (© Malcolm Fife)
Map of East Lothian by Helen Stirling

ISBN: 978-1905769-64-3

Printed by MBM Print SCS Ltd.

For my mother, Dona V. Fife

Contents

RELIGION

THE ECONOMY

DOMESTIC BUILDINGS

TRANSPORT

MISCELLANEOUS

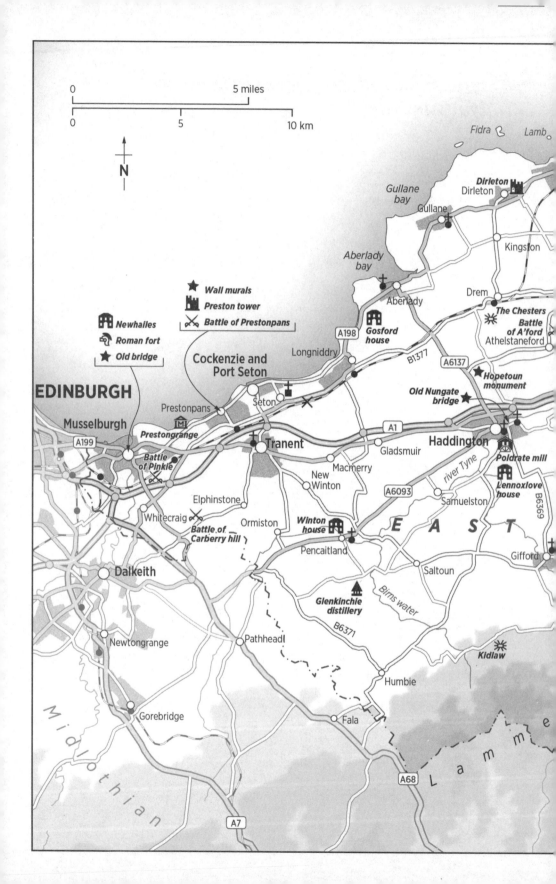

0   5 miles

0   5   10 km

N

Legend:
- ★ **Wall murals**
- 🏰 **Preston tower**
- ✕ **Battle of Prestonpans**
- 🏛 **Newhailes**
- 🛡 **Roman fort**
- ★ **Old bridge**

Fidra   *Lamb*

Gullane bay

Dirleton
Dirleton

Gullane

Kingston

Aberlady bay

Drem

Aberlady

The Chesters
Battle of A'ford
Athelstaneford

A198   **Gosford house**

Longniddry   B1377   A6137

★ **Hopetoun monument**

Cockenzie and Port Seton

Old Nungate bridge ★

EDINBURGH

Prestonpans

Seton

Haddington

Prestongrange

Musselburgh

A199

Battle of Pinkie

Tranent

Poldrate mill

Gladsmuir

river Tyne

Lennoxlove house

B6369

New Winton

Macmerry

A6093

Samuelston

E A S T

Elphinstone

Whitecraig

Battle of Carberry hill

Ormiston

Winton house

Pencaitland

Saltoun

Gifford

Dalkeith

Birns water

Glenkinchie distillery

Newtongrange

B6371

Kidlaw

Pathhead

Humbie

Gorebridge

Fala

Midlothian

A68

Lamme...

A7

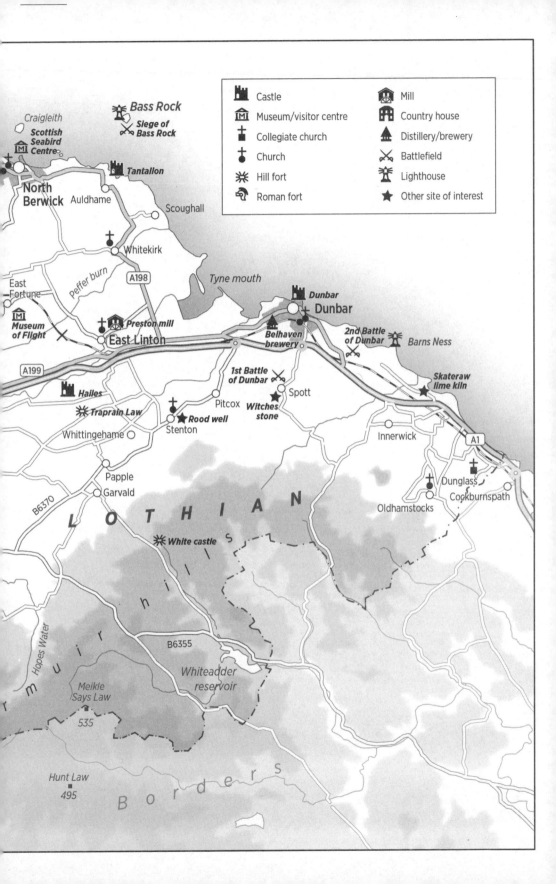

Craigleith
Bass Rock
Siege of Bass Rock
Scottish Seabird Centre
North Berwick
Tantallon
Auldhame
Scoughall
Whitekirk
Peffer burn
A198
East Fortune
Tyne mouth
Museum of Flight
Preston mill
East Linton
Dunbar
Dunbar
Belhaven brewery
2nd Battle of Dunbar
Barns Ness
A199
Halles
1st Battle of Dunbar
Spott
Skateraw lime kiln
Traprain Law
Pitcox
Witches stone
Rood well
Stenton
Whittingehame
Innerwick
A1
Papple
Garvald
Dunglass
Cockburnspath
Oldhamstocks
B6370
L O T H I A N
White castle
L a m m e r m u i r   h i l l s
Hopes Water
B6355
Whiteadder reservoir
Meikle Says Law
535
Hunt Law
495
B o r d e r s

Legend

Castle	Mill
Museum/visitor centre	Country house
Collegiate church	Distillery/brewery
Church	Battlefield
Hill fort	Lighthouse
Roman fort	Other site of interest

ENVIRONMENT

1. LANDSCAPE

Today's tranquil East Lothian landscape gives little indication of its violent and explosive origins 350 million years ago, when there was intense volcanic activity. Few other comparable places in Europe experienced as many eruptions as central Scotland. In East Lothian, prominent physical features such as the Bass Rock and North Berwick Law were formed from lava that solidified inside the vent of the volcano, which would have been many times the height of the current hill. In time, the elements eroded the surrounding slopes, leaving just the plug of very hard rock, which was once underground.

Not all lavas managed to reach the surface before they solidified and became rock. Some became trapped underground and formed dome-shaped masses of rock as they tried to escape upwards. Traprain Law, 700-feet high, was formed in this manner; resembling a beached whale, it is one of the most distinctive landforms in East Lothian. Other features formed in the same manner include Craigielaw Point, Gullane Point, Hummel Rocks, Black Rocks and the island of Fidra.

The Garleton hills near Athelstaneford are formed from volcanic rocks, like much of the other high ground in East Lothian.

The origin of the Lammermuir hills, which cover extensive tracts of East Lothian, predate the volcanic era, going back five hundred million years. The distinctive softer sandstone rocks that are found on the lower parts of East Lothian were formed after this, when the land experienced arid desert climates with sand dunes 370 million years ago.

Over the last two million years, Scotland has experienced several Ice Ages. The last Ice Age ended around fifteen thousand years ago and was responsible for moulding the landscape seen today. Glaciers up to a mile in height had buried East Lothian for thousands of years. The weight of the ice alone had a dramatic impact on the land, gouging out deep scars and removing entire hill tops. All traces of previous features, such as lochs and rivers, were removed. When the ice sheet began to melt, the Lammermuir hills became free of ice first, while the low-lying ground was still covered by stagnating glaciers. Huge amounts of water were channelled between the edge of the uplands and the remaining blocks of ice, carving deep valleys that form part of the present landscape.

In some cases, water followed the contours, while in others it cut deep gullies as it escaped underneath the remnants of the glaciers. Streams still flow along large valleys, which were carved out by flows of water hundreds of times their current size. Some of the most impressive examples of these actually cut across the present river watersheds. The northern slopes of the Lammermuir hills are scarred with deep valleys and gullies created during this dramatic period in geological history. Separating Deuchrie Dod from the Lammermuirs is a channel two hundred feet-deep, cut into solid rock.

When the glaciers finally retreated, they left behind deposits of sand and gravel along with large boulders that had been transported by the glaciers from other parts of Scotland. The movement of the ice also left its mark on the west side of North Berwick Law, which, in consequence, is rockier and steeper than the east side, where the glaciers deposited earth and gravel as low-lying ridges. Hills shaped by ice in this manner are known as 'craig and tail' features; another example is the rock on which Edinburgh castle stands.

The East Lothian coastline is one of great contrasts, with long sandy beaches punctuated in places by tall cliffs. The soft sedimentary limestone rocks immediately south of Dunbar create a low-lying coast adjoining gentle slopes of arable farmland. Tantallon castle, on the other hand, sits on a former volcanic vent, which gave rise to extremely

18

hard rock. No fewer than fourteen sites of former volcanic vents have been identified along the East Lothian coast. The Scottish Seabird Centre at North Berwick stands on a rocky promontory formed from three lava flows each 30-foot thick; the nearby paddling pool has been scooped out of rocks that originated from red volcanic ash.

The valley of the Hopes water in the Lammermuir hills was carved out at the end of the last Ice Age.

The main physical regions of East Lothian include the northern coastal plain, dominated by the isolated conical hill of North Berwick Law. The plain is generally under 250 feet in height. To the east, the low-lying ground continues in the form of the Dunbar plain and the narrow eastern coastal plain, which extends down the coast towards Berwickshire. In contrast, the southern edge of the county is occupied by the Lammermuir hills, with heights from 1,000–1,750 feet; they form a plateau that tilts south-eastwards. The summits of the hills are generally smooth and rounded, creating a uniform skyline when viewed at a distance. The Lammermuir foot platform, which consists of a mixture of low ridges and level ground, runs along the edge of its lower slopes at a height between 500 and 700 feet. It merges into the South Tyne plateau, which, like the Lammermuir hills extends across the country from the south-west to the north-east. The Tyne plateau is 400 to 500 feet in height, except where Traprain Law intrudes. Beyond it is the Tyne valley itself, separated from the northern plain by the Garleton hills, in which glacial drainage channels have formed numerous gulleys. On the west side, the ground descends into a smooth, flat-topped ridge extending to Tranent and beyond.

2. COASTLINE AND ISLANDS

The coast at Seacliff, with Bass Rock in the distance.

East Lothian's fertile coastal plain is rimmed with forty miles of golden beaches, punctuated by high cliffs and rocky outcrops. Around 350 million years ago, when there was intensive volcanic activity, East Lothian was part of a coastal plain covered by forests. There were numerous lagoons and it was not unlike the Gulf Coast of America today. Slow-flowing rivers meandered across the land with their waters heading towards a sea located to the north-east, where they formed large deltas.

In the last Ice Age, enormous quantities of water were locked up in the form of glaciers. The glaciers eventually melted, leaving the land still depressed by their weight. About 12,000 years ago the sea level of the Firth of Forth was over a hundred feet higher than it is now. As the land rose, the difference was reduced, although, five thousand years ago, waves were still breaking on the East Lothian coast some thirty feet higher up than those of today. Large areas of many of today's coastal towns and villages would still have been under water.

These variations in sea level have played a major role in shaping the coastline. Raised beaches are a relic of the higher sea levels, often forming a low-lying area just beyond the current shoreline. Waves have at some time carved sea caves into the base of cliffs, which now stand a few hundred yards from the shoreline. At Dunbar Winterfield golf course, the raised shore platform extends a thousand feet inland, terminating at the foot of a cliff. In the past, when Prestonpans had many market gardens, most of them were located on the raised beaches, which extended up as far as the 100-foot contour. Traces of the 75-foot raised beach can be found just north of Gullane.

Scotland's land mass continues to rise. As a result, at Aberlady bay, sand and mud have accumulated as the high-water mark has moved about 1,600 feet to the south-west over the last five thousand years. Most of what was shoreline on the east side of the bay is now dry land, erasing the once important harbour. It now is a place of refuge for birds, particularly in winter months when pink-footed geese reside here in their thousands. Skylarks and reed bunting also nest here annually, as do eider, shelduck, lapwing, lesser whitethroat and redshank.

Aberlady bay and Gullane have extensive areas of sand dunes that were once the sole preserve of rabbits, but have now in part been put to good use as links golf courses. As the sea level began to drop, large beaches were exposed. Sand from these was blown inland, sometimes obliterating raised beaches and platforms and forming the links areas along the coast. The movement of sand further inland was ended by the planting of vegetation to stabilise the dunes.

Between Musselburgh and Prestonpans, the coastline has been extensively altered by man. Large areas of land have been reclaimed from the Firth of Forth and protected behind concrete barriers. However, further to the east there remain extensive areas of broad sandy beaches,

The coast near Torness, with sea arch visible (*top*).

including the sands at Seton, Gosford and Gullane. Near North Berwick is Broad sands; to the east of the town the coast is more rugged, with rocky headlands in the vicinity of Tantallon castle. There are further large expanses of sand around Belhaven bay at Dunbar as well as between Seacliff and Tyninghame. Much of the coast to the south of Dunbar, as far south as Berwickshire, consists of rocky shore platforms and cliffs, punctuated by the occasional stretch of sand.

The coastline of East Lothian has a number of well-developed shore platforms, a flat rocky area between the shore and the sea, up to 1,640 feet wide. A small number of them were created around five thousand years ago, from which more modern platforms were fashioned by the sea. The cliffs of East Lothian also have a complex history, being a product of current erosion by the sea as well as being subject to similar activity in the past when the sea levels were at a different height.

East Lothian has a small number of islands. One is **Bass Rock**, a Scottish landmark, just over a mile off the coast. The origin of its name is unclear. It possibly comes from a man named Bass, mentioned in the *Chronicles of the Scots and Picts*. In AD 952, a naval battle was fought between the Scots and the Vikings, close to Bass Rock, the invaders being defeated. The island is a volcanic plug of phonolite rock of some

22

nineteen acres; it is a similar feature to North Berwick Law, which stands on the shore. The cliffs rise vertically out of the sea to a height of just over 350 feet, so that despite being little more than a mile in circumference, it can be seen from a distance. Its surface slopes steeply down on the south side in a series of three terraces towards the only landing place. The most remarkable natural feature of the Bass Rock is a huge cavern that extends right through the base, from west to east. It is 560 feet long, and, in places, 30 feet high, with the sea flowing through it.

In the Middle Ages, the Rock had a castle, later used as a government fort and prison. The most recent structure is the lighthouse, which, somewhat unusually, is located not at the summit but on the southern slope, a short distance above the sea.

Somewhat closer to the shore is **Craigleith island**. Its name possibly comes from the Gaelic *liath*, meaning grey or greyness. Its highest point is 168 feet above sea level, and it is steep on all sides. Although this description of it was written in 1839, much of it still holds true: 'Directly opposite to the town of North Berwick, a mile from the shore, is an island, about a mile in circumference, called Craigleith. It is a bare rock, inhabited only by rabbits and sea-fowl. The jackdaws are in immense numbers and it is a favourite residence of the Tommy Norrie, alias the Coulterneb or Puffin.'

Lamb island is even smaller, lying to the west of Craigleith and half a mile from the coast. Its highest point is only 79 feet above sea level. It is flanked by two rocky skerries, one known as North Dog and the other as the South Dog. Like Craigleith, it has little vegetation. In 2009, magician Uri Geller purchased the island because, in his words, 'This island has links not only to the pyramids but to King Arthur, King Robert the Bruce and to the Ancient Kings of Ireland too.' Rather a tall claim for a small, insignificant rock in the sea, little more than three hundred feet in length.

At the western end of this chain of islands is **Fidra**, far and away the biggest of the three. It has been suggested that its name is derived from old Norse, meaning 'feather island'. Fidra rises to 113 feet above the sea and consists of two rocky outcrops connected by a natural causeway. Like the other islands, its rocks are volcanic in origin, dating back 335 million years. There is a large, natural arch that cuts through the north cliffs, sometimes referred to as 'The Lady of Fidra', as it is said to resemble a veiled female figure when viewed from a certain point against a cloudy sky. At high water, the sea flows under the arch. In the twelfth century, the church of St Nicholas was built on the island, the north wall of which is extant. There is also a natural feature called Castle Tarbet, a 40-foot, flat-topped column of rock that rises sheer from the sea on three sides, not unlike the Giant's Causeway; it may owe its name to a man-made fortification once built on it.

Literary giant Robert Louis Stevenson frequently visited East Lothian and it is thought that Fidra may have been the inspiration for his novel, *Treasure Island*. No pirates or any other human beings live on it today. The last residents were the lighthouse keepers who left when the light was automated towards the end of the twentieth century. Like the other islands off the coast of East Lothian, it is now the sole preserve of seabirds.

3. RIVERS, STREAMS AND WELLS

The upland areas of East Lothian are dissected by numerous valleys and gullies. It is not unusual to find a small stream flowing through a wide valley, which it could not possibly have created itself. At the end of the last Ice Age, when the glaciers covering East Lothian began to melt, huge quantities of water were released. Enormous torrents, many times the size of the present rivers, carved out large channels as they flowed to the sea. The legacy of these forces is valleys, some completely dry, which are now features of the landscape around Garvald and along the northern edge of the Lammermuir hills.

There are a great many streams in this upland area. Some run down the northern slopes to swell the waters of the Tyne; others flow into the Biel water. A number of other short, fast-flowing streams, including the Thornton, Oldhamstocks and Dunglass burn, flow in a north-easterly direction from the Lammermuirs crossing the narrow coastal plain south of Dunbar before flowing into the North Sea.

The **Tyne** is East Lothian's main watercourse, twenty-eight miles long; it rises near Tynehead in the Moorfoot hills, Midlothian. The name 'tyne' is possibly derived from *tin*, the Celtic word for river.

Streams flowing down the northern slopes of the Lammermuir hills swell its waters. Two of its most significant tributaries are the Birns water, which enters it near Pencaitland, and Colstoun water, which confluence is a short distance west of Haddington. The headwater of the latter is the Hopes water, after which the stream crosses the northern edge of the Lammermuirs in a deep ice-worn depression, unlike any other valley in East Lothian.

The Tyne at Knowes mill on a spring day.

The Tyne flows the length of the coastal plain before entering the sea not far from Dunbar. At East Linton it encounters an outcrop of intrusive igneous rock, which hinders its smooth flow. The river drops about twenty feet as it cascades over a natural barrier called the Lynn, from which the village name is derived. In 1835 the lower reaches of the Tyne contained large trout, eel, flounder and many small salmon. Unfortunately, at the end of the eighteenth, or in the early-nineteenth, century, an unsuccessful attempt was made to create a channel through the rocks to encourage salmon to venture further upstream.

On the north bank of the Tyne there are few streams of any size, due to the low rainfall and the geology of the coastal plain. The rocks here are more porous than those of the Lammermuir hills. The main watercourse on the northern plain is the **Peffer burn**; the name comes from the Welsh *pefr* (pure or radiant). Its source are ponds located three miles south of North Berwick. It flows in a westerly direction for 5.5 miles, flowing into the sea at Aberlady bay. It has two tributaries both called Mill burn – the first flowing into it about a mile south-east of Fenton Barns and the other a similar distance south of Gullane.

Confusingly, there is also a **second Peffer burn**, two miles south of the other. It rises close to the Garleton hills and flows in the opposite direction before turning north-east towards Whitekirk and entering the North Sea near Scoughall. Around twelve East Lothian streams and rivers flow directly into the North Sea, among the largest being the Tyne and the Biel water. The latter starts life as the Papana burn on Moss Law in the Lammermuir hills; it later becomes the Whittingehame water, before flowing into the sea at Belhaven as the Biel water.

A small number of watercourses in East Lothian do not flow north into the Tyne or North Sea. The Whiteadder, which also has its source in the Lammermuir hills, flows south into the Tweed basin, being fed by the tributaries Monynut, Bothwell and Faseny waters. Its course has been obstructed to form a reservoir which bears its name. Although the **river Esk** has a significant flow of water, it passes through East Lothian only in its final stages at Inveresk and Musselburgh. The name Esk comes from *isca*, meaning water. Not too far away is Cuthill, a suburb of Prestonpans. According to local tradition, a small stream known as the Red burn once ran on the west side of Cuthill village, before it entered the sea. Mining activity in the area is said to have caused subsidence, resulting in the stream changing its course and cutting the small hill on which the settlement stood into two parts. The village derived its name, 'Cut-Hill', from this event.

Although East Lothian does not receive significant rainfall, its low-lying areas are prone to flooding. The northern slopes of the Lammermuir hills have shallow soils and little vegetation, allowing rainwater to run rapidly down the slopes and into tributaries that feed the Tyne, causing it to rise rapidly. During its history, Haddington in particularly has suffered from several devastating floods. It is vulnerable as it stands on a low-lying plain only a few feet above the Tyne. In September 1358:

The Esk near Whitecraig. A short distance away it is bridged by the A1.

. . . there happened a most extraordinary inundation, the rivers swollen by excessive rain, rose above their banks and swept away many villages, houses and bridges and many persons lost their lives whilst endeavouring to save their property, not only cattle but tall oaks and other large trees were torn up by the roots and carried off to the sea. As it approached the Abbey of Haddington a nun snatched up the statue of the Virgin and threatened to throw it into the water, unless Mary protected her Abbey from inundation. At that moment the river retired and gradually subsided within its limits.

Another devastating flood took place in 1421. Many houses were damaged in Haddington and people travelled to church in a large boat. On 4 October 1775, the town suffered from a further immersion when the Tyne rose 17 feet in less than an hour, flooding more than half the town and devastating the suburb of Nungate. The elegant Chinese Bridge, built of wood some fifteen years earlier, was swept away, as was a mill. Many residents fled to the safety of the nearby fields; fortunately, there was no loss of life. The probable cause was a couple of hours of torrential rain that fell on part of the Lammermuir hills and which was funnelled downstream in the Colstoun water, the water level in the upper reaches of the Tyne being little affected.

There were floods in 1928 and 1953, but the worst was in 1948.

August started with heavy rain, nearly five inches falling in the Haddington area by the eighth of the month. Over the next five days, a further five inches fell, most of which occurred on the thirteenth. Crops were flattened and small bridges swept away. Biel water flooded low-lying land around West Barns and great damage occurred along the banks of the Whiteadder water extending into Berwickshire. Haddington suffered one of its worst floods. With the ground saturated, the Tyne overflowed its banks, flooding some 450 houses. At its peak it was 10 feet above its normal level, inundating an area three-quarters of a mile wide, extending from the town house in the west to the gates of Amisfield park in the east. When the waters receded, a foot of mud was left in some places. This momentous event is recorded on a plaque located at the junction of High Street and Sidegate, where the water rose six-feet-two-inches above the pavement. About six yards further along the Sidegate there is another plaque to the 1775 flood, which states that 'on the fourth day of October 1775 the river Tyne at three o'clock afternoon rose to this plate'.

The Tyne nearly claimed the life of one of Scotland's monarchs. In 1595, James VI fell into the river from his horse while chasing Francis Stewart, a former associate. Weighed down by heavy armour, James was in danger of drowning when his escort managed to haul him out. Less fortunate was Robert Broun, who in 1703 was on his way back from Edinburgh with his two sons. They were caught in a flash flood and swept to their deaths in the Coulston water.

There are at least two wells named after St Baldred in East Lothian. One of them can be found a short distance to the south of Prestonkirk church, East Linton, next to the Tyne. By far and away the most famous holy well in East Lothian was located a short distance to the south of Whitekirk church. According to legend, Marjorie Comyn, countess of Dunbar, fled Dunbar castle to avoid capture by the English during their invasion at the end of the thirteenth century. While embarking for Fife in a boat, she sustained a serious injury. The winds prevented her party from crossing the Firth of Forth and they were forced to put ashore near Whitekirk, or Fairknowe as it was then called. While she was praying to the Virgin Mary, a hermit approached and informed her that, if she had faith to drink from the holy well, she would find relief. She followed his advice and, on drinking its waters, her bruises were healed:

> This miracle she made known to Andrew de Foreman, Prior of Coldingham, and in the year following she built a chapel and chantry in honour of our Lady

and endowed it with 10 merks a year for ever. The number of miracles at this
well was so great that in 1309, John Abernethy, with the assistance of the monks
at Melrose, procured a shrine to be erected and dedicated to the Holy Mother.

In 1413, no fewer than 15,653 people from many countries visited
Whitekirk church and its holy well. Unfortunately, the well disappeared
around 1830 when agriculture improvements were carried out and the
drainage improved.

In the sixteenth century, many pilgrims visited the holy well at
Loretto, Musselburgh. The construction of the chapel could not begin
until a stone, on which the Angel Gabriel was said to have stood, was
transported from Loretto in Italy.

The interesting Rood well stands by the road at the east edge of
Stenton village. Unlike most of its counterparts, which have been
reclaimed by nature, the wellhead is covered by a circular stone
structure, crowned by an apex in the form of a cardinal's hat. The well
is thought to date from the fourteenth century, possibly created by the
monks of Melrose, who had lands here. According to tradition, the
tenure of the Biel estate, on which the well was situated, depended on
its owner keeping the stone cap in good repair.

A few miles to the east, in a field next to the village of Spott, is St
John's well, which may date back to 1300 and allegedly had connections
with the Knights Templars who, according to tradition, held lands
around Spott and may even have had a hospital in Standing Stone field.
A 1933 letter in a local newspaper by Revd Lothian Gray, minister for
the village, relates the following:

> St John's Holy Well is situated 200 yards below Spott Kirk and in medieval
> times was visited by not hundreds but thousands of pilgrims. There is a
> passageway inside, round which the pilgrims passed and from under their feet
> gushed a constant stream of pure, cold water the source of which always
> remained unknown.

Spott valley is on a fault line and water comes to the surface at several
locations. In 1767, pipes were laid from the well to supply Dunbar
with water, two miles away. By 2004, this well had been almost
completely reclaimed by nature, but over the course of the following
year the silt had been removed and the entrance restored. There is a
footpath to the well entrance. There were many other wells in East
Lothian with possible healing properties. For example, the waters from
Kisthill well, in the parish of Spott, was reputed to cure scurvy.

In a field to the east of Aberlady, near Luffness house, is a tall square tower resembling a folly. It is actually a water tower constructed in the early-nineteenth century. There are stone drinking basins on the external walls at ground level. In the late-nineteenth century, local wells were still the source of East Linton's water supply. A good example of a working public fountain can be found in Haddington town centre at Court Street; it was converted in 1998 from a non-operational drinking fountain erected in 1924 to an ornamental fountain.

Although water may not be revered as much as in the past, it still is an attraction. In the square at East Linton stands a handsome cast-iron fountain, erected in 1882. It was a gift from a former resident of the village, John Drysdale, who had emigrated to Argentina, where he had become a wealthy cattle owner. The fountain was cast by George Smith and Co. at the Sun foundry, Glasgow. It stands on the site of a well, which, until 1881, supplied residents with water.

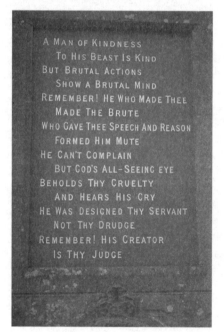

In contrast to the prominently displayed fountain at East Linton, there is a memorial drinking fountain and horse trough on the edge of a minor road a short distance to the west of Innerwick. It was commissioned by Richard Hunter of Thurston to comme-morate Queen Victoria's golden jubilee in 1887. There is a plaque set above the trough, with words of advice not to be cruel to beasts of burden (*photo on left*). Horses no longer drink at the trough these days, which was once fed by a spring, but now is sometimes filled with flowers.

4. LOCHS AND PONDS

Large, natural lochs are almost absent from East Lothian. Danskine loch is probably the largest; two miles south-east of Gifford, it is a third of a mile long, little more than a large pond. Today it is used for carp fishing. There is a circular footpath around it.

The *Blaeu Atlas of Scotland*, published 1654, depicts a number of small lochs in East Lothian that have long since vanished. They included two shallow, marshy lochs on low-lying ground to the south of Gladsmuir. At one time there was a hamlet called Gladesmoore loch nearby. The now vanished Lochend house took its name from the great loch of Dunbar, which was drained in the seventeenth century. Lochhill farm, on the Longniddry–Ballencrieff road, preserves the memory of a small loch that once existed in its vicinity. By the time the *Military Survey of Scotland* was completed in 1755, these lochs had disappeared, possibly drained as a result of agricultural improvements. A small loch is shown on one of their maps, on low-lying ground to the south-east of Dirleton. In a field on Phantassie farm, East Linton, there was once a small loch that supplied the local distillery with water. In the first half of the nineteenth century, this enterprise employed fifty people and produced half-a-million gallons of whisky annually, sold as far away as London.

During the Victorian era, many small lochs were artificially created by landowners as features in the grounds of large country houses. The loch at Balgone house near North Berwick, originally a mile in length, was created to drain marshy ground. It can be seen from the John Muir Way, which passes close by. Gosford house has a large water feature in its gardens, equal to that found anywhere in Scotland.

Smeaton mansion house, near East Linton (demolished in the 1950s), has been survived by its ornamental lake. Although on a private estate, there is a footpath that runs around this feature. It was a popular venue for curling in Victorian times, along with ponds at other country houses including Balgone, Johnstounburn, Stevenson, Yester and Whittingehame. The large pond at Smeaton is unusually called a lake, not a loch. Another example in East Lothian is Pressmennan lake, just south of Stenton, constructed as a reservoir in 1819. It is nearly 1.5 miles long and three hundred yards wide. At one time it was the largest body of fresh water in East Lothian. It occupies a deep, narrow valley excavated by a powerful stream of water at the end of the last Ice Age.

The woodland in the surrounding valley was cut down in 1623 by a servant of Isobel Hepburn, the mother of the owner. The Privy Council halted the felling, arguing that the woods were home for deer for the king's sport. The lake is now open to the public via walkways in surrounding woodland.

For most of their history the towns and villages of East Lothian relied on local streams and wells for water. Demand grew with the increasing population, meaning water had to be transported from farther away. Donolly reservoir (built in 1886) was among the first of the small reservoirs constructed on the northern slopes of the Lammermuir hills. It occupies a glacial-melt water channel and is dammed at both ends. Thorters reservoir, a mile south-east of Garvald, was completed in 1900; it extends to fourteen acres, the dam composed of an earthen embankment. It was followed by Lammerloch, near Kidlaw in 1905 and Stobshiel in 1914. All of these were small-scale projects, but, in the interwar years, Hopes, the first of two large reservoirs, was established. Stone from the demolished Calton jail in Edinburgh was employed in its construction; previously East Lothian's reservoirs had been built of brick. Opened in 1935, few people are aware of its existence, as it is almost completely encircled by some of the highest slopes in the Lammermuir hills. A large, grass-covered dam, blending into the surrounding landscape, spans the valley. There is an inscription on the stonework stating: 'The arch of this bridge and the walls of this waterworks which it spans were brought from the Calton Jail Edinburgh upon its demolition 1930–31.'

In the flood of 1948, the reservoirs of Thorters, Stobshiel and Spott were breached. The latter was abandoned and the valley allowed to revert to its original state. In the 1950s, the demand for water was still growing, both for domestic and industrial use, as well as for agriculture and golf courses. The planned Cockenzie power station would place a further burden on the water supply, requiring 650,000 gallons of water per day for steam production. To meet this demand, it was decided to build a new reservoir on top of the Lammermuir hills. This required damming the Whiteadder water with a structure 660 feet long and 90 feet high. Work began in 1964 and was completed in 1969, creating by far the largest body of fresh water in East Lothian at just under three hundred acres. Unlike the other reservoirs, it involved the relocation of a small community with the demolition of Millkowe farm and the local school, which stood on ground that was eventually flooded.

Whiteadder reservoir, Lammermuir hills, pictured in autumn.

With low rainfall and sandy soils, many farms supplement their water supply by having their own irrigation ponds. Sometimes these are fed by artesian wells, while others collect surface water.

A series of ponds have been created at the historic site of Markle, near East Linton, catering for trout fishermen. New golf courses, like Archerfield, incorporate water features. On the coast between Musselburgh and Prestonpans, the ash from coal-fired Cockenzie power station has been used over several decades to reclaim land from the Firth of Forth. A concrete seawall was built offshore and slurry pumped into the area between it. As the ash dried it was landscaped and turned into reclaimed land covering 330 acres; it has been planted with grass and trees and turned into a park and nature reserve. Around six large shallow pools lined with clay have been created a short distance to the north-east of Musselburgh racecourse. They attract many species of wading birds and wildfowl. Rare species noted here include the royal tern, western sandpiper, American golden plover and citrine wagtail.

5. CLIMATE

The fertile soils and benign climate of East Lothian have made it one of the leading farming areas in Scotland. Being on the east coast, it is sheltered from the prevailing south-west winds, which are moderated by the intervening hills and undulating ground across the breadth of Scotland.

The summits of the Lammermuir hills are subjected to the highest wind speeds in the county, hence their attraction for wind farms. The south-east wind often brings storms and gales, usually confined to autumn and winter months. More frequent, particularly in the spring, are winds from the east and north-east, which bring periods of cold weather often accompanied by cloud.

In 1698, there was an 'unkindly cold and winter-like spring', which caused a famine as well as the death of large numbers of sheep and cattle. At the time it was considered a divine punishment for drunkenness and Sabbath-breaking. The synod of Lothian and Tweeddale ordered a fast and 'solomn humiliation' for 17 May; an edict on the same date banned the export of food. These actions did little to ameliorate the situation, with the cold weather causing untold hardship for local people.

In the course of a year there are about 175 days on which rain falls on the coastal plain of East Lothian, but it has the distinction of being one of the driest areas of Scotland, along with St Andrews and the Moray Firth. The clouds carried on the south-west winds from the Atlantic have deposited much of their moisture on Ireland and the west coast of Scotland before they arrive. Dunbar gets around 22 inches of rain a year, whereas some locations on the other side of the country receive four times that amount. February to June are among the driest months; July, August and October the wettest.

The Lammermuir hills have a similar amount of rain to the rest of the central lowlands. Unlike most of the British Isles, East Lothian has its heaviest rain – as heavy showers and sometimes thunderstorms – in July and August. In June 2009 sixteen bullocks were killed by a lightning strike near Pencaitland. A more serious incident took place at Gladsmuir in July 1789, when the schoolhouse was struck by lightning during a thunderstorm, demolishing its roof; two boys perished in the school ruins.

In the Lammermuir hills, autumn rains are usually followed by fairly heavy winter rains through to January. The summits receive almost twice

Rain shower over Gullane.

as much precipitation as the low-lying areas, but not usually more than forty inches. When the east wind blows, the Lammermuirs are prone to snowstorms, which sometimes block roads. Even a small difference in altitude can make a great difference in the duration of lying snow. Dunbar experiences snow on about five days per year, but in the upland areas it can be thirty days or so and on the highest parts even more. Haddington and the neighbouring countryside can sometimes be under a few inches of snow, while there is none on the coast.

East Lothian is as far north as the Canadian prairies and the Russian steppes, but does not experience either their extremely cold winters or hot summers; close proximity to the sea acts as a moderating influence. The mean daily maximum temperature for the county in July is 17.5 °C, but inland Scotland has temperatures around 2 °C higher. The lack of exceptionally warm days in East Lothian allows golf to be played in reasonable comfort and there are few other areas in Scotland that experience as much sunshine. Dunbar has the highest amount of sunshine in Scotland and the fourth highest in the United Kingdom; in June it averages six hours per day, dropping to just below two hours in January. Winter in East Lothian is unusually mild for Scotland, with a daily temperature of around 7 °C and a night temperature about 2 °C.

In summer, the daytime temperatures are around 18.8°C, dipping to 11.4°C at night. Temperature extremes recorded at Dunbar include a sweltering 31°C in August 1990 and a freezing minus 12°C in January 1982. Often Edinburgh can lie under extensive layers of cloud while there are blue skies over East Lothian, only a few miles away.

Low-lying areas and valleys are more susceptible to frost than those on the coast; East Linton experiences twice as many frosty days as Dunbar. The average number of days with air frost on the coast does not reach forty a year but is over ninety per year on the upper Lammermuir hills. Ground frost is far more frequent than air frost and can occur on as many as 150 days per year on the tops of the upland area. East Lothian suffers from a coastal fog known as the haar; the wind blowing from the east in the spring and summer crosses the cool North Sea, so a fog is formed. Sometimes it extends only a mile or two inland and often appears in the late afternoon. While visibility on the coast can be reduced to a few hundred yards, the rest of East Lothian can be bathed in sunshine. Very occasionally, the haar extends across the central belt of Scotland as far as Glasgow and can persist for several days.

A haar engulfs North Berwick Law.

Other factors can cause fogs, including cold, dense air sinking into low-lying valleys. During winter months on frosty days, fog can form at the bottom of the Tyne valley. In 1837, the minister for Morham parish,

Revd James Forsyth, observed that on spring or autumn mornings the local inhabitants, 'were enjoying bright and pure sunshine, while Haddington and the vale of the Tyne lie beneath their eye buried in dense fog'.

6. TREES AND WOODLAND

When the glaciers retreated the first species of trees to colonise the land were birch, juniper, hazel and Scots pine. They were followed by oak but the Scots pine later disappeared from lowland Scotland, possibly due to competition with broadleaved trees. Although the clearing of woodland for agricultural purposes started before the Romans, some tracts of large woodland survived into the medieval period. There is mention of a substantial forest around Roslin, south of Edinburgh, inhabited by large numbers of deer and other wild beasts. Saltcoats, in Dirleton parish, was said to contain a large area of woodland, in which there were wild boars. Further evidence also comes with an account of the great flood of Haddington of 1358, which records that many large oaks were swept away.

However, by end of the Middle Ages most natural woodland had been cleared. In the sixteenth century the county was producing a surplus of barley, which was taken to Edinburgh for malting. The landscape would have been almost totally open and some early travellers noted the absence of trees. In 1598, Fynes Moryson wrote: 'I rode to Edenborrow seated in Lodonay [Lothian], the most civill [sic] region of Scotland being hiley and fruitful of corne but having little or no wood.'

Bleau's map, compiled around the same time, shows only a few woods remaining, notably in the vicinity of Keith, Humbie, Ormiston and Winton. Most trees in the landscape were either in the grounds of country houses and mansions or in the steep valleys on the Lammermuir hills; the latter generally were the remnants of ancient forest. As the threat of conflict declined, the gentry abandoned their castles and tower houses for the comfort of new country houses. They also developed an interest in adorning their grounds. In the opening years of the eighteenth century, the Hays of Yester were among the first to plant trees around their residence for ornamental purposes. In 1722 John Macky wrote: 'The palace of Yester stands in the middle of the best planted park I ever saw. The park walls are about eight miles in circumference and I dare venture to say, there is a million of full-grown trees in it. In short, it's larger, as well walled and more regularly planted than Richmond in Surrey.'

Non-native Scottish tree species, including beech and sycamore, were also introduced around this time. The sixth earl of Haddington, at his wife's instigation, established Binning wood, a short distance to the north of their residence, Tyninghame house. Work began in 1707. The earl eventually planted around eight hundred acres of woodland, areas of which extended almost down to the sea. Over the next hundred years, many of the mature oaks and larches were eventually felled to provide timber for shipbuilding. It was the first large commercial plantation in the Lothians and was laid out on a barren moor composed of sandy soils. There was initially much scepticism that trees would grow on this ground. The earl first became interested in trees when he was planting shelter belts around Tyninghame house to protect it from

Spring sunlight sparkles through a group of beech trees, Binning wood, near Tyninghame.

the cold east winds, but his involvement did not stop at planting. He wrote a handbook entitled *Forest Trees, Some Directions about Raising Forest Trees*, published posthumously in 1761.

In the first half of the eighteenth century there were around seventy significant woods in East Lothian; some were exploited on a commercial basis and the timber sold locally. The construction of the New Town in Edinburgh required large quantities of softwood, but almost all of it came from foreign sources. A record of wood sales at Saltoun, which had large tracts of woodlands in its vicinity, shows that most of it was used on the estate itself or by neighbouring tenants and wrights. The rest went to places like Aberlady, Gladsmuir and Prestonpans. A heel-maker in Cockenzie purchased eight alders, the wood for this tree being relatively immune to dampness. In 1757, thirty-two loads of bark from Saltoun were purchased by a tannery in Tranent, with a similar number the following year.

Woods were often looked after by foresters, or 'fosters' as they were known. As early as 1654 there is mention of Lord Hay of Yester employing a man to look after his woods at Snawdone. He received two bolls of oatmeal, a shilling sterling and half the fines levied in the Sheriff Court for every person he brought to book for cutting down or destroying trees.

In the late-eighteenth century, the parish of Pencaitland had 155 acres of what was said to be natural wood consisting of oak and birch, with 191 further acres planted with 'forest trees'. On a less positive note, the young trees on the estate of Fountainhall were suffering from the depredations of squirrels, which had been introduced at Dalkeith a few years earlier and had spread to this part of East Lothian. They had caused considerable damage to the elms and to a lesser extent the Scotch firs.

Much of the coastal plain is devoted to agriculture, with land at a premium. Woods today can be found on the steep river banks, particularly around Innerwick and Dunglass. The greatest concentrations are on the edge of the rich farmland, where the land gradually rises towards the Lammermuir hills. There are extensive tracts south of Haddington and around Gifford. Further west, the river valleys to the south of Pencaitland are adorned by woods and forests. As the altitude increases, so the number of trees decreases. Almost all the higher parts of the Lammermuir hills are covered by heather with trees found only in the sheltered valleys and around Whiteadder reservoir.

The two world wars caused further depletion, as timber could not be easily imported and had to be obtained from local sources. Binning wood was clear-felled in the Second World War, its wood being used in the manufacture of De Havilland Mosquito fighter-bombers. It was replanted in the 1950s to the same plan as the original, with a high proportion of oak and beech. Saltoun Big Wood was another casualty, but it too has been restored. Sadly, many of the old hawthorn hedges were uprooted in the mid-twentieth century for agricultural improvements.

By the end of the twentieth century the woodland coverage of East Lothian had increased to just under 8 per cent, but only about 1 per cent was native species. On the banks of Pressmennan lake, there are a number of old oaks, which represent the remnants of the original woodland that once covered the whole county. Timber is still commercially exploited here and in other woods in East Lothian. In 2020, two large sawmills still operate in the western part of the county: one at Petersmuir, specialising in processing larger and longer logs not suitable for other mills; the other at Windymains, concentrating on timber for fencing. In past centuries, waterwheels on the banks of the Humbie water provided power for this industry.

Between 1961 and 1981, Sitka spruce was planted extensively on the slopes of the Lammermuir hills. At the same time, forested areas took on an increasingly important conservation and recreational role. They serve as havens for wildlife in a heavily farmed landscape and many are accessible by foot.

The Scottish Wildlife Trust manages a number of small woods on the north-eastern edge of the Lammermuir hills. Brock wood, a short distance south-west of Spott, is composed of a mixture of native oak, ash and alder as well as some conifers; it covers 42 acres on the banks of Brock burn. The valley bottom once contained a small reservoir. In 1948 the dam gave way in a flood and was abandoned. The wood is now home to numerous plant species, including the rare hoary plantain and early dog violet.

The 154-acre Woodhall Dean is another wood owned by Scottish Wildlife Trust. It lies 1.5 miles to the south of Spott and has the largest area of genetically pure sessile oaks in the east of Scotland. The trees cling to the slopes of two steep valleys that extend upwards into the Lammermuir hills. These gorge woodlands are the best remains of ancient woodlands in East Lothian and Berwickshire. In the early-twenty-first century, native woodland made up 20 per cent of the county total. A short distance to the west, the Woodland Trust has a 210-acre site on the southern edge of Pressmennan lake. It is about a mile south of Stenton on the northern slopes of Deuchrie Dod; access is along a narrow track. From the fifteenth century its trees were in demand for the building of ships at Leith. In the eighteenth century, bark from here was used in the tanning industry.

At Longyester, south of Gifford, the privately owned 100-acre Blinkbonny wood offers walks among mature pine and broadleaf trees. Moving away from the edge of the Lammermuir hills, Saltoun Big Wood (or 'Saltoun Forest' as it is shown on the OS maps) stands on the bank of the Birns water, close to where it meets the Humbie water. It is close to East Saltoun village and is one of the biggest blocks of woodland in the county; dissected by footpaths, most of its trees are conifers. Around three miles to the north-west is Pencaitland. Close by is Winton house and its extensive grounds covering some 208 acres. Parts are covered with old deciduous woodland, which can be explored using its twelve miles of paths.

Due to intensive farming, there are few large tracts of trees in the centre of East Lothian. One exception can be found a short distance to the south of Gladsmuir village: Butterdean wood stands on what was once a marsh and the ground is still waterlogged in winter; birch and ash occupy the dampest part of the site. There is also an area of willow trees on the south edge of the wood, which is particularly unusual. An added attraction are four imaginative metal sculptures next to the footpaths, including a Celtic wild boar and a wood wasp. The 105-acre forest is managed by the Woodland Trust.

There is a small area of woodland underneath the Hopetoun monument on the Garleton hills to the north of Haddington. The trees are an obvious feature as they crown the steep slopes overlooking the neighbouring fields. There is a good mixture of mature species including beech, oak, birch, ash, hawthorn, elder, Scots pine and sycamore. Some of the trees are of a considerable age. The footpath to the Hopetoun monument snakes its way up through the woodland.

By contrast the wood at Thornton Glen is hidden away in a deep valley. In an area of rolling fields of farmland on the coastal plain, the Thornton burn has cut a deep, narrow gorge on its journey to the North Sea. Most the trees here are ash and elm, which cling to the steep slopes. The remains of Innerwick castle (private property) guards the head of the nature reserve, which is managed by Scottish Wildlife Trust. There is a narrow footpath along the side of the glen but in places there are steep drops. It can be accessed at the hamlet of Crowhill, a short distance to the west of Thorntonloch.

Further up the coast there are extensive tracts of woodland at Tyninghame. To reach the beach from the car park at Tyninghame Links involves a fifteen-minute walk, much of it through woodland consisting both of deciduous and conifer trees. Further inland lies the famous Binning wood, easily accessible from the Whitekirk–North Berwick road. Covering three hundred acres, it is one of the largest woods in East Lothian. Most of the trees were planted just after the end of the Second World War; they are generally conifers, but there is also a 10-acre beech plantation. Within the woods are several circular clearings with walks radiating from them, including the Bruce's circle. There are links to Newbyth wood, which is found on its western margin; it extends across a further 139 acres and has been recently planted with native species.

At North Berwick there is a woodland walk along the Glen on the eastern edge of the town. It extends to twelve acres and is composed of beech, oak, elm and sycamore. Further along the coast at Yellow Craig, near Dirleton, fringing the beach and the sand dunes, is an area of woodland that includes old beeches and sycamores from the late-nineteenth century. The majority of trees are more recent, being planted in 1960. There is a large variety of both conifers and deciduous species including ash, elm, Corsican pine, Scots pine, silver birch, western hemlock and Norway spruce. Such areas of woodland next to the coast were usually planted to stabilise the sand and prevent it from drifting inland.

East Lothian also possesses one of Scotland's more remarkable trees – the ancient yew tree at Ormiston. One of the largest of its type in Scotland, the huge central trunk measures 23 feet in girth. By the fifteenth century, the yew was recognized as a local landmark. John Knox is reputed to have preached his early sermons within the secluded interior of the yew's evergreen canopy. It is difficult to locate, standing close to the site of Ormiston hall, around a mile to the south of Ormiston village. A track that leads in the general direction of the tree starts near the lodge of Ormiston hall, some 450 feet west of the junction of the A6093 and B6371.

7. WILDLIFE

With its diverse range of habitats ranging from rocky islands to upland moorland, East Lothian has abundant wildlife, but it comes as a surprise that this small Scottish county possesses one of the twelve wildlife wonders of the world, according to naturalist Sir David Attenborough.

Attenborough is referring to the colony of gannets on the Bass Rock, which by 2010 was the largest in the world. With a wingspan of more than 6 feet, the gannet can live past thirty and is Britain's largest seabird. The colony here has long attracted the attention of travellers. In the past, the gannet was often referred to as the 'solan goose'. In 1535, Peder Wave, a diplomat, was on a mission to Scotland and anchored under the Bass Rock. In his diary he records:

> We saw a fortified place called Basth [Bass Rock], situated on an immense rock. There are found birds which the Scots call gannets, of white colour, but mixed with black and in such multitudes that they could not be easily estimated. From the feathers and fishes which these birds carry on to the rock the commander of the fort is said to be able to collect an annual sum amounting to 400 gold pieces.

In 1548, the French dispatched an army to Scotland in an attempt to dislodge the English garrisons stationed there. Jean de Beaugué, a friend of D' Esse (André de Montalembert) who led the force, said of the Bass Rock:

> The place where they made their first attempt [to retake] was the Isle des Magots so called on account of the large white birds like swans [that] make their nests there. The Scots receive it as a fact that the hundred or hundred and twenty soldiers who form the ordinary garrison of the Castle of the Bass, which is built on the island, live for the most part on nothing else than the fish daily carried thither by these birds and burn no other wood than what these wild geese bring in spring to build their nests with, this being sufficient to last them for a whole year.

It is unlikely that the gannets deposited large quantities of wood on the Bass Rock, as they invariably used seaweed and grass for their nests.

This story is repeated by other writers, who portray the birds as having almost mythical properties.

There were many other misconceptions about the gannet; for instance, that its eggs were attached to the steep cliffs by a glutinous substance. The name solan goose was said to have been derived from the belief that it brooded its eggs with the soles of its feet! In the 1830s, the gannet was a source of meat, its feathers prized. Between 700 and 1,700 birds were caught on the Bass Rock each year. In 1945, there were only ten thousand gannets on the Bass Rock, but, by 2015, their numbers had exploded to 150,000. They have taken over most of the island, although small numbers of other seabirds including shags, razorbills and guillemot nest on the lower ledges. In autumn, the gannets migrate south to the Bay of Biscay and the west coast of Africa, some venturing as far as the equator. When they depart, the Bass Rock literally changes colour; this is because the birds nest so close together they give the impression that the rocks are white.

Ravens were also present on the Bass Rock in the first half of the nineteenth century, but have long since disappeared. To the west, Fidra

Gannets on Bass Rock.

island has some 1,500 pairs of puffins, along with guillemots and shags. On the small islands of Craigleith and Lamb, a wide variety of seabirds make their nests, including cormorants, fulmars, guillemots, kittiwakes, puffins and razorbills. Perhaps the most unusual resident of the Bass Rock was a black-browed albatross, which first appeared in 1967, some nine thousand miles from its normal habitat in the southern oceans. Two years later it disappeared, only to turn up in Shetland, where it remained for the next thirty years. In 2005, an albatross was spotted in the Western Isles, thought to be the same creature.

Seals are a common sight in the Firth of Forth and can often be seen on island rocks. The most common species is the grey seal, although there are also small numbers of harbour seals. In recent years, the latter has become an increasingly rare sight. Bottlenose dolphins and harbour porpoises also visit the Forth. Other species of dolphins have been noted from time to time, including the common dolphin and the Risso's dolphin. Whales are seen occasionally and their appearances are becoming more frequent: in 2015, a small pod of orcas (killer whales) was spotted close to May island; two years later, a young humpback whale was seen off the Fife coast. In the past there have been some notable stranded whales on the East Lothian coast. During 1950, 147 pilot whales became beached on the coast at Thorntonloch near Dunbar, eventually dying or being humanely put down; thirty thousand people descended on the beach to witness the tragedy. More recently in 1992, a minke whale was washed ashore near Thorntonloch and, in April 2019, the corpse of a young humpback whale, thirty-feet long, was found on Tyninghame beach.

In October 1831 a dead, 78-foot-long blue whale was discovered floating in the Firth of Forth near Dunbar. It was towed to the shore at North Berwick, where the carcass was purchased by Robert and Frederick Knox. The skeleton of the whale, weighing 28 tons, was displayed in the museum at Chambers Street, Edinburgh from 1864–2008 and was one of the main attractions. It was, however, permanently removed from display when the exhibition halls were refurbished.

Boats trips from North Berwick around the Bass Rock enable the gannets and sea life to be seen close up. Next to the harbour is the Scottish Seabird Centre, opened in 2000 by Prince Charles. Housed in a distinctive building, with a roof resembling a bird's wing, it is one of East Lothian's leading attractions. Inside there are interactive live cameras on which the birds and wildlife can be observed on Bass Rock and May island, at the mouth of the Forth. Standing close to the entrance is an impressive statue of a tern and several other sculptures close by. One is appropriately a life-size birdwatcher, cast in bronze, gazing at the Bass Rock through binoculars. Lying on a rock is 'Sandy the Seal', one of its flippers raised in the air, as if waving. A sculpture of a group of penguins by local artist the late George Graham, seems out of place as these birds are found only in the southern hemisphere.

Statue of Arctic tern, Scottish Seabird centre.

East Lothian has a diverse coastline, which attracts a wide variety of bird species. Aberlady bay nature reserve, established in 1952, was the first of its kind in Britain. In contrast to the rocky islands of North Berwick, it is centred on the mouth of the Peffer burn, extending northwards towards Gullane Point. It encompasses a diverse range of habitats including salt water, salt marsh, mudflats, a small marl loch and sand dunes. Over 250 species of birds have been recorded here. In autumn, on the open expanses of the saltmarsh and seashore, there are often large numbers of waders, including lapwings and golden plovers. Off Gullane Point one often finds a variety of species of duck including common scooter, eider, red-necked grebe and long-tailed duck floating on the open sea. In winter, large numbers of pink-foot geese descend on Aberlady bay from Greenland and Iceland, where they spend the summer. Redshank live in the saltmarsh with jack snipe, snow bunting and twite also being found there in winter. Water rail and lesser whitethroat reside at Marl loch. Birds that breed at the bay include eider, shell ducks, lapwings and redshanks. Short-ear owls also hunt over the area. In spring, ospreys are also occasionally seen in the skies above.

Further to the west at Musselburgh, the river Esk enters the Forth and attracts large numbers of seabirds. These include divers, eiders, grebes, scoters, curlews, redshanks, mergansers, turnstones and goldeneyes. Other species seen here have included little stints, golden plovers and curlew sandpipers. The shallow artificial lagoons created on reclaimed ground at Levenhall Links on the eastern side of Musselburgh are a magnet for birds. The mouth of the Tyne, which opens out into Belhaven bay, is also rich in birdlife. On its banks are a diverse range of habitats including Corsican pines, broadleaved woodland, grassland and salt marshes. The large sheltered expanse of water attracts ducks, particularly wigeon, in winter along with pink-footed geese and swans. Canada and barnacle geese migrate through here in early autumn. Common and great black gulls are also seen in large numbers in winter. Mute swans live in Belhaven bay all year round and are joined by whooper swans in winter. In the shallow waters, wading birds found during the colder part of the year include oystercatchers, grey plovers, lapwing curlews and redshanks. Goldeneye often feed at the mouth of the river Biel. The saltmarsh on the edge of Belhaven bay is home to curlews, linnets and skylarks. In the broadleaved woodland on the north side of the estuary lurk the great spotted and green woodpeckers. Birds of prey that regularly hunt over Belhaven bay include the peregrine, sparrow hawk and merlin.

Close by, at Dunbar, kittiwakes occupy the rocky ledges beneath the ruined castle. Less welcome are herring gulls, which sometimes nest on the tops of buildings. Further down the coast, birds migrating across the North Sea often make their first landfall in the vicinity of Barns Ness lighthouse, while in the grasslands here live a small population of common lizards. At the southern extremity of the coast close to the boundary with Berwickshire, fulmars nest on the cliffs at Bilsdean and Dunglass. On the rocky shore here and elsewhere on this part of the coast there are herring gulls and black-beaked gulls, cormorants, turnstones, redshanks, curlews, oystercatchers and a variety of types of ducks.

Situated between the coast and the Lammermuir hills, the intensively farmed plains are challenging for wildlife. Over the last fifty years, bird numbers have declined in common with most other regions of Britain that are dominated by arable farming, a situation exacerbated by the removal of hedgerows. There are fewer lapwings, sparrows, song thrushes and skylarks, while summer visitors such as house martins and swifts are less frequently seen. In autumn large flocks of pink-footed, greylag and barnacle geese can be seen feeding in the fields. Many are in the process of migrating to their wintering grounds further south, but some remain in East Lothian. There are also smaller numbers of whooper and mute swans. With shooting less frequently practised than it was in the mid-twentieth century, the numbers of crows and rooks have increased in farmland areas in contrast to many other species. Roe deer are even present in intensively farmed areas and sometimes can be found within a short distance of towns such as Tranent.

The Lammermuir hills provide a very different environment for wildlife. By the mid-twentieth century both brown and mountain hares had almost been hunted to extinction, but numbers have recovered. There are also rabbits and stoats along with larger animals, including badgers and roe deer. There were once also pine martin and wildcat, but these are thought to have disappeared by the 1800s.

Birds found on the open heather moorland are red grouse and partridges. Other species include the curlew, snipe and golden plover, sky lark, meadow pipet and short-eared owl. Birds of prey, including buzzards and sparrow hawks, once rare, are now frequently seen in the open skies over the Lammermuir hills. In Victorian times there were also sea eagles, ravens and hooded crows but they were hunted to extinction. Britain's only venomous snake, the common adder or viper, is also present on the uplands, easily recognisable by the zigzag pattern on its back. Beekeepers now bring their hives to the Lammermuirs when the heather is in bloom. Heather honey is much in demand and more expensive than that from blossom.

The few remaining areas of woodland in the valleys on the edge of the uplands are particularly rich in wildlife. Great-spotted woodpeckers and tawny owls live in the oak woodlands of Woodhall Dean. Redstarts also nest in the trees here and dippers can be found by its streams. Roe deer, foxes, stoat, weasels and foxes are found in the vicinity of Pressmennan lake, as are smaller species such as voles, mice and bats.

Small numbers of red squirrels were still present at Dunglass and Saltoun Big Wood in the early years of the twenty-first century. Another mammal whose numbers have dwindled greatly in recent decades is the hedgehog. Otters have reappeared in the Tyne and some of its tributaries, although less welcome is the appearance of mink on the banks of some streams as they are destructive to native wildlife. Kingfishers are occasionally seen by streams in more remote parts of East Lothian, but herons are fairly common.

HISTORY

8. THE STONE AGE AND THE BRONZE AGE

In 2002, a major discovery was made at East Barns. Former cement-plant quarry workings were being restored when evidence of Scotland's earliest house was unearthed, a timber framework of a burnt structure dating back to 7,600 BC. Discovered with it were some thirty-thousand stone artefacts, indicating the long-term occupancy of the site, including numerous pieces of flint used to make tools. Burnt hazelnut shell fragments were also found, the waste from prehistoric roasting to improve flavour and meat preservation. The site also yielded 'bevelled pebbles', stone tools thought to have been used in the working of animal skins.

By 3,500 BC, farming was well-established. Over the next thousand years, the inhabitants left their mark by building tombs, stone circles and cairns. It is puzzling that many of the surviving monuments of the early farming communities are found in upland areas, such as the Lammermuir hills, as today the most fertile farmland is found on the coastal plain. Perhaps these early inhabitants concentrated on rearing livestock and avoided low-lying areas that were prone to be waterlogged and covered in marshland. Another explanation is that many of the Stone Age monuments on the coastal plain were obliterated by centuries of intensive farming.

The most obvious monuments are standing stones. The 10-foot tall 'Long Stane' stands on the slopes of Pencraig hill, in a field next to the main road a short distance from East Linton. Several miles further along the same main road, close to the junction with the North Berwick road, a tall, slender stone can be seen in the middle of cultivated fields near Kirklandhill farm. Heading east again, another standing stone occupies a prominent position at Easter Broomhouse, a short distance south of Dunbar. The red sandstone monolith is 9-feet tall and has carvings on its west side. Standing in fields that are cultivated for much of the year, it can be seen on the skyline from the road to Spott. A short distance south-west of Traprain Law is the Loth stone; this is not its original position. Legend relates that it covers the remains of Loth, king of the Lothians, but he hailed from the much later Dark Ages. The stone has been scientifically excavated, but nothing was found that could date it (*see photos on page 54 and in plate section*).

Loth (or Lothus) according to one source, was king of the Gododdin and lived on Traprain Law around AD 528. His daughter Princess

Above

Kirklandhill standing stone, near Tyninghame. It is speculated that it acted as a marker linked to North Berwick Law, over which the sun would set at the summer solstice.

Left

The Loth stone, south-west of Traprain Law.

Theneva, or Denw, became pregnant after an illicit encounter with her cousin, King Owain, who ruled part of Galloway. On discovering this, Loth was furious and had his daughter bound to a chariot, which was launched off a precipitous slope on Traprain Law. Theneva, however, survived the fall and fled East Lothian, later giving birth to a son; he became St Mungo. King Loth is the origin of the name Lothian.

The surviving stone circles in East Lothian are nothing like the impressive Stonehenge; many could have been constructed by a single Stone Age man on his day off from hunting! Their exact purpose remains unknown; they may have been memorials, boundary markers or navigational aids. With difficulty, some circles can be found on the Lammermuir hills. These are generally composed of stones no more than a foot tall, often lost in the undergrowth. Approximately thirty small stones, some fallen down, make up a stone circle on the north-west slope of Kingside hill, close to the Gifford–Cranshaws road, not far from Whiteadder reservoir; it had a small burial cairn at its centre. There is a large concentration of other stone circles, cairns and hut circles in the vicinity of Kingside hill, Penshiel, Mayshiel, Johnscleuch and Spartleton hill at the source of the Whiteadder water and its tributaries, the Faseny and Bothwell waters.

Many are thought to date from around 3,000 BC, towards the end of the Stone Age. There may have been a network of trackways across the uplands centred on the Whiteadder valley, leading to the profusion of early monuments in this area. Another small stone circle exists on the aptly named Nine Stone Rig hill, opposite Kingside hill. Stone cairns exist on the surrounding hills, including one that crowns the summit of Priestlaw hill.

Unfortunately, no trace of some of the more interesting monuments exists above ground. At Drylawhill, East Linton, aerial photos have identified the existence of a 'cursus', one of only three in south-east Scotland. Dating from 4,000–2,000 BC, it was thought to have been used for ceremonial or ritual purposes; it consisted of two long, parallel ditches, perhaps over a mile in length and some 280 feet apart. Evidence of a huge timber wall and the remains of a mortuary house, in use six thousand years ago, were discovered near Eweford cottages, Dunbar; the bodies had been buried in urns after cremation. The site continued to be used as a cemetery into the Bronze Age and it is a site of national significance. Evidence of another cursus has been found to the south of Inveresk.

The Bronze Age brought significant change. The dead were buried in stone cists (a stone box in the ground), with the body placed in a crouched position. Beside it was placed a tall ornamental vessel; this gave rise to the name 'beaker' people. Numerous cists have been unearthed across East Lothian, mainly on lowlying ground; later on, bodies were cremated and placed in the urn itself.

The Iron Age hill forts of East Lothian began to emerge at the end of the Bronze Age. A fortified settlement was established on Traprain Law around 1,000 BC; five hundred years earlier it had been used as a Bronze Age burial place, with a stone burial cairn.

9. THE IRON AGE

Iron Age people left their mark on the landscape with hill forts. Stone walls enclosed the summits of both North Berwick Law and Traprain Law. To protect their interests, tribes constructed forts with earthen and stone walls, sometimes with strengthened wooden frameworks. There are over thirty hill forts in East Lothian, most of which are on the northern slopes of the Lammermuir hills, with no less than fifteen being concentrated in the area to the south of Gifford.

The largest Iron Age fort in East Lothian was on Traprain Law. This hill was known as Dumpelder (from the Brythonic, or Welsh, 'Hill of Shafts') until about two hundred years ago, but 'Traprain' is not out of context as it was a name of a village close to the Law and it too is derived from the same language – *tra pren*, wooden town. There is evidence that this distinctive natural feature was important long before a hill fort was built on its summit, as rock carvings dating back to the Stone Age have been discovered on the steep southern cliffs. The first ramparts were probably constructed around 1,000 BC. On a ledge on the south side of the hill, four bronze axes were discovered in the early twenty-first century, perhaps an offering to the gods. From 800 BC, and for several centuries thereafter, there is little evidence of habitation on Traprain Law, although some ramparts were constructed in this period. They were followed by an increasingly complex set of defensive walls

Traprain Law, site of the largest Iron Age fort in East Lothian.

and ditches enclosing the summit of the hill. The protected area was extended from around 10 to 40 acres over a thousand years.

By the time of the Roman invasion of Scotland it was occupied by the Votadini tribe, who would have also controlled numerous other East Lothian hill forts. It is thought that Traprain Law was their capital, and, at that time, it was densely populated, both round and rectangular houses lining the streets. The Votadini are thought to have cooperated with the Romans, as there is almost a complete absence of forts and camps of this occupying power, other than at Inveresk.

In 1919, one of the most significant archaeological finds in Scotland was made on Traprain Law when a hoard of late Roman silverware was unearthed. It dated from the reign of Emperor Honorius (AD 395–423) and consisted of silver bowls, dishes, flagons and plates cut into pieces. It may have been a form of payment to keep the Votadini onside at a time when tribes were rebelling or perhaps by this time the Votadini too had changed sides and had begun stealing from the Romans. Some of the treasure is on display in the National Museum of Scotland.

As the Roman empire fell into chaos, a large defensive wall was built to protect Traprain Law. By around AD 500 the site had been abandoned;

it is not known why. There have been suggestions that the Votadini, who by now had become known as the 'Gododdin', migrated the short distance to Castlehill in Edinburgh. At this time the Anglo-Saxons were beginning to infiltrate southern Scotland.

There was another fort on top of North Berwick Law, and, like Traprain Law, it has been home to people since the Bronze Age. There are eighteen hut circles and field systems on the south side of the hill, which date from around 2,000 BC; the remains of stone dykes and ramparts can also be seen. A stone wall enclosed the top of the hill 50 feet below the summit; there was a second wall below it, and, on the lower slopes, a third.

Not all the Iron Age forts are located on hill tops. One of the best surviving examples is Chesters fort, near Drem, which had twenty to thirty circular stone structures enclosed by a complex series of earthworks and ditches; it is thought it was occupied in the second century AD or later. The site is one of the more accessible Iron Age forts in East Lothian, located on the edge of sloping ground, close to where it meets the coastal plain. The fort is overlooked by high ground, calling into question its purpose. An attacker could presumably have launched missiles into the fort from the vantage points above. It is possible that the oval series of ramparts and ditches were constructed as much for prestige reasons as for defence. Another theory is that such forts may have served as ceremonial centres and meeting places. The inner ramparts still stand, to a height of around six feet. Evidence has been discovered of an early field system close by.

To the south of Gifford, in the valley of Hopes water, we find not only the highest hill fort in East Lothian but also one of the largest. With an elaborate system of earthwork defences, it stands on a 1,350-foot spur on the northern slope of Harestone hill, near Hopes reservoir. Streams flow down either side. The site is defended by three ramparts, outside of which there are a further two unfinished ramparts and ditches; its defences are further enhanced by a scree-covered slope about 250 feet high. A mile to the west, on the opposite side of the valley, is another hill fort, this time close to the summit of Harelaw hill. Located at an altitude of 1,150 feet, it looks down on most other East Lothian hill forts. What distinguishes it is that its inner wall contains traces of stone walls that were subjected to intense temperatures, fusing the stones together. It is not known if this was done deliberately, or when the fort was attacked and the timber framework set on fire, but it would have needed an extremely high temperature to melt stone. There are in total some sixty vitrified forts in Scotland, forts where the stone has melted. How this was achieved was long a mystery. Conspiracy theorists have claimed that some sort of superweapon was used to create the extreme temperatures. The explanation is more mundane as recent experiments have shown that if the timber superstructure on top of the stone walls was set alight, the fire burning down on them could heat them up like an oven.

Further to the west, on lower ground, are four hill forts within a short distance of each other – Castles, Kidlaw, Stobshiels and Witches Knowe. The most significant is Kidlaw, situated just above the hamlet of the same name. Two circular earth and stone ramparts enclose an area 370 feet in diameter, making it one of the largest Iron Age forts in East Lothian. A third rampart has been created in places to further enhance defences. There is evidence that three stone homesteads were built in the fort between the second and seventh centuries AD.

Situated a mile to the south-west, close to the road, is Stobshiels fort. Like a number of other hill forts, it exploits natural features for protection, being situated on a promontory. Witches Knowe, to the south of Kidlaw fort, is small compared with the others yet was heavily defended. There are also a number of open Iron Age settlements in the area, evidence that not everyone lived behind walls. About a mile to the east of Kidlaw fort is Castles hill fort, also situated on a promontory. Three miles to the east are another two hill forts on the lower slopes of Dod Law. The larger of the two still has a rampart, 10-feet high, on which are the traces of the stone wall that once surmounted it.

Close by are a further two hill forts, a short distance to the west of the Gifford–Duns road, as it begins a climb up the northern slopes of the Lammermuir hills. Black castle stands on top of a hillock and is almost circular in shape. The inner defence is a stone wall, some 18-feet thick; it still stands some 10 feet above the ditch and was probably twice this height when built.

A short distance to the south-east is Green castle fort, which exploits the natural features of the area, being located on an area of level ground between two streams. It is among the better-preserved examples in East Lothian and, like the other hill forts there, the grass-covered ramparts are assimilated into the landscape. In many cases, hidden beneath them, are the remains of massive stone walls up to 20-feet thick. Many walls may have also been 20 feet high and would have had their defensive properties further enhanced by a ditch. The stone and earth from the excavation was sometimes used to construct additional ramparts.

At the eastern edge of the Lammermuir hills there is an incomplete hill fort near Innerwick on the summit of Blackcastle hill, easily distinguished by the large radio mast that stands on its summit. The inner rampart was completed but a further four walls and ditches were abandoned during their construction.

The most accessible Iron Age hill fort on the slopes of the Lammermuir hills is White castle, said to date from 600 BC (*see plate section*). White castle occupies the summit of a peninsular promontory, thrusting out into the valley from a nearby hillside; the road from Garvald to Whiteadder reservoir passes within a few yards. This earthen fort is oval in shape and consists of three ramparts and ditches; traces of houses can still be seen within the enclosure. Many of these earthworks have been given the name 'castle', but they are not 'castles' in the true sense of the word, as these belong only to the Middle Ages.

While most of the visible traces of the Iron Age in East Lothian is in the form of hill forts, it would be incorrect to conclude that life in this epoch was only about them. There is increasing evidence that, by the end of the Iron Age, the low-lying areas of East Lothian had numerous settlements. While some of these were defended by wooden enclosures, many were not, indicating that deterring attacks was not necessarily the top priority. In the vicinity of Traprain Law there were more than a dozen unenclosed settlements. The fort on the nearby hill may have served as a refuge of last resort in times of crisis. Also, in some cases, the term 'hill fort' is misleading as some were situated on low-lying ground or at the edge of the sea shore.

The Iron Age way of life did not die out when the Romans arrived. Many hill forts were occupied for several more centuries and only gradually abandoned; some have vanished without trace, like a number of the Stone Age monuments. There was a 'Danish or British' camp on Dodridge Law, near Ormiston, all traces of which vanished by the end of the nineteenth century.

Broxmouth Iron Age hill fort stood on the coastal plain a short distance from Dunbar, next to the minor road that leads to the caravan site and Barns Ness lighthouse. No trace of it remained above ground before it was consumed by the quarrying of limestone at Oxwellmains in the late 1970s. This was not before it had been excavated by archaeologists and had shed important light on its Iron Age inhabitants. The site was occupied from 2,000 BC to around AD 200. The first building was a large circular timber house. It was followed by a hill fort with a single rampart, which underwent four major and several minor phases of modification. At first the enclosed area was just over half an acre, defended by a palisade, with a single entrance followed by a more extensive area being defended by several ramparts extending over five acres. The remains of five houses were found within its walls. Animal bones indicated the importance of cattle in the lives of its inhabitants.

The most remarkable find at Broxmouth was iron artefacts dating from 490–375 BC, made from high-carbon steel. They had been deliberately heated and quenched with water, the earliest evidence of the use of steel in Britain. There is also limited evidence for copper alloy and gold working. Fragments of human skulls were found throughout the site; they could have come from severed heads or body parts taken as trophies and brought back to Broxburn.

In 2016, a further Iron Age site consisting of five roundhouses was excavated at East Barns, half-a-mile east of Broxmouth hill fort. Quantities of animal bone and red-deer antler were discovered, including many examples with butchery and tool marks. Other items found included a dozen rotary querns (grinding stones), two possible ingot moulds and cobbler tools.

10. ROMAN OCCUPATION AND THE DARK AGES

From AD 138–163 (the Antonine period) the Romans established a number of permanent bases, including a fort at Inveresk (Musselburgh) in AD 140, thought to have been home to a cavalry regiment. Excavations have unearthed numerous horse harnesses and some Samian vessels bear graffiti with Thracian or Dacian names, hinting that the unit may have originated in this part of the Roman empire.

In 2007, the tombstone of a Roman cavalry man was found in a field near Carberry, a short distance to the south. The inscription names him as Crescens, who at the time of his death was serving with the *equites singulares*, the governor's bodyguard, which was drawn from the *socii*, Rome's Italian military allies. It is thought that the Roman governor of Britannia spent some time at Inveresk fort.

Another recent significant discovery was two altars to the east of the fort on a ground now used for cricket; both were dedicated to Gaius Cassius, who was possibly a centurion seconded to take command of the fort's auxiliary garrison. Located on a small hill, the garrison enjoyed commanding views. Its defensive position was enhanced by the river Esk, which flowed around its base on three sides. The initial structure was timber, but this was quickly replaced by stone. The fort was heavily defended, having two defensive ditches on the west side and possibly on the other sides. A road passed through the gate here and headed towards the Esk, perhaps to a bridge or to the harbour. A short distance to the north, the river flowed into the Firth of Forth. The Romans would have received some of their provisions by ship, possibly ferried up the Esk. Despite its large size – 600 feet by 475 feet – there are no traces of the fort above ground. Its site is now occupied by the cemetery adjoining Inveresk church and as nothing other than tombstones from recent centuries occupy the site it is possible to get a good feel for it.

There are no other remains of Roman fortifications in East Lothian. The main military road was Dere Street, which ran north from the Tweed valley via Soutra towards the fort at Cramond. Rather surprisingly, no Roman road seems to have been constructed along the coast of East Lothian to link it to southern provinces.

Under Roman authority, the lives of the Votadini remained relatively unchanged. They continued to live on the hill-top fortress at Traprain Law and did not found new settlements or adopt new farming methods. There was, however, a large civil settlement known as a *vicus*, built on the south-east side of Inveresk fort's wall and overlooking the river Esk; this covered ten acres and was the nearest equivalent in Scotland to a Roman town. Laid out in a grid pattern, it had at first timber and later stone-strip buildings lining its streets; in it lived merchants and craftsmen, who made a wide range of pottery. Beyond the houses were ditched enclosures where animals were grazed and crops grown. There may have been a parade ground and amphitheatre on the ridge to the east of the fort.

The Romans abandoned the Inveresk fort towards the end of the second century AD. There is some evidence that it was retained as an outpost fort at the northern end of Dere Street, a major military route until AD 180. The Roman name for the fort is not known; Ptolemy's Curia has been suggested, or Coria, or perhaps Evidensca.

When the Romans left Britain, the island fragmented into a number of regional kingdoms. The Votadini regained authority over their East Lothian territories and by the mid-fifth century appear to have abandoned Traprain Law, possibly in favour of Din Eidyn, now the site of Edinburgh castle. Here they are thought to have become the Gododdin.

Dark Age buildings and monuments are remarkably thin on the ground in East Lothian. The Pictish kingdom arose on the northern shore of the Firth of Forth (the Sea of Iudeu). There are no physical remains of the Pict culture in East Lothian but there is some evidence that the Picts once had a presence here. The word *pevr* (radiant and beautiful), is the origin of the place name Peffer burn. Around AD 600, the Gododdin marched south under King Mynyddog, in what may have been an attempt to stem the advance of the Anglo-Saxons. They were, however, annihilated at the battle of Catraeth, probably Catterick in North Yorkshire.

For the next four centuries or so East Lothian fell under the control of the Anglian kingdom of Northumbria ('the people or province north of the Humber'). By AD 638 Traprain Law had fallen and even the fort at Edinburgh was under siege by King Oswald of Northumbria. Place names show the influence of the Angles: the incorporation of *ingaham* in a name, as in Tyninghame – the settlement of the people by the Tyne; Lyneryngham, the old name for East Linton – the settlement of people by the *linn* (pool); and Whittingehame – the settlement of the people of *Hwita* (an Anglo-Saxon personal name). Haddington is also Anglo-Saxon and means 'the settlement of the people of Hoedda'. These were long-established settlements, perhaps dating back as far as the seventh century and in time they all became the basis for parishes. The incorporation of the word *ham* in a place name is also thought to date from the same period; examples in East Lothian include Morham, Auldhame, Oldhamstocks and Hamer (the old name for Whitekirk).

Large wooden halls (*bothl*) were the centre of Anglo-Saxon life. Elements of this word are incorporated in the name 'Bolton', a small village near Haddington, and 'Eldbotle', an abandoned medieval settlement near Dirleton. It was long believed there was a rectangular timber hall from the sixth century on Doon hill, possibly the work of native Britons. This was thought to have been replaced by a seventh-century aisled hall attributed to the Northumbrians. Although the timber structure and defensive palisade have long since rotted away, the outline of their foundations has been marked out by a broad concrete line. In 2018, a re-evaluation of this archaeological site was undertaken and the long-held assumptions about it were proved to be wrong. Only one of the timber buildings was erected in the Dark Ages. The primary hall is thought to date back to 3,800 BC, making it amongst the earliest timber structures to have been discovered in Scotland. Around that time there was a move from a hunter-gatherer economy to farming and permanent settlements.

Concrete marks out the perimeter of the timber halls on Doon hill.

The Anglo Saxons had a coastal fort on the headland at Dunbar, which contained a central royal hall surrounded by smaller buildings. It stood in the vicinity of the leisure pool, not far from the castle. In 2016, the remains of a further enormous Anglo-Saxon building were unearthed a short distance to the north of Aberlady parish church. It too was rectangular, measuring130 feet by 65 feet, and partly constructed in stone. It may not have been just a hall but, given its size, a palace or possibly a monastery. It dates from between the seventh and ninth centuries, when East Lothian was part of Northumbria.

The southern shore of the Firth of Forth was the limit of Northumbrian power in Scotland. In May 685 Ecgfirth, king of Northumbria, led an army into the Pictish heartland in Angus, possibly in an attempt to extend the frontiers northwards. Brude, king of the Picts, scored a major victory over the invaders at the Nechtansmere, thought to have been near Dunnichen, Angus or Dunachton in Badenoch. For the next three centuries, East Lothian was on the fault line between the two kingdoms but generally remained under the control of the Anglo-Saxons. Their grip over the area came to an end when the kingdom of Scotland was formed at the beginning of the eleventh century and, around the same time, Northumbria was absorbed into England.

11. BATTLEFIELDS

East Lothian lies on a main invasion route from England, so it is not surprising that it has been the scene of several significant battles in Scotland's history.

Battle of Athelstaneford, AD 832

One of the first documented accounts of Scottish history (by medieval chronicler Walter Bower) mentions a battle in the Dark Ages at Athelstaneford and relates that the key player was King Hungus MacFergus of the Picts, who fought the Northumbrians in 761. Other sources date this battle to the tenth century. The generally accepted date is 832 AD. At that time the kingdom of Northumbria extended as far north as the Firth of Forth, with East Lothian under its control; beyond it lay the kingdom of the Picts.

Hungus had led a force of Picts and Scots on a punitive raid into the enemy territory of East Lothian. According to Bower, it was a great army that caused immense devastation. After several days marching, the Picts retired to what was described as a pleasant plain in Lothian, not far from the river Tyne. Here they pitched camp in order to replenish their supplies. When the commander of the Northumbrian army, Athelstan (who was perhaps a king, but more likely a prince or warlord) got word that his enemies were resting, he attacked. The Picts and Scots, taken by surprise, were encircled by the Northumbrian army.

At that time there were extensive marshes surrounding the river Peffer, which flowed across the plain with the main ford at Prora, not far from the present site of Athelstaneford village. Trapped by a far superior force, Hungus prayed to God and St Andrew for divine intervention; Andrew then appeared to him in a dream, promising victory. His enemies would be routed because an angel bearing the standard of the Lord's cross would proceed in front. On awakening, Hungus revealed his vision to his companions, emboldening the Pictish warriors.

East Lothian county sign, Dunglass: note the association with the battle of Athelstaneford and the saltire.

Pressed against the Peffer, the Picts and Scots stood their ground. As the two armies clashed, tradition relates that two narrow bands of white cloud formed a diagonal cross in the blue sky, forming the colours associated with St Andrew, who was martyred on a diagonal cross. The Picts and Scots saw it as a good omen, and, despite overwhelming odds, defeated the Northumbrians, most of whom fled. Only Athelstan and a small band of his Northumbrian warriors held their ground, but were killed in the first clash. According to one story, Athelstan was buried in a grave at a ford of Cogtail burn. However, Walter Bower avers his head was cut off and placed on the highest point of Inchgarvie island, near South Queensferry, to be seen by travellers crossing the Forth. The victory was taken as a sign that the Scots and

Picts had been favoured by God. St Andrew's emblem, a diagonal white cross on a blue background known as the saltire, was adopted as the flag of the victors in gratitude. Two centuries later Scotland came into existence, with the saltire as national flag. It is believed to be the oldest flag in Europe still in use today.

Of all the place names in East Lothian, none has stronger Anglo-Saxon roots than the village of Athelstaneford. In the church grounds is the saltire memorial, a granite slab on which a scene from the battle is carved, with the cross of St Andrew visible in the sky. The flag-heritage centre is housed in an old lectern dovecote located in the north-west corner of the churchyard. The battle is thought to have been fought on low ground around the Peffer burn, approximately one mile north of Athelstaneford, close to Prora farm. One of the enclosures here is still called 'Bloody Fields', and at the farm (on private property) stands the Boar stone. There is some suggestion that it marked the site of the battle, but most sources state that it indicates where the last wild boar in the area was slain. The 6-foot shaft of sandstone has been relocated to its present position from a nearby field.

Athelstaneford parish church, home to the saltire memorial and to the flag-heritage centre.

The Vikings raided East Lothian but they do not appear to have established a permanent presence, as there are only a handful of place names that might have a Norse origin. The only recorded incursion was by King Olaf Gothfrithsson, who landed his army on Scoughall sands in AD 941. He then plundered the church of St Baldred and burnt the village of Tyninghame.

Throughout the tenth century, the Picts and Scots tried to wrest control of the Lothians from Northumbria. Around AD 973, the English king, Edgar, granted this region to Kenneth II, king of Scotland, but it was not until Malcolm II comprehensively defeated the Northumbrians at Carham, near Coldstream, in 1018, that the area between the Forth and the Tweed was secured for Scotland.

Battle of Dunbar, 1296

Blood was again spilled on East Lothian soil during the Wars of Scottish Independence. John Balliol, who had been installed by Edward I in 1295 as the puppet ruler of Scotland, rebelled against his English overlord, signing a treaty with England's enemy, France. Enraged by these actions, Edward sent his army north, laying siege to Berwick-upon-Tweed, an important Scottish port. As the town was defended only by wooden walls, it was not long before the English forced their way in, massacring 7,500 of the 12,500 inhabitants. At the same time the Scots launched a diversionary raid into northern England, burning villages as far south as Hexham, before hastily withdrawing and seeking protection in Dunbar castle. The English army had re-commenced its march northwards and the garrison dispatched a plea for help to John Balliol, who was camped near Haddington with the main Scottish contingent.

There was a brief truce once the English army had surrounded Dunbar castle, as it was hoped that the Scottish king would instruct the garrison to surrender. He responded by dispatching John Comyn, earl of Buchan, with a force of cavalry. On 27 April 1296, the force took up a commanding position on the edge of the Lammermuir hills in the vicinity of Doon hill, overlooking Dunbar. The English army left Dunbar to meet this challenge and forded the Spott burn. The advancing army disappeared from view of the Scots, giving the impression that it had retreated. The Scottish cavalry left their commanding position and charged downhill straight into the English knights. Taken by surprise the Scots army was resoundingly defeated, one English chronicle putting its dead at over ten thousand men from a force of forty thousand. This account is wildly exaggerated, as neither army fielded more than a few thousand men; a recent estimate puts the English at 2,300 and the Scots at 2,000–3,000. In fact, only one Scottish knight is reliably known to have been killed!

The first battle of Dunbar was fought here in 1296, in the vicinity of Spott.

However, a hundred Scots were captured, among them John Comyn and the earls of Atholl, Mentieth and Ross. Those that managed to escape the battlefield fled towards Ettrick forest. The next day, Dunbar castle surrendered, although it is suspected that treachery may have been involved.

The battle was fought in the vicinity of Spott village, close to where the stream of the same name cuts a depression on the edge of flat arable fields that stretch towards Dunbar. The site is marked on Ordnance Survey maps but there are neither monuments nor plaques on the ground.

Scottish resistance re-emerged the following year. William Wallace was supported in East Lothian by Lauder of Tyninghame and Lyle of Stoneypath near Garvald. Gospatric, earl of Dunbar, sided with the English and fled to Dunbar after his numerically superior forces were defeated by Wallace in a battle near Innerwick.

The conflict continued for decades. After his defeat at Bannockburn in 1314, Edward II fled south along the roads of East Lothian. He reappeared in August 1322 with a large army, intent on revenge. Robert the Bruce had taken the precaution of laying waste to the countryside to deprive his enemy of food and shelter. So thorough was this tactic that the English soldiers were unable to locate any livestock except for a lame cow at Tranent. Their commander, the earl of Surrey, is reputed to have said 'this is the dearest beef that ever I saw'. After a month starving in the Lothians, the English were driven south.

In February 1356, Edward III ravaged East Lothian, burning Haddington along with its monastery and its then famous church, 'the Lamp of Lothian'. In 1400, Henry IV reasserted the English claim to Scotland and passed through East Lothian with a large force, said to have been thirteen thousand-strong; it was the last time an English king led an army in person. The army halted at Haddington, but spared it further destruction, before proceeding to Edinburgh castle, which it failed to take. This invasion lasted only fifteen days, but the relief of the population of East Lothian would be short-lived as in the following year an English force of two thousand men made its way north across the Lammermuir hills led by Henry Hotspur, son of the earl of Northumberland, along with the exiled earl of Dunbar. It made two attacks on Hailes castle and burnt the villages of Hailes, Traprain and Markle. While camped at East Linton and Preston they were surprised by an army that had marched from Edinburgh castle overnight. The

English fled south along the coast to Berwick, with many stragglers slaughtered at Cockburnspath.

The conflict with England simmered during the fifteenth and sixteenth centuries, but East Lothian saw only one large-scale engagement. In 1482, an English army made its way to Edinburgh in support of Alexander, James III's brother, but after drawn-out negotiations withdrew to England. In his quest for power, Alexander seized Waughton castle, near North Berwick, which fragmented ruins survive. Before he fled south to England, Alexander killed Sir Anselm Adornes, a companion of James III, close to this town.

Battle of Pinkie, 1547

In 1544, because the Scots had rejected his proposal that his son, Edward, marry Mary, the infant daughter of the recently deceased James V, Henry VIII sent a large army north under the earl of Hertford. Towns, villages and the countryside of south-east Scotland were laid waste. The following summer, the English army returned to continue the destruction, this episode being known as the Rough Wooing.

Realising that this tactic would never subjugate the Scots, Hertford proposed stationing a permanent garrison in the Edinburgh area until the Scottish lords agreed to Henry VIII's plan for the amalgamation of England and Scotland. Unconvinced, Henry ordered Hertford to mount a further punishing raid across the border. Henry died in January 1547 before this could take place. The Earl of Hertford, now Duke of Somerset, became regent and was in a position to invade Scotland and establish bases there. In 1547, he led an army of eighteen thousand along the coast, crossing the Pease burn at Cockburnspath and passing through East Linton on the way to Edinburgh. The Scots, numbering twenty-three thousand, blocked the route. They were camped on Shire Haugh, Inveresk, close to Musselburgh, where they had built large defensive earthworks to protect their position from bombardment by English ships. On 9 September, the English army deployed its forces on the slopes of Carberry hill and Falside, overlooking Scottish positions, the armies separated by an area of marshy ground called Howe Mire. The Scottish cavalry, numbering 1,500, crossed the river Esk and approached the English positions. As the Scots wheeled around to feign retreat, the English horsemen charged and effectively destroyed their opponents.

The following day, the English advanced on Pinkie Cleugh with the intention of taking the high ground where Inveresk church stands. The Scottish pikemen advanced to meet the English and initially the English cavalry made no impression on the wall of pikes. But as the Scots moved forward, huge gaps were torn in their ranks by the guns of the English fleet anchored off Musselburgh. An orderly retreat soon became a rout as casualties mounted; the Scots infantry, fleeing towards Edinburgh, were cut down by English cavalry. By nightfall, the Scots had lost six thousand men, while English casualties did not exceed eight hundred. Much of the fighting took place close to where the Edinburgh–London railway now runs, just south of Musselburgh and Inveresk. An English government official, William Patten, present at the battle, noted the pitiful sight of the Scottish corpses, 'some their legs off . . . others the arms cut off . . . of sundry the brains pashed out, some others with their heads quite off.'

Battle of Pinkie memorial, near Wallyford.

The English consolidated their victory by building strongpoints at Dunglass, Haddington, Ormiston, Saltoun and Yester. It was intended to turn Edinburgh and its hinterland, including East Lothian, into a

Scottish pale, similar to the pale surrounding Dublin. The Scots, with the assistance of French troops, resisted, so that virtually all English troops had been driven south by 1550.

The A1 crosses the southern edge of the Pinkie battlefield, but few drivers would know that perhaps the biggest battle ever fought on Scottish soil took place here. There is only a small stone memorial, south-west of Wallyford, close to the road to Whitecraig just before it passes under the A1. In addition, there is a stone plaque mounted on top of a wall in Lewisvale park, with the inscription, 'The Protector, Duke of Somerset encamped here, Sept. 1547'. There is some doubt as to the accuracy of this, as it is thought the actual camp site of the English on this date was about a mile to the east.

Battle of Carberry hill, 1567

Carberry hill – a battle in name only – was near the site of Pinkie Cleugh. On one side were forces led by Mary, Queen of Scots and her third husband, James Hepburn, earl of Bothwell; on the other a force led by James Douglas, earl of Morton, who had the support of most of the aristocracy as well much of the Scottish population.

Mary and Bothwell's force took up a position on Carberry hill, and, on seeing the commanding position of her army, the opposition decided against a full-frontal assault and veered towards Dalkeith, later reappearing on high ground close to the royal army. From eleven in the morning until five in the afternoon, there was a stand-off, during which time the French ambassador attempted to negotiate a peace treaty. It was also suggested that the situation could be resolved by single combat, in which Bothwell would fight an opponent from the enemy army, but Mary forbade this.

As the day wore on, the Queen's soldiers began to desert and her husband also took the opportunity to flee. After long negotiations, Mary agreed to the demands of her nobles, allowing herself to be taken prisoner. Meanwhile Bothwell sailed to Denmark, whose king had him imprisoned in solitary confinement in a castle near Copenhagen, in which conditions were so bad that he eventually went insane.

The site of this confrontation is marked by a tall, stone plinth with the following inscription: 'M.R. 1567. At this spot Mary Queen of Scots after the escape of Bothwell mounted her horse and surrendered herself to the Confederate Lords.' It is located close to the summit of Carberry hill, at a point shown as 'Queen Mary's Mount' on maps. The monument is well concealed at the edge of woodland, immediately north of the road between Carberry and Elphinstone. It can be reached by a footpath that heads up the hill from a car park some distance to the south of Carberry house.

Battle of Dunbar, 1650

Although many Scots had opposed the policies of Charles I, they were shocked by his execution in 1649 and declared his son, Charles II, the ruler of Scotland. Lord Protector Oliver Cromwell saw this as a threat and his army crossed into Scotland on 22 July 1650, progressing along the coast into East Lothian. At his arrival outside Edinburgh he was defeated in a number of skirmishes. On 30–31 July there were clashes between rearguard units of the English army and advanced parties of the Scots at Musselburgh. With his army short of supplies and many of his soldiers ill, Cromwell was forced to retreat to Dunbar.

The Scottish army, twenty-thousand strong, was commanded by David Leslie, a distinguished soldier. All was not well within his army, which suffered interference from religious extremists, many of whom were Edinburgh lawyers! The Scots thought their country the most progressive on earth when it came to reformed Christianity and soldiers who had in the past supported the Royalists were dismissed. It was thought that God would more readily grant victory to an army purged of those lacking in faith. In consequence, more than three thousand experienced officers and men were replaced by raw recruits.

Leslie manoeuvred his army onto Doon hill, near Dunbar, while the English army was camped on the narrow plain below, sandwiched between the sea and the edge of the Lammermuir hills. It was effectively trapped and David Leslie could have starved it into submission or allowed a retreat into England. However, against his advice, the ministers and politicians in his ranks were eager for battle and moved the army to the lower slopes of Doon hill. The Scottish army was funded by the church, which was eager not to delay the battle so that it could save money. Estimates put the strength of the English army at fifteen thousand, half of them cavalry – with the Scottish force at twenty-two thousand, of whom six thousand were cavalry.

On 3 September 1650, the English launched a surprise attack on the right flank of the Scottish army. The initial assault was repulsed, but the better-disciplined English force eventually broke through and the Scots fled; it was all over in a couple of hours. Scottish casualties were eight hundred killed, according to one Scottish officer, although Cromwell claimed they were as high as three thousand. Cromwell also stated that ten thousand Scots were taken prisoner but the correct number is closer to six thousand. While a number of the sick and wounded were released and allowed to go home, the others were force-marched to Durham. Along the way, up to two thousand Scottish soldiers died of hunger, exhaustion and disease. On reaching their destination they were imprisoned in the castle and the cathedral, both of which were disused. Held in appalling conditions, 1,700 of the 3,000 prisoners perished. In 2016, mass graves were unearthed in Durham, thought to contain the remains of captives. Many other prisoners were sent to America and forced to work as indentured labourers.

Dunbar was one of Cromwell's greatest successes and over the next two years he subjugated the rest of Scotland. The site of the battle is commemorated by a stone memorial and plaque by the road leading into Dunbar, in the hamlet of Broxburn (*photo in plate section*). Many of the dead were buried in the vicinity of Spott Dean.

Battle of Prestonpans, 1745

The last revolt of the Jacobites was in 1745 when Bonnie Prince Charlie landed in Scotland. The Jacobite army arrived in Edinburgh on 17 September 1745, the same day that government troops disembarked at Dunbar. The government commander, Sir John Cope, then marched across East Lothian to Tranent, where he awaited reinforcements from Berwick. His forces were deployed on an east–west line behind a marshy area known as Tranent meadows, near Prestonpans. The Jacobite forces decided not to make a full-frontal attack but overnight marched from Birsley brae to the hamlet of Riggonhead. Next morning, they launched a surprise attack from the east; the battle was over in fifteen minutes. The 2,300 Highlanders killed or wounded 800 government troops and captured a further 1,500, almost all the survivors. The crushing defeat was attributed to the element of surprise and the ferocity of the Highland charge.

The site of the battle is immediately to the east of the town of the same name. A modest stone memorial cairn, erected in 1932, about 10-feet tall and on the south side of the road next to Longniddry, marks the spot. Close by at Meadow mill, an artificial mound has been created from the remains of mining operations there. On top there is a flagpole, on which the standard of Prince Charles's army is flown. For one week in the year it is replaced by the Union flag to mark the anniversary of the birth and death of George II. There are commanding views of the surrounding views of the local area from the top of the mound, on which there are information boards. Up until the early years of the twentieth century, the only reminder of the battle was an old hawthorn tree marking the spot where Colonel Gardiner was mortally wounded and the fighting most ferocious.

A re-enactment of the battle of Prestonpans.

A second memorial to Prestonpans has recently been erected on its site. It is found near Preston Crescent, a short distance to the north-west of the 1932 monument, close to a children's playground. It is inscribed: 'During the Battle of Prestonpans fought on twenty-first September, 1745, Colonel Gardiner of Bankton was fatally wounded beneath a Hawthorne Tree in this area.' There is another much older monument to Gardiner – an obelisk with four ornamental lions lounging at its base, dating from 1853. It stands next to the railway line a short distance from Bankton house, where Gardiner lived. By sheer coincidence his home was a stone's throw from the site of the battlefield on which he perished. He had joined the army at the age of fourteen.

12. CASTLES AND TOWER HOUSES

Although Scotland is often thought of as a land of castles, many familiar examples, such as Balmoral and Glamis, are really grand country houses. There are only a small number of major medieval castles that still stand in anything like their original form. East Lothian is lucky to have several examples – Tantallon, Dirleton and Hailes have all withstood the rigours of time. Only fragmentary ruins exist of Dunbar castle, once an important stronghold.

Castles

The first castles were built of wood. An artificial mound was fortified with a timber tower and the area around it enclosed by a wooden wall. While the earthworks of several hundred of these fortifications still exist in Scotland, they are almost unknown in East Lothian. A ground survey uncovered evidence of a motte and bailey castle around six hundred feet to the north of Gladsmuir church. Some of the stone castles such as Dirleton may have started life as a timber fortification, but successive rebuilding has destroyed the evidence.

The sole surviving earthwork mound of a timber castle can be seen close to the seashore at the east end of North Berwick. It was built in the thirteenth century by the MacDuffs, thanes of Fife. At the time of Bannockburn (1314) an English garrison was installed here, but abandoned it on hearing the news from the battlefield and fled to Dunbar castle. In the late fourteenth century, an oblong stone tower was built on the site but has long since vanished. North Berwick castle was possibly abandoned in favour of Tantallon castle by around 1420.

Dunbar castle was the most strategically important such structure in East Lothian. Located on a rocky outcrop on the seashore, it guarded the narrow coastal plain that was the gateway to central Scotland for invading English armies. By the seventh century, long before the medieval castle was erected, the Anglo-Saxon kingdom of Northumbria had a fort here. In 835, according to a rather dubious tale, the fort was gifted by Kenneth MacAlpin, a Pictish king, to a famous warrior called Bar, from which the name Dunbar (*dun*, fort) is said to have derived. For most of the thirteenth century, the earls of Dunbar held the castle, but it was captured by the English in 1296 and used as a base for their troops. After Bannockburn, Edward II sought refuge here before sailing to Berwick-upon-Tweed.

The most famous episode in the castle's history occurred in 1338 when it held out for five months against a besieging English army. Even more remarkable was that the resistance was led by a woman, Black Agnes, the countess of Dunbar, so named for her olive complexion and black hair. Agnes taunted the English from the battlements and on one occasion, when the walls were enduring a bombardment of large rocks, she responded by having her maids dress in their best clothes and led them to the outer walls where they pretended to dust away the damage each time a hostile missile struck. The castle defied all attempts by both the English army and navy to crush it and even a personal visit by Edward III had no effect. The English retreated.

Scotland lost Berwick-upon-Tweed to England in 1483. The town had been the country's most important port and this role was now partly fulfilled by Dunbar. As Dunbar castle had been owned by the earls of Dunbar, some of whom were sympathetic to the English, it was annexed by the Crown and, in 1488, Parliament ordered it to be destroyed to the extent that it could never be repaired. A few years later, this decision was reconsidered, as one of the country's main harbours now had no defence. When war broke out in 1496, James IV had the castle rebuilt. It was completed by 1501 and included a chapel dedicated to St John, as well as a vaulted hall. It was reserved for the King, and the earldom of Dunbar was now held jointly with his queen. During the reign of James V, it was adapted for artillery with a blockhouse being built on a separate rock in the sea, linked to the main structure by a bridge.

The situation changed after the conflict between Mary, Queen of Scots and the earl of Bothwell on one side and most of the Scottish nobility on the other. Dunbar castle was a base for Bothwell and when

The blockhouse of Dunbar, perched on the rocks.

he and Mary lost the power struggle, the Scottish Parliament ordered it to be pulled down to prevent it becoming a thorn in the flesh again. This time the destruction was final, and only fragmentary ruins now crown the cliffs overlooking Dunbar harbour. In addition, over the centuries, the elements have wrought damage on these remains. In 1869, a large section of wall collapsed into the sea during a gale.

Tantallon castle is also on the coast and has stood the test of time. Built of red sandstone, and with the Bass Rock close by, it is one of the most impressive redoubts in Scotland. The structure – unusual for a medieval castle – is little more than a gigantic wall flanked by towers on either end that cuts across a promontory of land surrounded on the other three sides by steep cliffs over 100-feet high. Despite the protection of these natural features, a curtain wall once enclosed the other three sides. Recent excavations have indicated that, unusually, the courtyard itself was divided into two by a further wall. The north-western tower had seven storeys and provided high-status accommodation. There was also a small harbour at the foot of the cliff so the castle could be supplied by sea. North Berwick was one of a number of estates held by the powerful Douglas family. William Douglas built the present castle in the latter part of the fourteenth century, possibly to replace the castle at North Berwick. He had spent his youth at Chateau Gaillard in Normandy and the design of Tantallon was influenced by French military architecture.

The enormous walls of Tantallon castle.

The first written reference to the castle occurs in 1374 when William, first earl of Douglas and Mar, writes 'our Castle of Temptaloun' and mentions two voyages to St Andrews that were described as being 'in great danger from the sea'. It may not have been the first fortification on the site; a map dated before 1300 shows a castellated site here bearing the name 'Dentaltoune', possibly derived from *din talgwn*, Celtic for 'high-fronted fortress'. The emblem of the Douglas family, a bloody heart on a stone shield, stands over the entrance. Towards the end of the fourteenth century, the family split into two factions, the Black and the Red Douglases. The latter took the title earls of Angus and made Tantallon their main residence.

Tantallon has witnessed much conflict. For example, in 1526, Archibald Douglas, sixth earl Angus, held his stepson, the 14-year-old

James V, in virtual captivity for two years. The young king eventually broke free and when Douglas fled to Tantallon castle, James laid siege, requisitioning several artillery pieces from Dunbar castle. After twenty days, the royal forces withdrew, but as the artillery was trundling back to Dunbar, the garrison mounted a raid and captured it. The guns were hauled back to Tantallon for use against the royal forces. James only gained control of Tantallon when Archibald Douglas fled to England and a compromise was reached with the governor, Simon Panango. The damage done by the artillery was repaired and the stronghold remained in the control of the king for the next fourteen years. The wallhead was rebuilt to take heavy cannon and the outer defences were improved, while the towers and chambers were filled in to strengthen the structure.

Another assault on Tantallon took place in the seventeenth century. After the battle of Dunbar in 1650, Oliver Cromwell set about occupying Scotland. In south-east Scotland, 'moss-troopers' began to harass his army; they took their name from armed bands in the Borders, who made a living by robbery and stealing cattle. Moss-troopers now had a new connotation, being used to describe small groups of mounted soldiers loyal to the Royalist cause and Cromwell threatened severe reprisals against anyone who assisted them. In 1651, a band of moss-troopers took possession of Tantallon castle, from where they very effectively attacked the English. Cromwell sent General Monck with a force of several thousand to attack Tantallon; opposing him were ninety-one moss-troopers inside. For twelve days, Monck's cannon battered its walls, while warships blockaded it from the sea. The English prevailed and the castle was then garrisoned by Parliamentary soldiers until the restoration of the monarchy in 1660. The damage done by the artillery was never repaired and by the end of the seventeenth century, Tantallon had been abandoned and left to decay.

For a brief time at the beginning of the nineteenth century, East Lothian was again terrorised by the occupants of Tantallon. A gang of robbers led by a sailor who had been wrecked on Fidra island took up residence in the ruins. After dark they descended the castle walls by means of a rope ladder and plundered the mansion house of Seacliff and the farm at Scoughall. Eventually, all but one of the thieves drifted away. The sole remaining culprit was caught by local men, sent for trial in Edinburgh and transported to the colonies.

Dirleton castle, unlike the two previous strongholds, is a mile inland. This imposing ruin stands on a rocky outcrop of no great height, but with commanding views across the surrounding flat lands. The oldest part extant is from the mid-thirteenth century and consists of a cluster of towers on the south-west corner. The castle was built by the de Vaux family, who were granted the barony of Dirleton in the twelfth century. It is possible there may have been an earlier timber castle on the site, or that the family's first castle may have been at Eldbotle, a short distance to the north-west. John de Vaux was responsible for constructing the stone castle, in the years after 1240. Like Tantallon it was influenced by French design, particularly that at Coucy-le-Chateaux. At that time, it stood in an area of marshland, which enhanced its defences.

When Edward I invaded in 1298, he established a large camp at Kirkliston to the west of Edinburgh. Foraging parties setting out from there were coming under attack from the Scots in Dirleton castle, which had been bypassed in the invasion. Edward's army attacked but the garrison fiercely resisted and as the siege wore on the English troops ran out of food, resorting to eating peas from nearby fields. Eventually, however, Dirleton was captured; the defenders were spared and allowed to leave with their property.

In the early-fourteenth century, Earl Aymer Valence of Pembroke was given orders to put an end to the rebellion led by Robert the Bruce. As part of the campaign, he was ordered to seize Dirleton castle, now controlled by the Scots. Once this was achieved, his brother John Kingston took command and until 1311 it was garrisoned by English troops or their supporters. The Scots eventually managed to wrest back control, and, in accordance with Bruce's policy, Dirleton was 'slighted' to prevent further use by the enemy, its three large stone towers demolished almost down to their foundations.

Around 1350, ownership passed to the Halyburton family, who rebuilt what had become a ruin. They added a new gate-house, kitchen and a great hall was built over the foundations of the original three stone towers. The castle was being warded by the crown in 1363 when it was seized by William Douglas, 1st earl Douglas, in a brief revolt against David II for the alleged misuse of public money. He was defeated at the battle of Lanark by forces loyal to the king and Dirleton was returned to its rightful owners.

In 1515, ownership of Dirleton castle passed to the notorious Ruthven family through marriage. Like the Douglases, they were involved in a

Dirleton castle: west side. The large windows indicate adaptation for residential use.

number of plots against the Scottish monarchy: Patrick, Lord Ruthven, had a hand in the murder of David Rizzio, secretary to Mary, Queen of Scots; his son William, earl of Gowrie, was involved in the kidnap of the16-year-old James VI in 1584. For a brief period, William ruled in the King's name; he was pardoned for this treachery but later executed for plotting to seize Stirling castle. His lands and Dirleton castle were confiscated but had been returned to the family by 1586. In the interim, it was occupied by the earl of Arran who entertained James VI in the requisitioned property. By this time Dirleton had been gentrified with the building of a residential range resembling the town house of the Ruthvens in Perth on top of the medieval fortifications.

By offering the castle to Robert Logan, the Ruthvens enlisted his help in an abortive plan to kill or capture James VI. Alexander and John Ruthven, brothers, died in the attempted regicide at Perth in 1600 and the castle was given by a grateful king to Thomas Erskine, who was responsible for killing the plotters in the ensuing fight. It has been rumoured that John Ruthven was the grandson of James IV, which, if true, meant that he had a stronger claim to the throne than James VI.

In 1649, Manny Haliburton and her husband, Patrick Watson, were accused of witchcraft and underwent examination in Dirleton castle by witchfinder John Kincaid. He claimed to have found the 'evil sign' on them. They were tried at Haddington, found guilty and burnt at the stake.

As with many of the Lothian castles, Dirleton's defences were last put to use when Cromwell invaded in 1650. Some thirty moss-troopers took over the castle and rode out from here to disrupt English supply lines. Again, General Monck was dispatched to deal with the problem. On 9 November, Dirleton was surrounded by 1,600 soldiers and the following day was bombarded by mortars. Dirleton was captured and used as a hospital before being slighted to prevent its use as a base by anti-government forces. With the restoration of the monarchy, Dirleton became the property of the Nisbet family. In the latter part of the seventeenth century, a new mansion house was built at Archerfield and Dirleton castle, like Tantallon, was forsaken as a place of residence.

Hailes castle, unlike those mentioned above, does not figure prominently in the landscape but is well concealed at the bottom of the Tyne valley not far from an important river ford (*photo in plate section*). In many ways it resembled an English fortified manor house but was actually a castle of enclosure. Along with Dirleton and Yester, the castle is one of the oldest in Scotland, probably built by Hugo de Gorlay, scion of an important Northumbrian family, shortly before 1300. The family, backed by the English, supported John Balliol's successful claim to the Scottish throne, but when Balliol refused to obey Edward I's demands, Edward invaded Scotland. The eventual defeat of the English by Robert Bruce led to the Gourlays having their possessions confiscated and Hailes castle passed to new owners. According to tradition, Adam Hepburn rescued the earl of Dunbar from an attack by a vicious horse and was rewarded with the forfeited castle; it remained in his family's possession for the next 250 years.

Additions were made to the western side of the structure including a large tower with a pit prison. Captives were lowered into it from the roof above, making escape near impossible. The castle was attacked twice in 1401 by English troops led by Henry 'Hotspur' Percy but both attempts to capture it failed. However, it fell to the pro-English Archibald Dunbar in 1446, whose soldiers put its defenders to the sword. James IV paid a visit in 1507 while building work was in progress and ordered drink silver to be distributed to the masons. Being a mason could be a hazardous occupation; in 1974 the remains of a finger were found wedged between two stones at the entrance. Bothwell, third husband of Mary, Queen of Scots, may have been born in Hailes castle around 1535. The couple spent the night here in May 1567 while making their way to Dunbar castle. Later the same year, Mary was taken prisoner by the Scottish lords at Carberry hill, while Bothwell fled abroad. The properties of the Hepburns, including Hailes, were confiscated by the Scottish Parliament. James VI then granted the castle to Hercules Stewart and later it came into the possession of the Setons.

After the defeat of the Scottish army at Dunbar in 1650, the soldiers guarding Hailes castle abandoned it. For a time, it was used to garrison Cromwell's troops, but was later demolished to prevent it being occupied by Scottish Royalist forces. As with the other great castles of East Lothian it ceased to have a military role after this date and fell into disuse. In 1835, it was being used as a granary.

Dirleton, Tantallon and Hailes castles are managed by Historic Scotland and welcome visitors.

Other castles

The ruins of Innerwick castle.

The ruins of a number of other castles are scattered across East Lothian. The remains of **Innerwick castle** are perched on a rocky outcrop at the edge of the deep gully of the Thornton burn, not far from the border with Berwickshire. Although protected on three sides by steep slopes and on the fourth by an artificial ditch, it suffered a turbulent history, being fought over for centuries by Scotland and England. Thornton tower stood almost opposite Innerwick castle, also on the edge of the deep river valley, and, in 1547, was much fought over and damaged by cannon fire directed by the English and blown up by them when it fell into their hands. Almost no trace of the tower remains today.

A short distance to the south, there was another castle that stood on the steep banks of the Dunglass burn. It occupied a strategic position on the invasion route from England, at a point where there was only a narrow strip of low-lying ground sandwiched between the sea and the edge of the Lammermuir hills. There had been a castle here since the 1300s. In 1544, during the Rough Wooing, it was besieged and again in 1547, when it was defended by twenty-one soldiers. The English took possession and razed the fortification using no less than four hundred pioneers. So strong was its construction that they had to resort to blowing up its walls with gunpowder. Reflecting the importance of this location, the English constructed a large earthwork fort of their own on the hill overlooking the ravine and site of the castle. When the English had retreated from Scotland, Dunglass castle was rebuilt on a grander scale. James VI stayed here in 1603 with five hundred of his retinue while journeying south to be crowned king of England and Scotland. In 1640, the castle suffered a major disaster during the Second Bishops War, the prelude to the outbreak of the Civil War, when ammunition exploded, killing the earl of Haddington and a number of other Covenanters who were in occupation.

The castle was acquired by Sir John Hall in 1687 and appears to have been rebuilt. It was described as an L-shaped house, probably a tower house around a courtyard. All remaining evidence of the castle was swept away when Dunglass house was constructed on its site but it too has gone the way of the castle. Although the site where they once stood is private, it is only a few hundred feet from Dunglass collegiate church.

Although better known for its association with the supernatural, **Yester castle** was once a significant stronghold. Unfortunately, other than its subterranean Goblin hall – allegedly created by goblins on the instigation of Hugh de Gifford – only a few fragments remain above ground and are concealed in woodland. The castle was built on a promontory formed by the confluence of the Hopes water and a tributary close to Castlemains farm, two miles south-east of Gifford. Its position was reinforced by a ditch around 100 feet wide and 20 feet deep, and a second ditch some 30 feet wide and 15 feet deep cut across the north end, which further isolates its position. It was one of the first stone-built castles in Scotland, with a stone keep constructed some time before 1267. Prior to this, there was a timber motte-and-bailey castle on the site. It was probably built at the end of the twelfth century when William the Lion granted land here to Hugh de Gifford, who was of Anglo-Norman descent. At that time, nobles with this heritage were encouraged to settle in Scotland in return for military service.

Alexander III visited Yester castle in 1278, as a guest of de Gifford. Soon after the outbreak of the Wars of Scottish Independence, Edward I entered Scotland at the head of a powerful army, capturing Dirleton and Yester castles in 1298. The latter was given to Adam de Welles, a knight from Lincolnshire. In 1308, Yester was retaken by the Scottish army and demolished to prevent it being used by the enemy, a common occurrence. After Robert Bruce achieved victory over the English, the fortification was rebuilt, this time as a courtyard castle. It followed a triangular plan similar to the previous structure. In 1357, its ownership passed to the Hay family, also of Anglo-Norman ancestry. Towards the end of the fifteenth century John Hay was created a lord and to reflect his new status he began a major rebuild of Yester.

Like many other East Lothian castles, Yester came under attack by English forces during the duke of Somerset's invasion of Scotland in 1547. A small pioneer force left the main column, marching up the east coast and laid siege. Their attempts failed thanks to John Hay, 4th lord of Yester, putting up a resolute defence. Not long after, the baron fought at the battle of Pinkie but was captured after being thrown from his horse as the defeated Scots fled; he spent the next three years imprisoned in the Tower of London. In the meantime, his castle was captured by English troops, assisted by some Scots, as they tried to increase their grip on south-east Scotland with the establishment of a large base at Haddington. Only a short time elapsed before it was back in Scots hands. Yester castle was abandoned permanently in 1557, when William Hay, 5th lord of Yester, built a new tower house a short distance down the valley. A hundred years later the castle was in a ruinous state.

A further two ruinous castles can be seen not far to the north of Haddington. The sixteenth century **Garleton** – a courtyard castle with a gabled hall house and possibly a tower house enclosed by a curtain wall with drum towers – stands on the north edge of the hills of the same name (*see photo in plate section*). The great sixteenth-century playwright, Sir David Lindsay, may have been born here; his works include *The Satire of the Three Estates*. There is a legend that William Wallace hid in a small cave on the north side of a hill, immediately above the castle, to rain arrows down on the pro-English troops within. While concealed, he thought he had been discovered when a hunting dog approached him, but tied around the animal's neck was a bag of food sent by one of his supporters. Nonetheless, he decided not to linger in the cave for long. The present Garleton castle was built three centuries after Wallace's time but, as in many cases, it was probably constructed on the site of an older fortification. The row of cottages here made use of stone from the original castle. There is no access to the ruins but they can be seen from the roads that run close by.

About a mile to the east, on a ridge overlooking Athelstaneford, are the enigmatic remains of **Barnes castle**, sometimes referred to as 'the Vaults'. Despite covering an extensive area, some 160 feet by 126 feet and flanked by towers, the walls do not rise much above 12 feet. Its owner, John Seton of Barnes, died in 1594 while the castle was in the early stages of construction, hence its unfinished appearance. While most landowners were still building tower houses at this time, the design for Barnes castle was very advanced with its buildings being positioned around a symmetrical courtyard.

Toward the coast, near Gullane, stands the distinctive ruin of the late-sixteenth-century **Saltcoats castle**. The west side survives, consisting of two five-storey towers linked by an arch, giving the ruin its characteristic appearance. It was inhabited until 1790, when it became a quarry for field dykes, much of the structure being removed for agriculture improvements. The only consolation was that the vandals who pulled it down did so with great difficulty; the stones are said to have been 'sheathed in steel', so firm was the old cement. The castle belonged to the ancient family of Livington, or Livingston, the head of which is said to have slain a marauding wild boar at a small stream, Livingston's ford, on the north bank of the Peffer burn. Other accounts state the incident occurred near Prora farm, Athelstaneford, where the 'boar stone' marked the site. For removing this scourge, the Livingstons

Above

Barnes castle, near Athelstaneford.

Right

The ruins of Saltcoats castle.

were awarded extensive lands, stretching from Gullane Point almost as far as North Berwick Law. The spear and helmet worn by the Livingston who killed the boar hung in Dirleton church until around 1830, when they disappeared. The ruins are private but can be seen from a footpath that runs close to its western side.

Tower houses

The first tower house in Scotland dates from 1285. In the following century, numbers increased, particularly in the Borders, where raids were an ever-present danger. The basic design was nothing more than a square or rectangular tower. In time, outbuildings were added and enclosed by a protective wall, making the distinction between them and a castle somewhat academic. East Lothian has many tower houses, but few exist in their original state. When their protection was no longer needed many landowners constructed country houses, incorporating the tower into the design. In some cases, such as Winton house, there is little trace of them, with the new structure being built over an older tower house. At Yester, the sixteenth-century tower house was completely demolished when a new country house was built a century later.

However, at **Lennoxlove house**, near Haddington, the tower house still forms a major part of the building. It is first recorded when David II granted the lands in 1345 to Robert Maitland, who was killed the following year fighting the English. The massive tower standing today dates mainly from the fifteenth century but incorporates parts of an earlier structure. It was once enclosed by a wall forming a courtyard but this did not prevent it being burned by the English in 1549. William Maitland of Lethington, secretary to Mary, Queen of Scots, resided here. John Maitland, duke of Lauderdale, lived here in the seventeenth century; he fell out of an upper window of the tower as a child, but was unscathed. The grounds were enclosed by a grand stone wall constructed after the Duke of York – later James II of England – made a sarcastic remark to him implying that Scotland did not even possess a park (for a country house). The wall, originally 12-feet high and enclosing grounds of more than a square mile, was said to have taken just six weeks to build. When John Maitland died, Stewart, Lord Blantyre, purchased the estate.

Lennoxlove house, formerly a tower house.

At that time, it was still known as Lethington. Its name was changed to Lennoxlove in 1703 in memory of Frances Stuart, duchess of Richmond and Lennox, sometimes referred to as 'La Belle Stuart', and the model for Britannia on British coins. When Frances Stuart died, she left money to William Stewart, Lord Blantyre – a relative who was virtually bankrupt – to purchase the tower house and estate. It later passed to the Bairds and in 1947 became the property of the duke of Hamilton, since when it has become his family seat after the demolition of Hamilton palace in Lanarkshire. Lennoxlove house is open to visitors in the summer months.

In Musselburgh, **Pinkie house**, one of the most impressive seventeenth-century mansions in southern Scotland, incorporates an L-shaped tower house at its northern end. It dates from the previous century, but may contain an earlier fortification. Originally, it was the country seat of the abbots of Dunfermline. Pinkie house is now part of Loretto school and there is no access. The building can be seen in the distance from High Street.

To the south of Musselburgh is **Carberry tower**, an impressive baronial mansion. It began life as a sixteenth-century tower house, to which has been added a much larger residence. The lands originally belonged to the monks of Dunfermline abbey but passed to Hugh Rigg in 1543. He built a small tower house which, again, may incorporate parts of an older building. Four years later, the battle of Pinkie was fought a short distance away. It is recorded that Hugh Rigg advised the commander of the Scottish army, Regent Arran, to alter the position of his soldiers. According to John Knox this was not done for military reasons but with the intention of keeping the fighting away from his tower house. Not long after the Reformation, the lands and tower of Carberry were annexed by the crown, as it appears Rigg had Catholic sympathies. In 1760, John Fullerton became the owner and began adding extensions; further additions were made in the nineteenth century to create the mansion house. From 1800, the Elphinstone family owned Carberry house, in addition to the tower house that bore their name. In 2020, the building is an upmarket hotel.

A number of tower houses have remained relatively unchanged since falling into disuse. One is **Redhouse castle**, a landmark next to the

Redhouse castle, almost intact, save for the roof.

Longniddry–Ballencrieff road. A tall, ruined tower house forms the nucleus of a sixteenth-century courtyard castle, with ornate additions in the following century. It takes its name from the Reid (red) Friars who owned the property and may have had an earlier building on the site. John Laing, deputy keeper of the signet, built the oblong tower house on the north side of the courtyard. It was then extended into an L-plan building with ornamentation when Sir John Hamilton became the owner. The family, who still owned the property at the time of the 1745 rebellion, forfeited Redhouse for supporting the Jacobites. The building was then purchased by Lord Eilbank but he neglected it, preferring to live in Edinburgh. It fell into ruin, although fortunately it has not been used as a quarry for its stone like other abandoned buildings.

A few miles to the west of Redhouse is Preston tower house at Prestonpans (*see photo in plate section*). Preston village belonged to the influential Scottish family, the Hamiltons, from the latter part of the fourteenth century. The L-shaped tower house was built in the following century, around 1460, although parts of it may date from the previous century. During the reign of James II, the Black Douglases precipitated a rebellion. They initially had the backing of the Hamiltons, who later changed their allegiances and rallied around the monarch. For their support in defeating the king's enemy, they were well rewarded. In 1503, James Hamilton was elevated to the position of earl of Arran. The family owned several castles across central Scotland, Preston tower being one of their less-important possessions.

In 1544, the town and castle were burned by the English army commanded by the Earl of Hertford. The Hamiltons rebuilt Preston tower house after this act of destruction. Sir John Hamilton (1565–1644) was responsible for building the upper extension to the tower in 1626. It was torched again in 1650 by troops led by Oliver Cromwell in an act of revenge, as Sir Thomas Hamilton had commanded a troop of cavalry, raised at his own expense to fight against him. It was again set on fire in 1663, this time by accident, and gutted. From this time, it was abandoned by the Hamiltons, who moved to a house close by. Despite this, Preston tower is still an impressive building, reaching a height of about 90 feet, much greater than most other similar buildings. It stands in a small park, which makes it possible to view the exterior close-up.

While both Redhouse castle and Preston tower are roofless, several East Lothian tower houses have been restored. They include the

L-shaped **Stoneypath tower house**, a short distance to the east of Garvald. It stands on a promontory above the Papana water with steep slopes on three sides and is built out of attractive red stone with walls that are nine-feet thick in places. It may have been built around 1350, when it was first held by the earls of Dunbar (originally known as the Gospatricks). It was one of no less than seven fortifications held by this family in East Lothian, referred to as 'warsteeds'. By the end of the fourteenth century, it had passed to the Douglases and after that to the Lyles.

Like most of the other castles and fortifications in East Lothian, Stoneypath suffered during the Rough Wooing. It is thought that Stoneypath tower was captured in 1548, but retaken later that year by the Hamiltons. During Cromwell's campaign against Scotland, his troops removed its roof and there is an unproven claim that the fortification was blown up in the 1650s. Archaeological evidence points to an explosion inside Stoneypath tower, which may have occurred at this time or possibly during the earlier conflict. Up until the end of the twentieth century this was a ruin but has been restored and is now a private residence. It can be viewed externally from a nearby footpath.

Around a mile to the north-east is the well-preserved **Whittingehame tower**, on the north bank of Whittingehame water. It is rubble-built, with three-storeys, and dates from the late-fifteenth century. During the reign of Mary, Queen of Scots, it was the property of James Douglas, who later became regent of Scotland. It is believed he planned the murder of Henry Darnley, the Queen's husband, while travelling between Lennoxlove tower and Hailes castle with the earl of Bothwell. In 1581 justice eventually caught up with James Douglas; he was executed in Edinburgh by the maiden, an early form of guillotine, and his head placed on a spike on the tolbooth, where it remained for eighteen months. Whittingehame tower is still a private residence, hidden away in woodland to which there is no access.

Nearer the coast is **Fenton tower**, standing on Kingston hill, a rocky outcrop surrounded by arable fields. For several centuries it was in a ruinous state until it was restored at the turn of the twentieth century. The current structure was built by Patrick Whytelaw, son of Lord Ruthven, around 1550 and was a typical fortified tower of the time. There had, however, been a tower on the site since the eleventh century. Ownership of the building was forfeited to John Carmichael in 1587. Four years later, James VI, while residing in Falkland palace, was almost captured by a rebel army led by the earl of Bothwell. The inhabitants of the town came to the support of their monarch and enabled him to escape. He fled to East Lothian, taking the ferry to North Berwick and the Carmichaels gave him refuge in Fenton tower. When Cromwell invaded Scotland in 1650, the tower was sacked by English soldiers. At that time, it was owned by the earl of Dirleton, Sir Maxwell of Innerwick. By 1663 it had become the property of Sir John Nisbet, by which time it was probably in a derelict state. A short distance to the north there is a medieval burial site and the remains of the foundations of one of the earliest Christian chapels in Scotland. Good views of Fenton tower, now a private residence, can be had from the road to North Berwick, which passes within a short distance.

Fenton tower, on Kingston hill.

Falside castle also occupies a commanding position, standing on a ridge at a height of 474 feet overlooking Musselburgh and the Firth of Forth (*photo in plate section*). It has in the past been known by a number of names including Fawside, Fauxside and Fawsyde. The first fortification is thought to have been erected here as far back as the eleventh century.

The monks of Newbattle granted land at Falside to Saer de Quincy, 1st earl of Winchester, in 1189. The early castle was attacked in 1288 by Sir William Douglas. Alan la Zouche of Ashby, a distant relative of Saer de Quincy, was its owner at the time. He later made the mistake of supporting the English during the first War of Scottish Independence. Robert the Bruce seized the castle, along with many others, and the Seton family were given control in return for their support. At the end of the fourteenth century it was sold to the Fawsides, who owned it for the next 260 years. They constructed a tower, which forms the oldest part of the present structure; its walls are 6–8 feet thick. In the fifteenth, or early-sixteenth, century an L-shaped tower house was added. The lands of the Fawsides bounded those owned by the Hamiltons of Preston.

A dispute between the two families concerning the grazing of cattle came to a head in 1540. Cattle belonging to the Hamiltons were allegedly poisoned after drinking from a small stream which rose on the Fawsides' land and then flowed through their estate. The Hamiltons attacked Fawside castle, killing some of its guards and setting fire to its gates. The Fawsides retaliated by raiding their neighbour's territory. While fighting against the Hamiltons, the elderly head of the Fawside family became separated from his followers and was dragged from his horse and killed where he fell. His followers wavered and fled back towards Falside castle. The wife of their slain leader rallied the defenders to repel the onslaught. They sallied forth on several occasions, attacking their besiegers and retreating to the tower. The following morning, the Hamiltons realized that their cattle had died of distemper and had not been poisoned. They made all the reparation they could to the widowed Lady Fawside.

Falside castle was again under siege seven years later, this time during the duke of Somerset's invasion. The English had drawn up their forces along the ridge to face the Scottish army at Inveresk. For several hours, Falside held out while the battle of Pinkie raged around it. Lady Fawside organized its defence, having previously defended it against the Hamiltons. Her defence was unsuccessful and the tower house was set on fire with its garrison perishing.

Fawside was repaired in the years after the battle of Pinkie. The ghost of Lady Fawside is said to stalk the building and the battlements. The Fawsides continued to live in the castle, but not without incident. In 1616, John, the only son of Robert Fawside, was murdered by one of the family servants, who attacked him with a knife; he was later tried for his crime and beheaded. There is a plaque in Tranent churchyard in memory of John. Robert Fawside sold the castle a few years later. By the eighteenth century, it had become a ruin. After narrowly escaping demolition in 1960, it has been restored and is now a private residence. A minor road passes close to Falside castle, from which it can be viewed.

There is a tradition that underground passages link Fawside tower with **Tranent tower house**; such stories occur frequently but there is little evidence. Tranent tower house, unlike most other examples, does not stand in open countryside but is surrounded by houses standing at the end of a lane a short distance to the north of Tranent town centre. It is thought to have been built at the end of the sixteenth century, perhaps on the site of an older fortification. At the beginning of the twentieth century, it was used as a stable but since then has been in a ruinous state despite attempts at restoration. It is private property but can be viewed from the nearby road.

Not all of East Lothian's tower houses have fared so well. **Elphinstone tower house** was almost completely demolished due to mining subsidence. Up until the mid-twentieth century, it was a local landmark standing on top of a hill and could be seen from miles away. The tower itself was just under 60-feet high, and, prior to its destruction, was one of the most complete examples of a tower house in the Lothians. Only some parts of its lower walls remain, located on private ground. To the south lay Ormiston tower on the south bank of the Tyne, dating from the fifteenth century, but it too has disappeared. At one time there were tower houses at a number of other locations, including Athelstaneford and Kilduff of which no trace remains today.

Time has taken a toll on a number of other East Lothian strongholds. Only a fragment remains of the once-powerful **Waughton castle**, two miles south of North Berwick. During the reign of James III, his brother, the duke of Albany, tried to seize the throne. His attempt failed but not before he had captured Waughton castle, which under David Hepburn had held out for the king. The castle was again captured in 1548, this time by the invading English army during the Rough Wooing. In 1567 the Hepburns of Waughton fought at the battle of Carberry hill in support of Mary, Queen of Scots and her husband, James Hepburn, 4th earl Bothwell. By the beginning of the eighteenth century, the castle had been abandoned, its buildings quarried for stone. The sparse ruins, which once rivalled Hailes in size, can be seen from a nearby minor road, but there is no access to the site.

The fragments of Gamelshiel castle, Lammermuir hills.

Seacliff tower, near Seacliff house, another ruinous structure, stands on an exposed position overlooking the sea and the Car rocks; the remains of its walls are only a few feet in height. The building was oblong and is thought to date from the sixteenth century but little else is known. Almost all East Lothian castles are located on its plain or low-lying ground. **Gamelshiel castle**, in the heart of the Lammermuir hills, is the exception. Only a few stumps of masonry exist on the lower slopes of Spartleton hill, a short distance north of Whiteadder reservoir. Some of its stones have been used to make sheep pens. Little is known of its history. It appears to have been little more than a small tower, thought to date from the sixteenth century, which possibly guarded the track across the Lammermuirs. There is a story that the lady of Gamelshiel castle was killed by a wolf as she walked near her home one evening.

13. FORTS AND FORTIFICATIONS

The arrival of gunpowder and cannon heralded the decline of the castle. By the sixteenth century, refinements in artillery meant their impregnable walls could be breached in a matter of days. Instead, walls made of soil were built to absorb the impact of cannonballs. The main difference between a castle and a fort is that the former was both a defensive structure and a residence, while a fort was solely for military purposes.

There are two surviving mounds at Inveresk, one of which is in the churchyard of St Michael's and a second in private grounds to the north-east. They were reputedly thrown up as gun emplacements by the English army around the time of the battle of Pinkie in 1547 and would have overlooked the vital bridge across the river Esk. Oliver Cromwell's army is said to have put them to use again in 1650. There may be some substance to this, because Cromwell stayed in Inveresk house and used St Michael's church next door as stables. Excavations have found bones and relics in the mounds, which may be Roman in origin, but could still have been used as an artillery fortification in more recent times.

The best-preserved military earthwork sits on a hill above Dunglass collegiate church. In 1547, the Scots had suffered a devastating defeat at the battle of Pinkie Cleugh but fought back with the support of French troops. The laird of Ormiston's house at Saltoun was successfully mined, retaken from the English garrison and the governor hanged. Hailes castle was also recaptured. In response, the English commander, the duke of Somerset, had a sophisticated fort built at Dunglass in 1548 to guard the narrow coastal plain. Designed by Sir Richard Lee, it cost £2,300, the most expensive fortification constructed in this campaign. It was star-shaped and dominated by four projecting bastions, with thick ramparts and gun emplacements to provide flanking fire. It housed 686 light cavalry and infantry armed with an early form of handgun. The garrison withdrew in 1550, when a peace treaty was signed. The earth ramparts and deep ditches enclose a triangular area, now surrounded by trees (absent in the sixteenth century). A summer house built in 1718 stands on the highest point of the fortification; it can be accessed from the footpath that leads to Oldhamstocks.

The French also built a number of earthwork fortifications; one such example was at Dunbar. The French king, Henry II, sent troops to assist the Scots against the English occupation on condition that he would get control of various strongholds, including Dunbar. The French landed ten thousand soldiers at Leith in June 1548, and, during the same month, took over Dunbar castle and almost immediately began improving the town's fortifications. A motte (defensive mound) was built in front of the castle. The French intention was to fortify the entire town but the plans did not come to fruition.

When Elizabeth I acceded to the throne of England in 1558, it encouraged more strife in Scotland. The French built a fort at Dunbar in 1560 to reinforce the castle. The Scots Protestants were encouraged by the English to oppose Mary of Guise, who died the same year. The Treaty of Edinburgh stipulated that French troops should leave Scottish soil, with their forts at Leith and Dunbar dismantled. The French captain was reluctant to demolish his fort, which could accommodate over five hundred soldiers, with a 'cave' for supplies. The Scots eventually sent a hundred labourers to undertake its removal. By 1561, the French had gone and a few years later Dunbar castle was abandoned. The fort stood at Castle Park on the shore to the north of Lauderdale house, immediately facing the blockhouse of Dunbar castle. No trace remains today.

The French also constructed another fort in the summer of 1549, at Luffness, east of Aberlady. This was done to stop the English garrison at Haddington receiving supplies through the port. In 1552, instructions were given to destroy the fort as it was no longer required, with the artillery relocated to Dunbar. Some earthworks survive around Luffness house, which is not accessible to the public.

By far the largest earthwork fort built in East Lothian was at Haddington after its capture by the English in early 1548. It was the first appearance in Scotland of the *Trace Italienne*, a bastion fort designed to defeat conventional siege tactics of bombardment, sapping and storming. It had an outer wall about 27 feet tall enclosing the whole town and extending south to a point near St Mary's church. Each corner had a large, turf-faced bastion mounted with cannon. An inner fort was erected around the town house, a tall, stone structure, to which the defenders could retreat if outer fortifications were captured. These fortifications were on a completely different scale to the medieval town wall that had previously defended Haddington. The new earthworks were based on a square and appear to have been superimposed on the town with little consideration for its layout.

A number of the town's buildings, which stood on the banks of the Tyne, were demolished. Timber was brought from the nearby woods of

Colstoun for the construction of the ramparts. When completed, a French mercenary serving on the English side was said to have remarked that it was almost as impregnable as Turin. The completed fort was occupied by five hundred cavalry and two thousand infantry soldiers. The Scots were determined to oust the English from Haddington and sent a force of more than five thousand under the command of James, earl of Arran and regent of Scotland. The result was one of the longest sieges in Scottish history.

Despite the deployment of large numbers of soldiers on each side, including ten thousand French troops in support of the Scots, Haddington did not fall. Much blood was spilt, but neither was able to declare victory. However, as the siege dragged on, the English garrison, wracked by plague and hunger, decided the game was no longer worth the candle. A strategic retreat was organised and in September 1549, eighteen months after the siege had begun, they were gone. Haddington was once again in Scottish hands. In March 1550, a peace treaty between Scotland and England was agreed.

The large earthwork fortifications were dismantled not long after and today there is little evidence of the fiercely fought battles around Haddington. St Mary's church is about the only building still standing that witnessed the siege, although it was not unscathed, having part of its roof removed, damage that was not put right for four hundred years. At the end of the sixteenth century, work began on a stone town wall around Haddington. It was not intended to repel invading armies, but for controlling the influx of beggars and undesirables. A few fragments remain today – on the north side of the town between Newton Port and Hardgate, in the vicinity of St John's church.

The fortress on Bass Rock

Another castle adapted for the cannon was that on the Bass Rock, founded by Sir Robert de Lavedre, who was granted the island as a supporter of Malcolm III against Macbeth in the late-eleventh century. It was rebuilt several times, but not much is known of its early history. In March 1406, Robert III sent his son, Prince James (later to become James I), to the safety of the Bass Rock because Robert's brother, the Duke of Albany, was plotting to seize the throne. Not long thereafter the young prince boarded a ship for France but it was captured by the

English thanks to information supplied by Albany. When James eventually returned to Scotland – nineteen years later after payment of a ransom – he had his enemy, Walter Stewart, eldest son of the duke of Albany, held in 'close custody' on the Bass Rock. At this time, the castle was described as 'a fortress, a stone castle with a curtain wall over the landing stage'.

The fortress played an active role in harassing English supply ships during the siege of Haddington. In summer 1548 it was bombarded by twenty-five warships but to little effect. Although the Scottish army was resoundingly defeated by Cromwell at the battle of Dunbar in 1650, it was not due to lack of effort by the Bass Rock garrison. Its soldiers bombarded supply ships bound for Leith and the *John O' London*, carrying Cromwell's personal baggage, was captured. The garrison held out against the furious Cromwell until April 1652, when it was starved into submission.

In 1671, the Bass Rock was purchased for use as a prison for Covenanters. More than forty Covenanters, many of them ministers, passed through the Bass Rock gates, serving sentences from two months to six years. It was described as 'a base, cold, unwholesome prison, all the rooms ordinarily full of smoke like to suffocate and choke them . . . prisoners were necessitate many a time to thrust head and shoulders out of the windows to recover breath'. The prisoners had a meagre diet, consisting mainly of dried fish, and, because only the guards were given fresh water, they were forced to drink from puddles in the rocks.

By the mid-1680s, with the death of Charles II, the prison on the rock had become largely redundant. But it would not be long before it was at the centre of events once again. The Glorious Revolution of 1689 saw the Catholic monarch James VII/11 deposed and William of Orange crowned king, a move that enjoyed widespread support in Scotland. However, there were pockets of support for the deposed monarch. Highland clans raised an army, but their progress south was halted with defeat at Killiecrankie. The Duke of Gordon held Edinburgh castle for King James, but surrendered after a short siege. The entire kingdom was now under the control of William of Orange with the exception 'of one small lonely isle'. This was the Bass Rock, the last place in Scotland to fly the flag for James.

The rock's garrison, under Sir Charles Maitland, held out for nearly two years and during this time, raids were mounted by his men on the coasts of Fife and the Lothians. The government was so concerned it gave instructions that twenty soldiers be kept as a constant guard at Castleton immediately opposite the Bass Rock. Inducements were offered to the garrison; Maitland, for example, was offered indemnity if he gave up. When this did not work, a bribe of three months' pay was mentioned but it did not have the desired effect. The garrison was eventually starved into submission.

In a twist of fate, the new government decided to maintain the fortress as a state prison; its first inmates were sympathisers of the exiled King James. In 1690, General Buchan had been sent by James to drum up support among the clans but the venture was a failure. When confronted by government troops the rebels were routed. Four captured Jacobite officers were dispatched to the Bass Rock and placed in cells recently occupied by the Covenanters. They were given a degree of freedom, being allowed to wander about the island behind the fortifications. Only a few weeks after their arrival a ship docked with a cargo of coal for the prison; the governor was away and some of the garrison were ashore at Castleton. While the remaining soldiers were occupied unloading the coal, three prisoners shut the main gates and appeared on the battlements armed with muskets. They taunted the soldiers stranded on the landing stage, telling them to leave the Rock. Having no alternative, they embarked on the coal ship for the mainland.

On hearing about this daring act, Jacobite sympathisers dispatched ammunition and supplies to the Bass Rock. The rebellious prisoners had their ranks swelled with the arrival of sixteen supporters, including two Irish seamen. When word reached James VII, he threw his weight behind the enterprise and dispatched supplies and muskets. In no time, raids were being again being mounted from the Bass Rock on the coast for livestock and supplies. Merchant ships sailing up the Firth of Forth were also intercepted and looted of their provisions in the name of 'the King across the sea'.

Despite the loss of some of their colleagues during government incursions, the rebels continued their forays ashore. On one occasion, they stole sheep on May island that belonged to the lighthouse keepers. King William was becoming increasingly exasperated by this show of defiance so two frigates were dispatched to attack the rebels, but the mission ended in failure. It was found that the ships' cannon could not hit the fortifications on the Bass Rock: they were beyond the elevation of the guns, perched high up the cliff face. The rebels managed to inflict some damage on their assailants with their ordnance and killed several sailors. After two days, the frigates gave up and withdrew.

With the siege entering its third year in August 1693, the *Lion*, a small Royal Navy warship, and two other ships, were ordered to enforce the blockade. One day, a French man of war was seen heading up the Firth of Forth but instead of attempting an interception, *Lion* beat a hasty retreat. The French warship then anchored close to Bass Rock and proceeded to unload supplies for the rebels. A message from the deposed James VII was delivered to Captain Michael Middleton expressing gratitude for his support and promising further provisions.

The government responded by strengthening the blockade. By now, anyone collaborating with the Jacobite rebels faced the death sentence. A man named Trotter was caught near Whitekirk and sentenced to be executed. The place of execution was to be the nearest point on the shore to Bass Rock, as a warning to the rebel garrison. When the fateful day came, a large crowd of onlookers gathered around the gallows. Before the sentence could be carried out, they were sent fleeing in all directions when cannon on Bass Rock opened fire. Trotter was later hanged in a field out of range of the rebel guns and the location became known as Gallows Field.

After enduring the long, hard winter of 1693–4, the garrison's spirits were lifted by another letter from James VII. He promised to send them further supplies together with a military adviser and a priest. It is not known if either man ever set foot on Bass Rock, but further provisions arrived on a small Dutch vessel. The garrison was so depleted that there were not enough men to bring the supplies ashore so ten sailors from the Dutch vessel disembarked onto Bass Rock to assist. Seven bags of rusks had been landed when the *Lion* appeared. This caused panic among the sailors on board the Dutch vessel. They cut its landing ropes and immediately put to sea and such was their haste that they left ten of their crew behind on the island.

The rebels were now in a dire situation, as they now had ten additional mouths to feed. Provisions were so low that everyone was put on a ration of two ounces of rusks per day. In April 1694, Middleton made it known that he was willing to discuss terms of surrender. To conceal their dire circumstances, coats and hats were placed on the battlements by the rebels when a Major Reid arrived to negotiate. He was offered French wine and biscuits to give the impression that there was no shortage of food or drink. The rebels were offered lenient terms;

they could go either to Dunkirk or Havre de Grace. Alternatively, after a month, those who wished could continue to live in Scotland. The siege came to an end on 18 April 1694.

In 1701, William III ordered the demolition of the fortifications on Bass Rock, but the government reserved the right to refortify the island at any time should circumstances dictate. Some of the old cannon remained; one was used to fire a salute when George IV sailed up the Forth to visit Edinburgh in 1822. Bass Rock did not have any permanent inhabitants until the construction of the lighthouse on top of the old fortifications some two hundred years later.

The castle and later fort relied chiefly on the sheer cliffs of the island for defence. The main function of the man-made fortifications – covering a small area close to sea level on the south-east side of the island – was to guard the only landing place and passageway. The sixteenth-century castle walls with their gun loops still exist today; they were incorporated into the fort, which was built a century later. The prison buildings and garrison accommodation blocks, which resembled houses, stood a short distance behind them, but have now disappeared.

The fortress on Bass Rock, with gun loops visible.

At Dunbar harbour, a small stone fort still stands on Lamer island and, unlike the castle, is in a good state of preservation. Towards the end of the eighteenth century, shipping and harbours at the mouth of the Firth of Forth were threatened by marauding pirates. The most notable of these was John Paul Jones, of Scottish birth, who had joined the fledging American navy during the fight for independence. In command of the *Ranger*, in 1779 he led his fleet of five ships to Dunbar, intending to burn it to the ground. A gun battery was hastily cobbled together using cannons from whaling vessels at Kirkhill to the eastern side of the harbour. When Jones met with opposition, he changed his plans and sailed up the Forth towards Edinburgh but unfavourable winds put paid to this plan as well.

In May 1781, Captain Fall, an American commanding a French privateer, fired cannonballs into Dunbar and attempted to capture a fishing vessel entering the harbour. Cannon were again requisitioned from the whaling vessels tied up at the quays and brought to bear on the hostile vessel. They bombarded the enemy from the castle and Lamer island. Captain Fall fired back but with little effect and he too abandoned his plan to raid the town. He then sailed to May island, where he stole some sheep before leaving the Firth of Forth. In response to these events, it was decided to establish a fort next to the harbour on Lamer island, which initially had twelve cannon, increased to sixteen during the Napoleonic Wars. The small, sandstone structure still survives today and is little changed. This was not the only East Lothian port to be protected by a stone fort: Morrison's Haven at Prestonpans once had a fort, but no trace of it remains. It was built around 1547, not by the government but by the owner of the harbour, Alexander Acheson. It was rectangular, with walls 9-feet thick; an underground passage several hundred yards-long ran south-east from it. The stone fort was believed destroyed by Cromwell's soldiers in 1650. Today its site lies buried under the road that runs between Prestonpans and Musselburgh, next to Prestongrange industrial museum.

At the beginning of the nineteenth century, with Napoleon threatening to invade, the government took additional anti-invasion measures. Wooden huts capable of housing large numbers of infantry were erected overlooking the sea at Aberlady bay, with further accommodation for cavalry near Belhaven. Locals were told to flee to the Lammermuir hills should the French set foot on the beach. When the threat receded, the barracks became redundant and by 1814 had been removed. The only relic of this invasion scare is the small signal station on top of North Berwick Law, now a ruin. There was once another example on the Garleton hills.

In 1855, the militia artillery established a base at Dunbar using Lauderdale house as its barracks. An artillery battery was established on the site of the present swimming pool with its guns pointing out to sea. It later moved to a site near the war memorial before being removed from the town in the 1930s. In 2005, a preserved 25-pounder QF mk. II artillery piece, one of the army's most successful weapons of the Second World War, was placed on the cliff top, close to Bayswell Road. Appropriately, its muzzle faces the blockhouse of Dunbar castle. This was built in the early-sixteenth century and was the first of its type in Scotland. Standing on a separate island, its construction was an attempt to drag the medieval castle into the age of gunpowder. It was originally octagonal in plan, measuring 54 feet by 60 feet, with walls 8-feet thick in which there were recessed gun platforms. It was reached by a passageway from the main buildings, which was some 70 feet in length.

14. THE WORLD WARS

First World War

Before the outbreak of war in 1914, there was concern about the threat from Zeppelins. During the summer of 1915, several sites in East Lothian were considered for an aerodrome to defend the important Rosyth naval base: these included Dunbar, but eventually a field at East Fortune was selected. The first aircraft arrived in September and were initially housed in tents. Throughout 1916 it had the distinction of being the only Royal Navy airfield in Scotland. By the end of the year, there were seventeen duty pilots, with five aircraft available for defensive purposes. There were also a few other patrol aircraft.

On the night of 2 April 1916, a RNAS Avro 504 took off from East Fortune in an attempt to intercept two Zeppelins heading for Edinburgh. The pilot was unable to locate them and crashed while attempting to land at East Fortune. Over the next two years, the airfield expanded rapidly with the improvised accommodation for both men and machines being replaced by permanent hangars and barrack blocks. In 1917, it became the shore base for aircraft carried on warships. The following year, torpedo training was undertaken, with a temporary landing ground established at Belhaven bay. At least sixteen pilots had to be rescued from the sea while making practice torpedo drops.

At the start of the war it was thought that Zeppelins would wreak havoc on both civil and military targets, but the real menace was the submarine. In an effort to counter this threat, the navy developed airships to patrol sea lanes; they had the ability to remain airborne for many hours at a time. The first two coastal-class airships arrived at East Fortune in 1916 and were housed in purpose-built sheds, much larger than aircraft hangars. The coastal airships were small in comparison to R.24, the first rigid airship to be based at East Fortune, and the British equivalent of a Zeppelin. A 700-foot-long shed was constructed at East Fortune to house the rigid airships. In addition, there were numerous ancillary buildings to support their operation, including windbreaks and a plant to manufacture gas.

Another rigid airship, the R.29, also based at East Fortune, was patrolling off the coast of north-east England in September 1918 when an oil slick was sighted – the tell-tale sign of a submarine. A number of bombs were dropped and the submarine was sent to the bottom. The R.29 is the only British rigid airship to have the distinction of destroying an enemy submarine. Less fortunate was the smaller North Sea-type airship, NS.3, which, a few months earlier, was returning to East Fortune when a south-westerly gale blew up. It struggled for several hours to make any headway towards the coast, eventually crashing into the sea a few miles north-east of Barns Ness lighthouse. Five of the crew were rescued but the remaining five drowned, trapped in the wreckage.

At the end of the war, East Fortune looked to have a bright future. The newly delivered R.34 airship departed in July 1919, heading for the USA amidst much publicity. It returned to England just under two weeks later, having made the first successful return crossing of the Atlantic by air. There were few airfields in Britain that could handle airships of the size of the R.34. RAF Howden in Yorkshire was one of them and the RAF decided to concentrate its airship fleet there and not at East Fortune. There was an outcry in Scotland, with questions raised in Parliament. East Lothian was dealt a further blow with the disbanding of the torpedo school in 1920 and the closure of the airfield not long after. The large airship shed – one of the biggest buildings ever constructed in Scotland – was torn down, as were most of the other airship facilities.

A short distance from East Fortune airfield was an emergency landing ground at West Fenton that became a major First World War airfield in its own right. Towards the end of the war, the Royal Flying Corps selected it for a training depot to meet the urgent need for more pilots. A large building programme was undertaken on a site of around thirty-six acres, with the construction of six aircraft hangars as well as various workshops. It was officially known as Gullane airfield, although in the Second World War was renamed Drem. In the summer of 1918, there were over eight hundred personnel stationed here. Accidents were commonplace, with aircraft frequently ending up in the Forth, while one pilot misjudged his height and flew into a concrete building on the airfield. The undercarriage of another caught on high-tension wires while coming into land, causing the Sopwith Camel to crash and burn, killing the pilot. American pilots were also trained at RAF Gullane before heading to the front. The airfield closed in 1919, like most others in Scotland.

In autumn 1916, 77 Home Defence squadron, Royal Flying Corps, was formed to defend the airspace over the Firth of Forth and as far south as Berwick-upon-Tweed. Most of its aircraft were initially based at Turnhouse, Edinburgh, but some were later transferred to Penston, near Macmerry. The airfield was located on the east side of a minor road, just to the south of Penston and close to Butterdean wood. By this time, Zeppelins were rarely seen over Britain and 77 Squadron was given the additional role of supporting the army should the Germans invade. During 1918, the remainder of the unit had arrived from Turnhouse. Several small landing grounds, for use in an emergency, were scattered across the countryside, including Townhead, near Gifford, Skateraw and South Belton at Dunbar. The one at Skateraw was located in a field just to the west of Torness nuclear-power station. There is a small memorial to it close to the car park at Skateraw. Penston airfield closed in 1919 when 77 Home Defence squadron disbanded. No trace of either the small hangars or other buildings remain, the land being returned to agriculture.

The Germans had no plans to carry out an invasion of Britain during the First World War. East Lothian, however, has a rare survival of 1914–

18 beach defences constructed to defend the coast. On the seaward side of the wood at Hedderwick, close to the surviving pill box at Tyninghame, is a trench system. About two thousand feet of the original system can still be traced here although much survives only as a long, zigzag depression. At the north end the actual trench survives to a depth of around four feet. Even Belgium does not have an example of a front-line trench system of this length.

Second World War

For most of the interwar period, East Lothian was devoid of military airfields. In the mid-1930s, as a consequence of the looming threat from Germany, the RAF began an expansion programme. The former airfield at Gullane was renamed RAF Drem and completely rebuilt, the original buildings of the First World War being swept away. In 1939, 13 Flying Training School began operations at the airfield with a fleet of Airspeed Oxfords, Hawker Harts and Audax. Due to its strategic position between the North Sea and Edinburgh and the Royal Navy base at Rosyth, Drem was transferred to Fighter Command shortly after the declaration of hostilities. Spitfires of 602 City of Glasgow squadron were the first of many front-line units to be based here.

In the opening months of the conflict, the Lufwaffe concentrated much of its attention on Scotland and it was not long before 602-squadron aircraft were in action. On 16 October 1939, it fought an air battle against twelve Junkers 88s that were attacking shipping in the Forth, with two enemy aircraft shot down. On 28 October, a lone Heinkel 111 was spotted flying over the Forth and Spitfires of 602 and 603 squadrons were sent in pursuit. They riddled it with machinegun fire, wounding the pilot, who managed to make a forced landing on the Lammermuir hills between High Latch and Kidlaw to the east of Humbie; two of the crew of four were killed. This was the first German aircraft to be brought down on the British mainland in the Second World War and received much press attention.

Early the following year, another He.111 was forced down by 603-squadron Spitfires and landed at Rhodes farm, North Berwick, completely intact. The capture of this bomber provided the RAF with invaluable intelligence on enemy aircraft. One important discovery was the *knickebein* ('crooked leg') blind-bombing system used for locating targets at night. By the end of 1940, the Germans had switched their attention to the south coast of England and sightings of enemy aircraft became increasingly rare. Nevertheless, a succession of squadrons flying Spitfires and Hurricanes regularly patrolled the skies over East Lothian until the end of 1944. During the war no Drem aircraft were lost to enemy action, but many were destroyed in accidents, both in the air and on the ground. One of the worst, on the airfield itself, was to a visiting Flying Fortress, which failed to get airborne in February 1944, killing its four American crew and two British passengers.

Drem airfield gave its name to the Drem lighting system, invented by station commander Richard Atcherley. It guided fighter pilots approaching the airfield at night towards the runway and had the added advantage that it was invisible to enemy aircraft flying directly overhead. Further experiments were undertaken at RAF Drem, including the development of equipment known as 'Serrate' in 1943; this was a homing device that locked onto the radar transmissions of night fighters and could then be used to locate them. Drem was selected for such trials because it was far enough away from German territory to avoid electronic eavesdropping. For the same reason, the Admiralty's establishment for testing methods of jamming German radar was perched on a cliff top immediately to the north of Tantallon castle; it was in use until 1984.

From 1942, the Fleet Air Arm also had a squadron based at RAF Drem to train night-fighter pilots. It made use of the radar station at Dirleton, which also supplied directions to aircraft attempting to intercept German bombers at night. With the defeat of the German forces in Europe, the RAF began to run down its operations, but as it was thought that the conflict with Japan might go on for years, Drem was transferred to the Fleet Air Arm in April 1945.

In May 1945, three white-painted Junkers 52 transport aircraft touched down at Drem. On board was a delegation of German officers, there to arrange the surrender of their forces in Norway. The following year, Drem was returned to the RAF. It was closed not long after, never to be used as an airfield again. Unlike many Fighter Command airfields, many of the buildings associated with RAF Drem still remain in 2020. A number of the accommodation huts form a small retail park, while the remaining hangars and technical buildings to the west are used by businesses. Parts of the perimeter track remain, although the grass runways have long since been ploughed and returned to agriculture.

The former First World War airfield at East Fortune was initially opened as a relief landing ground for RAF Drem in the summer of 1940. By the following year it had become an airfield in its own right, its task to train night-fighter aircrews for Fighter Command. Twin-engined Bristol Blenheims and Beaufighters were used for this purpose along with single-engine Bolton Paul Defiants. Trainee airmen came not only from Britain but also as far away as Australian and New Zealand. With much of the flying carried out at night by inexperienced pilots there were frequent accidents. On 15 August 1941, a Bolton Paul Defiant hit a farm building while attempting to land at RAF Drem. As German raids on Britain diminished, it was decided to transfer RAF East Fortune to Coastal Command. Bristol Beauforts and Beaufighters flown by 132 Operation Training Unit were employed to instruct crews in anti-shipping strikes. Many later took part in attacking vessels off the coast of Norway flying from bases in north east Scotland. In May 1946, 132 Operational Training Unit was disbanded and RAF East Fortune was transferred to Fighter Command, but closed not long after.

Unlike at RAF Drem and East Fortune, almost all traces of RAF Macmerry have been obliterated. In the mid-1930s, a small airfield was laid out on land near Tranent for Edinburgh Flying Club. It was located a short distance to the north of the site of the First World War airfield at RAF Penston. In 1936, Macmerry also began to be used by passenger aircraft operating between Aberdeen and England. For a brief time, it became the civil airport for Edinburgh. In 1941, the RAF took over the site and built a single large hangar, along with eight smaller 'blister' hangars. A detachment of Hawker Hurricanes was briefly based here from RAF Drem and it also served as a satellite airfield for RAF East Fortune. A number of other squadrons, several of which specialised in supporting army operations, also used the airfield. One pilot said Macmerry resemble a postage stamp compared with their previous airfield at RAF Thruxton in Hampshire. This was despite the fact that the airfield had been greatly enlarged in 1942.

Cuncliffe-Owen Aircraft had a works on the eastern edge of the airfield for overhauling Lockheed Hudson aircraft and later the SMT company repaired Corsair aircraft here. In 1946, Macmerry airfield was reopened by the Edinburgh Flying Club. It closed in 1953, and over the next fifty years most of its buildings were removed, although some remain a short distance to the south at Penston. When the A1 was improved, the new dual carriageway was driven through the centre of the airfield, running almost parallel to the previous site of the main runway, a few yards to the north. RAF Macmerry also had a sinister secret; it had underground storage tanks that contained mustard gas, which would have been sprayed on the beaches by aircraft of 614 Squadron in the event of invasion. A live practice with the gas was carried out in October 1942. The new A1 now runs over the site of the tanks, which were on the northern edge of the airfield.

In early 1941, the RAF established a minor airfield a short distance to the south of Haddington at Lennoxlove, its purpose to store aircraft away from major airfields. The runway was initially very short, but was extended by tearing down a section of the boundary wall of the estate and building the runway across the Haddington–Gifford road. By 1944, there were nearly 120 aircraft stored here, but, by late 1945, this minor airfield had closed and today there is little evidence of its existence.

Unlike in the First World War, there was serious concern about an invasion and hasty preparations were made to fortify the coastline. The chain of defensive works extended along the east coast as far north as Scotland; with Norway also under enemy control, it was thought an invasion could be launched across the North Sea. The public were no longer allowed onto the extensive sandy beaches, such as Belhaven and Tyninghame. In a list drawn up in June 1940 Aberlady and Belhaven bays were ranked second and third in priority on a list of thirteen vulnerable Scottish beaches.

Mines were laid on the vulnerable parts of the coastline, both onshore and offshore, while large concrete blocks were placed just above the waterline to impede the advance of armoured vehicles. There was concern that troops might be landed by gliders on level areas of land. Wooden poles were erected to act as a deterrent to such an action; almost all of them have long since been removed but a few still exist and can be seen at Hedderwick sands on the edge of Belhaven bay and there are also examples in Gosford bay, including one mounted on an upturned concrete block. Many are barely visible, extending only few feet above the mud.

A coastal battery was constructed on the coast near Dirleton to defend the approaches to the Forth. There was also one opposite, on the Fife coast. Known as the Fidra battery, although it was on the mainland, it was equipped with two six-inch guns removed from a former warship; roofs were constructed over the guns to conceal them from the air. In 1940 five more former naval guns were located much further inland, at Spott, at the height of the invasion scare. The skies over East Lothian were protected by anti-aircraft guns, supported by searchlight batteries at Keith, near Humbie, and at Whitburgh, near Pathhead. There were additional anti-aircraft searchlight positions near Dirleton, East Linton, Garvald, Gifford, Haddington, Innerwick and Oldhamstocks. A less conventional form of defence was the 'flame fougass'; if enemy ships had entered Dunbar harbour, its waters would have been flooded with petrol and then set alight.

There were similar traps alongside the roads. The obstacles included concrete road blocks, a few examples of which survive, including one in Tyninghame Links wood. Machinegun posts were set up across East Lothian, some enclosed in small fortifications built out of brick or concrete, known as pillboxes. Seven were constructed in the vicinity of Wallyford and Whitecraig. The steep ravine at Dunglass on the border with Berwickshire with its vital road and rail bridges was also heavily defended with a series of earthworks and pillboxes. Most of these have been demolished, but examples survive at Drem on the site of the former airfield, as well as at Scoughall Links and Tyninghame near St Baldred's cradle.

East Lothian also had some forty observation posts. The best-known example is a concrete-and-brick structure close to the summit of North Berwick Law. Had the Germans managed to advance inland there were specially trained units that would remain hidden and attack from the rear; in Janefield wood at East Linton there was an underground base with arms and ammunition. There were further examples nearby at Drylawhill and Smeaton, which were filled in at the end of the war.

East Lothian was also home to more conventional troops, many of whom were Poles. In February 1942, the 1st Polish armoured division was established with one of its units based at Haddington. Much of the training was done on the open spaces of the Lammermuir hills, where anything that stood in their way was liable to be demolished. Shelling was practised at Mayshiel and Faseny, close to where Whiteadder reservoir is today. Early in the war, Polish soldiers were responsible for undertaking much of the concrete work on the anti-tank blocks that once lined the seashore. Although some of the blocks were later removed, many still can be seen on the coast at Gosford bay, Gullane, Ravensheugh sands, Tyninghame and Belhaven bay. There is little other evidence that Polish soldiers were once present in East Lothian, other

Anti-tank concrete blocks, west of Gullane. They date from the early years of the Second World War.

than a small memorial hidden in Ormiston wood, where there was once a camp.

After D-Day, large numbers of Germans were captured and new camps had to be hastily opened. In the grounds of Gosford house more than three thousand German prisoners were held, living in huts accommodating fifty men each. Even this became overcrowded and a smaller satellite camp was opened at Amisfield, Haddington, which could hold a further thousand.

The most obvious reminder of the conflict is the airfields. Like the other wartime airfields in East Lothian, RAF East Fortune closed not long after the end of the war. In the early post-war years, the runway was extended with the intention that it would become a base for American bombers, but this came to nothing. Later, fire engines were stored here along with other emergency supplies to be used in the event of hostilities with the USSR. In 1961, the runways of East Fortune came to life again when they were briefly used by passenger aircraft while Edinburgh airport was undergoing repairs. More recently, the site has been used as a venue for a Sunday market and motorcycling events.

Much of the Second World War airfield at East Fortune has been preserved intact. The former technical area, which includes the hangars and many smaller buildings associated with maintenance and servicing, is now part of the Museum of Flight. The runways still exist, along with the control tower, but are no longer in use except for a very small stretch used by microlight aircraft. Unfortunately, little trace remains of the First World War structures that were situated on the northern side. Some of the former barrack blocks were converted into a tuberculosis sanatorium in 1922. From the 1950s it housed patients with learning disabilities before eventually closing in 1997. Twenty-odd years later, the East Fortune hospital, dating back to the early years of the twentieth century, is in a derelict state. There is no access to the buildings.

Today, East Fortune is best known as the home of the Museum of Flight, Scotland's leading collection of preserved aircraft, housed in Second World War hangars on the south side of the former airfield. It started life as a storage collection for the Royal Scottish Museum, but then became an offshoot of it, opening to the public for the first time in 1975. There is one hangar devoted to civil aircraft and another to military aircraft. The third is used for aircraft renovation.

Many of the aircraft displayed have connections with Scotland, including a Loganair Beech 18, which once flew scheduled services to the Highlands and Islands. There is also a Scottish Aviation Twin Pioneer along with a British Aerospace Jetstream, both of which were built at Prestwick. On the military side, the Hawker Sea Hawk, De Havilland Sea Vampire and De Havilland Sea Venom all once served with the Fleet Air Arm at RNAS Lossiemouth, Morayshire.

As at 2020, the Museum of Flight had over thirty preserved aircraft plus a number of aircraft noses. The largest machines – which include an Avro Vulcan nuclear bomber, a de Havilland Comet C.4, and a BAC 111 – stand in the open air. In pride of place is the Aerospatiale BAC Concorde, which has the fourth hangar to itself. The aircraft was transported to its present location by sea in 2004 on a barge that berthed at the jetty at Torness power station. It was then moved overland, the final stages along an improvised track to reach East Fortune as the roads were too narrow for the Concorde to negotiate. The Museum of Flight air display has become a major annual attraction since it was first held in the closing years of the twentieth century; the RAF's premier aerobatic team, the Red Arrows, are regular performers.

RELIGION

15. ST BALDRED

Scotland's patron saint, Andrew, has been closely associated with East Lothian, since a cloud in the shape of a diagonal cross was seen over the fighting armies at the battle of Athelstaneford. There is another saint associated with East Lothian, namely Baldred. Unfortunately, his connections with the county are vague; a handful of references survive in medieval manuscripts, but the details are often contradictory. According to one version, he was a follower of the great missionary, St Kentigern, in the late-sixth century. Initially, he worked in the west of Scotland founding houses for monks and eventually succeeded Kentigern as Celtic bishop of Strathclyde. The East Lothian churches of Auldhame, Tyninghame and Prestonkirk were said to have been founded by him. Baldred's career was cut short because of turmoil in the kingdom of Strathclyde and he lost his spiritual authority.

Prestonkirk church, East Linton. It stands on the site of a medieval church dedicated to St Baldred.

Another account, written in 1510, depicts Baldred as a hermit who spent his life on Bass Rock. It was not uncommon for early Christians to seek out isolated islands for religious contemplation. However,

Holinshed's chronicles depict someone with a more active role in society. This sixteenth-century account states he died in AD 607 but this is at odds with the twelfth-century historian, Simeon of Durham, who gives his death as AD 756. His later years were spent at Tyninghame monastery. This Baldred is associated with the see of Lindisfarne, on Holy island. At that time, Tyninghame had authority over an area of territory similar to that occupied by the county of East Lothian today.

To add to the confusion, some historians have claimed Baldred was also Bilfritt or Bilfrid, a hermit goldsmith who was responsible for creating the cover of the book, *The Gospels of St Cuthbert*, now in the British Museum. It was made in the time of the rule of bishops Eadfrid and Ethelwold of Lindisfarne between 678 to 740. The relics of saints Bilfrid and Baldred were placed in St Cuthbert's shrine at Durham, but later removed to the shrine of St Bede in 1104. Over time, reports of his life became greatly embellished and Baldred is attributed with supernatural power, probably with the encouragement of the medieval church. The most significant evidence proffered for this is that, on his death, the parishes of Auldhame, Tyninghame and Preston all vied for Baldred's remains. To the astonishment of all, next morning it was discovered that there were three identical bodies. Thus, he could be interred in all three locations, thereby resolving the dispute.

Up until the Reformation, the church at Preston, East Linton, was dedicated to Baldred. A large statue of the saint was destroyed accidentally in 1770; a stone mason was attempting to incorporate it into one of the new walls when the church was reconstructed. A short distance to the south of the church, overlooking the Tyne, a plaque marks the site of St Baldred's well, from which the 'purest water flowed'. Close by in the river itself is a pool called St Baldred's whirl. At Auldhame, another well to St Baldred is found in the middle of a field but is now capped; its waters were renowned for making a good cup of tea.

Such was his influence that several other natural features bear his name. At a rocky headland on the north side of the mouth of the Tyne, at Tyninghame, there is a fissure 14-feet deep called St Baldred's cradle, which, at its mouth to seaward, is 6-feet wide. In stormy weather the sea bursts in with considerable force, spraying water into the air. Legend has it that when the rocks were subjected to extreme elements, they swayed like a cradle. Around three miles to the north, at Seacliff, is St Baldred's cave; it is at the foot of a cliff standing on a raised beach. George Sligo, the owner of Seacliff house, discovered it around 1830 when he removed the sand covering its entrance. Unearthed in it were the skeletons of two children, along with many animal bones including that of a horse; there was also a large, flat rock at the back of the cave. This gave Sligo the idea that it had been an altar on which human sacrifices had taken place; he speculated that the shallow cave may have been a pagan temple, perhaps to the Norse god, Balder, a son of Odin. There are a number of similarities between him and Baldred.

There is some evidence that the Vikings at one time may have settled in the area. The local name Scoughall is not unlike the Icelandic word *skogall*, which signifies rocky promontory. The truth is perhaps more mundane as some artefacts were found in the cave dating from the Iron Age, when it may have been used as a shelter. The cave itself faces onto a reef, known as St Baldred's boat. According to legend, this extensive area of large rock was not always in the same place. It used to be further offshore and caused many ships to run aground. Baldred was upset by this destruction and placed himself on this rock; at his nod, the rock lifted itself up and headed towards the shore, moving like a ship. It has to the present day remained close to the beach, as a reminder of this miracle.

St Baldred's beacon (or cross), Seacliff beach.

Standing close by on the South Car Rock is St Baldred's beacon, a circular structure not unlike a small lighthouse crowned by a cross (*photo on page 121*). It serves as a warning to mariners of the hazardous coast. Monks originally placed a seamark on the reef and it was rebuilt in the late-nineteenth century. On the shore is Seacliff harbour, which claims to be the smallest harbour in Britain; it is 40 feet in length, with an entrance no more than 6-feet wide. The harbour was created in 1890 by the owner of Seacliff estate using a steam engine to carve it from the Ghegan rock, which appropriately means 'churchmen's haven'; it has been used by lobster and crab boats.

Further offshore there is also a ruined chapel, perched high on Bass Rock, dedicated to St Baldred. Although some believe he lived on the rock in the seventh century, the present building dates from c.1492. During the latter part of the seventeenth century, it was reduced to the role of a store for gunpowder and ammunition for the garrison on the Bass Rock. On the mainland, in North Berwick, Baldred has given his name to St Baldred's Crescent and St Baldred's Road. The Episcopal church built in the nineteenth century has also been named after him.

16. RELIGIOUS HOUSES

St Baldred founded the monastery at Tyninghame, whose territory extended east from Musselburgh and was bounded to the south by the Lammermuir hills. There were further monasteries at Auldhame and Aberlady, but little is known about them and no trace above ground exists today. Tyninghame monastery was raided by the Vikings in 941 and there is no further reference to it. The ruins of St Baldred's parish church are believed to stand on its site but are not generally accessible, being in the grounds of Tyninghame house.

It was not until the twelfth century that the next religious houses appeared in East Lothian and they were very different from those of the Dark Ages. The Scottish kings invited religious orders, such as the Cistercians, to establish monasteries, ensuring that Scotland did not become a spiritual backwater.

Haddington was home to one of the largest convents in Scotland, situated about a mile to the east of the town on the site of Abbeymill farm, next to Abbey Bridge; in its time it was also one of the wealthiest in Britain and Ireland. Unfortunately, no trace of the buildings can be seen today, with the exception of the ruins of the twelfth century St Martin's kirk on the edge of Haddington. For much of its early existence it belonged to the convent, standing close to the western entrance to its grounds. The nuns sometimes held courts in the building.

The ruins of the twelfth-century St Martin's kirk, Haddington. It belonged to the former Cistercian convent here.

The Haddington convent was run by the Cistercians. It was founded by Countess Ada, wife of Prince Henry, eldest son of David I and built between the death of her husband in 1152 and her own death in 1178. Ada also gifted extensive tracts of land to it as did other wealthy landowners. The prioress swore fealty to Edward I in 1291 and 1296, saving it from destruction during the English invasions at the end of the thirteenth century. The convent was burned by the English in 1356, with all records destroyed. In 1358, floods extensively damaged

Haddington, but the convent was allegedly saved when a nun threatened to throw a statue of the Virgin Mary into the water unless she protected the building. At that point, the water level began to drop.

In 1400, Henry IV entered Scotland at the head of a large army, the last time an English king led troops into Scotland, but, unlike previous incursions, little damage was inflicted. Henry stayed at the convent on his journey to Leith. Many women travellers were provided with accommodation, including Margaret Tudor, daughter of Henry VII of England, who, in August 1503, was on her way to Edinburgh to marry James IV. Later, Mary, Queen of Scots stayed here during visits to Dunbar castle.

After the death of James II in 1460, his daughter Margaret was sent to the convent. She remained there for around fourteen years; at the time there were twenty-four nuns in residence. In 1544, during the Rough Wooing, the convent was torched by the English army and again the following year. By the summer of 1548, when the siege of Haddington began, the convent had been rebuilt. During the siege, the convent was used as the residence of the French general, D'Esse, who was helping the Scottish army attack the English garrison in Haddington.

Just before the dissolution of the religious houses in Scotland there were still eighteen nuns in the convent. The last prioress was Isobel Hepburn, who held office for just a few months in 1566. After her departure the buildings fell into disrepair, although the village that had grown up around it remained. With the dissolution of the religious houses and their extensive land holdings, considerable effort was made by the Scottish lords to annex the land. In 1567, William Maitland of Lethington, secretary to Mary, Queen of Scots, received most of the convent's land with the consent of the chapter and prioress.

East Lothian's agricultural potential did not go unnoticed by the Cistercians and other religious orders. Although sworn to asceticism, their organisational ability, along with their ownership of land, ensured that they became successful entrepreneurs. Farms belonging to religious houses were known as granges and their managers as grangers. The nuns at Haddington convent owned no less than five granges; one was at West Hopes, not far from where West Hopes reservoir is today, and earthworks here may be evidence of the farm. The convent also had a grange at Byres, near Haddington, where a substantial, still-standing, rectangular stone structure may be a connection. The convent had a further grange at Nunraw on the northern slopes of the Lammermuir hills.

The remains of Penshiel grange.

The best-preserved example of a grange in Scotland belonged to the monks of Melrose abbey. It is located at Penshiel, overlooking Whiteadder reservoir on the Lammermuir hills. Only a few ruinous walls remain, probably dating from the first half of the fifteenth century; in most other cases no trace of such establishments survive. The monks of Melrose also had a further grange at West Bearford, north-west of Stenton.

At Friar Dykes in the Lammermuir hills, two miles north of Whiteadder reservoir, there was a religious house to which refractory priests from Melrose abbey were banished for bad behaviour. Granges themselves would rarely see a proper monk as they were usually worked by farm labourers and sometimes by lay monks.

East Lothian had a second major Cistercian convent at North Berwick. The ruined north range of the buildings still stands in a private garden and the top of the structure can be seen from the adjacent Old Abbey Road. It has survived because of its conversion to a laird's house in the early-seventeenth century, when a tower house was added. This important religious house was founded by Duncan, earl of Fife, around 1150, and originally stood in open countryside on a hillside overlooking North Berwick harbour. It received extensive grants of land, including that of the local manor.

The priory church was consecrated to the Virgin Mary in 1242 by David de Bernham, bishop of St Andrews. The order was also responsible for the hospital, which stood close to the harbour on a site in Quality Street and provided accommodation for travellers and assistance to the poor.

In time the nuns at North Berwick, like many other religious orders, probably strayed from strict Christian principles. They commanded considerable wealth, owning lands in East Lothian and in other parts of Scotland. Income flowed from their running of the Firth of Forth ferry as well as from the sale of pilgrim badges and mementoes and their revenues were further swollen by the export of wool from their harbour at North Berwick. Grain from its farms was milled in the Glen, now a public park in North Berwick. The ruins of three mills, occupied until the 1840s, still exist. They were powered by water from a dam that once stood at the entrance to the Glen near the present road to Dunbar. The convent was entitled to a portion of all the grain milled here.

The North Berwick convent suffered in the frequent conflicts between England and Scotland. To prevent it being plundered by English troops in the 1296 invasion of Scotland, the prioress transferred her allegiance to Edward I, but its buildings were damaged in the reign of James III. In 1492, Parliament agreed to make good the damage. In 1529, a further grant was made by the archbishop of St Andrews 'in consideration of its losses, due to Wars in which it was plundered and its church burnt'. The date may be incorrect, as there was no conflict with England at the time. It may refer to strife between the king and the Douglases, who owned Tantallon castle.

The site of the North Berwick priory church is unknown, despite excavations in the vicinity of the convent. During the Rough Wooing the English army burnt several Scottish abbeys and it is possible that North Berwick suffered the same fate; the prioress was granted £2,000 to carry out repairs a few years later. The convent in 1544 held twenty-two nuns along with the prioress, but this had dropped to eleven by the time of the Reformation. It was reported to be in a ruinous state by 1586, although there was still one nun there ten years later. The convent was formally abolished in 1597.

There was mention that Gullane once had a convent. It is stated that in 1369 the prior of Coldingham mediated in a dispute between the nuns of St Bothans and the nuns of Gullane regarding the lands of Fenton. Over a century earlier, the nuns of Berwick-upon-Tweed had been involved in a further dispute when they laid claim to Gullane parish church, which had been given to Dryburgh abbey. Although convents owned land here and around Dirleton, there is little evidence other than this that they had a community at Gullane.

Fidra island was gifted in 1220 to the monks of Dryburgh by William de Vaux, who owned the lands around Dirleton. A chapel, dedicated to St Nicholas, had been built on it in 1165. It became a place of pilgrimage for both the monks of Dryburgh abbey and the North Berwick nuns. Fidra may have also served as a place of quarantine for sailors and plague victims. There have been suggestions that there was a monastery on the island, but there is no evidence for this. Tradition states that the island is haunted by a hooded figure known as the Dark Monk of Fidra.

The Franciscans had a long association with Haddington. Unfortunately, in common with the convent, no trace of their friary remains. It stood close to the banks of the Tyne, a short distance north of Nungate Bridge and the Episcopal church by Elm house now stands on its site. It is uncertain when the friary was established, but it was in existence by the mid-thirteenth century. The earl of Athole, murdered in Haddington in 1242, was buried in its grounds.

There were two orders of Franciscans – the Observantines, who rigidly conformed to living in poverty as preached by their founder St Francis of Assisi, and the Conventials, who were less strict. It was the latter branch that established the friary at Haddington, which consisted of a 'church, houses, edifices, gardens and dovecotes'. Although the Franciscans generally constructed plain buildings, those at Haddington were among the most impressive in the town and its church was known as 'the Lamp of the Lothian' because of its outstanding architecture. This did not prevent it from being burnt by Edward III's army during the invasion of Scotland in 1356: this was the 'Burnt Candlemas', when numerous towns and villages in Berwickshire and East Lothian were torched.

In 1478, the establishment consisted of eight friars with a warden. During that year, Sir John Haliburton, vicar of Greenlaw, selected them to administer his charity for the poor. For this purpose, a tenement in the Poldrate was converted into an almshouse. In May 1544, the friary was burnt by the English and four years later heavy fighting took place around it during the siege of Haddington. After this, its endowments declined. Shortly before the Reformation there were only three friars and a warden. By 1572, the friary had been pulled down. The Dominican friars also had a house at Haddington but it was not founded until around 1470. According to one source it was devastated by the English and then around 1558 it was reduced to ashes 'by the rage of fanatics'.

Around half a mile from the medieval town of Haddington there was St Lawrence's hospital, first mentioned in records from 1327–8. Its function was to assist the poor, but it also housed lepers; it was re-founded in the early 1470s. There was also a chapel here dedicated to St Lawrence, with 82 acres, endowed by James V. The last traces were demolished in 1906 and cottages were built on the site, which is now close to the road to Edinburgh on the western edge of Haddington. During the building work, thousands of skeletons were uncovered of people who had died at the hospital. Although no trace remains of Haddington's numerous religious houses, their legacy lives on in place names such as Abbot's View, Priory Walk and Nungate Bridge.

There were other religious orders with a presence in the county. At Dunbar, an old dovecote in a good state of preservation can be found close to the town centre at the West Port; it started life as the medieval steeple of the church of the Trinitarian priory. The building is square and short, standing over the passage of the former choir and nave. The order of Trinitarian friars was established in the late-twelfth century to assist the release of Christians captured during the Crusades, who were often held to ransom. They were also known as Red Friars, as they wore white habits bearing a blue and red cross. The priory was founded in 1240–3 by the countess of Dunbar, Cristiana de Brus. It was a small house with one friar maintaining divine service and close by was a hospital for the poor, which was probably under the jurisdiction of the Trinitarian friars.

The Trinitarian order also had a house at Houston, a short distance to the south of Preston church, known as the 'Grace of God'. Its founders were Christina and Robert de Moubray, who owned land in the Fortune area. Alexander III confirmed its foundation in 1271–2, and may have visited the friary. By the 1530s the house had been reduced to one member. Its memory lingers on in local house names such as 'Red Friars' and 'Monks Orchard'; a minor ruin exists on the site of the Trinitarian house. This order may also have had a presence at Dirleton. The chapel of St Andrew is mentioned in 1507 as being held by the Trinitarians.

Hidden in woodland to the east of Aberlady, next to a footpath, are the ruins of the Carmelite friary of Luffness. The first references to it date from 1335–6, when it is recorded that the friars of 'Lufnok' received from the lands of 'Lufnok' ten marks yearly in virtue of a long-standing

In woodland near Aberlady, the tomb of the thirteenth-century knight in the ruins of the Carmelite friary of Luffness.

endowment. The friary may have been founded in the previous century, possibly by Patrick, earl of Dunbar. Only the foundations of the church survive, measuring 90 feet by 24 feet. In the north wall there is a recess that houses a life-size sculpture of a knight in armour; it occupies a position usually reserved for the founder's tomb. The last record of the friary dates from 1512, when it was in receipt of alms from the king. About a hundred yards to the north-east are two hollows, which once housed fishponds. It is possible that another Carmelite friary was founded in Dunbar in 1263, but the evidence is questionable.

The only house of the Bethlemite order in Scotland was the hospital at St Germain's, a short distance to the west of Longniddry. 'Hospitals' fulfilled a number of functions, including assistance for the poor and accommodation for pilgrims; in Scotland they were sometimes referred to as 'spittals'. The role of the hospital at St Germain's was to help the poor. The foundation date is unknown, but Ralph, prior of St Germain, is mentioned in a charter before 1219. By the end of the sixteenth century, its buildings, other than the chapel, were reported to be in ruins. As with all the other East Lothian hospitals, no trace of it remains today and St Germain's house now stands in its vicinity.

Another medieval hospital existed at Ballencrieff, dedicated to St Cuthbert. It was also known as 'Red Spittal', possibly after the red friars. It was said to have been founded in 1296 by relatives of Robert de Pinkeny, a contender for the Scottish throne five years earlier. The hospital had two mills as well as nine acres of land; by the end of the fifteenth century, it had ceased to exist. There is a place called Spittal today, close to Redhouse castle. Further to the east there was a hospital at Fortune in Athelstaneford parish. In a charter dated 1271–2, Alexander III confirmed the donation of 'the whole land which was of the hospital of Fortune' to the Trinitarian monastery of Houston by Christiana de Mubray, who founded it. It would appear that the hospital was already no longer in existence by this date.

There is evidence from a document dated 1480 that the collegiate church of Dunglass had a hospital associated with it for poor relief. It had a chapel dedicated to St Mary and St John the Baptist and was built by Sir Alexander Home, lord of Home and Dunglass, close to the collegiate church he founded. Although the collegiate church still stands there is no trace of the hospital.

Located a short distance from Garvald, on the northern slopes of the Lammermuir hills, is Nunraw monastery. Unlike the locations above, monks still live and pray here. The name Nunraw is derived from 'nun's row'. The lands here and extending across much of the parish of Garvald belonged to the Cistercian nuns at Haddington. They had a grange here and some sources suggest there was a convent in the area, but there is little evidence for this. At a much later date, in July 1547, when England was on the verge of invading, Lady Elizabeth Hepburn, prioress of the Haddington convent, was made keeper of the 'place and fortalice of Nunraw'. She was instructed to keep it 'surlie fra our auld ynemies of Ingland and all uthairis'. It was only to be given up to Regent Arran or, if necessary, demolished and made uninhabitable. Thanks to the Reformation, the Hepburns had gained possession of the lands at Nunraw and built a Z-shaped tower house here. In the 1860s, the building was reconstructed as a baronial mansion house.

In 1946, Cistercian monks arrived from St Joseph's abbey at Roscrea, Ireland, and purchased Nunraw tower. Here they established the first Cistercian community in Scotland since the Reformation. Prior to their arrival, there were no Catholics in the area and locals are reported to

Sancta Maria abbey, Nunraw

have been concerned about the 'terrible monks coming', and kept their doors locked. In 1954, the foundations were laid for the Sancta Maria abbey, with stone from Rattlebags quarry used in its construction. The monastery is of modern design, with a two-storey building laid out around an open square space. The refectory block extends from it on the south-west side. By 1969 it was ready for partial occupation, but construction work continued into the 1980s. The abbey church is still to be built.

The daily routine of the monks begins at 3.15 in the morning, with vigils, followed by meditation for half an hour, then community mass at 4.45 and breakfast at 5.30. During the day, their time is spent on farm work, studying or carrying out tasks such as cooking and maintenance. Time is found to pray seven times a day and the day ends at eight. The monks grow their own food and also keep livestock, including cattle and sheep. Cistercians have throughout history been known as 'white monks' because of their un-dyed robes of sheep's wool. They rarely leave the monastery, although in the past they accepted guests at Nunraw house, who went there on retreat. They sold this building in 2015 and it has now reverted to a private residence. The number of monks at the abbey had dwindled to around a dozen by 2016. Sancta Maria abbey stands close to the Garvald–Whiteadder reservoir road, from where it can be viewed. There is no public access to the monastery itself.

17. COLLEGIATE CHURCHES

The first collegiate churches were established in Scotland in the thirteenth century. Their main function was to house priests who would perpetually recite masses for departed souls to assist their progress to heaven. They were not monks but a self-contained secular community who lived next to the church and were independent of other religious houses. Collegiate churches became particularly popular with the wealthy as a means of ensuring their salvation. A further development was the construction of a collegiate church next to the lord's castle, which would be solely devoted to the family's spiritual needs. Sometimes the local parish church was nominated as a collegiate church by a wealthy sponsor, with the priests funded by tithes and revenues from the parish church.

The first **collegiate church** in East Lothian was at **Dunbar**, where the 9th earl Dunbar granted a charter conferring collegiate status on the parish church in 1342. It was staffed by a dean, an archpriest and eight canons, often known as prebendaries. At Dunbar, the dean was entitled to receive all the teinds and altar dues of the parish of Whittingehame. Each of the eight canons received a prebend from the chapels and churches in the following towns and villages – Dunbar, Pinkerton, Spott, Belton, Pitcox, East Linton, Duns and Chirnside (the latter two in Berwickshire). For his disloyalty to the Crown, the eleventh earl of Dunbar's lands were forfeited to the crown in 1435 and his collegiate church now came under royal authority.

As with other Catholic institutions, the collegiate churches ceased to exist after the Reformation. The medieval collegiate church at Dunbar continued to serve as the parish church. By the late-eighteenth century, the building was in a poor state of repair, with worshippers enduring dark and cold conditions. In 1819, the former collegiate church, built in the form of a cross and possibly dating as far back as twelfth century, was demolished. In the same year, work started on the new parish church, extant today; built from attractive red sandstone and with a tall tower, it is a local landmark.

Dunglass collegiate church

While most of the medieval churches of East Lothian have suffered the same fate as that of Dunbar's, the **collegiate church at Dunglass**, close to Berwickshire, is still standing. Although a ruin, it is almost complete; this is remarkable since it was on the main invasion route into Scotland and nearby Dunglass castle was destroyed on several occasions, no trace remaining today. The country house that latterly stood on its site has also gone. The walls of the collegiate church were built of ashlar and it was roofed with stone slabs. The structure is laid out in a cruciform plan and many of the original sculptures can still be seen in its interior.

On 30 November 1423, Alexander Home made donations to the chapel of St Mary of Dunglass situated next to his castle and 'the presbyters there serving God'. This chapel became the nucleus of the

Dunglass collegiate church, founded in 1443, its sole function to pray for the salvation of the Home family. It was staffed by a provost, two chaplains and four boy choristers, their salaries paid by the Home family, who also supplied them with a house and a garden with fruit trees. They could be dismissed if they failed to look after their gardens, for poor timekeeping or having concubines. The priests were instructed to wear long surplices with sheepskin-lined hooded capes. In 1491, there were also eight canons or prebends.

The Home family sold Dunglass in 1644. By early the following century the church had been converted into a coach house, stables, granary and pigeon loft. Its then owner, Sir James Hall, also pulled up gravestones. On a more positive note, one of his descendants constructed a 20-foot-high model cathedral on the estate, made out of willow rods to test the theory that Gothic arches were inspired by the properties of wood; its plan was based on the collegiate church. Today, Dunglass collegiate church is in the care of Historic Scotland, along with **Seton collegiate church**, another outstanding example. The latter is at the opposite end of the county, on the Prestonpans–Longniddry road, and is an interesting and unusually complete example of fifteenth-century ecclesiastical architecture.

Seton collegiate church

There was a parish church at Seton in the thirteenth century. It was a rectangular building that later became the nave of the collegiate church and whose foundations can be seen to the west of the surviving building. Around 1434, a chapel was built on to the south side by Lady Janet Dunbar for her deceased husband, the second Lord Seton; it included an altar where prayers could be said for him. Pope Paul II gave conditional permission to George, third lord Seton, for the parish church to be made a collegiate church once its rector left. Its staff were to include a provost, six canons, a clerk and two choristers. George died in 1478, but not before he had built the walls of the choir for the collegiate church at the east end of the parish church. Over the next thirty years, his son, the fourth lord Seton, completed the choir. It was during his lifetime that the Pope gave the final sanction in 1492 to establish a collegiate church here. It was to be dedicated to St Mary and the Holy Cross.

There is a legend that when the Seton church was being extended the master mason had problems with the vaulted roof of the nave. During his absence an apprentice solved this problem, producing diagrams of how it could be constructed. On his return, the master mason showed his gratitude by flying into a rage, striking the apprentice with a mallet with fatal consequences. Interestingly, there is a similar story concerning Roslin chapel, Midlothian with the master mason also killing an apprentice in a fit of jealousy after sculpting a pillar; following which murder he then committed suicide. It is, however, believed that the same master mason may have been involved in both incidents, fleeing Roslin and finding employment designing and extending Seton collegiate church in the late-fifteenth century. The fifth lord Seton was killed at Flodden, but not before glazing the windows and roofing the vault with stone slabs. His widow, Lady Janet Hepburn, added the north transept to the church after his death.

During the Rough Wooing, English soldiers damaged the Seton church, stealing the bells and organ then setting fire to the woodwork. Three years later, just before the battle of Pinkie in 1547, English troops again set fire to the church and stole its bell. Seton palace, home of the Setons, was also destroyed during these campaigns, but later rebuilt. Lady Janet Seton made good the damage to the ravaged collegiate church. She also demolished the south chapel and added a new south transept immediately opposite the north transept, which gave the church a cruciform plan. Finally, Lady Janet was responsible for the square tower crowned by the octagonal-slated spire. The top has never been completed, giving it a stunted appearance. Its brooch-style design is unusual for Scottish churches and more reminiscent of those in France.

Lady Janet Seton died in 1558, some forty-five years after her husband had perished at Flodden, and was buried in the church. After the Reformation, the building served for a time as a parish church, but by 1580 worshippers used the church at Tranent instead. A new bell, still there, was cast in the Netherlands. The Seton family continued to use the collegiate church as a private place of worship. Further damage was inflicted in 1715 as the Setons supported the Jacobite cause; the Lothian militia broke in, defacing monuments and opened coffins in search of treasure.

The earls of Wemyss eventually took possession of the Seton estate and spent considerable sums of money renovating the collegiate church, using it as a family mausoleum. Today it is in good condition, hidden behind a tall, stone boundary wall, looked after by Historic Scotland. In its grounds are the foundations of a building that may have provided accommodation for priests. Part of the structure was used as a brewhouse and after the Reformation may have been a mill.

There had been a **parish church at Bothans village**, now the site of Yester house, since at least the thirteenth century. Following a petition of Sir William Hay, the local landowner, and three co-lords, the church received collegiate status in 1421. It was dedicated to St Cuthbert with a provost and four chaplains, increased to six in 1443, assisted by two choirboys. By that time there were several altars in the church, including to the Virgin Mary, St Edmund – king and martyr – in the south transept, the Holy Cross, the Rood altar and one to St Ninian. After the Reformation, the Hay family continued to patronise Bothans church. It was later turned into a mausoleum when a new west front was built across the truncated nave in 1753–4. Yester house, a private residence, stands close by and there is no public access to it or Bothans collegiate church.

Sir Walter Haliburton, owner of **Dirleton castle**, founded a **collegiate church** within its grounds in 1444; the provost was John Burgon. It appears to have been a small foundation as there is no record of any canons being attached to it. No trace of the collegiate church remains above ground. There was also a chapel within the castle building.

It is suggested there was a **collegiate church at Markle** in 1450. St Mary is mentioned as the title of the provostry. Later records state there was a chapel here in 1511, but there is no evidence that it was a collegiate example.

The last church in East Lothian to be conferred with collegiate status was the impressive **parish church of St Mary's, Haddington**. Although it had eleven altars in 1450, it was not until about 1540 that it was formally constituted a collegiate church. Its existence was relatively brief with the Reformation only a few years away.

THE ECONOMY

18. FARMING AND FARM BUILDINGS

Farming

The lowland areas of East Lothian owe their characteristic appearance to arable farming, the origins of which go back to the Bronze Age. In prehistoric times, small patches of woodland were cleared to grow crops. By the time the Romans invaded Scotland, much of the woodland on the fertile coastal plain had probably come under the plough. This expansion in agriculture enabled larger settlements to be established.

By the medieval period there were numerous villages reliant on agriculture scattered across East Lothian. The population scraped a living from the land; there were no enclosed fields, just a patchwork of plots. However, by the eighteenth century, a radical transformation was underway in the form of the Agricultural Revolution and today's landscape owes much of its appearance to this. Around 1840, when East Lothian had become one of the most productive areas in Scotland, there were 386 separate farms of 60 acres and upwards, the average size being about 250 acres. About forty of them were owned by the farmer, most of them under pasture. The remainder were let to tenants.

A mosaic of fields near Spott, early autumn.

Wheat is thought to have been grown in East Lothian as far back as prehistoric times, but, by the seventeenth century, it was rarely seen. Around 1750, it was such an unusual sight that when a field near Edinburgh was planted with this crop, people flocked to see it. A century later, wheat was the staple produce of East Lothian, both white and red varieties being cultivated. The Chevalier variety of barley was introduced in the early-nineteenth century. At this time, potatoes were grown mainly for the consumption of the farmer and his family.

Crop rotation was at the centre of the new farming methods. On the fertile red sandstone soils, turnips were grown in the first year and used as cattle feed. Once the ground was clear, wheat was sown; barley the following spring. In the third year, clover or ryegrass was grown and sometimes left to be consumed by livestock. The final crop in the sequence was oats, but, depending on the soil, rotation was sometimes drawn out over five years with peas and beans also planted. With the exception of the Lammermuir hills, there was limited livestock farming, not unlike the situation today. Sheep, usually ewes, arrived in the area in autumn to feed on grass and turnips and were then sold the following summer. Some cattle were bred locally, often the shorthorn breed.

Several East Lothian landowners were at the forefront of agricultural reform. They included John Cockburn of Ormiston, who introduced crop rotation and winter-grown wheat to his estate. He was also in favour of long-term leases for farm tenants to give them an incentive to undertake improvements. The drainage of his farmland was greatly improved. His other improvements included tree planting, as well as a scientific approach to market gardening and fruit growing.

In the days before motorised transport and refrigeration, most towns and villages had extensive orchards. The monastery at Haddington is recorded as possessing an orchard of a considerable age as early as 1245. After the dissolution of the monasteries, fruit was grown on the estates of landowners. In the seventeenth century, pears were grown at Tyninghame, Stevenson, Biel, Redhouse and Gosford country houses. Patrick Neil, in his book *Scottish Gardens and Orchards*, published in 1812, mentions that there were orchards at Ballencrieff, Luffness, Ormiston Hall and Phantassie. He notes that the cultivation of fruit trees in East Lothian was handicapped by the cold east winds during April and May.

In 1900, there were around seventy-five acres of orchards in East Lothian but a hundred years later they have almost vanished. Apples grown on a fruit farm near Dunbar have been used for locally produced cider. An orchard has also been created by schoolchildren in East Linton, where apple growing was once important. The local landowner, Sir George Hepburn of Smeaton, wished to encourage tenants to increase their income by growing fruit and imported trees from France and North America. East Linton market gardens grew flowers, tomatoes and vegetables as well as fruit, until the 1970s. Long gone also are the market gardens that once were found just outside Musselburgh and Prestonpans, supplying produce to the Edinburgh market. In 1926 a rare example of a bulb farm was established at West Barns with assistance from the Netherlands, concentrating on daffodils, tulips, crocuses, lilies and dahlias. By the end of the nineteenth century, East Lothian's farmers were so successful that they were regarded as a model for arable farming. Around half the total land area of the county was under the plough. In the book, *The Gateway of Scotland*, the fertile red soils around Dunbar were described as, 'The cream of the county, probably the cream of the earth.'

In the mid-twentieth century, around a third of Scotland's vegetables came from East Lothian. David Lowe & Son was the largest grower of vegetables in Scotland when it ceased trading in 1976. Around that time, it had two thousand acres under cultivation in the vicinity of Musselburgh. Strawberries were once grown at Ormiston and supplied to Holyrood palace when a member of the royal family was in residence. Unfortunately, its market gardens have gone the same way as the others. At the end of the twentieth century there were still around 1,200 acres devoted to the cultivation of fruit and vegetables on East Lothian farms.

Cereal crops, including wheat and barley, are nowadays the prime produce of East Lothian's fertile soils; the mild climate enables crops to be grown throughout the year. In winter, the green shoots of the cereal crops give some colour to an otherwise bleak landscape. By early summer, the lowland areas of East Lothian are a sea of gold as harvest time approaches. Dashes of yellow can be seen across the county in spring, created by fields of oilseed rape. The mixed farms grow potatoes, peas and beans in addition to cereal crops, although in recent times such enterprises have become rare. The low rainfall in summer can cause problems for crops such as potatoes and cabbages, which are often irrigated.

With the closure of the sugar-beet factory at Cupar in 1972, this crop ceased to be grown in East Lothian. The acreage given over to turnips

Fields of gold at harvest time, East Linton.

used as a winter feed for livestock has also greatly declined over the last few decades, as has the area devoted to oats. In the mid-nineteenth century some parishes devoted more fields to growing oats than any other crop but now it is absent from most farms. Potatoes are still grown around Aberlady and Dunbar. Away from the fertile sandy loams of the coastal plain, the quality of the soils is variable and mixed farming takes place up to an altitude of five hundred feet. Cattle are brought here from other parts of Scotland to be fattened. It was Rennie of Phantassie who was responsible for introducing the shorthorn breed of cattle to the Scotland in 1818; he was also responsible for the first Scottish fat-stock show, held in Edinburgh four years later.

There were once livestock markets at East Linton and Haddington, but they ceased in the latter part of the twentieth century. Large numbers of migrant workers came to East Lothian seeking work in harvesting and sheep shearing. In 1890, John Martine gave the following description:

[East] Linton was long ago well known as a central hiring market or 'port' for shearers in the harvest months. On a Monday morning Linton Port ruled the wages for the county. Large crowds of Cavan, Leitrim, Roscommon 'boys' with lots of Highlanders from the Isle of Skye, etc, used to congregate to meet farmers. It was no easy task sometimes for farmers and shearers to come to terms. On one occasion, Ralph Plain, the constable, got his big red nose nearly cut off with a hook. For some seasons twelve dragoons were sent early from Piershill [Edinburgh] to keep order.

Machinery has now superseded manual labourers: the first combine harvesters arrived in East Lothian in the early 1930s. In the 1950s, most farms had half-a-dozen or so permanent workers to assist the owner. By the end of the century, most of the work was done by the owner with the assistance of perhaps one other person, sometimes a relative. Despite the reduction in workforce the yield of wheat and barley per acre had doubled within just fifty years, due to improved methods and artificial fertilisers.

The shallow soils and inclement weather of the Lammermuir hills present a hostile environment for arable farming. Instead, sheep have been grazed here since at least the Middle Ages. Blackface and cheviot, breeds suited to the harsh climate, are most common although in recent times they have been partially supplanted by cross-breeds. At the beginning of the twentieth century, there were 130,000 sheep in the county, but, by its close, numbers had declined greatly. Livestock of any form is rare on the fertile, low-lying plains of East Lothian, now almost totally given over to wheat and barley. On the lower, less-exposed slopes of the Lammermuirs there are some arable fields in which wheat and barley can be grown, along with fodder crops for sheep.

For hundreds of years, horses had toiled alongside man on the farms of East Lothian, integral partners in food production. In 1900 there were around four thousand horses in East Lothian, most of which were used to work the land or provide transport. In the years immediately after the Second World War, most farms still had several horses for work, including for ploughing, but they were rapidly replaced by tractors. By the end of the 1960s, the few remaining working horses had been retired. The growth in riding as a leisure activity has ensured that the animal is still to be seen in fields across the county.

Many farmers also had a few cows, which they used to supply milk to the family and workers, but, for health-and-safety reasons, these animals are no longer kept. The small number of dairy farms found in East Lothian in the second half of the twentieth century generally have become nothing more than a memory. By 2020 there were only two such farms remaining in the county. One of them is Yester farm dairies, which produces a range of dairy products from its herd of four hundred traditional black-and-white Holstein Friesian cows.

Farm buildings

Pre-eighteenth-century agricultural structures (other than mills) are almost totally absent from East Lothian. The one exception is at Whitekirk, just to the north of the church, in the form of a seventeenth-century tithe barn created out of a tower house. It has since been converted into a private house but can be seen from either the churchyard or the road.

With the expansion of agriculture in the eighteenth century, larger harvests and increases in livestock numbers made the old structures redundant. Substantial stone buildings appeared: the grand steading was the farm showcase, proclaiming its owner's success and the country-side's wealth, particularly in the most fertile areas around Dunbar and Haddington. Long, rectangular, stone barns with steep-pitched tile roofs formed an elegant quadrangle facing a central courtyard and this layout became a major feature in the landscape. Some were located on the site of the old buildings, but often new locations were chosen.

At Papple, to the south-west of Whittingehame, there is an impressive nineteenth-century farm complex a short distance from a minor road; it has an entrance arch crowned by a slate roof in the shape of a pyramid (*see plate section*). Some of the large farms powered their threshing machines with steam engines, their disused chimneys an unusual feature of the landscape. Other farms preferred horse power; the harnessed animal walked around in circles powering the threshing machinery, which was housed separately in a small, round building. Some examples still survive next to barns and granaries. In the 1840s, East Lothian had 386 threshing machines: 269 were driven by horse power, eighty by steam, thirty by water and seven by wind. Numerous examples of cart sheds are also still standing. These are instantly recognisable by the series of arches forming the entrance and now generally house vehicles and farm machinery rather than horse-drawn contraptions.

In the twentieth century, steel and concrete replaced the distinctive sandstone and red pantiles as the favoured construction materials for farm steadings. With the widespread introduction of large tractors, traditional stone buildings were too small. In the 1930s, concrete silage

There are some impressive farm buildings in East Lothian. Castellated building, Amisfield mains, next to the old A1 (*top*). Buildings, Castle Moffat, northern Lammermuir hills (*bottom*).

towers also began to appear on farms. Many of the redundant nineteenth-century buildings have been converted into attractive housing, forming small communities in their own right; one conversion at Innerwick includes the disused farm chimney.

The higher parts of the Lammermuirs are almost devoid of farm buildings or any other structures. This was not always the case; in the Middle Ages there were numerous farming hamlets on the tops of the hills. From the sixteenth century onwards, they were abandoned and the area became the preserve of sheep, robbers and vagabonds. Evidence of the lawless nature of the area is provided by Packman's Grave, not far from Whiteadder reservoir. It takes the form of five stones close to the road between Gifford and Preston. Tradition has it that a packman (a peddler or hawker), who was murdered by an innkeeper at Danskine, is buried here. There are two other packman graves in the surrounding hills.

19. WATERMILLS, WINDMILLS AND MODERN POWER

Watermills

Watermills, ponds and water channels were once a major feature of the landscape. A charter drawn up by David I granted lands to the abbey of Dunfermline and included Inveresk and its mill. In the 1230s, Alan de Sinton wished to construct a mill on the river Esk, close to that operated by the monks. He was given permission on condition it did not impede the flow of water through the monks' mill.

While the rivers Esk and Tyne provided the main source of power, there is an early reference to tide mills in East Lothian, a rarity in Scotland. A tide mill is driven by tidal rise and fall using a pond that fills with the incoming tide and is later released to power the mill. In 1526 Alexander Acheson was granted a licence to build a harbour near Prestonpans, which also included permission to erect tide mills inside it. This option appears to have been taken up, as by 1587 there were two tide mills (or 'sea mills' as they were known in Scotland) used to grind meal here.

By the mid-seventeenth century, Prestonpans and its port of Morrison's Haven had become an important industrial centre. In addition to its tide mills there were several watermills powered by the outflow from streams emanating from mine adits (horizontal entrances). There was also at least one windmill in the vicinity. The tide mills had a long life and were still in operation in the 1790s, although by then they had been converted to grind flint for local potteries. They probably had a secondary function helping to deal with the silting-up of the harbour. When the ponds were released to drive the watermills, this water flow would also assist in flushing away deposits on the harbour floor. Unfortunately, there is no trace of the tidal mills today; they stood close to the east end of Prestongrange industrial museum.

In the eighteenth century, East Lothian was noted for its milling innovation. The parish of Saltoun claims the first barley mill in Scotland, erected close to Milton Bridge on the Humbie water in 1712. For forty years it was the only one of its kind in Britain, Ireland and America. The structure is built of rubble and has three storeys. It continued to function as a mill until the early-twentieth century, but has since been converted to a private residence.

As the Industrial Revolution progressed, watermills were used for many processes. In 1747, building work began on a bleach field – where cloth was spread to be bleached by sun and water – for the British Linen Company at Saltoun. In that year, 123 cartloads of timber were delivered from Prestonpans, most likely having been landed at the nearby harbour of Morrison's Haven. During construction, over four hundred cartloads of raw materials were delivered. Some were sourced locally; lime for plastering roofs and cementing stonework probably came from Herdsmanston lime-works. Slating work on the mills and Dalkeith was carried out by an artisan from Dalkeith.

Advances in the chemistry of bleaching made this one of the earliest large-scale industrial activities. Robert Meikle, a first-rate millwright who resided nearby, was employed in this industry. The site selected was 'haugh land' (a low-lying meadow) near the Birns water. At that time Edinburgh was the centre of the linen industry and only fifteen miles away. Three waterwheels provided power and within a short time it became the most important bleach field in Scotland. By 1772, when chlorine began to be used as a bleaching agent, it had ceased production. Today there is little trace of the complex or of the numerous medieval mills that once hugged the banks of East Lothian's rivers.

Preston mill, with waterwheel clearly visible.

Close to East Linton is Preston mill, one of Scotland's earliest, watermills, preserved by the National Trust for Scotland. There has been a mill at Preston since at least 1599, but the current structure dates from the following century or perhaps even later. The atypical, but distinctive, Dutch-style conical roof on the attached kiln makes it one of the county's iconic landmarks. The structure has at some time (possibly in the late-eighteenth century) been raised to house additional machinery, possibly using stone from the demolished medieval church of Prestonkirk. It was one of the last working watermills in the county, ceasing to grind grain only in 1959.

In the mid-nineteenth century there were seventy-three watermills still in operation in rural East Lothian; thirty-four were corn mills, fourteen on the river Tyne. There was a particular concentration of mills at East Linton, where the Tyne falls over the Linn rocks. All have since been demolished or converted into houses.

All along the Tyne and on many of its tributaries there are former watermills converted into smart private residences, such as Colstoun old mill on the Gifford–Bolton footpath. While most have lost their waterwheels, one exception is at Tyninghame, standing a short distance from the Dunbar–North Berwick main road, on the southern approach to the village. The single-storey, rubble building, with diamond-panel windows dating from 1828, was once the sawmill for Tyninghame estate. Now a private house, it still has a wood-and-iron paddlewheel, but is concealed from public view. A short distance upstream is Knowes mill, standing close to a footbridge over the Tyne, in a ruinous state.

Poldrate mill, Haddington.

Haddington, with its rich agricultural hinterland, had numerous mills. The best-preserved example is Poldrate mill, one of the first buildings visible when entering the town from Gifford. Standing on the site of the medieval Kirk mill, the present buildings date mainly from the eighteenth century, but were reconstructed in 1842. They consist of a three-storey rubble block, with kiln and steam-engine house at the rear. Close by is a large, four-storey, granary block linked to the mill by two gangways. The all-iron, six-spoke waterwheel of the nineteenth century is still in position. Milling continued here until 1965, the buildings now serving as a community centre.

Further down the Tyne, close to the Victoria Bridge, is a large weir once used to provide water to the numerous mills on its banks. Now converted to housing, the attractive rubble-and-red pantile Glimmer's mill once had the only 'double-undershot' wheel in the county. Records show that milling has been conducted here since 1408. Adjoining this building is Bermaline maltings, a massive, red-rock-faced sandstone structure that towers over the surrounding area and in some ways resembles a castle; it was built in 1900 and produced only malt flour for baking. In the early-twenty-first century, it still functioned as a maltings, making the area probably the longest site in continuous industrial use in Scotland.

Haddington also had a thriving textile industry based on wool. The Scottish fine-woollen industry came to an end in 1713 with the closure of the New Mills manufactory, but the town continued to be a market for coarse wool produced on the Lammermuir ('moorland of the lambs') hills. Cloth was produced in the Nungate at a 'waulk mill', which cleansed the wool and removed its impurities. In the mid-eighteenth century, the Tarred Wool Company was formed, taking its name from the practice of using tar on sheep to prevent infection. Andrew Meikle was employed to survey the river Tyne and Colstoun water for a suitable site; he concluded that the best location for a new mill was on the Tyne, at Haddington. Although the ground had already been designated for a lint mill, it was made available to the Tarred Wool Company provided there were safeguards to protect the already functioning malt and waulk mill. During drought the former ran by day, the latter by night.

A two-stock mill, a freese mill and a teazer were all constructed and powered by water from the Tyne. According to the testimonies of three clothiers, the mill 'answered extremely well'. The freese mill was extensively used, not only by the company itself but also by other manufacturers in East Lothian. Broadcloth and blankets were manu-factured at the premises and mainly sold to Edinburgh and Glasgow markets.

Of 6,000 stone of wool brought to Haddington in 1776, some 5,000 were used in local manufacture. By the end of the eighteenth century, the Tarred Wool Company had experienced a change of fortune and ceased trading. An attempt to continue the manufacture of coarse woollen cloth on the premises was made, but it ended for good by 1814. The town's waulk mill fared somewhat better, surviving until the mid-nineteenth century, when it too closed due to lack of demand.

A large weir disrupts the smooth flow of the Esk at Musselburgh, a short distance upstream from the town centre. The sluice gate and mill lade (race) still can be seen next to it. Paper mills once relied on the power generated from the rush of its waters. The companies that thrived here are no more than a memory and most of their premises have long since been reduced to rubble. Fortunately, one outstanding example of a large industrial mill from the Victorian era has been preserved and converted into offices. This is Esk Net mills, 'an extraordinary complex' built for J. W. Stuart in the late 1860s.

The former Esk Net mills, Musselburgh, now business premises.

In 1812, Colonel James Paterson, a native of Musselburgh, invented and patented the first machine capable of tying knots for the manufacture of fishing nets. When he died, his company and the patents for the knot-tying machines were bought by J. W. Stuart. His firm became the world's leading manufacturer of nets for the fishing industry, at one time employing over six hundred workers in their net mill. Throughout the world, 'Scotch Weave Nets' became the generic name for machine-made nets. In both world wars, the company diversified into anti-submarine nets, but its fortunes went into decline with the introduction of fishing nets made of nylon and Terylene. Esk Net mills eventually closed in 1979, but, fortunately, a new use was found for the building. The four-storey mill, with its classical façade surrounding the courtyard, is capped by a small, brick, clock tower with a cast-iron crown. Built sometime after the main complex is a red-sandstone tower with a fish weathervane, which travellers on the nearby main road can hardly fail to notice.

Windmills

Although the traditional windmill, with a large tower and sails, is not now associated with Scotland, they were once widespread. By the late-eighteenth century, there were probably fifty in operation in lowland areas of Scotland, particularly where there was a shortage of fast-flowing streams. Parts of East Lothian fit this description and it is not surprising that around Dunbar, one of the driest places, there were once several windmills; a rare example of a horizontal windmill also existed there in the eighteenth century, its small sails parallel to the ground and located below the millstones. The stone tower of a pumping mill survives in a hollow close to the entrance of Oxwellmains lime-works; it could once be seen from the A1 but is now concealed by trees. At Belhaven, a ruined tower dating from the seventeenth century was reconstructed in 1907 and incorporated into a large private house, which stands on top of a hillock there.

The most conspicuous windmill tower to have survived can be seen in the middle of a field, a mile south-west of North Berwick, close to Balgone farm; its long-vanished sails once provided power to grind flour, but, by the late-eighteenth century, it had fallen into disuse and was converted to a dovecote. Many other examples have disappeared: Camptoun farm, on a hill near Drem, is recorded as once having both a thrashing windmill and a bone-crushing mill; a tower mill, some 35-feet tall with a wooden wind cape and four sails, stood behind Phantassie farm, near East Linton; at East Barns a ruined windmill was demolished in the mid-nineteenth century to make way for a threshing mill. *Fowler's Map of Haddingtonshire* (now East Lothian) published in 1824 shows other windmills at Athelstaneford Mains and Papple.

Finally, mention should be made of Andrew Meikle, the son of James Meikle, who built the first barley mill in Scotland, at Saltoun. He inherited Houston watermill, near Dunbar, where he devised many improvements for machinery used in watermills. His innovations extended to windmills and in 1750 he came up with the idea of the fantail, which kept the sails rotating at right angles to the direction of the wind. Later he devised the 'Spring Sail', which counteracted sudden gusts of wind.

Modern power

By the mid-nineteenth century most of East Lothian's windmills had ceased functioning, but it was not the end of wind being harnessed. Wind-pumps, a familiar feature in Westerns, were found on some farms. They were used to draw groundwater to the surface, but are now a rare feature, having generally been superseded by electric motors. One of the last examples was still pumping water to a small reservoir next to a minor road from Gullane–West Fenton in the early-twenty-first century.

Aikengall windfarm, Lammermuir hills.

This is the age of the windfarm. Wind turbines can be seen on top of the Lammermuir hills, silhouetted against the skyline. In 2009, the first windfarm in East Lothian began operations at Aikengall, three miles south of Innerwick (*photo page 155*). It initially had sixteen wind turbines, with a tip height of 410 feet. Since then it has been considerably extended with the addition of a further thirty-eight, 475-feet high. Although Aikengall is the only major example in East Lothian, just across the border in Berwickshire is Crystal Rig windfarm, one of the largest in Scotland, extending south for a considerable distance over the tops of the Lammermuirs. Although the giant turbines are confined to the uplands, small examples have begun appearing on lowland farms; several can be seen in fields between Drem and Dirleton.

In 2000, two of Scotland's five major power stations were situated on the East Lothian coast. Cockenzie power station was constructed in the 1960s for the South of Scotland Electricity Board, with much of the electrical equipment manufactured by Bruce Peebles & Co of Edinburgh. When it began operating, it was one of the largest power stations in Britain; it initially burned coal produced from the Midlothian pits but later supplies came from further afield. For fifty years, until its demolition in 2015, the power station was a major landmark. Its two chimneys, at just under 500 feet in height, towered over the nearby town of Port Seton. There were plans to replace the coal-fired power station by a gas-turbine plant around the time of its closure in 2013, but these have been abandoned.

Cockenzie is survived by Torness nuclear power station, on the North Sea coast to the south of Dunbar. Located close to the A1, the large glass-and-concrete structure is a local landmark. At first sight, its function is not obvious as it has neither tall chimneys nor cooling towers; it was first proposed in 1974 and preparatory work began in 1977. The decision to build a nuclear power station was not without opposition but construction got underway in earnest in 1980. At its peak, three thousand workers were employed on the site. As with all such facilities, a lot of water was needed for cooling purposes, hence its location by the sea. Just over a mile of coastal defences were built, with half-a-million tons of locally quarried rock being used for protection. A huge amount of earth was excavated during the site preparation and some two million tons of material were used in construction.

The more intricate work involved the creation of pre-stressed concrete vessels for the two reactors. In 1988, the first of the two advanced gas-cooled reactors went live and Torness was officially opened the following year by Prime Minister Margaret Thatcher. It was the last of the second-generation nuclear power stations to be commissioned in Britain. It and Hunterston nuclear-power station, situated on the other side of Scotland, were capable of providing half of Scotland's electricity. Torness was due to close in 2023 but its life was extended to 2030 to secure electricity supply. There is a visitor centre at Torness, which explains how electricity is produced by nuclear reaction.

20. BREWERIES AND DISTILLERIES

With East Lothian being an important region for grain, it is not surprising that brewing and distilling are long-established activities.

Breweries

Between 1700 and 1850, there was a proliferation of commercial breweries and even small villages in East Lothian had a brewery, although they were often little more than cottage industries functioning on a seasonal basis. At Tyninghame house, ale was home-brewed twice a year. In the nineteenth century there was a small brewery at Athelstaneford. The owner of a small-scale enterprise at Garvald travelled the county in his cart selling his 'small beer and tippeny' (mutton pies). According to tradition, Cromwell's soldiers on their march from Danskine to Dunbar consumed all the beer they found in the brewery at Whittingehame village. Many of the East Lothian towns had several breweries, but their number declined with improved transport links. North Berwick's brewery was demolished in the late-nineteenth century.

There have been some fourteen breweries at Haddington. They included Nungate brewery, opened for business around 1801. A further three breweries had been established by 1825. One of the largest was Sidegate brewery, located not far from Poldrate mill. New Nungate brewery, 'a substantial three-storey structure equipped with modern machinery', commenced production in 1882; it had refrigerators and a five-horsepower Otto gas engine. Owned by Mark Binnie & Co, it was the last of Haddington's breweries, closing in 1937.

Musselburgh and Fisherrow, a major industrial centre with large numbers of workers, had a ready market for its breweries. In 1697, there were twenty-six brewers and maltsters in the burgh, although most would be individuals working for themselves. The first commercial brewery was opened in the town in 1704 in Short Street. Ladywell brewery was constructed in the mid-nineteenth century on a strip of land that ran north from High Street to New Street. It was owned by John Young & Co until the company was taken over by Whitbread in 1968. When it closed three years later, it was the last brewery in Musselburgh. It has since been demolished along with Whitelaw's Fisherrow brewery, which closed in 1939.

Further along the coast, Prestonpans has long been associated with brewing. In 1754, there were sixteen brewers, but by the end of that century the number had dwindled to five. One brewery, which started production around 1720, came into the possession of the Fowler family in the mid-eighteenth century and had a reputation for quality ales. John Fowler did much to expand the business and by 1830 it was the second-largest brewery in East Lothian. In time, the town's other breweries went out of business but the Fowlers went from strength to strength. The White family acquired the business in 1865, but continued to trade under the name 'John Fowler and Co Ltd'. By the end of the nineteenth century, the ales it produced had become a household name. The company specialised in a rich, malty brew known as 'wee heavy'. At Prestonpans, men would drink a half-pint of beer and then add a 'wee heavy'. Despite having to compete with bigger companies, its reputation ensured a ready market across Scotland.

In the early-twentieth century there were only two breweries left in Prestonpans, including Fowler's. In the early 1950s, it was one of the biggest local employers, with 150 staff, including brewers, engineers, coopers, maltmen, boxmen and bottlers. The company was the subject of a takeover by United Breweries. The brewery, now only one of two in East Lothian, was shut down at the beginning of the 1960s with its machinery and production transferred elsewhere. The premises of John Fowler, which stood on High Street, Prestonpans, have since been demolished.

At Belhaven, Dunbar has the distinction of possessing East Lothian's last brewery. Monks are said to have brewed beer here since 1150. In the sixteenth century, Belhaven ale was supplied to the French expeditionary force commanded by Mary of Guise, part of which was garrisoned in Dunbar castle. The town had several local breweries in the eighteenth century, including one owned by Harry Knox, which ceased trading about 1770, and another in High Street, which went out of business in 1825.

Belhaven brewery, Dunbar.

Belhaven brewery is still in business in 2019, thanks to the reputation of its beer. It uses the best locally grown malt barley, together with traditional brewing methods. Established in 1719, control of this family business passed to Ellis Dudgeon around a century later; he was a family member but had higher aspirations for the business than previous owners. An advertisement displayed in *The London Morning Chronicle* in 1837 proclaimed that even the Emperor of Austria drank Belhaven ales and praised it as 'the Burgundy of Scotland and famed as Bavaria is for its strong beer'. By the late-nineteenth century most other Dunbar breweries had closed, but Belhaven continued to thrive with its distinctive brands, surviving a setback in 1887 when there was a devastating fire. Belhaven ale was supplied to the armed forces in both world wars.

In 2020 Belhaven is the oldest British brewery still in business. Although it has undergone modernisation, its older buildings are the core; they include three malting kilns with their distinctive steeply sloping roofs and a number of other stone buildings with pantile roofs. The old-fashioned skyline of the brewery is often used for marketing purposes.

Distilleries

As well as being home to one of Scotland's last breweries, at Glenkinchie, East Lothian possesses one of the last lowland whisky distilleries. In the 1800s, there were around two hundred distilleries in Scotland, half of which were located in the lowlands, several of them in East Lothian. The lowland distilleries earned a bad reputation by flooding the market with poor-quality spirit by contrast with those in Speyside, which produced high-quality whisky. Prior to this, high taxation had acted as a brake on the industry with whisky being produced in illicit stills in remote areas, including the Lammermuir hills.

One of the earliest legal distilleries was Mr Swinton's distilling house at North Berwick, which was in business in the first half of the eighteenth century; it stood in the grounds of the lodge house. Another distillery was built by the agricultural reformer John Cockburn at Ormiston in 1726. At Dunbar, there was once a distillery and a brewery, on ground behind the former West Barns inn. The brewery outlived the distillery, operating until almost the end of the nineteenth century, whisky production having ceased half a century earlier.

St Clements Well distillery stood at the foot of the slope crowned by Falside castle. According to a late-eighteenth-century description it was 'the most considerable distillery now in Scotland'. Despite this, it was out of business by the 1830s. On the coast at Prestonpans around the same time there was another distillery; it was a profitable concern but went out of business around 1850 when it was absorbed by Fowler's brewing company. Allegedly, it was closed down because its new owner had become a supporter of the temperance movement! Haddington had at least one small distillery at the end of the eighteenth century. In 1825, James Cumming opened the Nungate distillery, but many years later it was converted to a brewery, before closing. Westfield distillery was in business around the same time and may have been located close by.

East Linton was home to one of the largest distilleries in the region. It opened around 1783 and stood on the banks of the Tyne, close to Linton Bridge. Over fifty men were employed, when most other breweries and distilleries had but a handful of staff. It was capable of producing half-a-million gallons of whisky a year, sold as far afield as London. In 1835, around 92,000 gallons of whisky was exported from Dunbar harbour, most of it from Linton distillery. To meet its needs, not only did the distillery consume local barley, but also some from Berwickshire; large quantities were even imported through Dunbar harbour. From 1817, until it closed in 1852, it was owned by George Dunlop and Co, which also operated the Nungate and Westfield distilleries at Haddington.

Glenkinchie, a lowland distillery, south of Pencaitland.

By the early-twenty-first century, only Glenkinchie was still in business, one of three remaining distilleries in lowland Scotland. Its late-nineteenth-century buildings stand in farmland, 1.5 miles to the south of Pencaitland. The brothers John and George Rate established Milton distillery in 1825 using water from Kinchie burn (the name a corruption of 'De Quincy', the original landowners), which flows from the Lammermuir hills to the Tyne. They grew and malted their own barley, producing a distinctive malt whisky. In 1837, the enterprise changed its name to Glenkinchie. Around 77,000 gallons were produced annually, the spent wash being used to irrigate nearby fields. The production of whisky ceased in 1853 when John and George Rate went bankrupt and for the next twenty-seven years the premises was used as a sawmill. In the 1880s, the distillery was rebuilt under Major James Grey, who later founded Scottish Malt Distillers. In 1969, the distillery stopped malting its own grain and the malting floors were converted into a visitor centre. Today Glenkinchie is an important tourist attraction, with listed red-brick buildings, producing an internationally known brand of whisky, often referred to as the 'Edinburgh' malt.

An interesting reversal to the continual closures of breweries and distilleries has been the construction of NB distillery in 2017 at Halfland Barns, near North Berwick, which makes handmade gin from pure grain spirit.

There were once numerous maltings in East Lothian to support breweries and distilleries. In the eighteenth century, there were many barns and kilns scattered across East Lothian, but as brewing and distilling grew in scale, malting became concentrated at just a few locations. Several breweries and distilleries had an important side line in fattening cattle and pigs on the spent grain. In the 1950s, the manager of Glenkinchie distillery raised a prizewinning herd of Aberdeen Angus cattle on the product of malting and mashing.

Pentcaitland maltings.

There are now only a handful of maltings left in Scotland. One is located at Pencaitland; it is a local landmark, the tall, metal grain silos towering over the countryside (*photo on page 162*). The maltings were established on a greenfield site in 1964, the present plant built in 1978. The facility is supplied with local barley, which is dried on arrival. Pencaitland maltings has a production capacity of 47,000 tonnes a year, all the malt produced being destined for the distilling market.

21. DOVECOTES

More than eighty dovecotes exist in various states of preservation in East Lothian, one of the highest concentrations in Scotland. Apart from castles and churches, few other pre-eighteenth-century buildings survive in such numbers, one reason being that it was considered bad luck to demolish a dovecote. The Romans were known to have built towers for housing pigeons, but it was the Normans that introduced the dovecote to Britain. The dovecote, or 'doocot', provided an alternative source of fresh meat in times of scarcity.

By the late Middle Ages, most castles, tower houses and abbeys had their own dovecotes. The earliest form was the tun-bellied or beehive type; similar in style is the cylindrical structure. The second main type in East Lothian is the rectangular or square design. Occasionally, dovecotes were an integral part of the castle or house, as at the now-demolished Bothwell castle in Haddington.

The importance of dovecotes meant that they were strictly regulated by the old Scottish Parliament. The Haddington justices of the peace had a number of dovecotes demolished because their owners did not have the necessary qualifications. The beadle at Tyninghame church got an allowance for shooting the 'doos' as they fouled the church seats. A few churches actually had dovecotes incorporated into their towers, including those at Aberlady and Stenton. At the latter, the thirteenth-century church tower had accommodation for sixty pigeons. Dovecotes usually had nesting perches from floor-to-ceiling to afford maximum accommodation.

Dovecotes were still being built in Victorian East Lothian, but their importance had waned as meat was readily available from other sources. Many of the late examples were incorporated into the farm buildings themselves. An excellent example exists at Saltoun home farm, near Pencaitland, where the domed structure crowning the roof of the farm buildings that houses the pigeons can be seen from the nearby road.

Above left
'Beehive' dovecote, Dirleton castle.

Above right
'Beehive' dovecote, Phantassie, East Linton.

Left
Beehive dovecote: It originally belonged to Northfield house, Prestonpans.

A number of dovecotes in East Lothian have been well preserved and are readily accessible. A large beehive dovecote lies within the grounds of Dirleton castle, one of the oldest surviving dovecotes in East Lothian. Standing 25-feet tall it has walls 3.5-feet thick.

A similarly well-preserved example, dating from the seventeenth century, is located only a few feet from the main road at Prestonpans. Once the property of Northfield house, it is a seventeenth-century structure with walls 3-feet thick and a cone-shaped roof covered with stone slabs. A short distance from East Linton is Phantassie dovecote, preserved by the National Trust for Scotland. This tall stone tower stands alone in open fields. It did not start out life as a residence for pigeons, but was once a windmill. It has walls 4-feet thick and is crowned by an unusual, horseshoe-shaped sloping roof. Another tall structure clings to the slopes of Drylaw hill, just to the north of East Linton. It is one of the most substantially built dovecotes in East Lothian and can be seen from a considerable distance. Another less-accessible beehive dovecote can be seen from the passing road at the entrance to Luffness house, near Aberlady (to the south of North Berwick), which is private property.

East Linton has some of the oldest examples of square and rectangular lectern dove-cotes in Scotland. They are recognisable by their distinct-ive single roof, which usually faces south. They include the restored structure behind the church at Athelstaneford, dating from 1583, and one near the church at Tranent from around the same date. A dramatically situated example stands in front of Tantallon castle: it is of unusual size and has stone walls over 3-feet thick; within are 1,196 nesting places.

Dovecote of 1583, Athelstaneford church.

Preston tower also has a well-preserved square dove-cote dating from the seventeenth century, in a public space immediately to the north. The square structure has a thousand stone-built nests. There is also a well-restored rectangular example at Pencaitland, which stands a short distance to the north of the main street in the centre of the village and has accommodation for over 1,100 pigeons. Another easily accessible example stands in playing fields to the east of Pinkie house, Musselburgh.

Cylindrical dovecote, close to Nungate Bridge, Haddington.

Cylindrical dovecotes are relatively rare compared with the other two forms of design. East Lothian has some well-preserved examples. The first, of the eighteenth century, stands next to the road at Bolton in front of a group of farm buildings now converted for residential use (*see plate section*). A further example is found at Haddington, close to the west end of the Nungate Bridge, which was part of Lady Kitty's garden; it is topped with ornamental battlements, resembling a round tower on a castle. In the nineteenth century it served a dual purpose, with the lower portion in human occupation and pigeons living above. Another circular example can be seen in a field close to the road at Heugh on the east side of North Berwick Law, although it now has a concrete roof.

Not all East Lothian dovecotes have been well maintained and a number have been demolished in the last few decades as it is difficult to find alternative uses for them. There are also impressive examples in the grounds of some country houses, which are not accessible to the public; at least two have been converted into houses, with one located next to Humbie parish church.

22. LIMESTONE KILNS AND QUARRYING

One of Lothian's most distinctive man-made landmarks – visible many miles away – is the large industrial complex with its tall chimney at Oxwellmains near Dunbar (*see plate section*). This is the only place in Scotland where cement is produced. An essential ingredient is limestone, found on the coast immediately to the south of Dunbar and extracted from a large opencast quarry, several hundred feet deep. The current plant was built by Blue Circle Cement and opened in 1963. The limestone on this part of the coast was long known as the best in Scotland. It is also of interest to geologists as it contains many interesting fossils, including ancient corals. At Oxwellmains the limestone rocks are crushed and mixed with shale and sand; it is then burnt at 900°C to form calcium oxide ('burnt lime'). This is then heated to 1,400°C to create a hard clinker, after which it is cooled and ground down with gypsum to produce cement in a powder form.

In the past, limestone quarrying and coal mining were often found in close proximity. Most of these enterprises manufactured lime, which was applied to arable fields as a fertiliser, countering soil acidity. They were small scale and comprised just one kiln and a handful of employees. The parishes of Humbie, Ormiston, Pencaitland and Yester all produced lime at one time. Most of the quarries are now filled or overgrown and their associated kilns have long-since disappeared or fallen into ruin. The most interesting relics are to be found on the coast near the Oxwellmains cement works. A double stone kiln has been preserved close to the seashore at Catcraig, not far from Barns Ness lighthouse. Coke burning was introduced here in 1913 when lime was sent by railway to destinations as far away as Aberdeen and Ross-shire. The fires of the kilns were extinguished for the last time in 1921, when there was a coal-miners' strike. Limestone continued to be worked from this deposit, although it was no longer burnt on the site.

The Coltness Iron Company opened a mine at Oxwellmains in the late-nineteenth century, which continued operating until the 1950s. It supplied limestone for steelworks in the west of Scotland. The entrance was close to the present cement works and its tunnels continued under the A1, in the direction of Pinkerton.

Lime-kiln complex, Skateraw.

Another large, well-preserved kiln complex can be seen at Skateraw, close to Torness power station. Limestone had been burnt at this site since the early-eighteenth century. During the Napoleonic Wars, lime was sent to the Devon iron works, Clackmannanshire. In 1826, the three kilns here gave work to fifteen men and ten horses. A harbour was established between 1799 and 1825 with two piers, but few traces remain. Such facilities were not only important for exporting lime, but also for supplying the kilns with coal, which is absent from this part of East Lothian.

In the early-nineteenth century, in the summer, there were sometimes up to three hundred carts queuing at Skateraw waiting to transport lime south to Berwickshire. Many of them waited all night as there was a set hour to begin removing lime from the kiln and loading it onto the carts. Sometimes the drivers galloped their horses so they were first to get a consignment.

One night in December 1810, the Royal Navy frigates *Pallas* and *Nymph* were wrecked on rocks near Dunbar after mistaking a burning kiln at Skateraw for the coal-fired beacon on May island. The *Nymph* was a 36-cannon warship, returning from a patrol off Norway. It steered a course for what it thought was the May lighthouse, when in fact it was heading towards the coast. As it approached land, the crew became aware of their mistake and tried to set a new course, but were too late to prevent the warship running onto the appropriately named Devil's Ark rock, near Torness. Despite the hull being gashed open, the *Nymph* did not completely sink and its sailors managed to crawl ashore along its masts, which had been cut down. The captain was later court-martialled and severely reprimanded.

The *Pallas* was less fortunate, being smashed against rocks close to Broxmouth house. When dawn broke, the Dunbar lifeboat managed to rescue most of the sailors, who were clinging to the wreckage. Several lives were lost, including at least one of the lifeboat crew, which became overloaded and sunk while ferrying survivors ashore.

Another lime works was established in 1755 at Rhodes, a short distance east of North Berwick. There is an interesting local tradition that ships came here for lime from as far away as Ireland and that the made-up ground in front of Rhodes farmhouse was formed of ships' ballast. Lime from the kiln here was advertised in bills posted on the doors of local churches and in May demand was brisk. Limeworking at Rhodes ceased in 1862.

One of the earliest vertical limekilns in East Lothian, built by George Rennie of Phantassie, stands inland a short distance from East Linton, next to the road to Stenton. It is trapezoid in plan with vents 11 feet wide; the overall height is 22 feet and it is lined with dressed stone.

Old limestone kiln, Spilmersford, Easter Pencaitland.

Another easily accessible example of a limestone kiln survives near Pencaitland in woodland close to the car park at Spilmersford; the nearby quarry has long been filled in. Tenants included John Rate of Milton, who built Glenkinchie distillery in 1824. The Rates were the third generation of a Northumberland family that had settled as lime burners here. Further inland, at the foot of the Lammermuir hills, a limekiln in a poor state of repair can be seen in a field at Kidlaw, south-west of Gifford. There was also a large quarry here as evidenced by the disturbed ground in its vicinity.

Quarrying

Up until the twentieth century, most of the buildings in East Lothian were constructed from stone, with sandstone proving very popular. In 1900 there were eight quarries in the county, but this had fallen to one shortly before the Second World War. By that time many of the sources of suitable stone had been worked out and alternative materials were becoming available. The upper, old-red-sandstone strata in East Lothian produced a bright-red building stone; it was much worked between Dunbar and Garvald, giving the area its characteristic attractive houses. There were important quarries at Wester Broomhouse near Spott, which operated for over a hundred years, as well as Black Bank quarries and Garvald quarry. Sandstones in the oil-shale group, also red in colour, were at one time quarried at a number of locations including Thornton and Branxton near Innerwick.

The stone wrought from a quarry at Dunglass Dean, further to the south, came in shades from white to pale yellow. Several quarries in the Tranent area once worked sandstone in the limestone coal group, which was very popular with architects for ornamental work as it was almost white. There were quarries at a number of locations including Upper Birsley and Bankton. They had ceased working by 1911.

Although in the past there were numerous sandstone quarries in East Lothian, other types of rock were also used. These included grey-wacke and igneous rock, which were much harder to chisel into shape. The older part of Haddington was largely built from volcanic rock worked at Peppercraig quarry, situated half a mile to the north-west of the town centre. The stone varied in colour from purplish to brownish-grey. Old Abbey quarries, about a mile to the east of Haddington not far from the road to East Linton, yielded the light, porous, yellow-brown 'tuff', used extensively for local walls and buildings.

Many of the older buildings of North Berwick are built of phonolite, an igneous rock, which came from a quarry on the south side of North Berwick Law. Unlike numerous other workings, which have either been filled in or have disappeared, this quarry survives and is easily accessible. It produced rock with a rich, reddish colour. Porphyritis olivine basalt lavas have been used as a building stone at Dunbar and East Linton, being quarried at Markle quarry just to the west of the latter village.

Igneous rocks have also been extensively used in road construction. In the late-nineteenth century, numerous small quarries were opened beside the highways; a good example can be seen on top of Pencraig hill, next to the old route of the A1 and close to the lay-by, around a mile from East Linton. Another small, disused quarry can be found in at Galalaw, on the west side of Gullane, next to a bend in the road. The rock here is Gosford quartz, which provided a good quality roadstone. At one time, roadstone with excellent surface-wearing properties was obtained from Millstone Neuk quarry on the coast, two miles south-east of Dunbar. The site had one major disadvantage – it could only be worked at low-water spring tides!

After the First World War, most of the small quarries were closed and Traprain Law became the main focus for stone for road repair; in time much of the north-east slope was devoured by quarrying. Due to concerns that this important archaeological site was being destroyed, operations ceased in 1975. This large quarry still looks much the same as when it was abandoned; its rock face, several-hundred-feet high, can be seen for miles. Although there is no access to the quarry, it can be viewed close up from the road that runs along the north side of Traprain Law.

While Traprain Law was operated by the council there was another significant example operated by a private company, which also produced roadstone. It was Bangley quarry, on the western edge of the Garleton hills. By 1986 it had been in operation for fifty years and was turning out a quarter of a million tons of crushed stone to build roads. Thirty years later, the situation had changed dramatically, with the now-abandoned quarry works being flooded. There is no access to the site.

The sand and gravel resources of East Lothian have never been exploited on a major scale but the blue-laminated marine clay found on the coast was extensively worked near Belhaven, Dunbar in the mid-nineteenth century for use in Seafield brickworks. The former workings are now occupied by a large pond, a magnet for wildlife. Similar deposits were dug by a small brick-and-tile works that once operated three quarters of a mile from Aberlady, on the road to Haddington.

A deposit of blue clay on the site of a small glacial loch about a quarter mile to the east of Gladsmuir, close to the Haddington road, was used to make roofing and draining tiles in the later-nineteenth century.

23. COAL MINING

There are few traces of East Lothian's coal mines today, but the concentration of towns (Tranent, Prestonpans) in the north-west corner of the county indicates where the coalfields are.

In 1184, Robert de Quincy, earl of Winton, granted land around Tranent to the monks from Newbattle monastery in Midlothian, on which to graze sheep and extract peat and probably coal. Legend tells us that the monks became aware of the properties of the 'black stone' when they lit a fire while grazing their sheep. It ignited a seam of coal exposed on the surface. The monks dug coal from shallow pits in the vicinity of Tranent, an activity that soon extended across the landscape. A 1210 charter drawn up by Seyr de Quency gave the monks permission to exploit the coal commercially, the earliest reference to the exploitation of coal anywhere in Britain.

Salters Road connected Newbattle monastery with their coalfields close to the coast around Prestonpans. The monks continued to work this resource throughout the Middle Ages. Coal was consumed by the

Miners monument, Prestonpans, by Cockenzie-based sculptor Gardner Molloy. A reminder of the historical importance of the coal-mining industry to East Lothian.

local salt industry and some was exported from local harbours, including Port Seton. In 1531, a contract was signed between the abbots of Dunfermline and Newbattle to 'drive the coil of Prestongrange to the bounds of Pinkin (Pinkie) and Inveresk'.

As the more accessible seams were exhausted, workings became deeper. Miners were harshly treated, punished for trivial misdemeanours. James McNeill, who died in 1844, had worked in the pits around Tranent and related that the favoured punishment involved placing an iron collar round the neck of the offender and nailing him to a wooden support at the pit bottom, where he was left for at least a day.

When the coal deposit was worked out, pits were often abandoned without being filled in, a hazard to travellers. On one occasion, a farm servant from the vicinity of Haddington lost his way in the dark while going to Elphinstone to collect coal. His horse left the public road when he was just south of Tranent and plunged into a flooded pit. The cart was pulled in after it and both the servant and animal were drowned. Shortly after, the hole was filled in but the outflow of water was so great that for many years after it served as a drinking pond for local livestock.

After 1945, when the pits were nationalised, production was concentrated at a small number of large mines. The largest was Fleets, a mile south of Tranent, where operations began in 1866. It was re-sunk in the 1880s and production reached a peak in the late 1940s, with eight hundred men employed. It closed in 1961. There was a second short-lived drift mine (a tunnel into a hillside) at Bellyford, which was sunk in 1949, further to the south near Ormiston. It had a workforce of three hundred.

The National Coal Board also opened a further two drift mines at Meadowmill and Winton, but neither had a long history. The former, in which the deepest workings were two hundred feet below ground, was located near Prestonpans. It closed in 1960 and the site has since been cleared to make way for playing fields. Some of the soil from it was landscaped into a small hill, now a local landmark. Winton drift mine commended production in 1952 and was located to the east of Ormiston, next to the railway line to Gifford.

There were also two much larger mines accessed by vertical shafts close to Ormiston. One was Limeylands, which began production in 1895. Its three hundred miners produced 72,000 tons of coal in 1948; six years later, it had ceased production. Half a mile to the south-west of Ormiston was Tynemount mine, sunk in 1924. It was three-hundred-feet deep and in 1948 produced 84,000 tons of coal; a few years later, it too had been abandoned and demolished. At the eastern extremity of the coalfield was Glencairn mine, a few hundred yards to the south-west of Longniddry, not a place usually associated with coal mining. Opened by the Glencairn Coal Company in 1936, it reached peak production in 1948 with 190 miners. By the early 1960s, it had closed, along with the other deep mines in East Lothian.

Coal continued to be extracted from open-cast pits. The most notable operation was at Blindwells, north-east of Tranent. It opened in 1979, and, during its twenty-two years, produced 9.6 million tons of coal, some of which was consumed by the nearby Cockenzie power station. When Blindwells closed, it brought an end to over eight hundred years of coal mining in East Lothian. The huge hole created by giant earth-moving equipment has been filled in, the land returned to agriculture. Most of the earlier coal mines have gone the same way, with most visible traces of this key industry erased from the landscape. There is, fortunately, one exception: Prestongrange industrial museum, operated by East Lothian Council, has preserved some of the colliery buildings that served this important mine.

The nineteenth-century engine house of the former Prestongrange colliery, now part of Prestongrange industrial-heritage museum.

Coal mining had been carried on around here by monks. The more accessible seams of coal were becoming worked out by the early-nineteenth century. Sir James Grant Suttie inherited the estate of Prestongrange in 1818 and decided to revive its fortunes. Initially, the mine was leased to an English company owned by Matthias Dunn. A deep shaft was sunk in 1829, the first in Scotland, to exploit the great seam, which lay at a depth of 420 feet. It was difficult to work, being prone to flooding, and by 1840 the mine had been abandoned. The Prestongrange Coal and Iron Company took up the lease and invested large sums of money, with commodious cottages built a short distance to the east of the mine for the workforce. Morrison's Haven, the now-vanished harbour a short distance north of the mine, was enlarged for the export of coal.

The key to the success of Prestongrange was investment in new technology: a steam-powered Cornish beam engine was imported in sections and erected in 1874, with an engine house constructed around it. The beam engine had been built as far back as 1853, in Plymouth, and was responsible for the revival of mining at Prestongrange.

The steam-powered engine lifted the pump rod, which dropped down under its own weight, pumping water from the mine on each down stroke. On average it made 3.5 strokes per minute and was capable of pumping nearly a million gallons of water out of the workings per day. It operated for seventy-one years and only had to be shut down twice for repairs. The Summerlee Coal and Firebrick Company acquired the mine in 1895 and remained its owners until nationalisation in 1947. They brought in many Irish immigrant workers, who lived at Cuthill, Prestonpans. The mine was enlarged at the end of the nineteenth century and the brick, tile and fireclay works were greatly extended.

Shortly after nationalisation, Prestongrange coal mine was producing 167,000 tons of coal per year, with a workforce of 650. Production ceased in 1962, one of the last coal mines to close in East Lothian. Fortunately, some of its buildings were saved from demolition. The beam engine is the centrepiece of Prestongrange industrial museum, the only one of its type in Scotland. Close by stands the power-house building, which housed the steam boilers. Next to the main road is the steel head gear, which once stood at the end of a mineshaft lowering and raising cages full of miners. One of the most-impressive structures at the museum is the Hoffman kiln, with its chimney. Built in 1937 it was capable of producing thirty thousand bricks in one firing; each firing lasting up to fifty hours. There had been an earlier Hoffman kiln on the same site erected in 1910, its impressive chimney being incorporated into the new kiln. At one time there were also twenty-one beehive kilns here, but, unfortunately, they were demolished, the only trace some circular bases visible on the ground.

Although stone was the traditional building material, brickmaking began in the eighteenth century with the rapidly expanding demand for housing. Clay suitable for this purpose, and for making earthenware tiles and pipes for field drainage, was found between Portobello and Prestonpans. Their manufacture became associated with coal mining when it was discovered that waste fireclay and shale were particularly suitable for their production. By 1789 there were two sites in the vicinity of Prestongrange producing tiles and bricks, one near the Old Kirk and another using locally dug clay at Ravenscroft. Many of the bricks used in the construction of Edinburgh's New Town came from here.

When Prestongrange colliery was revived in the 1870s, the site also became a major producer of heavy ceramics. By the end of the nineteenth century, the brickworks here covered an extensive area. New kilns were built for glazed-pipe production and bottle kilns were replaced by downdraught kilns. Brickmaking continued at Prestongrange until 1975, but, as the colliery had closed over a decade earlier, raw materials had to be brought in from elsewhere, driving up costs.

In the seventeenth century, a commercial glass works was established close to the site latterly occupied by Prestongrange colliery, with German workers employed for some of the more complex processes. A short distance to the east, coal mining and other past industries have been commemorated on giant wall murals scattered across Prestonpans. In addition, 'tombstones' mark the locations of long-disappeared mines on the Pencaitland railway walk.

Iron ore was exploited on a small scale in East Lothian. At the beginning of the nineteenth century, ironstone was worked by the Carron company at Gullane Point and shipped to its blast furnaces near Falkirk. In the late 1860s, haematite was discovered on the Garleton hills. The earl of Hopetoun engaged a mining company from south-west England to search for ore on his lands; the quest met with success and a mine was opened a short distance to the south-east of Hopetoun monument. Initially, it was leased by Christie of Gladsmuir, who extracted large quantities of iron ore from the upper levels of the vein; much of it was used locally at Macmerry ironworks. Here it was mixed with ordinary black-band iron ore to improve the quality of the pig iron. Because of its high purity, some of the output was transported as far as Lanarkshire.

The Coltness Iron company took over the working of the mine in 1871 when the previous operator went out of business. Production was stepped up, with additional huts being erected to accommodate the expanded workforce. By 1873, around three hundred tons of ore was being delivered each week to the railway siding at Cottyburn on the Haddington branch line. The following year, the mine in the Garleton hills produced over ten thousand tons of high-quality iron ore. There were extensive underground workings, accessed by three shafts and numerous surface buildings, one of which housed a steam engine for draining the workings. By 1876, circumstances had changed dramatically and work ceased. Workings had been driven down to a depth of 280 feet but in places the vein of iron ore was only 20-inches wide. All the buildings were dismantled and no part of the mine remains except for some traces of the iron-ore vein on the surface. The blast furnace constructed near Macmerry to smelt locally worked ironstone also ceased functioning around this time.

DOMESTIC BUILDINGS

24. COUNTRY HOUSES

Given its small size, East Lothian has a large number of country houses. This is because of its proximity to Edinburgh and the fertile farmland, which yield considerable wealth. Since the Second World War, a number of the houses have been converted into hotels or divided into flats, while others remain in private hands. Many of those discussed below are not accessible: some can be viewed at a distance from public rights of way, but others are wholly concealed by woodland.

As the need for residences to be fortified diminished, the emphasis switched to comfort, as can be seen at Dirleton castle. Tower houses were no longer austere buildings and began to incorporate elements of domestic architecture: there is no better example than Preston tower at Prestonpans; a new house was built virtually on top of the defensive structure in an entirely different design.

While some owners added extensions to their tower houses and castles, others opted for a complete break. The location chosen for their new house was often close to their original residence, but, instead of a hill or rocky outcrop, it was sited out of view in a wooded river valley. Some of the earliest country houses retained many of the characteristics of a tower house, with Ballencrieff house a good example. It was built between the late-sixteenth and early-seventeenth centuries, burned down in 1868 and restored in the latter part of the twentieth century. The whitewashed house is private property, but can be seen at a distance from the surrounding roads.

The now-restored Fenton tower house, with its large windows, resembles a house more than a fortification. Close by is the modest L-plan Sydserff house, dating from the early-eighteenth century. For a long time, it was a ruin, but has been restored and can be seen from the nearby road.

Standing on a cliff top at Seacliff, next to the road to the beach and concealed by trees, is the ruin of a three-storey laird's house of the sixteenth century. The structure has defensive towers, and in some sources is referred to as 'Auldhame castle'. It incorporates stone from an earlier building that occupied the site prior to 1550. In its heyday, the gabled house had a yellow harling wash over its rubble walls and an orchard stood close by.

Overlooking the ponds of Markle fisheries, a short distance from East Linton, are the ruins of Markle manor, another laird's house dating from the 1600s. There was an earlier house, surrounded by orchards, gardens, ponds and pools on the site. In 1601, its owner, Robert Hepburn, was charged along with several associates of abducting the daughter of a John Carkethill from his house at Monkrigg. All of them escaped punishment. Markle manor was still occupied in 1726 with a small village close by.

These lairds' houses were fairly small and drew on traditional Scottish architecture. The seventeenth century saw a break with the past and the construction of large country houses, inspired by buildings in England and abroad. Sir John Nisbet purchased Dirleton castle and its estates in 1663. Instead of living in the castle, he built a new house around a three-sided courtyard at Archerfield, half a mile to the west. Bowmen of the English army commanded by Edward I camped here in 1298, hence the name.

Nisbet's house was built of roughcast stone and Robert Adam remodelled the interior in 1790. In the later-nineteenth century extensions were built around the original house. There is a local story that Winston Churchill and US President Franklin Roosevelt met here to discuss the D-Day landings, but there appears to be no truth in it. After suffering years of neglect, the house was restored at the beginning of the twenty-first century as a hotel, now part of the Archerfield golf complex. It can be can be viewed at a distance from the John Muir trail.

Few golf courses have a more impressive clubhouse than Royal Musselburgh, west of Prestonpans. Situated close to the centre of the course is the yellow-sandstone Prestongrange house. It started life as a sixteenth-century tower house, onto which a large house was added in the following century. Further extensions were built in the 1830s in the Scots baronial style, designed by the distinguished architect, William H. Playfair. This was made possible by money generated from coal mining and other industrial activities on the surrounding estate for its new owner, Sir James Grant Suttie. In time, the underground workings extended under Prestongrange house itself!

One of the earlier owners, who lived here in the eighteenth century, lost his money gambling and as a consequence turned somewhat odd. He concocted a theory that St John wrote *The Apocalypse* in an underground passage at Morrison's Haven, a short distance to the north of Prestongrange house. The golf course is open to visitors, who have a good view of the historic house when they play a round.

Standing on the north bank of the Tyne near Pencaitland is Winton

The majestic Winton house.

house, one of East Lothian's most majestic buildings and a fine example of Anglo-Scots Renaissance architecture. It was designed by William Wallace of Tranent, the king's master mason. Dating from 1620–9, it was not the first building on the site. Around 1480, George, 4th lord of Seton, constructed a four-storey tower house, protected by a curtain wall. In 1544, during the Rough Wooing, it was badly damaged by English troops who bombarded it then set it on fire. Some restoration was carried out shortly after 1600, but this work ceased when the first earl died. In 1620 George, 10th Lord Seton and 3rd Earl Winton, 'founded and built the great house from the foundation with all the large stone dykes about the precinct, park, orchard and gardens thereof'.

This family already owned the prestigious residence of Seton palace. Parts of the original castle were incorporated into Winton house. Among its more interesting architectural features are the tall Elizabethan chimneys adorned with spirals, and the roof slates, which are cut into patterns. The Seton family lost Winton house along with all their other properties when they backed the Jacobite rising of 1715. The house was bought by the Hamiltons, who had lived in the seventeenth-century Pencaitland house, a short distance away near the medieval bridge. Pencaitland house eventually burned down in 1878, but two of its pavilions have survived, having been converted into separate houses. Colonel John Hamilton added a Gothic baronial extension to Winton house in the early years of the nineteenth century. The last of the Hamiltons to live here was Lady Ruthven, renowned for her charitable work.

By the early-eighteenth century, country houses were no longer the sole preserve of the aristocracy. Over the next two centuries, wealthy lawyers and merchants acquired estates and built impressive mansions. One of the most accessible country houses in East Lothian is Newhailes, near Musselburgh, which has been owned by the National Trust for Scotland since 1997 (house undergoing renovation in 2020). The original structure was built for architect James Smith as his own home in 1686. In 1709 Sir David Dalrymple changed the name of the house from Whitehill to Newhailes (Hailes castle was also one of his properties). Around 1718 to 1720 a huge library was built on the east side of the house and was once known as 'the most learned library in Europe'; the book collection is now in the National Library of Scotland. Newhailes is an impressive house in the Palladian style that was visited by many leading figures during the Scottish Enlightenment of the eighteenth century (*see plate section*).

Early in the eighteenth century, many houses were built in the classical style, but, towards the end of that century, Neo-Gothic extravaganzas, often taking the form of castles, came into favour. Seton house, designed by Robert Adam, is one example: lawyer Alexander Mackenzie commissioned the house, built 1789–91 to the east of Prestonpans. This was not an altogether inappropriate location, as the sixteenth-century Seton palace was demolished to make way for the new structure, leaving only some of the boundary walls for the garden still standing. Seton house is in private ownership but can be seen from Seton collegiate church on its east side.

Situated a short distance to the south of Prestonpans and visible to motorists on the A1 is the brightly painted Bankton house. Of modest dimensions, it dates from the early-eighteenth century. It was originally known as Olivstob and was purchased by Colonel James Gardiner, later killed at Prestonpans in 1745 by the Jacobites.

Further along the coast, a short distance to the north of Longniddry, is the magnificent Gosford house, one of Scotland's most important country houses (*see plate section*). According to one nineteenth-century account, this large structure can be seen from Edinburgh, some twenty miles away. The earl of Wemyss could not play golf at his residence at Amisfield, so, in 1781, he purchased Old Gosford house, along with extensive tracts of coastal land. New stables and a coach house were erected before work began on the house in 1791. The enterprise was described as like constructing 'a palace on a rabbit warren', because of the sandy ground. Using high-quality yellow sandstone from a quarry near Dundee, the first phase was completed in 1800. The plans were drawn up by Robert Adam, one of Scotland's greatest architects, and the house is rightly regarded as one of his finest designs. Unfortunately, Adam did not live to see his plans come to fruition: he died in 1792.

On the owner's death a few years later, his successor decided to alter Gosford house and demolished certain parts, including the wings. The next earl considered pulling down the remaining part, despite huge sums of money having been spent; fortunately, he was persuaded against this course of action. Gosford house remained unoccupied for nearly a century until the north and south baroque wings were added for the 10th earl in the later nineteenth century. During the Second World War, the house and grounds were used by Polish forces training for D-Day and as a German prisoner-of-war camp. The central block suffered a serious fire in 1940 and was not reroofed until 1987.

In 2020, Gosford house is open to the public (entrance fee) and is well worth a visit. The neoclassical exterior is exceptional, as is the interior, with the grand marble hall the highlight. Completed in 1891, to a design by William Young for the tenth earl Wemyss, the marble hall incorporates a stunning double staircase leading to a picture gallery. The grounds at Gosford are extensive, stretching to five thousand acres, encompassing coastal areas and parkland and on payment of a fee can be accessed by walkers. There is also a first-class golf course, Craigielaw, designed by Donald Steel, which opened in 2001.

Inland, a mile south-east of Longniddry, close to a minor road to Gladsmuir, is Elvingston house. It was built in 1837 in the Jacobean Scots Baronial style. There was once an earlier house in the vicinity. Elvingston is still a private residence, but can be seen from the road standing on low-lying ground surrounded by arable farmland.

Luffness house overlooks the southern shore of Aberlady bay. In the latter part of the 1840s it was redesigned in the baronial style, but at the core of the structure is a sixteenth-century tower. The house is a private residence but it is sited close to the Aberlady–Gullane road, from where it can be glimpsed.

Overlooking the mouth of the Tyne is the pink sandstone Tyninghame house. There has been a country house here since 1628, but it had few features of note until it was extended and remodelled in the Scots Baronial style in the early-nineteenth century. Sir Walter Scott was a guest on a number of occasions. Until 1987, it was the residence of the earls of Haddington, after which it was converted into flats. Unfortunately, this large house, resembling a fairy castle with its numerous towers and turrets, can only be viewed from the surrounding countryside. John Muir footpath offers distant views, as does the minor road leading to the beach at Tyninghame.

Inland, about a mile to the north-west, is Newbyth house. Like Tyninghame, it has been converted to private flats and there is no access; the building can be viewed at a distance from local footpaths. The Gothic-style house dates from 1817, but probably stands on the site of an earlier residence.

Further down the coast, on the east side of Dunbar, is Broxmouth house. It is well concealed by woodland, but can be seen at a considerable distance from Doon hill. The present house dates from 1774 and stands on the site of an earlier residence; Queen Victoria visited in 1878.

Saltoun hall overlooks the Birns water, a short distance to the east of Pencaitland. This vast Gothic house, complete with turrets and battlements, dates from 1803 and was built around an earlier house. It is likely that there was a castle here as early as the twelfth century. The laird of Saltoun in 1547 was pro-English and was one of the Lothian lairds who placed his house in 'our auld nemesis hands'. This was very much in contrast to Andrew Fletcher, who resided at Saltoun hall at the end of the seventeenth century. He was a noted Scottish patriot who actively opposed the 1707 union with England, so much so that he was forced into exile in Holland before eventually returning to Scotland. In 1967 Saltoun hall was converted into flats, after being owned by the Fletcher family for 340 years. The grounds are private and the building can be seen from afar from local footpaths although, as it is surrounded by tall trees of a considerable age, from many locations only its rooftop is visible.

Situated on gently rising ground two miles to the south of Musselburgh, is Carberry tower. The oldest part of the structure is a sixteenth-century tower house, on which additions were made in the eighteenth and nineteenth centuries. These Georgian elements owe their present appearance to the addition in 1909 of Scots Baronial features, such as the turrets and the gargoyles on the roof. Nowadays it is a hotel.

About a mile to the south of Gifford is Yester house. It is among the earliest examples of the large, purpose-built, country houses in East Lothian as well as among the most impressive. The Hay family, whose original residence was Yester castle, replaced it with a new tower house a short distance away in the late-sixteenth century. Two wings were later added. Around 1670, John Hay, 1st marquis of Tweeddale, began to plant trees and landscape the land in its vicinity; within decades, the garden and grounds were among the most impressive in Scotland.

At the end of the seventeenth century, the tower house was demolished and work commenced on the construction of the present Yester house. This was a drawn-out affair and it was not completed until 1729, due to the death of its owner. The building then underwent a series of modifications, including the redesign of the roof to prevent the accumulation of snow. In 1789, the architect Robert Adam was commissioned to redesign the exterior, but only the north side was completed. More recently, in 1972, the Italian-American composer, Gian Carlo Menotti, purchased Yester house and lived there until his death in 2007. There is no access to the house and grounds, but it can be seen from afar from local footpaths.

While most of the country houses are situated near the sea or on the coastal plain, Hopes house lies in a valley overlooked by the Lammermuir hills. It is constructed from sandstone and was built around 1825, probably on the site of an earlier house. It can be seen from the track to Hopes reservoir, which passes close by.

By the start of the twentieth century, the country-house boom had ended due to high taxes and the rising cost of employing servants. There were a few exceptions. Greywalls house at Gullane was built as a holiday home for Alfred Littleton MP, using stone from Rattlebags quarry in 1901. He was a keen golfer and the building stands next to Muirfield golf course. Since the Second World War, this Arts and Crafts-style house has been run as a hotel.

Unfortunately, the twentieth century saw the destruction of several outstanding country houses. From roughly fifty East Lothian houses at the end of the nineteenth century, ten have been demolished. Dunglass house, built around 1810, was a magnificent house that stood on the edge of a deep ravine where there had been a castle since the fourteenth century; it was demolished by the English during the Rough Wooing. It had been rebuilt by c.1600, but was destroyed in an explosion in 1640. The house was reconstructed, but, by the late-eighteenth century, it was in poor condition. Alexander Nasmyth drew up plans for a new building, in both classical and gothic design. An amalgamation of both styles – which it was thought would blend in well with the landscape – was ultimately incorporated into the new Dunglass house. During the Second World War, Donaldson's School for the Deaf was evacuated here from Edinburgh. Disaster struck in 1947 when it was gutted by fire; the ruins being blown up in 1958. A modern two-storey house was later constructed on its site.

Not far to the north, about a mile from Innerwick, was Thurston house, of red sandstone. The original house was reconstructed in 1890, at which time it was described as 'a fine residence surrounded by fine old trees'. Despite being in a good state of repair, it was demolished in 1952. The site is now occupied by holiday homes and caravans, though its lodge house survives.

To the west of Dunbar, Hedderwick Hill house once overlooked the mouth of the Tyne. In 1938 it was requisitioned by the army. At the end of the War, it returned to private ownership, but a few years later the building was found to be in poor condition and demolished. In 1961 it was blown up by the Territorial Army.

Another long-forgotten realm is Belton house, which stood beside the Biel burn, three miles to the south-west of Dunbar. Like several other East Lothian country houses, it started life as a tower house with walls over 6-feet thick but was turned into a residential structure with additions in 1739 and 1865. *The Courier* described it as 'one of the most secluded and beautiful of the many fine country seats of East Lothian', although it was relatively modest in size. After its owner died in the 1950s, Belton house was neglected. Eventually its roof was removed and it was demolished in 1967.

Near East Linton, Smeaton house was demolished in 1949, its walled garden now a garden centre. Its residence dated from the early-nineteenth century and was built in a Georgian style.

At least two country houses near Haddington were demolished in the twentieth century. Clerkington house, which overlooked the Tyne south of the Pencaitland road, suffered serious damage while being used by the army in the Second World War and was eventually pulled down in 1966. It dated from the late-eighteenth century and replaced an earlier building, part of which was washed away when the Tyne flooded in 1775. Perhaps the greatest loss to architecture was Amisfield house, on the east edge of Haddington. Unlike most other country houses, which were demolished after the Second World War, it was pulled down in 1928 due to dry rot. It was once described as 'the most important building of the orthodox Palladian school in Scotland'. The land on which it stood is now a golf course, but originally it belonged to the convent at Abbeymill and had an interesting history, related below.

Haddington was for many centuries associated with the woollen industry. One of the first attempts to introduce manufacturing to Scotland was made by James Stanfield (later knighted for his encouragement of industry), who served in the English army under Oliver Cromwell. After military service, he settled in Scotland and initially lived in Edinburgh. In 1681, he purchased land at Newmills, now known as Amisfield. Workshops, fulling mills and dyeing houses were erected in what was hoped would become a major enterprise employing over two hundred people. From the start there was difficulty in recruiting skilled workers and some came from as far away as England. Before long Sir James's company was in financial trouble and matters came to a head in 1687 when he was found drowned in a well.

At first it was thought to be suicide but suspicion fell on his son, Philip, who had hastily arranged the funeral. Sir James's body was exhumed and strangulation marks were detected. According to an ancient tradition, if the accused is made to touch the deceased and the body bleeds, it is taken as a sign of guilt. This was the case with Philip, who was transported to Edinburgh to be executed. When he was hung, his feet remained on the scaffold and the executioner was forced to strangle him. Philip's head was cut was off and displayed at the East Port in Haddington; the remainder of his body was hung in chains at the Gallow Lee between Edinburgh and Leith.

Initially, attempts to continue the woollen business met with success, but union with England in 1707 dealt a fatal blow, as cheap cloth from across the border flooded the market. In 1713, the estate of

Newmills was sold to Colonel Francis Charteris, who was responsible for its present name of Amisfield, which was his grandfather's seat in Dumfriesshire. To his annoyance, the estate was inherited by his cousin. It was not, however, for the renaming of Newmills that Francis Charteris is best remembered, but for his debauched lifestyle. He became the epitome of evil for several contemporary writers. The poet and satirist Alexander Pope used his name in his *Moral Essays*. William Hogarth, the English painter and engraver, featured Charteris in the first plate of his *Rake's Progress*.

During his teens, Charteris joined the army but was thrown out of his regiment for cheating at cards. While serving in the Dutch army he was dismissed for stealing beef. He later rejoined the army, but while in command of the 1st regiment of Foot Guards he enlisted several criminals after taking money from them, the case eventually ending up in the House of Commons. With his military career at an end, he became a successful gambler. However, he lacked integrity and would do anything to win. By using mirrors, he cheated the Duchess of Queensberry out of £30,000 (in excess of £1 million in 2020) during one game of cards. Charteris was a skilled swordsman and sometimes fought duels, killing a number of his opponents with a smirk on his face. Furthermore, he was a womaniser and was convicted to a term of imprisonment in Newgate prison for raping his female servant, earning him the sobriquet 'Rapemaster General'. George II pardoned him on condition he surrender some of his lands. When he was dying, he offered £30,000 to anyone who could come up with evidence that hell did not exist. He also said that, if there was a heaven, he had no interest in it although he moderated his behaviour shortly before he passed away. When he died at Stoneyhill near Musselburgh in 1732 there was a frightening storm, which was taken as a sign of divine wrath. At his funeral there was a riot and so relieved were the citizens of East Lothian to see the demise of Francis Charteris that they threw dead dogs and offal onto his grave.

It was his grandson (also Francis Charteris) who was responsible for the construction of the Palladian house at Amisfield in 1755, with wings added in 1785. During the First World War, it housed officers from the Lothian and Border Horse and the Royal Scots, with other ranks housed in huts in the grounds. In 1924, it was stated that Amisfield house was going to be demolished and by the following year only the façade remained. Some of its stone was used to construct Preston Lodge high school and the clubhouse of Longniddry golf club. Although Amisfield house is no longer, many of its outbuildings, such as the stables and walled garden, remain. The extensive parkland associated with the house is accessible to the public and is used as a golf course.

Preston house stood close to the market cross at Prestonpans. The seventeenth-century house had numerous interesting architectural features, including pointed arched roofs on the pavilions that flanked either end of the structure. The four acres of grounds contained mazes and walks, which could take two hours to negotiate. During the battle of Prestonpans in 1745, its 10-foot-high walls initially provided protection to government troops, but they were overwhelmed by the Jacobite rebels, who killed many of them. For a time, it was a school known as Schaw's hospital, for boys from a poor background. By the early-twentieth century, Preston house, over 140 feet in length, was a ruin. It was eventually demolished and no trace remains.

A more unusual loss was Beech Hill house, which stood between Gifford and Haddington. In 1944, a De Havilland Mosquito on a training flight from RAF East Fortune crashed into the nineteenth-century residence, causing considerable damage and killing the crew of two. Four people inside the house also perished, including Lieutenant Colonel J. Haig and Mrs Ruth de Pree, the nephew and niece of Field Marshal Sir Douglas Haig. In 1952, a new house was built on the site but the original stables and walled garden remain.

About two miles to the south-west of Gifford lay New Newton hall. It also suffered in the Second World War during its use by the military. Described as a fine, late-eighteenth-century house in the Adamesque classical style, it was demolished in an explosion by the Royal Engineers in 1965. Old Newton hall, a hundred yards away, fared little better. It was a two-storey building measuring just over fifty feet in length dating from the sixteenth century. In 1971, the last traces of it were removed having been a ruin for over a century.

Some country houses, including Biel house on the banks of the Biel water, have been partially demolished to make them more manageable. This structure started life as a fourteenth-century tower house, which was incorporated into the latter structure. An extension was built to the west in the late-eighteenth century, with battlements being added at a later date to give the appearance of a castle. The architect William Atkinson added a 'vast monastic Gothic addition' on the east side between 1814–18. When completed, at five hundred feet, Biel house was one of the longest houses in Britain. In 1952, William Atkinson's Gothic structures were demolished, as was the large Episcopal chapel to reduce the size of the house. Biel house is concealed by woodland and there is no access.

While most ruined country houses have been demolished, an exception is Seacliff house. It dates from 1760, but was extended and embellished in the Scots Baronial style in the mid-nineteenth century. John Laidlay purchased the property in 1841 and it then passed to his son Andrew. He was responsible for carving the diminutive Seacliff harbour – reputed to be the smallest in Britain – out of solid rock. Catastrophe struck Seacliff house in 1907, when it burnt down and Andrew Laidlay perished in the blaze. However, the ruin of Seacliff house is still substantially complete and can be glimpsed through the trees from the nearby beach. There is no access to the building.

25. LODGE HOUSES AND OUTBUILDINGS

While many country houses are hidden behind high walls or concealed by woodland, their lodge houses, standing at the entrance to driveways, are sometimes the sole indication that a country house exists close by. In some cases, they are all that remains of a great residence.

On the eastern edge of Haddington, two whitewashed lodge houses of two storeys stand at the former entrance to Amisfield house. The lodge house for Dunglass house still stands on a minor road, although though the house has disappeared, having burnt down shortly after the end of the Second World War.

The giant, red-sandstone arch, with ornamental lodge house attached on one side, at the western entrance to Gosford house, is one of the most impressive entrances to a country house anywhere in Scotland. It faces Longniddry village and in the past visitors would arrive at the station here to enter the estate under the huge arch. A further magnificent gatehouse faces the seashore on the Longniddry–Aberlady road, also constructed from red sandstone; octagonal lodges with parapets stand guard on either side of the gateway. The entire structure in some way

A Christmas-card scene: summit of Garleton hills.

The south side of Traprain Law, which is a laccolith – a reservoir of lava solidifies underground and is in time exposed as the softer rocks surrounding it are eroded.

The isolated hill of North Berwick Law is the remnant of an old volcano.

Above

Bass Rock from the west. It is the relic of an ancient volcano.

Centre

Coast north of Gullane. In the background are large sand dunes, which have been colonised by grasses and small bushes.

Below

The coast at Yellowcraigs, with Fidra island in the background. The island was formed from a volcanic sill – an intrusion formed by molten rock which has forced its way sideways between layers of strata, wedging them apart.

Above

Pressmennan lake (an artificial creation) in late autumn.

Centre

The Tyne flowing through the Linn rocks at East Linton: sixteenth-century bridge with two stone arches.

Below

Sunset over Aberlady bay. In medieval times it had an important harbour linked to Haddington by road.

< Opposite, above

Golden autumn colours in woodland on the banks of Colstoun water near Gifford.

< Opposite, below

A tree-lined road near Yester Mains in spring. Many of the roads in the vicinity of Gifford and Haddington are enclosed by avenues of trees.

Above

Chesters fort (late BC or early AD) occupies the undulating ground below the gorse bushes. Huts stood on this small hill, enclosed by earth ramparts.

Centre

The moon setting behind the standing stone on Pencraig hill near East Linton.

Below

White castle is misleadingly named as it is a well-preserved Iron Age fort on the northern slopes of the Lammermuir hills.

Above A re-enactment of the Battle of Prestonpans. A large Scottish saltire being displayed by Highlanders had its origins at an earlier battle.

Below left The small stone memorial to the second Battle of Dunbar, 1650, next to the side of the road near Oxwellmains.

Below right A modern reconstruction of an eighth-century, Anglo-Saxon cross in the grounds of Aberlady church. It is based on fragments discovered in the vicinity.

Above

The church at Oldhamstocks ('old dwelling place') was rebuilt in 1701, incorporating parts of an older building.

Centre

Dunbar parish church is one of the largest and most impressive churches in East Lothian. It dates from the early-nineteenth century and stands on the site of the Collegiate church founded by the Earl of Dunbar in 1342.

Below

Whitekirk parish church was once one of the leading religious buildings in East Lothian, an important destination for medieval pilgrims.

Above

A small preserved eighteenth-century fort stands guard over the old entrance to Dunbar harbour.

Left

Preston tower dates from the fifteenth century. The extension on top was built by the Hamiltons two centuries later.

Below left

Tantallon castle from the sea. There was a small harbour at the base of the cliffs for supplies during sieges.

Below right

Dirleton castle from the south-west. The oldest part of the castle is the tower and adjacent buildings in the foreground.

Above

Falside castle: a restored, fifteenth-century, tower house near Musselburgh.

Centre

Hailes castle on the bank of the Tyne, its walls catching the last rays of the setting sun.

Below

The ruins of Garleton castle lie at the foot of Craigy hill, two miles north of Haddington.

Above

Fields of oil-seed rape make a colourful sight in May on the lower slopes of the Lammermuir hills, near Spott.

Centre

Fields in late summer near Garvald. Close to the edge of the Lammermuir hills, they lie near the limits of arable cultivation.

Below

The impressive Gothic façade of Papple farm, near East Linton.

Above A cylindrical farm dovecote (eighteenth century) stands next to the road at Bolton. There is no access to it as it has been incorporated into a residential complex.

Centre Located on exposed ground not far from North Berwick Law is the stump of a vaulted tower windmill (seventeenth century).

Below One of the best-known buildings in East Lothian is the preserved Preston mill near East Linton (seventeenth century). It is now in the care of the National Trust for Scotland.

The preserved colliery headframe against a wintry sunset at Prestongrange museum. It stood over the top of the mine shaft and operated the lifts.

Torness nuclear-power station viewed from Skateraw. Requiring large quantities of cooling water, it is on the coast.

The cement plant at Oxwellmains, near Dunbar, makes use of limestone quarried close by. An important Iron Age fort stood here.

Clockwise from top left

A large obelisk located on the edge of a rocky slope near Traprain Law commemorates James Balfour (1820-56), the father of A. J. Balfour, prime minister from 1902-5.

The Hopetoun monument crowns the summit of Byers hill (560 feet), north of Haddington. It was built of bricks in 1824.

The statue of the great conservationist, John Muir, as a boy, in High Street, Dunbar. It stands close to the house in which he was born.

This impressive Celtic cross is near the entrance to North Berwick harbour, a memorial to Catherine Watson who drowned in an 1889 rescue attempt.

A giant golf ball occupies the centre of a roundabout at Levenhall, Musselburgh.

< Opposite, above

The charming Cockenzie harbour.

< Opposite, below

Built around 1530, the 210-foot-long Nungate Bridge, in sandstone, spans the Tyne at Haddington.

Above

Late-eighteenth-century town houses, High Street, Musselburgh.

Centre

North Berwick viewed from North Berwick Law, with Craigleith island beyond.

Below

Wall mural, High Street, Prestonpans, depicting bygone life in the Summerlee district, which was built to house the migrant mining community. It is one of a large number of imaginative murals in the town.

Newhailes house, Musselburgh, built c.1686 and extended in the eighteenth century. Along with its extensive grounds, it is now preserved by the National Trust for Scotland.

Gosford house: based on plans by Robert Adam, perhaps Scotland's greatest architect, this neoclassical mansion was completed in 1808. Imposing exterior, and, on the inside, a stunning marble hall of 1890 by William Young.

Lodge house, facing Longniddry. It guards the west entrance to Gosford house.

resembles the entrance to a fort or castle. It is not unusual for country houses to have at least two entrances, often with lodge houses at each, but Gosford house has a third, near Aberlady; it is a much more modest affair than the other two and consists of a single cottage.

Inland, near Pencaitland, there is an elaborate lodge house at the northern entrance to Winton house. Located a short distance from the road to Tranent the structure takes its inspiration from the castles of the Middle Ages. Two circular stone towers dating from the early-nineteenth century stand on either side of the driveway. A later structure has been added, linking the towers.

The main gatehouse to Saltoun hall, south of Pencaitland, has evolved in a similar manner. Dating from the early-nineteenth century, it is on the Pencaitland–East Saltoun road. Initially consisting of two square, castellated, twin-gate lodges with crenellated parapets, around 1935 they were linked by an arch on which was built a residence, giving it a distinctive appearance (*photo on page 194*). The south lodge for Saltoun hall is built in the more conventional Scottish Baronial style. Dating from 1913, it was among the last lodge houses constructed in East Lothian.

The unusual lodge house at the entrance to Saltoun hall.

The stable block, with classical façade, Newhailes house.

Another imposing entrance can be found at Carberry tower. It takes the form of a stone arch over the driveway and a lodge house in Baronial style. On the other side of the county, the lodge house for Broxmouth Park is a red-stone building close to the road from Dunbar–Oxwell Mains (*photo on page 413*). It is of the eighteenth century and is in a good state of preservation. Broxmouth Park house dates from the same time. It is not accessible to the public and is well hidden by surrounding woodland. On the slopes of the Lammermuir hills near Garvald is Nunraw house, once part of the Cistercian monastery. The driveway to the house, which started life as a tower house, is guarded by a red-sandstone lodge house appropriately resembling a medieval fortification.

The stable block, another type of building frequently found in the grounds of country houses, could be a substantial structure, sometimes the size of a small mansion house. One of the most impressive examples is found at Newhailes house, near Musselburgh (*photo on page 194*). Built in 1790, the block has a classical façade at the entrance, opening onto a large courtyard. Gosford house also has a stable block built in yellow-brown stone around the same time. It is also in the classical style, embellished with stone carvings and reliefs. Carberry tower stable block dates from the mid-nineteenth century and has been converted into residential use.

As with the lodge houses, several stable blocks survive, while the original country house has long since vanished. They include those for Dunglass house, which burnt down in 1947. Built in a Monumental Classical style, the block is now adapted for residential use and can be viewed at a distance by visitors to the collegiate church. The stable block for Amisfield house still exists and is surrounded by a golf course. It is an impressive complex of buildings enclosing a courtyard, dating mainly from 1785.

Another feature of the country house was the walled garden. As well as having an ornamental purpose, the walls provided protection against frost and winds, creating a microclimate. The second largest in Scotland, enclosing nearly 8 acres, belonged to Amisfield house. It resembles a fort, being rectangular in shape with 16-foot-tall walls flanked by towers at each corner. It is being restored to former glories after many years of neglect. The walled garden at Dunglass, built in the 1800s, has also outlived the house it served. Yet another example can be found, appropriately, at Smeaton nursery near East Linton. Unfortunately, the house it was built for no longer exists. Numerous other walled gardens,

Walled garden, with tower, in the grounds of the now-demolished Amisfield house.

however, are hidden away within the grounds of extant country houses. One of the more accessible examples is at Hailes house, owned by the National Trust for Scotland.

Another country-house trapping was the folly, but very few were found in East Lothian. The main exception was Amisfield house. As well as having an enormous walled garden (*photo above*) it had two follies, which still stand. On rising ground on the south edge of Amisfield park is a small, castellated structure thought to date from the early-nineteenth century. Close to the river Tyne is a small, ruined building resembling a Roman temple. It was originally a summer house, with bowling green located a short distance to the north. In 1775, it was damaged when the Tyne burst its banks and swept away the surrounding statues. As part of the ornamental grounds of Amisfield house, the watercourse had been altered to form cascades. Further east, a tower stands near the coast close to Broxmouth Park house. It is crowned with battlements and dates from around 1850. Although not exactly a folly, there is a curious building built in the form of a pyramid on a raised rectangular base in the grounds of Gosford House. It was built by 1795 for Francis Charteris, 7th earl Wemyss, as a mausoleum; there are spaces for sixty-four coffins, but only he is buried within. The unusual design of the building is likely to have been influenced by the fact that Francis Charteris was grand master mason of the Freemasons of Scotland.

26. COTTAGES AND HOUSES

One of the most distinctive features of the East Lothian landscape is its cottages. They are found across the county, sometimes as individual buildings, others in small rows. They are made from red or yellow sandstone, with only a small number in brick. The majority were built in the eighteenth and nineteenth centuries as housing for farm workers and, to a lesser extent, for railway employees. Sir Harry Lauder, the great music-hall entertainer, spent his early years in a Musselburgh miner's cottage and the inventor of the ship's propeller, Robert Wilson, grew up in a fisherman's cottage at Dunbar.

During the Agriculture Revolution, landowners provided new accommodation for their workers. All the 'cots' in the parish of Whittingehame had been demolished by 1792. Not all farm labourers appreciated being moved out of their old homes, so cot houses built of turf and stone lingered on in some parts of the county well into the nineteenth century.

In parts of Whittingehame a remedy was found with the building of new, two-room cottages at Morham Mains. By the end of the nineteenth century, the cottar houses had disappeared, replaced by fewer, more substantial, stone cottages. They are a feature of the Victorian age as in the early-twentieth century the need for large numbers of farmworkers dwindled along with the need to house them.

Domestic buildings from the Middle Ages are notable by their absence in southern Scotland, as towns and villages were devastated during the English invasions of the 1540s. Made of wood they burnt well and could be hastily rebuilt, but the houses that survived were swept away by later modernisation. They were replaced with stone structures, but retained the rectangular plan favoured in earlier times; most now had windows in the front wall on either side of a door. Two-storey buildings had similar symmetrical frontages with the windows of the first storey placed directly above those on the ground floor.

One characteristic of many East Lothian houses and cottages is their red-pantile roofs, not found in other regions. It is believed that the red tiles were first imported on board ships trading with the Netherlands.

Slate, transported from the west coast of Scotland or Wales, was the other main roofing material. Prior to the introduction of these materials, many roofs were thatched; this is now almost unknown in East Lothian, with one exception, Bolton Muir, a large Arts and Crafts house built in 1930, which lays claim to the largest thatched roof in Scotland. This oddity stands a short distance to the west of Gifford, on the road to East Saltoun, from where it can be seen at a distance. It is a private residence.

Many villages, such as Athelstaneford and Tyninghame, consist of little more than rows of single-storey cottages, grouped together. One notable exception is Gifford, where the original buildings were constructed to a height of two storeys. Outside the main towns, three-storey houses were almost unknown prior to the twentieth century. While medieval houses in towns like Dunbar and Haddington are long gone, their legacy is retained in the layout of present structures. The frontages of individual properties in the high streets are the same width as they were eight hundred years ago.

The centre of Haddington in some ways resembles Edinburgh Old Town, having tall structures fronting the main street, with narrow closes running underneath. In the late-nineteenth century, *The Ordnance Gazetteer of Scotland* described Haddington thus:

Old houses, Church Street, Haddington town centre.

> Though still a comparatively small place and though for a long period of a some-what mean appearance, is now one of the neatest and cleanest towns of Scotland, with spacious and straight main thoroughfares, containing an abundant array of shops and with good, sometimes even handsome, edifices among which a few curious ancient houses still remain.

The 'ancient houses' include Haddington house, in Sidegate Street, built in the seventeenth century. It is instantly recognisable with its balus-traded stair and canopied doorway and is the oldest house in the town. Kinloch house is another good example of early domestic architecture, standing next to the junction of Market Street and Hardgate. It dates from the eighteenth century and has a Dutch gable facing onto the street. There are several buildings in East Lothian that have been influenced by Dutch architecture, including Gifford parish church.

At first sight, Prestonpans appears to be composed entirely of modern houses, but, at its heart, it has several interesting examples of vernacular architecture. Hamilton house dates from 1626 and is a two-storey house built on an L-plan; it is now owned by the National Trust for Scotland and has been converted into flats. Standing on the opposite side of the street is its contemporary, Northfield house, an impressive, whitewashed mansion house with corner turrets and high chimneys overlooking Preston Road. It is currently a private residence.

Charming cottages of the early-nineteenth century, Inveresk.

199

Strung out on either side of Inveresk main street are numerous impressive mansion houses, most of which were built in the eighteenth century. In contrast, there are rows of whitewashed cottages at the eastern end of this suburb (*photo on page 199*). A short distance to the north is High Street, Musselburgh, which contains a number of eighteenth-century buildings. There is also 'the French Ambassador's house', dating from the seventeenth century.

High Street, Dunbar owes its appearance to buildings of the Georgian period. At its north end is Lauderdale house, built in 1734 for Captain James Fall MP, and extended in the latter part of that century; it is on a scale that would put many country houses to shame. Many large villas were built at Gullane and North Berwick in the early-twentieth century, when golf and seaside holidays became popular. Some of these introduced a distinctive English element to East Lothian architecture. For example, Gullane has villas with mock-Tudor timbering while North Berwick has a number of houses in the English-cottage style.

Golf again provided the incentive to construct luxury villas in the late-twentieth century at Archerfield, near Dirleton. In contrast, former mining villages such as Macmerry and Wallyford contain large numbers of semi-detached, two-storey houses built by the council in the mid-twentieth century. They are built to a similar design and are a feature of many former industrial towns across Scotland.

TRANSPORT

27. ROADS AND TRACKS

A rural road on Doon hill stretches into the distance.

The traditional view of prehistoric people is that they did not move far from their local area, but recent discoveries prove that some travelled great distances. For instance, a stone axe discovered at Tranent is thought to have originated at Langdale Pikes in Cumbria, where such items were made in substantial numbers. It is probable that there was an ancient track between the Forth and Tweed river basins via the Whiteadder water valley in the Lammermuir hills; it may have been favoured by early travellers, as the coastal plain to the south of Dunbar is dissected by a number of deep gorges around Dunglass.

In the seventh century, St Aidan of Iona was invited by King Oswald of Northumbria to establish a monastery in his kingdom. Monks and pilgrims travelling to this new religious centre at Lindisfarne probably landed at Aberlady, before heading south across the Lammermuir hills via Yester and the Whiteadder water valley. A more recent track crossing this upland area is the 'Herring Road'; a favourite route of modern walkers, it runs from Dunbar in a south-westerly direction towards the Borders. Its name relates to its use: from at least the mid-seventeenth century, salted herring was transported along it from the coast and, as a result, V-shaped gouges worn by laden pack horses can be seen in some places on this track.

Little is known about medieval roads, when pilgrims covered great distances on foot. Each year, thousands landed at North Berwick and made their way along the tracks of East Lothian to the holy well at Whitekirk, on the pilgrim route from St Andrews to Santiago de Compostela in northern Spain. In the mid-twelfth century, Malcolm IV granted Keith church and the lands surrounding it (now located in Humbie parish) to the monks of Kelso. The deeds mention a road that ran between here and Haddington. Another charter, dating from 1230, refers to a road called 'Ricardisrode' in the Lammermuir hills, the route of which follows the boundary of Whittingehame parish for some distance. The monks of Newbattle abbey worked coal from an early date and it was taken to Prestonpans along a route known as Salters Road for export. The road today follows a similar route.

By the eighteenth century, Highland cattle was an important meat source for lowland towns, with herds walked to market along 'drove roads'. Many of the drovers made for Gifford, before heading south across the uplands. One route went to Longformacus and another directly south in the direction of Lauder, via Lammer Law. Bleau's map, compiled at the beginning of the seventeenth century, shows only one road in East Lothian, starting at Musselburgh and heading east to Preston. It then turns inland, before passing close to Haddington and terminating at Dunbar.

The Union of Crowns in 1603 was a catalyst for the improvement of the road network, particularly between England and Scotland. Until then, there had been little incentive to improve communication between the two countries as the main traffic had been invading armies. In 1603, James VI and his retinue of five hundred nobles snaked their way south through East Lothian towards London, where he was to be crowned ruler of the two countries. Three hundred years earlier, Edward I took a similar route south after subjugating the Scots in the Wars of Independence. After leaving Edinburgh, the road to England went through Musselburgh then on to Preston, Seton, Cantyhall, Seton Hill, Cottyburn, Pencraig and East Linton, crossing into Berwickshire at Dunglass. Rather surprisingly it did not go through Haddington but skirted it to the north, going across the Garleton hills.

Close to Barnes castle the sunken tracks formed by the repeated pressure of cartwheels and horses' hooves are still visible. Fourteen years after his coronation, James VI/I made a return trip to Edinburgh. In 1610, he had instructed his Privy Council to improve the roads in Scotland, which were in a far worse condition than in England. Justices of the Peace, including those of Haddingtonshire, were made responsible for maintaining and repairing the highways. The work was to be undertaken by voluntary labourers, who were to devote four days a year to this task. This, unsurprisingly, proved ineffective.

When James made his way north from Berwick-upon-Tweed in 1617, many landowners hastily made repairs to the road on which he would be travelling. That at Preston was described to be in such poor condition that it would become impassable the moment it rained. Another monarch, Charles I, made his way along the Great North Road in 1633. The constables of East Lothian were instructed to supply the King's master of carriage with no fewer than 146 horses. The destination was Holyrood palace, where Charles was to be crowned king of Scotland.

By 1700, the few existing East Lothian roads were in a dire state. In 1669 a further act had been passed requiring inhabitants of a parish to undertake repairs on their local roads for six days a year. This piece of legislation – like the first – was often ignored. Around the same time, landowners were given the power to enclose their fields with hedges and fences; no longer would tracks and paths take the most direct routes between two points. Instead they had to conform to the layout of the fields, skirting around their edges and taking corners at right angles, in time creating the present road pattern. Despite the lack of good roads, James Lauder (the Sheriff Clerk) and two associates were given permission in 1678 to run a stagecoach from Haddington–Edinburgh. It was to operate twice a week, all-year round, and was to be the sole coach service on this route.

Travellers not only had to contend with muddy surfaces and huge potholes, but also bandits and thieves. 'Crockers Hedges', planted in the second half of the eighteenth century by the owner of nearby Beanston farm, was a notorious spot on the old Great North Road from Haddington–East Linton. Robbers, known as 'whilliwhaes', concealed themselves in the hedges and relieved unsuspecting travellers of their possessions.

In the seventeenth century, a postal service was established in Scotland, although deliveries were at first limited to the road from Edinburgh–Berwick-upon-Tweed, as part of the line of communications with London. In 1690, Andrew Cockburn, referred to as a 'postboy' despite being 44 years old, was travelling on the road between Cockburnspath, Berwickshire and Haddington. When approaching Hedderwick Muir he was waylaid by two masked, and armed, men on horseback; they threatened to kill him unless he handed over his post bags and black box. The highwaymen then tied Cockburn up and rode off in the direction of Garleton house, near Haddington.

The stolen items contained government communications, along with private correspondence. This was a serious crime, motivated by politics. Suspicion immediately fell on James Seton, youngest son of Viscount Kingston, and John Seton, brother of Sir George Seton of Garleton. (Incidentally, at this time the Seton family owned extensive tracts of land across East Lothian linked by the Great North Road.) It was not long before the two suspects were detained. They were sent off to Bailie Lauder's house at Haddington and confined to a room.

Being a Sunday, Lauder left for church with the town officers, who had been guarding the prisoners. The Setons took the opportunity to escape and got clean away. Unfortunately for Bailie Lauder and the town officers, the Privy Council ordered them to be arrested and detained in Edinburgh tolbooth. A few days later the magistrate was found guilty of connivance and declared unsuitable for any public employment. John Seton was soon after seized by Captain James Denholm on board a merchant ship bound for Holland and imprisoned in Edinburgh castle. He underwent trial in July 1691 and was surprisingly acquitted. Two months later, Parliament declared that robbing the post was such a serious crime it would in future be punishable by death.

The introduction of turnpike roads, charging tolls, was the first step towards the creation of a modern road network. Legislation was passed in 1750 to transform part of the Great Post Road into a toll road. This stretch of highway became the first toll road in Scotland, but progress was frustratingly slow. The Whittingehame farmers originally had to take their produce to Haddington market on pack horses, but, when the roads were improved in the second half of the eighteenth century, they could use carts, which could carry a far greater load.

The situation in the parish of Tranent still left a lot to be desired. In the late-eighteenth century, many of its roads were in a poor state and some – because of their intense use by carts hauling coal – almost impassable. One of the schoolmaster's additional duties at this time was to collect toll money from the Great Post Road, which ran through the locus. Many travellers resented having to pay for public highways, with evasion common. To discourage this, walls and fences were often erected along the sides of the turnpike roads to stop people taking detours across fields.

Some toll keepers were overzealous. In 1760, an attempt was made to demand payment from a troop of cavalry travelling along the road at Ravenshaugh; for this, the toll-keeper received a severe beating, as did some women standing close by. One of the most extreme measures taken to avoid the payment of tolls was the construction of a stone-lined tunnel over 130 feet in length on the south-west corner of Prestongrange estate. It still exists today under a fenced-off section of the old course of the B1361 road. It may have been constructed by Sir William Grant so he could transport coal from his colliery to Morrison's Haven, without having to negotiate the turnpike road.

By the mid-nineteenth century, stagecoaches linked the major centres of population in East Lothian with Edinburgh. There was a daily coach from North Berwick, the journey taking three hours. It passed through Aberlady, where a contemporary account stated the roads were all in good condition with smooth surfaces, in contrast to their poor state forty years previously.

By 1859, East Lothian had a total of 141 miles of turnpike roads with thirty-six tolls in place. There were a further 295 miles of statute labour roads (public roads maintained by unpaid work required by law). With the building of the railways, turnpike roads lost their importance and the payment of tolls disappeared.

It was not until the early-twentieth century that road surfaces were radically improved; tarmac was laid and they took on their current appearance. The Great Post Road (also known as the Great North Road) became the A1 in the 1920s when the newly formed Ministry of Transport began allotting numbers to roads. East Lothian had the distinction of having the first stretch of dual carriageway in Scotland,

A reminder of the early days of motoring, these quaint 'finger' signposts are found on many of East Lothian's rural roads.

albeit a very short one from Seton–Cantyhall on the edge of Longniddry. It was built in 1935 when the old A1 was realigned on the north side of the railway immediately west of Longniddry and is still in use today.

Many of today's roads follow the network laid out in the eighteenth and nineteenth centuries. Others, such as those that traverse the Lammermuir hills, may emulate the routes trodden by prehistoric people. To this day, walking is important in East Lothian, albeit for recreational purposes and many new paths and tracks have been created in the last few decades solely for this purpose. The most notable is the John Muir Way along the East Lothian coastline, which is 134 miles long, running from Dunbar in the east across Scotland's heartland and terminating on the west coast at Helensburgh.

A number of preserved cars and commercial vehicles are on view at Myerton motor museum, established in 1966. It is situated in the country-side off a minor road, a short distance to the south east of Aberlady.

28. RAILWAYS AND TRAMWAYS

Railways

Many travellers' first impressions of Scotland come from the carriage of an express train as it makes its way across the border through Berwickshire and East Lothian. The vital Edinburgh–London route has traversed East Lothian since the 1840s, and is the only main line in the county.

After the Jacobite rising of 1715, the landowners that supported the rebellion had their estates confiscated. The coalmines of Tranent came into the ownership of the York Buildings Company of London and it was this English company that constructed what was probably Scotland's first railway. A wagonway with wooden rails, 2.5 miles long, was laid to the harbour at Cockenzie on the Firth of Forth. It required the construction of a large embankment along part of the route and is still visible today. Nothing more than gravity was needed to propel the wagonloads of coal; horses, however, pulled the empty containers back up the slope to the mines. There is, however, a claim that this wagonway existed as far back as the late-sixteenth century and was the idea of the 8th Lord Seton and not the York Building Company. By a strange twist of fate, the wagonway became involved in the second Jacobite rising in 1745 when government troops placed cannon on the track to confront Bonnie Prince Charlie's army at Prestonpans. This must have been the first time that a railway was involved in a conflict.

After nearly a hundred years in operation, the wagonway was extensively rebuilt using iron rails with a gauge of 3 feet 3 inches replacing the wooden ones. It could now be used by wagons loaded with coal weighing two tons each. On the return journey horses would pull five wagons back up to Tranent making three round trips a day. Even when steam locomotives were introduced and the Edinburgh–Berwick line was opened, the wagonway still continued to operate in a truncated form. Wagons now delivered coal to the sidings at Meadowmill. The wagonway was also now extended a short distance south at Tranent to Windygoul, where there were further railway sidings. It ceased operation around 1880. It is possible to trace the route of almost the entire route of the wagonway, as most of it has been converted into a footpath. There is access to it from the Edinburgh road, a short distance west of Tranent town centre. It is then possible to walk to Cockenzie on it.

In 1825, engineer Robert Stevenson drew up a plan to connect Edinburgh with Dunbar and Paddington station in London using steam locomotives. His scheme came to nothing as did an initial proposal in 1842 by John Learmonth, chairman of the Edinburgh and Glasgow railway, to build a line to Dunbar. Two years later he put forward a scheme to extend the line to Berwick-upon-Tweed, and successfully raised the finance. Royal assent was given, construction being a straightforward matter in East Lothian as the route crossed the northern plain with therefore relatively few engineering works required. In 1850, trains were running from Edinburgh to Newcastle and beyond with the opening of the Border Bridge across the river Tweed during that year.

By the late-nineteenth century, most of the main settlements in East Lothian had their own stations. The densest part of the rail network was in the west of the county, where there were numerous short lines serving the coal mines, particularly around Tranent. In the 1920s and 1930s, the railway monopoly was challenged by the improvements to rural roads and the introduction of buses. As a consequence, in 1932, the Aberlady–Gullane branch line was among the first in Scotland to lose its passenger service. It had not opened until 1898, long after the railway to North Berwick, which was carrying traffic by 1850.

Initially, traffic on the Drem–North Berwick line did not reach expectations and in 1856 steam locomotives were replaced by a horse-drawn service known as a 'Dandy Car', in an effort to save money. It only lasted six months before proper trains were back on the route. So many visitors were arriving from Edinburgh in the latter part of the nineteenth century that North Berwick council asked the railway company to restrict the number of tickets sold. There was a petition in 1915, advocating that the branch line from Gullane should be extended to North Berwick, but nothing came of it. During the Second World War, when George VI visited Edinburgh, the royal train halted at Aberlady station and the monarch retired to it at night. The Gullane branch line remained open for freight until 1964; in its last years it was often used to carry locally grown sugar beet.

A steam excursion train heads south on the main Edinburgh–London line at Ballencrieff.

In the early years of the Second World War, an armoured train was based at Longniddry. With invasion appearing imminent, locomotives pulling wagons armed with weapons were given the task of patrolling sections of the railway network. Armoured Train-K was responsible for covering south-east Scotland, including the lines in East Lothian. It was powered by a single locomotive and armed with two 6-pounder guns, six Bren machine guns, two Vickers machine guns, four Thompson submachineguns and manned by troops armed with rifles. In 1942, Scottish command decided to transfer the armoured trains to the Home Guard, and Train-K was allocated a new depot at Edinburgh. If an emergency arose it would be deployed to Drem.

In 1945 there were almost eighty miles of railway track in East Lothian, but by the end of the century it had shrunk to about half this, essentially comprising the Edinburgh–London main line. By the 1970s, manual signal boxes had been replaced by a signalling centre in Edinburgh. The track was electrified in the 1990s and much of the railway has been reconstructed. Dunbar station, the only stop for long-distance trains in the county, looks much the same as when it was built in 1845. In 2002, old mine workings were discovered close to the Musselburgh–Prestonpans track, which had to be realigned to avoid a potential hazard.

Other stations that are found on the main line include Drem, Longniddry, Prestonpans, Musselburgh and Wallyford, all served by commuter trains. The branch line to North Berwick narrowly escaped the widespread closures of the rail network in the 1960s and is now a well-patronised route. Many people commute to Edinburgh on its electric trains.

The network of lines that served the coalfield in the western part of the county have long since closed. The Macmerry line closed in 1960, although it had lost its passenger services as early as 1926. Considerable quantities of coal were still being transported along the east-coast mainline from other parts of Scotland to Cockenzie power station until it closed in 2013. For many years the waste generated by the citizens of Edinburgh was taken by rail to a landfill site at Oxwellmains cement plant, near Dunbar, but this ended in 2017.

Two former branch lines have been converted into footpaths. The first is the old track bed of the branch from the mainline at Longniddry to the former terminus at Haddington, which closed in 1969. When the Edinburgh–Berwick-upon-Tweed railway was built, Haddington lobbied unsuccessfully for the mainline to pass through the town. The inhabitants were further dismayed as the branch line to their town stopped around half a mile away from its centre. The footpath commences immediately to the east of Longniddry and is four miles long; it forms a wildlife refuge in what is otherwise an intensively farmed area.

The second path is on part of the route once occupied by the Gifford and Garvald light railway. This was one of the most scenic branch lines in southern Scotland, with trains chugging their way through the rural landscape of East Lothian to Gifford at the foot of the Lammermuir hills. Light railways were not subject to the same rigorous standards; regulations had been loosened to encourage the construction of lines in those rural areas bypassed by the main network. Originally, it was intended that the railway from Pencaitland–Gifford would run in a straight line, but, due to a dispute with the Fletchers of Saltoun, it was forced to take a meandering route heading up the valley of the Humbie water, before turning east towards its final destination of Gifford. When plans were drawn up, it had been intended that the line would continue as far as Garvald. At a time when almost all towns and villages had a railway station, *The Haddingtonshire Courier* commented that Garvald, 'is yet as innocent of the railway whistle as the man in the moon is of bagpipes'. It never got its station as at an early stage it was decided to terminate the line at Gifford.

The single-line railway opened in 1901 and carried agricultural products and whisky barrels from Glenkinchie distillery, as well as passengers. The trains often travelled along this line at speeds not much in excess of the walkers who now follow its former route. The train drivers had to open and shut the level-crossing gates themselves.

There were two passenger trains a day from Gifford–Edinburgh. These services were discontinued as early as 1933, due to competition from motor coaches. Gifford continued to be served by freight trains until 1948 when the bridge at Gilchriston over the Birns water was washed away in a flood. There were four bridges on the route between Ormiston and Gifford, including a three-arch bridge and a viaduct over the river Humbie. The line then continued to operate in a truncated form, continuing as far as Humbie station where potatoes, cattle and grain were loaded onto freight trains. Horses were sometimes brought here in the summer by a Glasgow company to give them a rest from work.

At Saltoun station, whisky from Glenkinchie distillery was handled. It was not unknown for the barrels to be smashed while being hauled onto the wagons, sometimes with a helping hand. Not to let their contents go to waste they were collected by the onlookers armed with a variety of containers. For almost its entire existence, steam locomotives were used and there were only a few weeks when diesels were seen on the line. Declining freight traffic led to permanent closure in 1965.

The last rays of the setting sun reflect on a local train from North Berwick–Edinburgh.

There is a car park on the north-east side of Ormiston village, from where it is possible to walk along part of the former railway line as far as Pencaitland and Saltoun. Some of the semaphore signal posts still stand, but in a rather derelict state. There is also a footpath in the opposite direction along the former railway line from Ormiston–Cousland, built in 1867 to carry coal. Later, trains travelling from Gifford–Edinburgh made use of it but it was not part of the light railway that terminated at Ormiston. The sites of the coal mines which it served are marked by stone markers resembling gravestones.

There are no preserved railway lines in East Lothian, except for a short length of track at Prestongrange mining museum, where a few railway wagons are on display. At East Links family park near Dunbar there is a modern, narrow-gauge railway about a thousand yards in length. It gives visitors rides around the attractions, which include a pirate ship, fortress and farm animals.

Tramways

In 1871, Edinburgh began operating a network of horse-drawn trams, later converted to a cable-drawn system. Musselburgh opened an electric tramway system in 1904, which was extended from the town's eastern edge at Levenhall to Port Seton in 1909. Trams from Edinburgh served Musselburgh until 1954 when the network closed completely. The Levenhall–Port Seton line had ceased operating as far back as 1928.

A small section of the tramway, around two hundred feet in length, has been preserved at Morrison's Haven, on the south side of the main road and immediately to the east of Prestongrange industrial museum. It was part of a passing loop as most of the tramway to Port Seton was a single line due to the narrowness of the streets.

29. BRIDGES

East Lothian's geographical features are rather tame and do not require large-scale engineering works to pacify them. Nevertheless, there are several old and interesting bridges.

The old, sixteenth-century bridge over the Esk in the centre of Musselburgh. It replaced a medieval structure.

The old stone footbridge across the Esk, in the centre of Musselburgh, is sometimes known as the 'Roman bridge', as the Roman fort at Inveresk once overlooked this site and may have had a crossing here. The bridge is just under 250-feet long and may date from the early-sixteenth century, replacing an earlier medieval structure. This crossing point played an important part in Scottish history as it was on the main Berwick–London route. The Scottish army crossed over the Esk here in 1296 on their way to Dunbar. Eighteen years later, the English army retreating after Bannockburn would have passed this way. Stuart kings and Mary, Queen of Scots would have been familiar with the bridge as they made their way to Seton palace. During the battle of Pinkie in 1547, several Scottish soldiers were killed by shot fired from English ships lying off the mouth of the Esk. Nearly two hundred years later, the Jacobite army made its way to Prestonpans by this crossing. The bridge marked the west port, or gate, to the town of Musselburgh. The structure was on occasions repaired by forced labour. Today the Old Bridge, as it is now known, is for pedestrians only.

The Old Bridge has been supplanted a few hundred yards to the north by the New Bridge, designed in 1806 by the famous East Lothian-born engineer, John Rennie. It was opened in 1808 and there is a plaque on the north parapet commemorating him. Built of freestone, the bridge has five low arches. Unlike many earlier structures, which had a hump in the middle, the New Bridge at Musselburgh was noted for its low, almost flat, profile. Early users commented that they did not realise they had just crossed a bridge, thinking they were still on the highway!

Since then, several other bridges have been constructed across the Esk at Musselburgh. The second main road bridge carries the A6095 along the banks of the Esk and into Musselburgh on the route of the now-closed railway branch line. The old railway bridge has been replaced by a more modern structure for vehicles at the same crossing point. A short distance upstream is an elegant iron footbridge, constructed in 1923 for workers at nearby Esk Mills. Downstream to the east of New Bridge is another footbridge, known as Store Bridge because it stood close to the Co-operative buildings in High Street. It also stands close to an old fording place across the Esk; in the nineteenth century, there was a timber bridge here that was replaced by an iron example in 1897 and then by the current concrete structure. The final two bridges are the Old Jubilee and the Electric bridges, downstream of those mentioned above and close to the mouth of the Esk. The former was originally built in 1897 for Queen Victoria's diamond jubilee; it was swept away in a flood in 1948 but replaced by a new iron footbridge.

The unusually named Electric Bridge was built by the electricity board in the mid-1960s to transport large turbines to the now-demolished Cockenzie power station. Once the power station was built, the bridge was offered to Musselburgh town council as an additional crossing over the Esk but the proposition was declined due to the cost of maintenance. Since then, its gates at either end have remained locked, except when there is racing at Musselburgh when it is made available to relieve traffic.

Haddington boasts several handsome bridges. The earliest is Nungate Bridge, spanning the Tyne at the eastern edge of the town (*see plate section*). Built of red sandstone, this three-arched structure dates from the sixteenth century, possibly around 1530. It is over two hundred feet long and its masonry details are similar to the Old Bridge at Musselburgh. There had been a crossing here since the thirteenth century (if not before) by an earlier bridge, which was probably made of wood.

Condemned criminals were once hung from a hook inserted above the arch of the bridge closest to the west bank. At the funeral of the duke of Lauderdale in 1683, according to tradition, money was distributed among the beggars. While this was taking place, a man named Bell stabbed another person to death. He was soon apprehended and several stolen items were found upon him. To ascertain if he had committed the crime, he was made to touch the corpse of his victim; the wound was said to have bled again, a sure sign of guilt. The following day, he was hung from Nungate Bridge. The hook – last used in 1745 when a supporter of the Jacobite cause had his arm chopped off and displayed on it – is still there. Fighting took place around the bridge during the siege of Haddington in 1548, when it sustained extensive damage. During the eighteenth century, it was extensively repaired and further arches added to its eastern extremity.

Bridges were not the only means of crossing the Tyne at Haddington, as it was still just possible to ford it, although not without danger. One such ford existed just below Nungate Bridge. Around 1797, a four-wheel carriage attempting to negotiate it was carried away by the current, drowning the driver and a Mr Brown from East Linton, along with the horses. Some years later, a post-boy and his two horses were drowned at the same point.

Another well-preserved bridge of similar antiquity to the Nungate can be found about a mile to the east of Haddington, also spanning the Tyne. It is the Abbey Bridge, approximately 130 feet long and 16 feet

Abbey Bridge, near Haddington.

Victoria Bridge, over the Tyne at Haddington.

in breadth, and dates from the early-sixteenth century. Unlike the Nungate, it is still used by motor vehicles. It takes its name from the medieval abbey that stood close by and may have financed its construction. The west side of the bridge has been rebuilt in a different style from the east side.

On the southern edge of Haddington is the single-arched Waterloo Bridge, opened in 1817, and named after the famous battle two years earlier. Built of stone from the nearby Colstoun estate, it carries the road leading south to Gifford. A short distance to the west is Stevenson footbridge at West Haugh, built in 1948 after the previous bridge was destroyed in a flood. Further upstream, a mile south-west of Haddington, is Westfield footbridge, built in 1912 and one of the earliest reinforced-concrete structures in Scotland.

To enhance communications to the east of Haddington the Victoria Bridge was opened in 1900 and named in honour of Queen Victoria, whose diamond jubilee was three years earlier. It is a steel, twin-arch bridge with ornamental façades. A new bridge had been considered here since the mid-nineteenth century; at that time there was a timber bridge to the corn mill a short distance downstream. It was originally erected in 1732 but washed away in a flood in 1775 and was rebuilt. In the 1880s, there was a plan to use the girders salvaged from the first Tay railway bridge, which collapsed during a storm, in the construction of the new bridge here.

Another fine example of an early stone bridge can be found downstream from Haddington over the Tyne at East Linton (*see plate section*). A substantial structure, dating from the sixteenth century, it has a length of 125 feet and consists of two stone arches. For centuries, it was the lowest bridging point of the Tyne before it flowed into the sea. This made it a strategic point during times of conflict, such as the siege of Haddington in 1548 when it was partially destroyed to slow down the English army. By 1560, the damage to the bridge appears to have been repaired, as Lord Grey's English force was able to cross. In 1619, it was in a very poor state of repair and there was concern it could fall down. Towards the end of the seventeenth century, tolls were charged: prices included 2 pence for a single horseman and 4 pence for a flock of sheep. Due to its poor condition, carts were discouraged and instead had to cross the Tyne using a nearby ford.

Major reconstruction work took place on East Linton bridge in 1763, and, until the 1920s, it carried the Great North Road. An elegant, three-span, steel-plate girder bridge was constructed a short distance to the south, which diverted traffic around the southern edge of East Linton. Between the old and new road bridges is the bridge that carries the main Edinburgh–London railway line. The first railway structure was carried away in the great flood of September 1846, its failure attributed to poor workmanship. A certain Robert Ballantyne was standing on the old sixteenth-century bridge watching the event unfold when someone shouted a warning that it could suffer the same fate. He came back with: 'Linton brig fa'doun, ye idiot. Linton brig will stand for evermore.' To this day, it carries vehicles across the Tyne. In contrast to this old stone structure is the bridge that carries the rerouted A1, now a dual carriageway, across the Tyne, half-a-mile west of East Linton. It is a three-span, concrete, box-girder bridge, suspended on splayed leg piers. It was completed in 2004 and is one of the longest bridges in the Lothians.

One further example of a sixteenth-century bridge can be found at the opposite end of East Lothian, at Pencaitland. It is still used by the main road through Pencaitland to cross an embryonic river Tyne. Its three-pointed arches rise only a few feet above ground level and it is not as impressive as the other examples. On it is a carved shield with an

The sixteenth-century Pencaitland Bridge, with its three, pointed arches.

engrailed cross, the coat of arms of the Sinclair family, and the date '1510', which is not very legible.

Just to the east of Aberlady is one of the more unusual bridges in East Lothian. Constructed of timber and carrying only pedestrians, it links the car park next to the main road with Aberlady nature reserve. The experience of walking across the long, narrow structure must be similar to that of crossing a medieval bridge. A bridge, now fallen down, was erected at the end of the nineteenth century to give access to the newly laid-out Luffness golf course on the opposite side of the river Peffer. It lay a short distance upstream of the modern timber structure, which had to be rebuilt after a storm in 1990. The author, Nigel Tranter, who lived close by and often walked across it, referred to it as the 'footbridge to enchantment'.

The first bridge across Humbie water was built in 1645 by local landowner Sir Adam Hepburn. The single, stone-arched bridge still carries the main road over this watercourse. Over the next two centuries, landowners built numerous similar bridges to the same principles, but in time lighter bridges were constructed, with flatter arches, crossing many small rivers and streams. Most of them are still in use today. Samuelston Bridge, south-west of Haddington, dating from c.1793

Samuelston Bridge, an attractive, late-eighteenth-century, arched crossing on the Tyne.

with a span of 55 feet, is a particularly fine example. Further upstream is Saltoun Bridge, another single-arch, stone structure.

Heading downstream towards the mouth of the Tyne is Tyninghame bridge, a short distance to the south of the village of the same name. It dates from 1778. Andrew Meikle, the millwright and inventor, was recorded as 'giving advice and attendance during its construction'. Initially it was called the 'Boat House Brig', because the boatman lived here and operated the ferry across the Tyne before the bridge was built. Another example of a single-stone-arch bridge can be found just below Oldhamstocks village; it probably dates from the eighteenth century, but may predate this. Unlike many other similar structures, it stands in open fields spanning the Dunglass burn and is not concealed by woodland.

At Dunglass, nature has created a formidable barrier, which has led to no fewer than five bridges being built in very close proximity; in fact, four are so close together that they are visible from each other. The bridges are located where the eastern edge of the Lammermuir hills roll down to the coast. The main road and rail links from Edinburgh to England converge here, into a narrow strip of low-lying ground between the uplands and the sea. Communications are further hindered by the Dunglass burn, which has carved out a narrow but very deep gorge, which, in bygone centuries was a major obstacle to invading armies. This unusual land formation poses a major challenge to civil engineers yet over the centuries a series of bridges have been constructed.

The most impressive crossing at Dunglass is the viaduct that carries the main railway line to London. It was constructed as far back as 1846 and consists of five spans of 30 feet and a large main span of 135 feet, which is just over 100 feet above Dunglass burn. It is one of the largest stone arches in Scotland. Good views of the railway viaduct can be had from the New Bridge, immediately to its west. Despite its name, New Bridge was built in 1797, but collapsed a short time afterwards. It was reconstructed the following year and sits some 77 feet above Dunglass burn. Like most bridges of its time it consists of a single stone span and is crowned with crenellated parapets. (Interestingly, around half a mile to the north-west on the same road – Old Post Road – there is another bridge of similar style to the New Bridge, this one over a different water course, Bilsdean burn. That makes it six bridges in this small area!)

The eighteenth-century New Bridge was superseded by an out-standing example of an early reinforced-concrete bridge: this was built

The deep ravine formed by Dunglass burn is spanned by no fewer than four bridges, the oldest dating from the late-eighteenth century (there is a fifth bridge, of the seventeenth century, a short distance to the north-east). In the foreground is the railway viaduct, which carries the Edinburgh–London main line. Behind it is the 1932 road bridge for the A1.

in 1932 to carry the A1, its arch reaching 160 feet in length. Fifty years later, serious structural problems were discovered and it was thought that it would have be demolished. It is extant today, though no longer in use, having been replaced by a modern bridge that was completed at the end of the twentieth century, and which stands just a few feet away. This modern crossing, the fourth of our bridges here, was built to carry the A1; it has two asymmetric spans consisting of twin, steel-plate girders with a single, central, steel universal beam supporting a reinforced-concrete deck.

The oldest of the five bridges spanning Dunglass burn is found a short distance to the east of the other four, near the seashore. It is a solid, stone structure with a very small single arch, built sometime before 1617 with pink and yellow rubble. By 1648, it was in danger of falling down and needed extensive repairs. It was damaged by floods in

1794 when parts of the wall fell down and major reconstruction work was carried out. There were at one time two toll houses, which stood at either end. Unlike the other bridges across the Dunglass burn it sits lower down in the valley and at no great height above the water that flows underneath it.

30. LIGHTHOUSES AND SHIPWRECKS

By the sixteenth century there was a primitive form of lighthouse at some harbours in the form of an open brazier, mounted on a long pole. One is known to have existed on the coast at Aberlady, then an important harbour. Some of the rocks close to Dunbar harbour have iron poles embedded, from which lanterns were hung as warnings to sailors.

Despite these measures, many vessels met their end off East Lothian, on the coast between North Berwick and Torness. One of the earliest-known shipwrecks was that of the *Litill Martyne*, wrecked on the shore near Innerwick in 1528, its cargo looted by mounted followers of Douglas, earl of Angus. Whatever was left then fell into the hands of local people. A Flemish merchant later took out a summons for compensation.

Mariners also had to face man-made attempts to shipwreck them, from 'wreckers', who operated on isolated stretches of the East Lothian coast. One particularly ruthless gang – the Pagans of Scoughall – had their base on the coast at Scoughall, near Whitekirk. They lured sailing ships onto the reef known as the Great Car, using misleading lights. Many years later, Robert Louis Stevenson would spend his childhood holidays at Scoughall farm, where he heard gruesome stories on which he would later base his novel, *The Wreckers*.

Royal Navy ships faced the same hazards. On 14 November 1745, the man o' war, *Hope*, foundered off Dunbar. It had set sail around the time of the battle of Prestonpans and was carrying a large number of Jacobite prisoners, all of whom perished with the crew, a total of 140 men. The warship was also carrying valuables belonging to local land-owners, said to have been fleeing the advancing Jacobite army.

The rotting wooden hulk of a fishing boat, Seton sands.

Shipwrecks were a common occurrence throughout the nineteenth century. *Ceres*, a sailing ship of Aberdeen, was totally wrecked with all crew being lost off Dunbar in February 1838. A crew of four perished when the *Ariel*, carrying wheat, was driven ashore at Thorntonloch on 1 April 1853 in a south-easterly gale. Three months later, another schooner, the *Ino*, foundered in a gale at the mouth of the Tyne. In April 1855, the *Early* sunk near Thorntonloch, with the loss of four lives; the drowned sailors were buried in Innerwick churchyard. A further fatal wreck occurred on 4 January 1857, when the *Maria Annette* struck Scoughall rocks in a south-easterly force-11 gale. The crew of four perished.

By the second half of the nineteenth century, steamships were becoming increasingly common. One of the first to be wrecked on the coast of East Lothian was the *Aberavon* in February 1878. It got lost in fog and was stranded at Thorntonloch; the vessel was carrying a cargo of cast iron and was only a year old. On 6 December 1893, while steaming between Grangemouth and Middlesbrough, the cargo ship, *Bull*, carrying four passengers, collided with steam trawler *Rossyln* between Craigleith and Lamb island and sank, the only casualty a *Rosslyn* crewman. In October 1899, the Danish iron barque, *Eliza*, was driven onto rocks on the same stretch of coast during a fierce gale. The ten crewmen all drowned.

It was not until the 1880s that the first lighthouse was constructed on the East Lothian coast. The Scottish Shipmasters Association had presented a petition, signed by a large number of shipmasters sailing to Forth ports, calling for a lighthouse and recommended that the best location was Fidra island. Thus, in 1885, a lighthouse was built there. Like many of Scotland's lighthouses, it was designed by David Stevenson, a cousin of Robert Louis Stevenson. Situated on top of the rocky island, the tower is of no great height, having the natural advantage of a commanding position over the surrounding waters. In May 1909, a smack set sail from Granton for Fidra island lighthouse with supplies. As it left the landing jetty, after unloading, it encountered a heavy swell, which smashed the craft onto the rocks. The crew of six were hauled to safety by the lighthouse keepers and taken to North Berwick in a fishing boat.

In the early-twentieth century two more lighthouses were built. Unlike the light on Fidra, the lighthouse on Bass Rock is situated halfway up the rocky, south-facing slope. It was decided that the best situation for the new building was the gun platform of the long-abandoned fort. When work on the foundations began, part of the fort collapsed so the retaining wall had to be rebuilt. A light was first shown from this location on the evening of 1 November 1902. Its white tower, some 66-feet tall, can be seen from the nearby shore. The last lighthouse keepers left when it was automated in 1988, ending human occupation

Fidra.

Bass Rock.

With shipwrecks common on the East Lothian coast throughout the nineteenth century, the clamour for lighthouse provision grew stronger. The three lighthouses pictured here were built between 1885 and 1902: Fidra, Bass Rock and Barns Ness.

Barns Ness.

of Bass Rock. A ghost of a former lighthouse keeper is said to stalk the tower, checking that its light is functioning.

The third, and most accessible, lighthouse is at Barns Ness on the mainland, three miles south-east of Dunbar. First operational on 1 October 1901, its 121-foot tower is by far the tallest of the three lighthouses in East Lothian. Barns Ness had the distinction of being one of the first places in Britain to be subjected to an enemy machinegun attack (from the air!) in the Second World War. In 2005 it was decided permanently to turn off the light. During daylight hours it still serves as a landmark, its tall, slender, white tower visible for miles, particularly when bathed in sunlight.

Modern technology has drastically reduced the number of shipwrecks in the Firth of Forth. In Victorian times they were a frequent occurrence but by the twentieth century were relatively rare. There were, however, some notable incidents. In October 1908, the *Prosum*, a 200-foot Norwegian steamship going from London to Grangemouth, was driven ashore and broke in two on Bathe Reef, near Torness. One of the largest ships to be wrecked on the coast of East Lothian was the British-owned ship, *Malabar*. It was nearly two thousand gross tons and on its way from Almeria to Leith with a cargo of esparto grass and silver lead ore, when, on 3 April 1920, it ran aground on the Goatness rocks near the Barns Ness lighthouse shortly after ten at night. While its crew of twenty-four were rescued with great difficulty by the Skateraw lifeboat, the ship was badly holed and later broke in two. Much of its cargo of silver lead ore was salvaged.

In June, 1941, the cargo ship, *Royal Fusilier*, was attacked by German aircraft. The crippled vessel was taken in tow but later sank without loss of life not far from the Bass Rock. At the end of the conflict, HMS *Ludlow*, a destroyer of First World War vintage, was beached at Broad Sands near Dirleton. In early July 1945 it was used for target practice by RAF aircraft firing rockets and completely destroyed; the remains lie a few hundred yards off the beach, east of Longskelly point. On days when there are very low tides, its bows and other parts become visible above the waves.

Since 1945, only a handful of ships have been lost in the Forth. One of the largest was Spanish chemical tanker *Metanolt*; its cargo of nitric acid leaked through the storage tanks and onto the inside of the hull. Water leaked in and the vessel sank, close to the coast between the islands of Lamb and Fidra on 5 January 1974. It was raised a few months later and beached.

MISCELLANEOUS

31. MONUMENTS AND MEMORIALS

While most memorials and monuments are found in towns and villages, there are some notable exceptions. The Hopetoun monument, which crowns the highest point of the Garleton hills north of Haddington, can be seen from many miles away (*see plate section*). Resembling a Doric column, it has been described unkindly as 'looking like a large brick chimney'. Squared and coarse igneous whinstone was used in its construction. The foundation stone was laid on 3 May 1824 on the summit of the 560-foot Byres hill. A now-illegible inscription on marble near the base of the 100-foot tower once stated: 'This monument was erected to the memory of the great and good John, Fourth Earl of Hopetoun, by the affectionate and grateful tenantry in East Lothian. MDCCCXXIV [1824].'

There is a viewing platform at the top of the monument reached by a climb of over a hundred steps, contained in a poorly lit circular stairway. There are panoramic views across the northern plain and beyond to the Firth of Forth. While other monuments in Scotland commemorate obscure landowners, little liked by their tenants, Sir John Hope was a distinguished soldier and highly regarded. He was actually born outside of the county – in Hopetoun house, near South Queensferry, in 1765. The Hope family owned land in East Lothian, having not long before purchased the estate of the well-known agrarian innovator, John Cockburn of Ormiston. At the age of eighteen, Sir John was commissioned as a sub-lieutenant in the 10th Light Dragoons. Six years later, he became MP for Linlithgowshire.

When war broke out with France in 1793, John Hope was serving with the army in Devon. Two years later, he was ordered to the French West Indies, which the British were intent on capturing. While on Grenada he became ill and had to return home. The following year, he was back in the Caribbean where he was commended for bravery under fire. At the battle of Alexandria in Egypt in 1801, the French army was defeated but at great personal cost to Sir John, who sustained a serious wound; nonetheless, he was given the task of arranging the surrender of the French. On returning to England he was stationed on the south coast, ready to repel a possible landing by the enemy.

In 1807 Napoleon invaded Spain instead and British troops were sent to engage him. Sir John arrived there the following year, but with the French capture of Madrid, the British were forced to retreat. An army of nearly thirty thousand, led by General John Moore (also a Scot), marched across mountain ranges in the depths of winter, heading towards Corunna where they were to be evacuated. With the French in hot pursuit, a rearguard action was fought, and, although the enemy was defeated, Moore was killed. Sir David Baird, of Newbyth, East Lothian assumed command, but soon after was badly wounded. It then fell on John Hope to evacuate the last troops on the mainland. To ensure that none of his soldiers were left behind, he rode through the streets of Corunna before sailing for Britain.

The Duke of Wellington praised Sir John and he was thanked by Parliament. In 1813, he returned to fight in the Peninsula War but was wounded at the battle of Nivelle. The following year, he suffered a further misfortune, being captured at the battle of Bayonne, but was released not long after. Although the Napoleonic Wars came to an end in 1815, Hope stayed in the military, becoming a general. He was also appointed Lord Lieutenant of Linlithgowshire, the location of his home, Hopetoun house. While visiting Paris in 1824, he died suddenly, at the age of fifty-eight. Most unusually, there is a second monument to Sir John, almost identical to that in East Lothian. It is found on the opposite side of the Firth of Forth and was built two years later, in 1826. Located a short distance north-west of Cupar, it too stands on top of a wooded hill. If this is not enough to preserve his memory there is also a statue of him dressed in Roman costume leaning on a pawing charger. It stands in front of the Royal Bank of Scotland in St Andrew Square, Edinburgh. At one time Sir John Hope was vice-governor of this financial institution.

Another wholly different monument stands on top of North Berwick Law. It is a whalebone arch, which a couple of centuries ago was a popular form of ornament. There were once several hundred such examples across Scotland, but today only around twenty-five are extant. The North Berwick Law arch is the most dramatically situated of them all. The original arch was erected c.1789. Although some sources mention North Berwick's involvement in the whaling industry, there is little evidence to back this up. The original bones came from vessels operating out of Dunbar harbour. The first arch was replaced around 1860.

The second arch was replaced in 1933 when the bones, in an advanced state of decay, fell down during a gale. The two, 23-feet-long replacements were hauled up the Law by horses. Due to names being carved on the new arch, an iron railing was placed around it for

Whalebone arch memorial, North Berwick Law, made of fibreglass.

protection. At the turn of the century, the whalebones were again weathering away, and by 2006, the arch was dismantled. With whaling now banned by most countries, it was impossible to obtain new bones. For a while it looked as if this landmark would be no more, but an anonymous donation funded the construction of fibre-glass replicas, which were placed in position in 2008, a helicopter lifting them to the summit. It was the first time in Britain that a whale arch had been renewed with artificial materials.

Obelisks were first created by the ancient Egyptians but their monuments were copied and obelisks began to appear in Britain, often as memorials to the deceased. James Maitland Balfour is commemorated by one; it stands next to the Haddington–Whittingehame road, on top of a rocky hillside overlooking Traprain Law (*see plate section*). His father was responsible for constructing Whittingehame house, two miles to the east, with the fortune he made in India. It was considered one of the finest neo-classical houses of its time. Like his father, James had considerable business acumen and accumulated a fortune of his own; he was a director of the North British Railway when railway mania was at its height. From 1841–7 he was also Conservative MP for Haddington and commandant of the East Lothian yeomanry cavalry.

233

While overseas, he caught tuberculosis and died at Funchal, Madeira at the age of thirty-six. His son, Arthur James Balfour, eclipsed his achievements, becoming prime minister in 1902. Two years after James Maitland Balfour's death in 1858, the red-sandstone obelisk, with heartfelt inscription, was erected in his memory.

East Lothian has a number of other commemorative obelisks. In the grounds of Newhailes house, near Musselburgh, there is a tall, slender example erected in 1746 in memory of Sir John Dalrymple, second earl Stair. Another stone obelisk, not readily accessible, can be glimpsed from a distance in the grounds of Tyninghame house. Appropriately, it commemorates Thomas Hamilton, 6th earl Haddington (1680–1735), best known for the planting of large numbers of trees on his estate. This obelisk was erected in 1856, well over a century after his death.

At the east end of Ormiston there is a 21-foot obelisk chiselled out of Aberdeen granite and mounted on a base of Peterhead granite. It commemorates the life of Dr Robert Moffat, a distinguished African missionary, born here in 1795.

In contrast to the above monuments, which catch the eye from a distance, that for John Rennie the elder (1761–1821), one of Scotland's

This slender obelisk in the grounds of Newhailes house commemorates Sir John Dalrymple, second earl Stair.

Monument to the distinguished engineer, John Rennie, near East Linton.

most distinguished Victorian engineers, can be easily missed. It stands on the eastern extremity of East Linton, close to the road junction with the bypass. Set back from the road is a bronze memorial portrait of Rennie, mounted on the back wall of a small, curved, ornamental masonry pedestrian area. In front of it stands a single baluster recovered from the demolition of the original Waterloo Bridge, which once spanned the Thames. Rennie was born at Phantassie farm, located just behind his memorial. This quaint name is sometimes said to be French, or even Greek, in origin; more likely, it is derived from the Gaelic, *Fan t Easan*, which loosely translated means 'gentle slope at a small stream'. James, John Rennie's father, employed the innovative mechanical engineer, Andrew Meikle, on his farm and it was at Houston mill, close to Phantassie farm, that he perfected a threshing machine able to separate corn from straw. On his way to school, young John would often stop at his workshop and watch him work.

At the age of twelve, Rennie began working in the workshop as an apprentice, but later returned to school and attended Edinburgh University. On completing his education, he headed south and was first employed by James Watt, famous for inventing the steam engine. John Rennie did not stay with Watt for long; he travelled to London to assist with the installation of a steam engine for the Albion flour mills at Blackfriars. The machinery he designed used iron instead of wood for many of the parts. Soon after, in 1791, he set up a mechanical-engineering business of his own and over the next thirty years was involved in many prestigious construction projects. Almost all were connected to water, perhaps because he grew up close to the river Tyne.

Initially, Rennie worked on expanding Britain's canal network; he helped develop the Lancaster canal, Rochdale canal, and, in Scotland, the Crinan canal. In the early-nineteenth century, he devoted several years to draining operations in the Lincolnshire and Norfolk fens. He was also noted for his stone bridges with their wide, low arches. In Scotland, his fine bridges can be seen spanning the Tweed at Kelso and the Esk at Musselburgh.

Rennie's best-known creation was Waterloo Bridge in London. At the time it was described as 'perhaps the finest large masonry bridge ever built in this or any other country'. His last project was London Bridge, but he did not live to see it completed. Docks at Hull, Liverpool, London, Greenock and Leith were also designed by him and he improved numerous other harbours including Chatham, Portsmouth,

Holyhead and Ramsgate, as well as constructing a mile-long breakwater at Plymouth. To increase the depth of the harbours, he used a steam dredger with a chain of buckets. Some sources credit him with this invention and he was certainly the first person regularly to use it. Such was John Rennie's reputation, that, after his death in 1821, he was buried in St Paul's cathedral. Two of his sons went on to become famous engineers.

At Skateraw, next to the seashore at Chapel point, is a modest memorial consisting of a wooden cross mounted on a stone cairn. It commemorates six members of the St Giles (Canongate) boy's club, who used to camp here, but were killed during the Second World War.

32. MARKET CROSSES

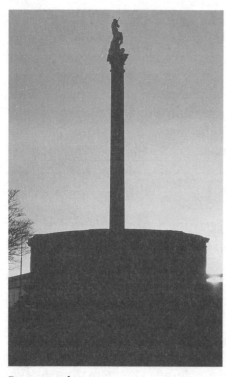

Preston market cross.

East Lothian has one of Scotland's best-preserved market crosses, at Prestonpans. The Preston market cross (now part of Prestonpans) was probably built in 1617 when the village was granted the privilege of holding a weekly market and an annual fair. The stone column, crowned by a unicorn, is mounted on a substantial stone base; it is known as a cross house and was sometimes used to hold prisoners. An internal staircase ascends to the platform from where announcements were made. In July each year from 1636, the powerful Guild of Pack Men, peddlers, the travelling sales people of their day, converged on the market cross at

Preston for their annual meeting. They sorted out their affairs here and elected their 'king' for the forthcoming year. In the eighteenth century, all members were sworn not to take less than four pence in the shilling profit on the sale of their goods and, if possible, much more! In 1851 they were still meeting at 'our ancient cross of Salt Preston where we . . . hold our Court and thereafter proceed to witness the sports and pastimes of the villagers.'

By Victorian times, the market cross had lost much of its significance. Boys would climb up its shaft with handfuls of stones and try to knock the horn off the stone unicorn; on at least one occasion, the attempt met with success. Despite the attention of vandals, the Preston market cross is one of the best-preserved examples in Scotland and unlike many other surviving examples it still stands at its original location. Unfortunately, most of the contemporary buildings around the cross have disappeared and it now stands somewhat isolated next to a local road.

A good example of an even-earlier market cross can be found in the centre of tree-lined Main Street, Ormiston. Dating from the mid-fifteenth

Ormiston market cross.

century, and one of the oldest in Scotland, it is unusually cruciform in shape. There is evidence that there was once an iron collar at head height, used to chain offenders, and a gossip's bridle. The latter resembled an iron muzzle with often a spiked plate inserted into the mouth to stop the victim speaking. A fair was held at Ormiston on the first Tuesday of July, but by 1805 it was of little importance. Paradoxically, the present village of Ormiston was created three centuries after the cross was erected. It originally stood in close proximity to a chapel and possibly owed its location to being at a meeting place of tracks.

Pencaitland market cross.

A few miles away is Pencaitland cross, situated at a road junction in the centre of the village. It is composed of a stepped pedestal and an octagonal shaft, crowned by a weathered sundial. Pencaitland was raised to the status of a burgh of barony in 1505 by a charter issued by James IV in favour of Jon Sinclare of Herdmanstoun. As was normally the case, the market dues were paid to the local landowner or ecclesiastical authority. In 1695, an Act of Parliament granted Sir Robert Sinclair of Stevenson a weekly market and two free fairs. One of the last cases of bodysnatching took place in Pencaitland: two body-snatchers were caught in the act; one was tied to the market cross and subjected to the anger of the crowd, which included a number of women.

Further to the east, another impressive market cross can be found in High Street, Haddington. It is relatively recent, dating from only 1881, but stands near the site of an earlier cross first referred to in 1425. In 1693, stones were purchased by the council for building a new cross, its shaft crowned by a unicorn. In 1811, an Englishman attempted to climb it, and, in the process, pulled over the shaft, which broke into pieces. This seems to have been a popular pastime undertaken at many of East Lothian market crosses around that time. A wooden post, some twelve feet high, was erected as its replacement until the current stone example supplanted it. Unlike the earlier cross, it is capped by a goat.

Musselburgh's proposed elevation to a royal burgh in 1632 was successfully challenged by Edinburgh, but it continued as a burgh of barony. Its market cross stands close to the tolbooth and consists of an eighteenth-century Tuscan shaft supporting a small lion with the burgh arms. The earlier cross was removed in 1774 but is likely to have stood close by. High Street at this point is very wide, enabling it to accommodate the markets.

Further along the coast, at Aberlady, is the stump of a market cross at the east end of High Street, recalling its status as a burgh of barony. It consists of a square pyramid of stone steps, surmounted by a stone pillar.

North Berwick was granted the status of a royal burgh in 1373 by Robert II. It now had the right to levy the king's custom duties using a tron (public weighing beam) operated by its overseer, known as a tronar. With the original charter having been destroyed, James VI issued a replacement that confirmed the rights and privileges held by the town since the fourteenth century. They included the right to erect a market cross and to have a market there every Wednesday for the sale of 'leather skins, wool and other merchandise'. The market cross was located in the centre of Quality Street at the junction with High Street but has long since vanished. A war memorial in the form of a market cross was erected in 1921 and stands at the southern end of Quality Street.

The market cross in front of Dunbar's tolbooth is a composite. Its base possibly came from a cross that stood at Dunbar castle but was destroyed when the fortification was demolished in the late-sixteenth century. The medieval heads attached the top of the present shaft were believed to have been found in a garden at the back of High Street in the early-twentieth century. The original market cross stood at the West Port where most of the tolls and taxes were collected. By 1736, it had become redundant. Eight years later, council records relate that the well at Kirkhill was to be lined with stones from the market cross. Markets were held on the first Tuesday after Whitsunday and Martinmas. In 1850, the principal articles sold were peddlers' wares and a few black cattle. A plaque (courtesy of the local Rotary Club) explaining the background to the market cross was placed at the town house in 2018.

Inland at Gifford, a more substantial example can be found standing prominently in front of the former town hall. The market cross here was raised in 1780, although now only the base dates from that time

Gifford market cross.

with the rest of it being reconstructed in 1952. On top of the shaft are the arms of the earls of Tweeddale, which combine the arms of the Hay and Gifford families. In the early-nineteenth century, the largest market fairs in East Lothian were held at Gifford. Cattle and sheep were sold, with many Berwickshire farmers attending.

At Oldhamstocks, another settlement of the edge of the Lammermuir hills, the market cross stands in the centre of the village green. It has been moved from its original position, which was nearer the crossroads at the eastern end of the village. Little, however, survives of the original cross other than the narrow shaft, erected in its current position in the 1950s. The carved stone ball that sits on top was added when it was reconstructed on the village green. In 1672, the Scottish Parliament gave Oldhamstocks the right to hold two fairs annually. Fairs were great social events and would have attracted farmers from miles around. In the early-nineteenth century, it is recorded that the fair attracted two hundred people. By around 1870, the fairs had ceased, overtaken by innovations in farming and improvements in transport.

Although Stenton never had the status of a burgh, it seems to have had a parish market. The circular stone base in the village with the wooden cross mounted on top – which could be mistaken for an old market cross – is actually a reconstructed tron. Very few now survive in Scotland and this is probably the best example. The tron has a close association with markets and market crosses as it was where stallholders weighed their goods.

One further piece of evidence of medieval markets can be found at the Hardgate, Haddington, in the form of the custom stone, originally located in High Street, now lying in a small public garden beside the road. A plaque beside it states: 'This ancient stone was for centuries the

Stenton's reconstructed tron.

seat of the jackman [attendant for a nobleman or landowner] when petty customs were levied in the burgh.'

33. SPORT

Golf

The fertile soil of the coastal plain made East Lothian an area of agricultural excellence, but the land adjoining much of the coast consisted of sand dunes riddled with rabbit warrens. With the rise in golf's popularity, sandy areas could be used productively and not conflict with other land uses. Many of the East Lothian courses were established between 1880 and 1900; they extend along the coast from

Musselburgh to Dunbar and include some of the country's most prestigious venues. There are now over twenty courses in East Lothian, attracting golfers from all over the world.

Golf has been played in some form on the east coast for centuries. James VI played golf on Musselburgh links, where he was informed of complaints by golfers who were not allowed to play on Sundays. He responded by issuing a decree stating that those, 'first done their duties to God' should be allowed to play. It is believed that when James VI became James I of England his courtiers brought the game of golf with them, inspiring the first English course at Blackheath, London. It is also related that Mary, Queen of Scots played golf and mall (an antecedent of croquet) at Seton house, near Musselburgh.

An account book kept by Sir John Foulis contains a note of a match played on Musselburgh links in 1672. At one time it claimed to be the oldest golf course in the world, although it is now generally accepted that this honour goes to St Andrews. The Royal Musselburgh golf club was founded in 1774. The original course had seven holes, increased to nine in 1870. Although the game was usually considered to be the preserve of men, fishwives played a match at Musselburgh links as early as 1791. The first documented women's golf competition was played here on New Year's Day 1811, in which the fishwives of Musselburgh again participated.

During the nineteenth century, three prestigious Edinburgh golfing clubs made it their home because of overcrowding on the city's courses. They were the Honourable Company of Edinburgh Golfers, which arrived in 1836, followed by the Edinburgh Burgess golf club in 1874 and the Bruntsfield Golfing Society in 1878. The railways enabled golfers to play away from their home courses, with tee times synchronised to the Musselburgh trains. The first British Open was held here in 1874, and by 1889 it had been hosted here a further five times.

Another lasting legacy of Musselburgh Old Course was that it was responsible for the diameter of a golf hole being exactly 4.25 inches. As far back as 1829, its members purchased a mechanical device from a local blacksmith to cut the holes on the green. It made holes exactly this size, and in 1893 when the Royal and Ancient wrote the rules of golf, it was decided this should be the standard size. Many well-known golf personalities were associated with this course, including one-time manager John Gourlay. He was a great authority on the rules of golf but his family became best known as a maker of 'feather' golf balls and a 'gourlay' became an accepted name for the best golf balls.

By 1900, the Musselburgh course was becoming very busy, with players having to sometimes wait forty-five minutes between each nine holes. Between 1890 and 1926, the four resident golf clubs migrated to new 18-hole golf courses. The Honourable Company of Edinburgh Golfers went to Muirfield and took with it the Open championship. In 1938, in an effort to regain its status as a golf centre, Musselburgh council built a new 18-hole championship course at Mortonhall. It occupies a bend on the river Esk, and, in contrast to the Old Links course, is set back from the coast. The original 9-hole links course is still in use today, coexisting with Musselburgh racecourse, which shares the same ground.

During its existence, the course has been home to some sixty golf clubs and societies. The Royal Musselburgh was the last of the four notable clubs in Victorian times to depart for a new home. Originally, it was hoped that land would be made available for it in the policies of Hailes house, but this was turned down. In 1926, respected designer James Braid laid out a course in the grounds of Prestongrange house for the Royal Musselburgh golf club, which included an area known as 'pit pony field'. The course suffered a major setback when part of it was ploughed up in the Second World War. Although it stands on a raised beach and a short distance from the sea, it is a parkland course, not a links. Few golf clubs can boast such impressive premises as Prestongrange house: the large baronial mansion has numerous ornamental towers and incorporates an earlier structure dating from the sixteenth century or possibly much earlier. A clubhouse of this age is probably appropriate for the sixth-oldest golf club in the world.

North Berwick golf club was founded in 1832 and established a course on the west links, next to the town centre. The sport was being played here long before this on the 'toune' links. There is a disapproving reference in *The Kirk Session Book* of 1611 to Thomas Gowan and Alex Lockart playing on a Sunday; they were punished by having to sit on pillory stools, while Thomas Bannatyne preached them a sermon. There is mention of further restrictions being placed on golfers in 1728, when the council prohibited them from playing during summer to allow the grass to grow for livestock. Towards the end of the eighteenth century, golfers were also required to have someone proceed in front of them while in the vicinity of Castle hill to warn walkers of the possible hazard of golf balls. The punishment for playing on the pasture ground was now a fine of 12 shillings.

Golf ceased to be played on the east links in favour of the west links by the early-nineteenth century. The course here was laid out on a raised beach, overlaid by windblown sand. Initially, it had only six holes, with a marquee being pitched for each meeting. The course was extended westwards in 1877 when land belonging to Ferrygate farm was acquired. Some of the ground was set aside for a ladies' course in 1867. By the end of the following decade, the west links course was home to several clubs including Bass Rock golf club (whose members were mainly artisans), North Berwick golf club, New North Berwick golf club and Tantallon golf club, which organised maintenance. In 1888, North Berwick women's club was formed but its members were not allowed to play the 18-hole course. For around the first fifty years of its existence they were confined to a separate nine-hole course with its own clubhouse and greenkeepers.

Despite the restrictions, many distinguished women golfed at North Berwick. They included Princess Helena Victoria, granddaughter of Queen Victoria, who played regularly in the 1920s. She usually stayed at Gullane and was driven the four miles in a chauffeur-driven car. Nancy Astor, the first female MP, also golfed here. Another important politician, future prime minister A. J. Balfour, became captain of North Berwick in 1899. Six years later, the British Ladies championship was held at North Berwick. The main 18-hole course had ten greenkeepers in 1915, but mechanisation arrived in the following decade with the purchase of its first tractor. During the Second World War, land in the vicinity of the ninth and tenth holes was incorporated into part of a target range for aircraft. In 1957, golf was allowed for the first time on Sundays. By this time, women had been playing on the 18-hole course for nearly two decades. The ladies' course was re-designated for children and claims to be one of the oldest surviving examples of a ladies' course in the world.

In 1894, a private 9-hole course was opened at the east end of North Berwick, close to where golf was first played several centuries earlier. There was an ever-increasing pressure on the town's west links, so it was decided to create another 18-hole course. The course, which extends from Tantallon Terrace to Canty bay, was designed by James Braid and Ben Sayers, the local professional. It opened for full play in April 1908 and became known in time as the Glen golf course.

There is a statue of Ben Sayers on the edge of the West Links course. Born in 1856, he spent most of his childhood in Leith, although he

Statue of Ben Sayers, West Links, North Berwick.

lived for a short time in Haddington where he was given his first golf clubs by an uncle. Sayers played golf regularly on Leith Links and was also a professional acrobat until the age of 16. In 1878, Sayers played in the Open championship at Prestwick. The following year he married Catherine Thomson of North Berwick. They lived in a row of pantiled cottages at Westgate where his wife made golf balls. The business received a boost when the editor of *The Scotsman* purchased a mould and golf-ball-making machine for him. Ben Sayers got to know him during golf lessons at Archerfield golf course.

Sayers taught many of the rich and famous, as well as royalty, including Queen Alexandra, the Prince of Wales (later King George V) and Princess Victoria. Some of his pupils went on to become famous golfers in their own right, including the great woman champion, Dorothy Campbell, and the Frenchman Arnaud Massy, the first overseas player to win the Open. Sayers's talents were not limited to teaching; he designed a number of courses, including the original course on Archerfield estate and Kilspindie golf course. During his life he patented several designs for golf clubs. His business expanded when he opened a shop in North Berwick High Street selling his golf balls and offering a repair service for clubs. When Sayers died in 1924, his son carried on the business.

For 124 years there was a factory in North Berwick that turned out gutta-percha balls. Golf clubs were also manufactured, with several innovative types being developed including the 'Benny Putter' (the first to have a square grip), the first set of carbon-shafted clubs and the first oversized driver, known as the 'Dreadnought'. Although Ben Sayers Ltd is among the oldest golf-equipment manufacturers still in business, it now has little connection with its founder. The North Berwick factory closed in 2003 and production was moved to China.

Golf courses spread along the coast to Dunbar, where the West Barns links was laid out in 1856, but the sport had been played here long before this. As in North Berwick, there was trouble with golfers playing the sport on the Sabbath, and, in 1616, Alexander Jackson and William Aitcheson were brought to book for this sin. Even an assistant minister in the Episcopalian church in Dunbar was caught out when 'apprehended while playing at the gouff' one Sunday in 1640. By the end of the eighteenth century, Dunbar Golfing Society was regularly playing on the links at West Barns but this came to an end with the advent of the Napoleonic Wars, when the land became a military camp with rifle ranges. For a long time after the end of the conflict golfers were absent from the locus.

In 1890, the local landowner, St Clair Cunningham, established a private course at West Barns, initially with nine holes and then extended to eighteen. Many of his distinguished friends were invited to the course and it was here that James Braid carded a round of 57, a world record. The Honourable Company of Edinburgh Golfers had considered the site for their new golf course before opting for Muirfield, as the Dunbar course was too far away from the nearest railway station. When Dunbar town council opened Winterfield links the course was no longer viable and it closed in 1937.

On the opposite side of the town, Dunbar golf club had established a course at Broxmouth – the East Links – by 1856. The course initially had fifteen holes, increased to eighteen in 1880. Initially, there was no clubhouse and players would meet at the George inn on High Street. The present clubhouse was built in 1902 and three years later the course was extended when Old Deer Park was acquired. This gave the Links Course some parkland characteristics. The current plan dates from 1922–4 when James Braid and Ben Sayers laid out an extended course.

With large numbers of golfers descending on Dunbar, the municipal Winterlinks course was opened on the west side in March 1935. It was another links course, laid out on a raised marine platform covered by sand, and, like many others, designed by James Braid. It was intended to provide an interesting challenge for both scratch players and novices. The course was closed during the Second World War when searchlights and lookout posts occupied the ground.

In contrast to the links courses, the first parkland course was opened on the grounds of Amisfield estate at Haddington in 1865, laid out on gravel terraces adjacent to the river Tyne. Although Amisfield house was demolished in the early-twentieth century, the course remains.

In the nineteenth century, residents of Aberlady played golf on the coast to the north-west of their village between Craigielaw Point and Harestanes Wood, on the 5-hole Wanster course. They had to compete with the Haddingtonshire Rifle Volunteers (formed in 1860), who used the same ground for rifle practice. After a while, the golfers decided to surrender the site and look elsewhere. In 1867, the owner of Luffness estate gave them permission to lay out a 17-hole course on the north side of the Peffer burn, on what is now part of Aberlady nature reserve, accessed by the wooden footbridge across the river. By 1872, an eighteenth hole was added, making it one of the earliest courses of its type in Scotland. Luffness golf club was the thirty-fifth registered golf club in the world.

After twenty-seven years, George Hope, the landowner, decided to create a new golf course slightly closer to Gullane. This proposal dismayed the Aberlady golfers. In time, the original Luffness course was abandoned, but two new courses were created to replace it. Old Tom

Morris laid out Luffness new course in 1894, which now almost merges with those of Gullane. For the next four years, old and new Luffness operated side by side until the lease expired on the former. Parts of it were then incorporated into the new course, including the fourteenth and seventeenth holes. The disgruntled Aberlady members then returned to the site of the old Wanster course. Here Willie Park laid out Kilspindie golf course, a flat links course on a raised beach. The plan of the course remains much the same as it was when opened at the end of the nineteenth century.

Although Gullane is at the heart of golf in East Lothian, the present 18-hole courses were not laid out until the late-nineteenth century. As with Dunbar and North Berwick, an early form of golf had been played here for many centuries. In the mid-seventeenth century, there was an annual golf competition between the weavers of Aberlady and Dirleton. It was held on 'Auld Handsel Monday', traditionally the first Monday after 12 January. Some of the Aberlady weavers had moved to Glasgow but walked back to Gullane during the night so they could continue to participate. The East Lothian golf club was formed in the early-nineteenth century, its members mainly local farmers and the brewers from Edinburgh who purchased their barley. A 7-hole golf course was established in 1840. It was later extended to fifteen holes and then to eighteen in 1884, to become Gullane no. 1 course, by far the most famous of the three courses here. Gullane no. 2 course was added in 1898. Twelve years later, Gullane no. 3 course opened, along with a children's course. All three are links courses standing on windblown sand, although Gullane hill, formed from volcanic rock, gives some variety to the terrain. The views from its top, which include the Firth of Forth and North Berwick Law, are among the best in East Lothian.

Dirleton Castle golf club, founded by shopkeepers and workers, is the oldest golf club still playing at Gullane. It was followed by Gullane golf club in 1882. At the end of the nineteenth century, horse training was still undertaken here, which led to friction with the golfers. Lord Low prohibited the exercise of horses on Gullane hill in 1892, making the area exclusively available for golf. Gullane no. 1 is regarded as one of the world's top courses and has been used for the qualifying rounds for Open championships. In addition, it has hosted numerous tournaments, including the Ladies Open in 1947, the Scottish amateur championship and the Scottish professional championship. The first clubhouse was built in 1889, but was superseded by the present one overlooking the first tee on no. 1 course in 1929. A clubhouse for visitors was added in 1993. Gullane's golf heritage is commemorated by a small golf museum located next to the pro shop. It is open only by appointment.

Of all the courses in East Lothian, Muirfield, on the east side of Gullane village, is the best known. It had hosted the Open championship sixteen times up to 2020 (most recently in 2013, the winner being Phil Mickelson) and many consider it one of the fairest Open courses. Jack Nicklaus, who won his first Open here in 1966, has described Muirfield as 'the best golf course in Britain'. It has also hosted Scottish amateur championships as well as Ryder Cup, Walker Cup and Curtis Cup matches.

Muirfield was established in 1891 when the Honourable Company of Edinburgh Golfers moved here from the Old Links course at Musselburgh. As far back as 1744, the club drafted the first thirteen rules of golf for a tournament on Edinburgh's Leith Links. The land at Muirfield was owned by the Rt. Hon. Nisbet Hamilton and had previously been used for horse racing and training. The first sixteen holes opened in May 1891, followed by the remaining two in December. The course was designed by Old Tom Morris, who also participated in many tournaments; his life was immortalised in the 2016 film, *Tommy's Honour*, directed by Sean Connery's son, Jason. The Open championship was played here in 1892.

A further fifty acres were acquired in 1923 and the course redesigned by Harry Colt, producing the layout that is in existence today. It departed from the conventional layout for a links course, being arranged as two loops of nine holes, one clockwise and the other anti-clockwise. This results in a different wind direction for every hole in the round. The layout also makes it particularly amenable for spectators. Numerous hillocks and hollows are interspersed in what is otherwise a flat course. The name Muirfield is derived from *muir* (Scots, moorland). During the 1892 Open championship, the golf professional was most uncomplimentary, saying that it 'resembled an auld water meadow'. There may have been a grain of truth in this because in the early years there was a curling pond north-west of the seventh fairway. The course has been improved beyond all recognition since those times.

In the eighteenth century, the 7th earl Wemyss and March purchased land at Gosford 'to be nearer the golf', but, 150 years later, it was the eleventh earl who built the 18-hole course at Longniddry. Harry S. Colt was responsible for its layout across 150 acres. Many thousands of trees had to be felled, some of which were in Boglehill wood, said to be the meeting place of witches and warlocks. The Longniddry course opened in 1921 with the inaugural match attended by four thousand spectators. Lying on top of a raised beach, it has many of the characteristics of a parkland course. Several significant changes have taken place in its design since it opened for play. During the Second World War, it was ploughed up for growing food. When the conflict ended, its layout was redesigned and the area occupied by the course now reduced to 106 acres.

Recent decades have seen a number of new courses established. In 1995, Whitekirk golf course was constructed on hilly and undulating ground, contrasting with the relatively flat links courses to the west; it was referred to as a heathland course. Twenty years after it opened, it closed. Around the same time, Castle Park course was opened a short distance from Gifford. It too was in danger of permanently closing in 2015 and reverting to agricultural land, but has since been saved, passing to new owners. The 9-hole Gifford course, on the other hand, has been in existence since 1904 although there is evidence that the game had been played here since 1889. In contrast to most other East Lothian courses it is located on rolling upland. It was designed by the famous golfer and landscaper, Willie Wart, of Royal Epsom, on land leased from part of Lord Tweeddale's estate. Mature woodland and a beech hedge surround the course.

Another new links course opened in 2001 at Craigielaw, a short distance to the west of Aberlady, although it has the appearance of a long-established golf course. It has a large modern clubhouse. The luxury resort established in the grounds of Archerfield house saw the creation of two new exclusive golf course – the Dirleton and the Fidra. Both were designed by golf architect David J. Russell, with the Dirleton winding inland towards Dirleton village and the Fidra heading towards the coast. In 2008, a third course was added – the Renaissance Club course, for one of the world's most exclusive golf clubs.

Archerfield has a long association with the game, with 'coarse golf' played here from the sixteenth century. The first modern course was laid out in the nineteenth century for the owners and estate workers and also for golf competitions. At first it had thirteen holes but in 1910 was extended to eighteen by Ben Sayers. When Archerfield estate was taken over by the Ministry of Defence during the Second World War, the course was neglected and fell into disuse. The Renaissance Club course was laid out at Archfield appropriately using some of the neighbouring Muirfield golf course. This links course was designed by Tom Doak, who has been responsible for many prestigious golf courses around the world including Pacific Dunes in Oregon.

East Lothian's association with golf is appropriately celebrated by a large sculpture of a golf ball standing at the centre of a roundabout next to the historic Musselburgh links (*see plate section*).

Horse Racing

This horse-racing sculpture stands on a roundabout at the entrance to Newhailes house, Musselburgh.

There are only five racecourses in Scotland that host regular meetings. East Lothian is fortunate in having one, at Musselburgh. Originally, this area was common land used for livestock. Racing began here in 1816 when a course was built.

Leith Sands, near Edinburgh, was the main venue prior to this, with races having been held there since 1504. The races were held in July or

August, attended by huge crowds noted for their frequently rowdy behaviour. The expansion of Leith docks and the increasing reluctance of horse owners to risk their animals galloping across wet sand often covered with water led to the site being abandoned. It was first proposed to make a new racecourse in 1805 and two new sites were suggested, one at Bruntsfield links, Edinburgh, and the other at Musselburgh links. The latter was chosen, it having been used for horse racing in 1777 and on a number of other occasions. The Royal Caledonian Hunt was so impressed with the new course at Musselburgh, that it instructed ten guineas be distributed amongst the labourers – they had undertaken much of the work on their own accord during their spare time. Although the official date of the opening of the course is usually given as 1816, a large event took place here two years earlier, attended by a large crowd. The Royal Caledonian Hunt continued to hold meetings here throughout the nineteenth and twentieth centuries.

It was not long before trouble followed. In July 1823, after a meeting, a dispute between an Irishman and a baker led to a pitched battle on Musselburgh links between Irish workers and local coal miners, in which three lives were lost. The new course failed to attract the large crowds that attended the Leith races as it was less accessible. There was, however, a great variety of races: in 1845, for example, there was a farmers' race, a hunter stakes and the Edinburgh Whip stakes. There was even a race in which horses normally employed in hauling stage coaches raced against each other and were ridden by their owners or the guards. Charles Carroll, a jockey, met with a fatal accident in 1867. Nearly twenty years later, Tom Bruckshaw rode the winner in the first race: his horse bolted a short time later, jumping over two railings and galloping into a quarry, breaking its neck. Tom Bruckshaw was taken to hospital where he read of his death in the local newspapers!

During the nineteenth century, the main event at Musselburgh was the September races, at which refreshments included shellfish, oysters, crabs, loaves called 'penny bricks' and ice cream. Racing was suspended during the First World War and not long after there were plans to find a site closer to Edinburgh but these came to nothing.

In 1963, a new threat to racing emerged. Off-course betting became legal, leading to the opening of betting shops. Attendances dropped, and, by the 1980s, Musselburgh's future looked bleak. Instead of closing the course, much effort was made to turn its fortunes around. Flat racing had taken place since the course had opened but National

Racing at Musselburgh.

Hunt was now introduced. The Edwardian grandstand was refurbished and new stables, pavilion and weighing room were built. By 2016, the effort had paid off with attendances almost doubling in twenty years. There are now around twenty-six flat and jump racing fixtures a year on its 1.25-mile oval track. The sandy, well-drained soil means that meetings are rarely affected by winter weather.

Musselburgh is not the only place in East Lothian associated with horse racing. There are records of a fixture at Haddington in 1553, although it appears to have ceased by the late-eighteenth century. In the 1860s, there was a steeplechase meeting held on the Garleton hills, described as the 'Scottish National Hunt'.

Racehorses were trained in the vicinity of Dunbar in Victorian times, when the seashore was much used for gallops. For a brief period, it had its own racecourse at Hedderwick, West Barns. The area was first used by the East Lothian yeomanry cavalry, which held an annual meeting there. The meetings were such a success that St Clair Cunningham, local landowner and trainer, was inspired to establish a racecourse in the late-nineteenth century and hold a National Hunt meeting in 1896. It became a popular venue, hosting the Dunbar handicap chase, the East of Scotland chase and the Tyninghame chase, among others. Despite this, Hedderwick closed in March 1906, shortly after Cunningham died as the result of a chill. He was also responsible for creating the adjacent golf course at West Barns. It lasted longer than the racecourse, with his widow taking over the running.

Gullane on the other hand, had a long-established racetrack where annual meetings were held as far back as the eighteenth century. It was located at the Hundred Acre park, on the east of the town, and Muirfield golf course now occupies the site. There were some natural sand hazards in its centre but the rest of the race track was described as being a fine stretch of turf. Heat races of 3–4 miles were then the order of the day. In 1832, there was an outbreak of cholera in Edinburgh so the Musselburgh races were run at Gullane. By that time the racetrack at Muirfield had fallen into disuse and had become a private gallop. Gullane village became best known, not for its racecourse, but as a training ground for horses. It was sometimes referred to as the 'Newmarket of the North'.

Training came to an end in 1890 when there was a quarrel between a trainer and the landowner, but by that time Gullane had long lost its prominent role in racing. Many top trainers had moved to England, attracted by greater prize money.

Other sports and recreational activities

Haddington lays claim to the first bowling green in Scotland, in Lady Kitty's Garden, near Nungate Bridge, dating back to 1662.

Hunting was the sport of kings and is still pursued in a limited form on the Lammermuir hills, where grouse and pheasant are shot. Access to some parts of the uplands is restricted when this activity in undertaken. For centuries, the Tyne has been a magnet for anglers; brown trout and sea trout are caught in its lower reaches, and, less frequently, salmon. Markle fisheries in East Linton has small spring-fed lochs, stocked with rainbow and brown trout. More remote are the Hope and Whiteadder reservoirs in the Lammermuirs, with brown trout. The latter location, the largest area of freshwater in the region, is also used for water sports, including canoeing and sailing.

Not all East Lothian's leisure pursuits are grounded in the past. East Fortune has become one of Scotland's leading locations for microlight aviation. There have been attempts to open the entire former RAF airfield to private flying, but these have proved unsuccessful. When the weather is fair, brightly coloured microlight aircraft can be seen in its skies, flying from the disused Second World War aerodrome; they land and take off from a small length of runway to the west side of the road that dissects the field. There were proposals in the early-twenty-first century to construct an entirely new airfield for light aircraft immediately to the south of Dirleton, but they have come to nothing.

Small sailing craft, North Berwick harbour.

Closer to earth, windsurfing has become popular. The North Sea can be whipped up by strong winds, which send large waves crashing onto the coast to attract surfers near Belhaven and Dunbar. Choppy seas are less welcomed by the sailing craft – ranging from dinghies to large yachts – which pack the harbours along the coast at Fisherrow, Port Seton, North Berwick and Dunbar. The sheltered inshore waters offer ideal conditions for novice sailors while the open waters of the North Sea can test the skills of the most experienced.

In the summer, bathers and swimmers are attracted to the sea. There were once outdoor swimming pools on the coast located at Dunbar (the largest in Scotland), Port Seton and North Berwick. North Berwick swimming club was founded in the late-Victorian era. Subscriptions were started for an open-air swimming pool with construction commencing in 1900. Changing rooms were added in 1929 when it assumed its art-deco appearance; at this time, it was one of twenty lidos in Scotland. Towards the end of the twentieth century, attendances declined and the pool was sometimes open for only for ten weeks in summer. Water heating was introduced in 1962, but being exposed to the cold air and the wind reduced its effectiveness. The end was in sight and it closed at the end of 1995. Demolition commenced the following year and the Scottish Seabird Centre now occupies part of the site. Port Seton open-air pool, at the east end of town, closed around the same time and was also demolished.

34. LOST DOMAINS

Although many of East Lothian's most historic buildings, such as Tantallon castle and St Mary's church, have stood the test of time, fate has been less kind to others. Some have completely vanished, while crumbling walls are all that remain of others. The relationship between historic buildings and their surroundings is not always apparent today. In the intervening years the ground may have been drained, trees planted or modern buildings erected. The important medieval harbour at Aberlady was watched over by a courtyard castle, where Luffness house now stands. Several hundred years ago, there would have been little, if any, woodland in the vicinity, giving the original castle commanding views. Another castle that has been totally erased is that of Longniddry, obliterated when houses were built on its site.

On the coast, the once important harbours of Aberlady, Belhaven and Morrison's Haven have all vanished, although their natural features are still recognisable. Even castles built to withstand sieges have been reclaimed by nature. Just to the north of the church at Aberlady there is a section of a ruined wall punctuated with gun loops, once the entrance to Kilspindie castle. These fragmentary remains replaced an early fortification on the site, which was once occupied by the Spence family.

Towards the end of the sixteenth century, Patrick Douglas had constructed a 'castell toure and fortalice' at Kilspindie. Its defences would have been enhanced by a surrounding salt marsh but this has long since dried up as the sea retreated. By the eighteenth century the castle had fallen into disuse with its stones being stolen for building purposes and some used in the wall next to the road that leads to Kilspindie golf course.

The remains of St Patrick's church: seashore north of Gullane.

Some churches have also gone the way of this castle. The chapel at Samuelston, where John Knox preached his sermons, has long vanished; even its original location is unknown. More fortunate is St Patrick's chapel, located above the waves on the coast to the north of Gullane. Its ruinous walls await discovery by the unsuspecting walker. As with many inconspicuous ruins, many will pass by not realising its significance.

Entire settlements have completely disappeared. Dirleton's forerunner was the medieval village of Eldbotle, located near the coast on land now occupied by Archerfield golf complex. Although shown on early maps, its exact location was unknown until excavations in 2003 uncovered the remains of timber and stone structures immediately north of Archerfield house and by the hillock next to the sea. Eldbotle comes from the old English *eldotl*, old dwelling place. Like several other settlements in East Lothian, it was originally British but was taken over by Anglo-Saxons from Northumberland. They established a royal manor at Dunbar but the status of Eldbotle at this time is unknown.

Eldbotle may have been in royal ownership in the mid-twelfth century, as David I visited at least once. In the early 1160s, Malcolm IV issued two charters from here. Around that time, Eldbotle was granted to John de Vaux, younger brother of a prominent Cumberland knight. In the following century, the de Vaux family constructed Dirleton castle and established a new settlement in the shadow of the castle. There is mention of a motte castle at Eldbotle, which was thought to have been located on a knoll close to the coast. It is possible that the John de Vaux may have built his first castle here and not at Dirleton or perhaps the kings of Scotland had already erected a fortification where they stayed during visits to Eldbotle.

The north wall, with doorway, is all that remains of the twelfth- or thirteenth-century church of St Nicholas on nearby Fidra island, now inhabited exclusively by birds. There are stories referring to 'the mysterious race of Congals', who lived on Fidra, being slaughtered by the Vikings in the ninth century. In medieval times, the island was part of the barony of Eldbotle and was known by this name. There was a castle here in 1220, which lends its name to the natural feature 'Castle Tarbet', a flat-topped column of rock.

Further to the east at Auldhame, near Tantallon castle, a medieval cemetery containing some two hundred organised burials lay undiscovered on the headland until 2005. Although now open fields, edged by a rocky coastline, there was once an early stone church here; it stood on the site of an even earlier timber example. A monastic settlement was thought to have been established here in the seventh century, possibly by St Baldred. It thrived until the ninth century and possibly suffered the same fate as that of the nearby monastery at Tyninghame – being raided by the Norsemen. The most significant find was the grave of a high-ranking Viking, fully dressed, with weaponry.

A Christian presence persisted on the headland, as in 1243 David de Berham consecrated the parish church here in the name Alda St Baldred. Any village associated with it has long since been abandoned. The only visible evidence of human occupation in the vicinity is the ruins of sixteenth-century Auldame house, standing next to the track to Seacliff beach. It was an L-shaped tower built by Adam Otterburn, an ambassador for James V. In 1651, it was attacked and severely damaged by Oliver Cromwell's troops, who were besieging Tantallon castle. A short distance to the south of Auldhame was Old Scoughall, another long-lost ancient settlement. It stood a short distance to the north of Scoughall farm and had its own chapel at the top of Chapel Brae.

Morham parish church, the centre of what was once a more substantial settlement.

Hidden away at end of a track, 2.5 miles south-east of Haddington, is Morham parish church. A few isolated houses in its vicinity are the only reminder that there was once a far more substantial settlement here. A castle once stood in a field to the south. There are numerous gravestones to the Knox family in Morham churchyard, leading to the belief that Morham may have been the birthplace of John Knox, but it is now thought to have been Haddington. The present small church dates from 1724, although it incorporates parts of an earlier example dating from 1685, including the bell tower.

Thomas Malherbe founded a church at Morham in 1180. Around the same time, the family built a castle here, which in medieval times overlooked an extensive village; the settlement declined after its castle was abandoned in 1574 with the death of Lady Agnes. She was responsible for concealing her husband, Archibald Douglas, in the building; he was involved in plotting the murder of Lord Darnley, second husband of Mary, Queen of Scots. The property of Lady Agnes was later confiscated by the Crown. By the eighteenth century, the village of Morham, south of the present church, had become deserted.

All that is left of the hamlet of Cottyburn are the ruins of two ivy-clad buildings of the eighteenth century. They are located next to the former Longniddry–Haddington railway, now a footpath. A minor road to Huntington also passes in front of the abandoned structures. The hamlet was thought to have been established here in the eighteenth century or possibly earlier. Although at one time it had a school, its population was never more than seventeen. By the early-twentieth century, it had fallen into decline. In 1960 the train with the royal carriage on its way to Hadddington stopped in the siding at Cottyburn, where the Queen's corgis were walked.

Place names offer clues to lost communities. For example, St Germains, near Prestonpans, takes its name from a Bethlehemite hospital that stood on the ground now occupied by a country house. The area, like many others, has a long history of occupation. Late in the twentieth century, the remains of both enclosed and unclosed Iron Age settlements were unearthed. A short distance to the east, Seton collegiate church is the only reminder of an extensive settlement that included a village and Seton palace.

In the Lammermuir hills, on the north side of Meikle Says Law, there are two small valleys bearing the name Wolf's Cleugh (*cleugh*, narrow valley), a legacy of a time when these animals once roamed the land. In more recent times, the remote uplands became a haunt of beggars and vagabonds and some estate owners took matters into their own hands. At Kidlaw farm, at the foot of the Lammermuirs, there was a small prison consisting of two apartments with walls 5-to-6 feet thick, which could hold a dozen people. The laird of Newtonhall estate would round up, and confine overnight, undesirable characters found on his lands. This practice continued until around the beginning of the nineteenth century. The 'lock-up' has long since vanished, along with the lawless characters who found refuge on these hills.

Also long gone is a tower house or old mansion house at Stobshiel, not far from Kidlaw, where a band of gypsies murdered the owner and occupied the building. James V (1512–42) was well known for often travelling across his kingdom disguised as an ordinary citizen. One evening, he came to the tower house at Stobshiel seeking shelter and encountered the gypsies. James gave his name as the laird of Ballengeich, instructing his only attendant to go to Eckieside mill to seek assistance. When he returned there was a furious fight in which the gypsies were captured and locked up at Kidlaw. The following day, the King ordered several of them to be hung from a nearby ash tree. The tree, like the prison, had vanished by the end of the nineteenth century.

Lochend house, close to Dunbar, was depicted on a map of the late-seventeenth century, together with Tyningehame and Yester, surrounded by avenues of trees, among the first in the area to be adorned in this manner. While the latter two houses are still standing, Lochend house has all but vanished. The only evidence of the existence of the two-storey mansion house are some ruined walls concealed in Lochend wood near Kellie Road.

Superstition has played its part in keeping the past alive. Close to the A1, at Dolphingstone just to the west of Tranent, is a dovecote with

Dolphingstone, close to the A1. A dovecote and the stone wall are the only reminders of the large country house that once stood here.

a tall, stone wall enclosing a sizeable plot of land. Within its walls once stood a large, seventeenth-century, country house set on an east–west axis. The barony of Dolphinstone (sometimes Dolphingstone) was formerly called 'Colthrople'. It was believed that bad luck would befall those who demolished a dovecote. Hence these buildings are sometimes the only indication that a country house or castle once stood in the immediate vicinity. The sinister reputation of another house, that also stood on the western edge of Tranent close to Birsley Brae, led to its destruction. The legend was recorded in *Tranent and its Surroundings*, by Peter M'Neill, published 1884:

That many years ago there stood on the site of this old pit head [Capon Ha Pit] a large building called the 'Hall' inhabited by a gentleman imbued with many peculiar traits of character. He would, for instance, have no wife, neither would he allow maid servant, nor grown-up man servant, within his door – all the work in his establishment had to be done by boys; further these youths had to be 'mitherless chicks' as he called them; for, said he, 'should a conflagration some day take place within the building and its inmates be consumed few will miss them'.

This eccentric gentleman is said to have dealt most tyrannically towards his boy servants. Not only did he mercilessly abuse them when in a fault but not a few of them, it was alleged, even when in no fault, had fallen a sacrifice to his violent temper. These victims to his spleen were said to have been buried within the walls of his establishment. The legend further tells that this curious individual was a great rearer of poultry and that on every day of the year nothing would serve but capon [domestic chicken] to dinner. One day, however, there was no capon provided for the miscreant and such an offence was too serious to be lightly passed over. That night the whole of his youthful servants were cruelly punished. The matter, however, did not end there. One of the 'chicks' more revengeful than his fellows proposed that they should 'burn the nest and roast the old bird before morning'. This was accordingly done. By midnight the Hall was in a blaze and in the morning nothing but a mass of blackened ruins met the eye. All the chicks are reported to have taken wing and escaped but the laird of Capon Ha' perished in the flames. By 1779 the lands of Capon Ha' were farmed by Mr Robert Pringle.

Of all the buildings to have disappeared in East Lothian, the greatest loss was Seton palace. Its destruction is made more bearable because of its replacement: Seton house, an outstanding design by Robert Adam. Seton house is built in the style of a castle, but unlike the building it replaced it has a relatively low profile and is concealed in the landscape. The name comes from the Seton family, who owned large tracts of land in East Lothian and for several hundred years were closely associated with Scotland's rulers. At some point after 1066 they built a castle on the site. The early building was a large, square tower that was rebuilt and expanded. By the mid-fourteenth century, it had become a large courtyard castle.

The Setons also owned numerous other fortifications including St Germains, Winton and Garleton, more modest but built to a similar style. The grand tower of Seton was called St Bennet's tower after St Benedict, the family's patron saint; later, the Wallace tower was added. By the late-fifteenth century, the castle was surrounded by an outstanding garden and orchards. During the Rough Wooing, in 1544, English soldiers burnt Seton castle and its orchards and gardens – 'the fairest in the country' – were destroyed.

Lord Seton fled and took up residence at Culross, where he died in 1549. His successors rebuilt the square great tower and round towers were added to the complex along with lavish extensions in Italian and French style. The gardens were recreated in an extravagant style. By the second half of the sixteenth century, it had become one of the most prestigious residences in Scotland and was now referred to as a palace, not a castle. Mary, Queen of Scots often retreated to Seton palace as did her son, James VI. On the second storey there were state apartments, which included three rooms whose ceilings were forty feet high. The furniture was covered in crimson velvet laced with gold. Paintings hung on the walls of the halls. Mary, Queen of Scots sometimes held court here, as did her son James VI. In 1617 – now as James I of England and VI of Scotland – he returned to spend a night here. Charles I was also entertained at Seton palace twenty years later.

In its final phase, Seton palace was set around a large, triangular court enclosed by freestone buildings at least seven-storeys tall, with various castellated towers, some influenced by French architecture. There was also a larger, and taller, octagonal watch tower. On either side of the main gate was a tower and further examples scattered throughout the complex. Some were built for defence, others added more recently for ornamental purposes. There was also a large walled garden in the twelve acres of grounds. In 1715, George Seton made the mistake of backing the Jacobite rising. Seton palace was fortified by rebels but an army of two hundred cavalry and three thousand infantrymen was dispatched from Edinburgh to subjugate this anti-government force. On arrival they found Seton palace so well defended that they withdrew.

Not long after, the Jacobite rebels were instructed to deploy to England. The Lothian militia took possession of the now undefended palace and, in view of its owner, it was set on fire, its painted, plastered and gilded walls and ceilings destroyed. Many of its paintings and other valuables were looted. George Seton was charged with treason and sentenced to death, but he managed to escape the Tower of London and fled to Rome, where he lived out his years.

The Seton family had all their property, including Seton palace, confiscated. This was in some way due to an unfortunate chain of events. It was said that George Seton had quarrelled with his father and took up with a gypsy woman who frequented his estate. He then disappeared for a long period, travelling with a band of gypsies. On the death of his father his whereabouts were unknown. When he returned to Seton palace to claim his inheritance, some of his nearest heirs refused to acknowledge his right to succeed. By then there was some question about his state of mind and it is likely that he did not calculate the consequences of backing the Jacobite cause. The York Buildings Company acquired his forfeited estate.

Further damage was done to Seton palace during the 1745 Jacobite uprising. Towards the end of the eighteenth century the company went bankrupt. The ruined palace was acquired by Alexander Mackenzie, a leading Edinburgh lawyer, who demolished it in 1790 and constructed Seton house, a private residence to which there is no access today.

35. WITCHES, FAIRIES, GHOSTS AND GOBLINS

Witches

One of the most significant incidents of witchcraft in Scottish history centred on St Andrew's church, North Berwick, which once stood on a tidal island near the harbour. Its fragmentary remains can be found a short distance from the Scottish Seabird Centre. In 1589, James VI was awaiting the arrival of Anne of Denmark, his bride to be, spending some of the time at Seton palace. As the days wore on and there was no sign of Anne he became increasingly concerned. Then a message arrived informing him that her ship had run into a storm and had to take shelter in Oslo. On hearing this, James decided he would set sail for Scandinavia, later said to be the one romantic gesture of his life! The King married his 15-year-old bride in Oslo, and while he was there learned of witch hunts across the country.

During the King's absence, David Seton, deputy bailie in Tranent and related to the wealthy Seton family, had his female servant Geillis 'Gilly' Duncan arrested. He was suspicious of her ability to heal the sick and her disappearances at night. When, after questioning, she revealed nothing untoward, Seton resorted to torture, crushing her fingers with thumbscrews. When that failed, he bound and wrenched her head with a rope, subjecting her to excruciating pain, but Gilly still refused to implicate herself.

It was believed that the Devil put a sign upon all his servants, which was recognizable by that part of the body being bloodless and insensible to pain. Seton had Duncan's body examined and the 'mark of the Devil' was found on her throat. At this, Gilly admitted that her work with the sick had been undertaken at the instigation of the Devil and her cures were brought about by witchcraft. She implicated thirty other people, many of them respectable Edinburgh citizens; one was Agnes Sampson, an elderly woman who lived at Keith in the parish of Humbie.

On 1 May 1590, James VI landed at Leith with his new queen. During the voyage their ship was battered by storms and there was suspicion that unnatural forces had been involved. The fears of the royal court were confirmed with the detention of Agnes Sampson, who had been accused of witchcraft by attending the sick and repeating rhymes over them. She was also alleged to have hauled the Devil up a rope, while standing on a small bridge over the Tyne just south of Ormiston. After being horribly tortured and stripped naked, the Devil's mark was found on her. She then corroborated Geillis Duncan's accusations that she was a witch.

Sampson then laid out her tale of witchery. She said that she had attended a meeting of two hundred witches at North Berwick's church on Halloween. The Devil was in attendance with Dr Fian – a young man normally known as Cunningham – acting as his secretary. The purpose of the gathering was to devise a plan to wreck the royal ship. Once the witches had settled on a course of action, they set sail in a fleet of sieves to rendezvous with the royal squadron. On their way, they encountered a ship called *The Grace of God*, which they boarded. Some of them were served with wine supplied by the Devil himself. After they finished feasting, they sent the ship to the bottom of the sea. When the King's vessel came into sight, the Devil handed a cat to Dr Fian, instructed him to throw it into the sea and to cry 'halo'. The royal vessel was then assailed by a tremendous storm.

Sampson continued her tale. The 'Devil's armada' returned to North Berwick where they disembarked and marched towards its church with the sieves in their hands, Geillis Duncan leading the procession. Then they attempted to enter the church but the door was locked. Undeterred, Dr Fian blew into the keyhole and the door flew open; he blew again and this time the candles inside the church burst into flames. The Devil then appeared in the pulpit dressed in a black gown. At the conclusion of a short service he requested the witches to kiss his tail as a token of their loyalty. They all then gathered in the churchyard, where they feasted on the dead.

So outrageous were these claims that even King James called the witches liars. But he changed his mind when he personally questioned Agnes Sampson, who told him the exact words that passed between him and the Queen on his first night of marriage. After that, he was impressed with her supernatural powers. Cunningham, a Prestonpans schoolmaster, was also implicated by Geillis Duncan in the conspiracy to sink the royal ship; he was 'Dr Fian', the Devil's secretary at North Berwick. It was said that he had previously chased a cat in a street in Tranent and then leaped over a wall like the animal, a feat no ordinary human was capable of.

At first, Fian/Cunningham denied the accusations. Then his legs were placed in bootikens, a torture device in which wooden wedges were hammered between the leg and a wood and iron boot with a mallet to crush the victim's bones. Still Cunningham would not confess. Despite being partially crippled, he managed somehow to escape from prison and make his way to Prestonpans. Unfortunately, he was recaptured and again tortured, by having his feet compressed, and, for good measure, his fingernails torn out with pincers. He again denied that he was an associate of the Devil but this did not save him from being burnt on Castlehill, Edinburgh. Gilly Duncan and many of the people she implicated were also sentenced to death.

On the north side of the churchyard at Tranent there is an old dovecote with a weathered inscription, 'David Seton 1587'. This was the same David Seton responsible for triggering the North Berwick witch hunt.

Until the trial of the North Berwick witches, accusations against witches were almost unknown. However, because of the alleged attempt to sink James VI's ship, a witch panic broke out. Between 1593 and 1705, an estimated six hundred people were tried for witchcraft in East Lothian. Once they were brought before a court, the location they came from was permanently identified as a locus of supernatural activities. There were few more notorious places than the hamlet of Samuelston on the north bank of the Tyne, three miles south-west of Haddington. A number of women were found guilty of witchcraft and burnt in a field called Birlie Knowe, situated on the south side of Samuelston and close to the river Tyne.

Although almost all of those tried were women, one of the most notorious wizards in East Lothian was the cattle herder, Sandy Hunter, whom it is said the Devil had named Hattaraick. He was known for curing diseases, both in man and in animals, by words and charms. This power was allegedly given to him when he met the Devil in the manifestation of an old, learned physician on the Garleton hills, just north of Haddington; Hunter, in return, had to acknowledge the Devil as his master. Many would give Sandy Hunter money or food, not because of his ability to cure sickness but out of fear. One day, Hunter was standing at the gate of Lady Samuelston's property when he encountered her brother, who exclaimed, 'You warlocke carle, what have you to do here?' The brother then struck Hunter on the face. As he made off, Hunter put a curse on him. Later that day, the assailant rode home, passing through a shady piece of haugh (riverside meadow) called Allers. It was not known what he encountered there, but the following day he was in such a state of delirium that he had to be bound.

Lady Samuelston immediately concluded that her brother's plight had been caused by Sandy Hunter; she sent her servants to find the wizard and bring him to her house. When they returned with Hunter, a large sack of meal along with beef and cheese was offered to him if he lifted the curse from her brother. His shirt was brought to him and the wizard performed a ritual that lifted the curse. There was not a happy conclusion as Hunter predicted that the brother would soon leave for foreign parts. On hearing this, Lady Samuelston made her brother sign over his share of the estate to her, which had the effect of defrauding his younger brother, George. For some time afterwards, Sandy Hunter made a lucrative living from his charms and cures. Eventually, he was arrested at Dunbar and taken to Edinburgh where he was burnt on Castlehill as a wizard.

This wall mural in Cuthill park, Prestonpans depicts the trial of witches from the town, held at Edinburgh tolbooth. James VI presided at the trial.

Prestonpans was another witchcraft hotspot. Witches were uncovered here for almost a century after a number of residents were accused in the plot to sink the King's ship in 1590. In 1607, a high-profile case involved Isobel Grierson, wife of a labourer. One of Grierson's hate objects was William Burnet. She was said to have devised all sorts of fiendish and ungodly means to deprive him of his life. He became sick and for months the Devil appeared in his house in the form of a naked infant who sat beside the fire with an enchanted image in his hand. Burnet wasted away, eventually dying in great pain from an unknown sickness. Isobel Grierson was found guilty of this and other acts of witchcraft and was sentenced to be strangled and burnt on Castlehill, Edinburgh.

The summer of 1628 saw over a dozen women in Prestonpans accused of witchcraft. Unfortunately, legal records give no indication of their fate. There were further accusations of women practising witchcraft here from 1658–62. A young beggar boy who spoke of fairies and witches was responsible for implicating several residents. The last outbreak of witch frenzy in the town occurred in 1678. Two elderly women – Agnes Kelly and her servant Majorie Andersone – confessed to being witches and were burnt. Before the sentence was carried out, they implicated others. Nine East Lothian women were condemned on their confessions and burnt – five between Edinburgh and Leith and four at Penston, near Macmerry.

By this time, witch hunters were falling out of favour. Katherine Liddel, an elderly widow, was seized by John Rutherford, bailie of Prestonpans. With the assistance of a number of other men, including two saltmakers, he barbarously tortured her in prison in order to obtain a confession. David Cowan, witch pricker, stuck 'pins in several parts of her body to the great effusion of her blood and whereby her skin is raised and her body highly swelled and she is in danger of her life'. In addition, she was deprived of sleep for several days, but refused to confess to being a witch. On her release, Liddel presented a petition to the authorities about her treatment. The government condemned Rutherford and his associates but they were let off without punishment. Less fortunate was witch pricker David Cowan, sentenced to imprisonment.

Scottish witchcraft trials were notable for their use of needles and pins to prick the suspect's flesh. Travelling around from his base in Tranent, John Kincaid was responsible for the deaths of many alleged witches. The needles he used were three inches long. Witch prickers were generally paid by results, giving them an incentive to find the accused guilty. His activities were brought to an abrupt end when the Privy Council ordered his arrest on the grounds that he had been responsible for the torture of many innocent victims. After prison, he was released on the grounds of old age and on condition he would not undertake any further pricking of suspects without a warrant.

It is not surprising that Kincaid's home town of Tranent had a reputation for also being home to numerous witches. Jonet Maglene, wife to William Naismith, gardener at Seton, along with Helene Mwere from Tranent were apprehended as suspected witches in 1622. Ten years later, another gardener's wife was pricked by James Balfoure and the mark of a witch was found on her arm. In 1649, Jean Craig was claimed to have bewitched farm animals in the vicinity of Falside castle, two miles south-west of Tranent: the horses dropped dead, the oxen ran mad and the cows gave blood instead of milk.

Like many of those accused of witchcraft, Janet Bruce of Tranent was involved in healing the sick. Although some of the people she treated seemed to recover after she ministered to them, her actions led to her being condemned as a witch. She was detained in the tolbooth before being taken to Castlehill, where she was strangled and her body burnt on 8 October 1657.

Dunbar saw at least sixteen put to death for witchcraft. In 1612, Robert Allane, a fisherman, and his wife were accused of witchcraft as evidence had been given against them by people who subsequently died. The following year, a further two persons from Dunbar were suspected of being witches, along with one person from Innerwick. Margaret Baxter and Marion Bathcat in East Barns were detained in 1628, having long been suspected of witchcraft. Five women were burnt on Castlehill in March 1659, having being transported from Dunbar; they had been found guilty of consorting with Satan and frequently dancing with the Devil. The last case of witchcraft at Dunbar occurred in 1688 when an old woman was condemned by a commission of the Privy Council.

In 1608, unusual goings on at Longniddry gave rise to one of the more notorious witch trials. Beigis Tod was accused of meeting the Devil at Deane-Fute beside a circle of now-vanished ancient standing stones, where she carried out witchcraft with several other men and women. The Devil had visited them in 1594, when they celebrated by drinking and singing. They then went back to Tod's home and participated in an unusual ceremony that involved passing a cat nine times through a large hook used for hanging the cooking pot above the fire. They then set off from Longniddry – at that time a village – for Seton. Here the cat was drawn nine times through an iron gate at Seton palace and then christened in a stream, being given the name Margaret. The 'witches' then returned to the stone circle, where the cat may have been offered as a sacrifice. A further accusation was that a boy called Alexander Fairlie suffered from a number of ailments, which Beigis Tod was said to have inflicted on him. She was also reputed to have visited him at night sometimes in her own shape and at other times in the shape of a dog. At the end of her trial, Beigis Tod was found guilty and strangled at the stake on Castlehill, her body then burnt.

As Haddington was the main administrative centre for East Lothian, it was the scene of many witch trials. John Carfra, his wife Alison

Borthuick and Thomas Carfra, his brother, were all tried for witchcraft in 1629. There were further trials the following year. Margrat Vaith was confined in the Tolbooth in the summer of 1649, having confessed to witchcraft. At the same time, permission was granted for the execution of a number of witches within the parishes of Haddington and Dirleton. Nine years later, Margaret Anderson was convicted of witchcraft and of making a pact with the Devil; she was strangled and burnt. In 1661, several women were named in Humbie parish as witches.

The final witch hysteria in Haddington was in 1677. Margaret Kirkwood hanged herself in her own house. Not long after, her servant, Lizzie Mudie, was said to have made a disturbance and counted out numbers aloud until she came to fifty-nine, when she cried out 'the turn is done'. Margaret Kirkwood had been fifty-nine when she died! Suspicion immediately fell on Lizzie, who was arrested and examined for witch marks. They were detected on her body and she confessed to being a witch. She was burned at Haddington in June 1677.

Despite being an important town in south-east Scotland, Musselburgh was not so affected by the witch craze. Those persons that were found guilty of witchcraft were executed at Bogie Hole. There were witch trials in 1603, 1609 and 1628. The last year in which they took place here was 1661 when Bessie Fouler was burnt as a witch. Records state that the Devil was so angry at her prosecution that he raised a great storm to prevent her execution.

At Peaston, a village south of Pencaitland, four women were found guilty of witchcraft on 13 September 1678, one claiming that she had metamorphosed into a crow. All were sentenced to be strangled at the stake until dead and their bodies burnt to ashes. Six people were burnt at Stenton in January 1650. Nine years later, Bessie Luost and four other women (the 'Stentoun witches') were interrogated in the old church tower; they were later transferred to Dunbar, then taken to Castlehill, Edinburgh where they were put to death. Three witches were uncovered at Whittingehame in November 1649 and burnt. A few months later a man was executed in a similar manner.

Spott was another settlement with its fair share of witches. In 1624, Marioun Boyd was implicated as one by several persons already arrested. Four women and two men were sent for trial in 1661 as 'self-confessed witches'. At the end of the seventeenth century, Marion Lillie, an elderly resident, was examined at length for alleged witchcraft. Other than being rude to some of her neighbours, there was little evidence against her. She is often referred to as the 'Rigwoodie' or the 'Ringwoody' witch, a term describing a tough, lean person. A few hundred yards to the south-west of Spott, on the edge of a minor road, is the witches' stone, marking the site where the executions took place. A plaque next to the stone states: 'Marion Lillie, the Ringwoody Witch was burnt here in 1698.'

The witches' stone is also reputed to stand on the site of the burning of the last witch in the south of Scotland. In 1705, 'Many witches [were] burnt on the top of Spott Loan' according to *The Old Statistical Account*, written later the same century. There is doubt about the validity of this

The witches' stone stands a short distance west of Spott, once notorious for its witches.

statement as it is not mentioned in the church records. Marion Lillie's fate is also in doubt. It appears she was not executed but died a natural death and was buried in the local churchyard. There was at one time another witches' stone at Thistley Cross, between West Barns and Stenton, but it has long since disappeared. By the early-eighteenth century, the East Lothian witch frenzy had fizzled out.

Fairies

Modern literature depicts fairies as small and beautiful, but they were originally perceived to be as tall as normal people and similar in appearance. According to legend, the west side of Traprain Law was a meeting place for fairies and at the top was a large rock known as the maiden stone. There was a belief that if a person squeezed through a narrow gap in the stone it increased fertility and good fortune would follow. This ritual was best performed during the solstices and equinoxes and was most effective if the individual was naked. Those involved in this ceremony ran the risk of having their clothes stolen by the fairies. To retrieve them from the mischievous creatures they would have to chase them across the countryside, risking embarrassing encounters with local residents.

At the edge of the Lammermuir hills there is a small, remote valley known as Fairy Dean. It was believed until not long ago that fairies dwelt here among the unusual rock formations. In Deans nature reserve below Aikengall windfarm, the Back water, which flows into Oldhamstocks burn, has carved out a valley in sandstone rock. It is an unusual physical feature, with steep, red, rocky slopes almost devoid of vegetation, resembling a canyon in the American west. There are also pillars of red rock known as the fairy castle. (Due to the relatively inaccessible location of Fairy Dean it should only be visited by experienced walkers.)

Ghosts

Ghosts are said to haunt a number of East Lothian's historic buildings, including Saltoun hall. For many years, the old village of Whittingehame was tormented by an 'unchristened wean'. An unmarried mother had murdered her child under a large tree not far from the village. Not long after, the ghost of the deceased child was seen running between the trees and the churchyard in a distracted manner and crying. The villagers believed the haunting was because the child did not have a name – no anonymous person could get a footing in the other world. Nobody dared mention the apparition from a superstitious dread of sudden death.

One night, a drunk was making his way home to Whittinghame when he encountered the ghost. Totally unfazed, the drunk cried out: 'Hoo's a' wi' ye this mornin' Short Hoggers?', as if he was greeting a normal person.

The ghost was delighted with this, exclaiming, 'Oh weel's me noo! I've gotton a name. They ca'me Short-Hoggers o' Whittingehame.'

After that encounter the supernatural child was never seen again. The name Short Hoggers denotes that the ghost was wearing short stockings without feet, as worn by coal miners. It may be that the ghost had worn out the feet of normal stockings by years of fruitless walking.

At the opposite end of East Lothian, a mysterious woman in white was often seen walking in the woods close to Humbie church. The belief was that she was a member of the Hepburn family, long associated with this parish. The grounds around the Lodge in the centre of North Berwick are reputedly haunted by a phantom white lady. She is not alone, as a hooded figure of a former pageboy, who was murdered in London, is also said to stalk the locus.

In the late-eighteenth century, a North Berwick weaver was haunted by the ghost of his late wife, who had died giving birth to her fourth child. Although very beautiful when alive, in death her corpse was grotesque. The weaver's friends believed this could only be explained by the actions of elves, who had carried away his wife and substituted a deformed body in its place.

As time passed, the weaver decided to remarry. One night, he awoke to find his late wife standing close to him. The apparition, dressed in white, informed the petrified weaver that she had not died but was alive and being held captive in Elfland. The ghostly figure claimed the only way she could escape was if her grave was dug up and her coffin opened. Once this had been done, she said she would spring from the coffin and sprint round North Berwick churchyard. The fastest runner in the parish, a blacksmith, was to give chase and grab hold of her; at this point she would be returned to mortal form. The weaver decided that it was just a dream and tried to forget about it, but the apparition reappeared. It pleaded with him to carry out the instructions and eventually said that if he failed to do so she would not return again. The weaver then confided his ghostly visitations with his minister, who listened carefully. The minister replied that he had no authority to open graves and that his late wife rested in peace. He advised the weaver to remarry as soon as possible; taking this advice, he did so and never saw the apparition again.

Haddington also has its own lady ghost, thought to be that of Catherine Charteris. She lurks, dressed in eighteenth-century costume, by the Abbey Bridge. This ghost has distinguished company: the duke of Lauderdale haunts St Mary's church and has been blamed for disturbing his own coffin in the crypt.

East Lothian was home to numerous religious houses and convents, so it is not surprising that the ghosts of monks and nuns have been seen. At Old Craighall (near Musselburgh) not only apparitions of monks have been witnessed but also that of a bishop and a woman in white. A ghostly nun has appeared in the vicinity of Trainer's Brae, North Berwick, where there was once a convent. In the wood at Luffness, where the scant remains of a Carmelite friary can be found, the ghost of a monk has been encountered.

One East Lothian ghost became the subject of a book. On the death of Mr Ogilvie, minister of Innerwick parish, papers were found in his desk describing his encounters with the ghost of a local landowner, Maxwell, laird of Coul. The laird died with a guilty conscience, having become rich by forging documents to cheat his relatives. On the night of 3 February 1722, the ghost appeared in front of Revd Ogilvie as he was heading home. The ghost realised that the minister was in such a state of shock that he would be unable to talk, so he said he would rendezvous with him later.

A month later, the laird's ghost appeared in front of the minister while he was on the road to Blarehead. The troubled ghost stated he had not yet appeared before God to be judged. The minister enquired whether people have guardian angels, to which the ghost replied that they do but also attendant devils. After this discussion the ghost vanished, only to reappear four weeks later by a ruin in Oldhamstocks; here he stated that he wished his widow to repay those he cheated. Ogilvie declared he did not wish to become involved and rode off. The ghost made a final appearance at Pease bay, Berwickshire, before vanishing forever. Mr Ogilvie never told anyone about the sightings but after his death, the ghostly encounters were published as *The Laird of Coul's Ghost*, based on his written records. It became a best-seller.

Goblins

Goblins are another supernatural entity with East Lothian associations. In Gifford main street is the long-established hotel, Goblin Ha' (*ha*, a hollow), which takes its name from a feature in the once-formidable castle of Yester, two miles to the south-east. The sparse ruins are hidden away in woodland, but there is a subterranean chamber, 37 feet long by 13 feet wide, which is still in good condition. As far back as the Middle Ages, concerns were expressed as to how it was created; Fordun, the medieval chronicler, stated it was formed by magical art. Sir Hugo de Gifford is thought to have been responsible for its creation in the thirteenth century. Despite being Alexander III's guardian, he was said to practise the dark arts, at times in the underground chamber. According to legend, he could raise a supernatural army to carry out his wishes in alliance with the Devil.

Goblins are credited with constructing Yester castle and the subterranean chamber giving it the name, 'Goblin hall'. The more mundane explanation is that it was built to ensure the stronghold had access to an underground water supply in times of a siege or simply as a place to store provisions.

Yester castle was still a significant stronghold in the sixteenth century, being fought over by Scottish and English forces during the siege of Haddington in 1548. In the following century it was abandoned and fell into ruin.

The Goblin Ha' hotel, Gifford.

TOWNS AND VILLAGES:
FROM ABERLADY
TO WHITTINGEHAME

ABERLADY

The picturesque village of Aberlady is located close to the point where the river Peffer empties into Aberlady bay. For many centuries it served as the port for Haddington, five miles to the south. It offered sheltered anchorage as the coast turns northward from this point and protects the bay from easterly gales and the stormy waters of the North Sea. Its name is thought to derive from the prefix *aber*, meaning the mouth of a river or the confluence of waters. 'Lady' is said to be derived from *Leddie*, the old name for the Peffer or a nearby stream; another explanation is that it refers to the church of Our Lady.

As far back as the Dark Ages, Aberlady was a place of some importance. Early church records refer to the diocese of St Cuthbert, centred on Norham, having a number of churches or monasteries located on the coast in the ninth or tenth centuries including Abercorn, Edinburgh, Pefferham, Auldhame, Tyninghame and Coldingham. The one at Pefferham is an early reference to Aberlady. There is evidence that it had important links to early Christianity, as it stood on a route tramped by monks from the monastery on Iona to Lindsfarne monastery on Holy island.

The remains of an eighth-century carved stone cross – now housed in the National Museum of Scotland – were unearthed at Aberlady; an impressive replica stands in the village gardens close to the church. A recent archaeological excavation revealed the foundations of a large wooden building standing close by, thought to have been an Anglo-Saxon palace or hall, dating from the time when the coast here formed the northern frontier of Northumbria.

On the opposite shore of the Firth of Forth was the kingdom of the Picts. Tradition has it that in ancient times the Culdees had a religious establishment at Aberlady connected with the Culdee monastery at Dundee. It was called Kilspindie, which in old British means 'the cell of the black heads or hoods'. In 1585, Patrick Douglas built Kilspindie castle, which stood between Aberlady village and the sea; only a few stones remain today.

In the Middle Ages, the lands of Aberlady, including the church, were under the authority of the bishop of Dunkeld. A toft (a house site and adjoining land) in the village was granted to the monks of Dryburgh by Bishop Richard in the early 1170s. A Carmelite friary was established a short distance to the east of the village and a few fragmentary remains

Aberlady parish church.

of its church survive. By contrast, the parish church stands prominently at the west edge of Aberlady; the oldest part being the tower, dating from the fifteenth century. In 1773, the rest of the structure was rebuilt, replacing a building that was a hundred feet long: this Georgian church was described as an ugly and ungainly structure; little trace of it remains. The present church dates from 1886, when it was rebuilt, and was described in a newspaper of the time as 'one of the finest ecclesiastical buildings in Scotland'. There is a good collection of eighteenth-century gravestones and table tops in the churchyard. At its entry there is a mounting stone, used by worshippers to mount their horses.

Adam Glass was minister at Aberlady but departed for London and became a member of the Church of England. He was the subject of a pamphlet published in that city in 1712, accusing him of insulting the Church of Scotland and denying that he ever had taken the confession of faith, although he had done so in front of hundreds of people at Aberlady. It made many other allegations, including neglect of ministerial duties, seldom visiting the sick and celebrating communion only three times in seven years. It also stated that he had a scandalous relationship with one woman while betrothed to another, played dice and cards and visited the homes of Catholics. If this was not enough, he had run up large debts, including to innkeepers for wine. Matters reached a head when he was denounced at the market cross. To avoid capture he hid in the abbey of Holyrood but still sometimes returned on Sundays to Aberlady to preach before departing for London.

The 'last thing one would associate with the inhabitants of this pretty English-looking village is that they should go down to the sea in ships'. It was, however, once a bustling commercial port, first mentioned in reign of Robert II (1371–90). There are no further records until the sixteenth century. In 1535, Haddington made £20 available to the kirk master to buy timber for the construction of a harbour at Aberlady. A beacon, the forerunner of the lighthouse, was erected in the bay in 1576.

In 1630, Haddington was gifted 600 merks by the convention of royal burghs to help repair the 'decayed' harbour of Aberlady. Further funds were made available in 1661 for three beacons, to be made of wood and placed on stone bases. Other than the beacons and a wooden pier, little investment was made to improve the harbour. Even so, it handled a wide variety of goods, including tar, lint, iron, kid skins, sheep skins, coal, salt, wheat, oats, peas, cod, skate and firewood. The main trading destinations were England, Flanders and Norway.

In the second half of the sixteenth century much of the timber imported at Aberlady was used in the construction of new buildings at Haddington, including mills and a town school. Sometimes entire tree trunks were unloaded from ships. In addition, large quantities of stone were quarried on the edge of Aberlady bay. In 1532–3, the inhabitants of Aberlady were instructed along with other burghs to send two horses with fish each 'fish day' to the Scottish army in the Borders. Another imposition on the village occurred in 1550 when all those who had suitable vessels were instructed to transport French soldiers back to France! A year earlier, a fort had been constructed around the medieval castle, a short distance to the east, where Luffness house now stands, to prevent the English garrison at Haddington receiving provisions through the harbour.

As ships increased in size, Aberlady harbour was at a disadvantage as the shallow waters of the bay were becoming increasingly silted-up. There was some recovery at the end of the Napoleonic Wars, but the construction of the railways during the nineteenth century was the last straw. In the second part of the nineteenth century, two trading sloops (the *Perseverance* and the *Eliza*) still sailed regularly to Leith to collect dung for the neighbouring farms. Skipper Thomson, who acted as a pilot to the last commercial vessels to use the harbour in the nineteenth century, vanished on a stormy night while out in his small boat. The only trace of him found was his wooden leg, retained by his wife until her dying day.

Today there is scant evidence that there was ever a harbour here. There is the former customs house, dating from 1710, near Aberlady Point and next to Kilspindie golf course. There are also the rotting remains of a number of nineteenth-century boats in the muddy shallows. A more permanent reminder is a ship carved on the side of an old house at the east end of the village, next to the main road where it turns towards the sea. There is the stump of a mercat cross not far from here in High Street. The village contains a number of single-storey cottages dating from the eighteenth century. There are also three rows of red-sandstone Gothic terraces, built by the Wemyss estate in the 1830s. Haddington Road also contains further examples of housing built by the Wemyss estate some fifty years later.

In 2011, Aberlady had a population of 1,514. As with other East Lothian villages most of its inhabitants work elsewhere. There are three golf courses in the vicinity and the Aberlady nature reserve, a short distance to the east, attracts many visitors. In the car park, next to the footbridge across the Peffer, there is a small memorial to author Nigel

Wooden footbridge across the Peffer burn at Aberlady bay.

Tranter (1909–2000), who wrote more than 140 works, including children's books and westerns. From childhood he was interested in Scottish castles and his first book, published in 1935, was on this subject. Not long after, he began to write novels on Scottish history, for which he became best known. Tranter spent much of his life in Aberlady, having moved here in 1938. He could often be spotted walking around Aberlady bay, inspiration for many of his works.

ATHELSTANEFORD

This attractive village stands on a low-lying ridge surrounded by rich agricultural land, three miles north-east of Haddington, with the Garleton hills lying between the two. The name originates from 'Athelstane', the commander of the Northumbian army, who was killed near here when his army was routed by Hungus, king of the Picts. According to legend, his remains were buried at the ford of Peffer burn, also known as the Cogtail.

Another less-dramatic theory as to the origin of the name is that *Ath-ail* in Gaelic is 'stone ford'. Until the nineteenth century, a narrow, stony path crossed the Lug Down burn. Anglo-Saxon settlers finding the 'Ath-ail' already in existence, added to the name in their own language, *stane ford*. Thus, the first and last portions of the name are identical in meaning but expressed in different languages. The lands on which the battle of Athelstaneford was fought and won were later gifted by the king of Scots to the Culdee priory of St Andrew in gratitude for the victory over the Northumbians. The village church stands at the western end of Athelstaneford; it dates from 1780 and is a modest structure with a bellcote on the western gable.

There has, however, been a church on this site since 1176 – *Ecclesia de Elstaneford* was said to have been founded by Countess Ada de Warenne, mother of William the Lion. The churchyard contains the flag heritage centre, consisting of a memorial next to which there is a tall flagpole flying the saltire. The cross of St Andrew was said to have appeared above the battlefield, inspiring the Picts and Scots to defeat the Northumbians in AD 832 and was later adopted as Scotland's national flag. The sixteenth-century dovecote at the back of the church has an interactive exhibition about the battle; it overlooks open fields sloping away to the north, on which the two Dark Ages armies fought.

Pantile cottages, Athelstaneford main street.

In 1799, Athelstaneford had four hundred inhabitants. It gained a new lease of life around this time when Sir David Kinloch encouraged rural craftsmen to settle here by granting them perpetual leases. Through to the end of the nineteenth century, weavers manufactured the much-valued coarse woollen cloth called 'Gilmerton grey'. The single-storey cottages, with pantile roofs, which stand on either side of the main street date from the early-nineteenth century although some may be older. The more recent houses are grouped at the east end of the village. Overlooking Athelstaneford are the ruins of Barnes castle, which stands on the eastern extremity of the Garleton hills.

Among the most notable residents of the parish was Sir John Hepburn, born here in 1598. After being educated at St Andrews, he travelled to Europe and became involved in the wars of religion in the Holy Roman Empire. Despite being a Catholic, he joined the Scottish contingent fighting for the Elector Palatine of Bohemia. When this army was disbanded, he served in the Swedish army of Gustavus Adolfus, fighting in Prussia, Hungary and Poland in command of a Scottish regiment. By 1631 this had expanded to four regiments, which fought successfully at the battles of Leipzig and Mentz. Despite this, while John Hepburn was camped at Nuremburg, King Adolfus insulted him for his Catholic faith; he retorted that he would never draw his sword for the Swedish monarch again. The following year he entered service with the French army. This large contingent of Scots became known as the *Régiment d'Hebron* and eventually evolved into the Royal Scots regiment. Hepburn was killed in 1636 while besieging Saverne; Cardinal Richelieu, who held him in great esteem, thought this a high price to pay for the town.

A more passive character was the portrait painter Archibald Skirving (1749–1819), born on his father's farm at East Garleton. He was a contemporary of Allan Ramsay and Henry Raeburn but never achieved their level of success, which was attributed to his eccentric nature; his best-known painting is a red-chalk portrait of Robert Burns. The earl of Wemyss became his patron during the 1780s when he was much in demand in Edinburgh. Skirving then spent some time with a community of Scots artists in Italy. On his return in 1794 he was detained and imprisoned by the French at Brest, accused of spying for the British. His friends petitioned for his release, claiming that they too had suffered from English tyranny. Eventually, Skirving was given his freedom, but during captivity he contracted an eye disease and was no longer able to paint miniatures. He died suddenly at Inveresk in 1819 and is buried alongside his father and grandfather in the churchyard at Athelstaneford.

One of the ministers of Athelstaneford church also achieved fame. John Home was born in Leith and graduated at Edinburgh in 1742. Three years later, he was fighting against the Jacobites. In 1746, he was taken prisoner and confined in Doune castle, but soon escaped. The following year he took up residence in Athelstaneford as parish minister and while living there wrote the play *Agis*, and later *Douglas*, based on a Scottish ballad. In 1756, *Douglas* was performed to great acclaim in the Canongate theatre, Edinburgh, such that a member of the audience is reputed to have cried out 'whaur's yer Wullie Shakespeare noo?' Home resigned from the ministry in 1757 following strong disapproval of the play by Edinburgh ministers. He served as private secretary to the earl of Bute and tutor to the Prince of Wales, later to become George III. In his later years he wrote a number of other plays including *The Fatal Discovery* and *Alonzo*, as well as a book on the Jacobite rebellion. He died in Edinburgh in 1808 and was buried in South Leith churchyard.

BOLTON

The hamlet of Bolton, with parish church.

This hamlet is found in farmland two miles south of Haddington. The Colstoun water flows along its southern edge for a short distance before it merges with the Tyne. A footpath follows the river upstream, along its wooded banks, and comes out a short distance to the north of Gifford. The name Bolton is said to be derived from *buaile* (an enclosure). There is an attractive church here dating from 1809, Gothic-style, with a pinnacled tower at its western extremity; the yellowish stone for the building came from Abbeymains quarry near Haddington. The present structure stands on the site of an earlier church, erected some time before 1244 and also long vanished is the original village that stood next to it. There was also a mansion house on its west side, some traces of which survived into the late-eighteenth century. Attached to it was an area of parkland, long referred to as The Orchard. The property was said to have belonged to John Hepburn, a friend of the notorious earl Bothwell, husband of Mary, Queen of Scots.

While these buildings have long gone, there are a number of monuments in the churchyard that predate the existing nineteenth-century structure. This includes the mausoleum for the Stuarts of Eaglescairnie, a country house, which stands on the banks of the

288

Colstoun water, a mile south-east of Bolton. In the centre of the churchyard stands one of the best-known gravestones in East Lothian, that of Robert Burns's mother, Agnes (Burns) Brown, who died in 1820 at the age of 88; his brother and sister are also memorialised here. Agnes outlived her famous son by more than two decades.

The family had moved from Ayrshire in 1800. Agnes (Burns) Brown lived with her other son, Gilbert, his wife, and eleven children, three of whom died at a young age and have their names also chiselled on the gravestone. Agnes Brown while living in Ayr employed Betsy Davidson, an elderly maidservant with great knowledge of East Lothian folklore. It is believed that the stories were passed on to Robert Burns and provided inspiration for his poetry, including 'Tam o' Shanter'.

Gilbert Burns was employed as a factor on the Lennoxlove estate by Lord Blantyre and was responsible for the planting of woods and other improvements. His large family lived in a two-storey thatched house at Grant's Brae on the Haddington–Bolton road. The building has long since gone but its site is marked by a memorial, Burns mother's well, which stands on the north side of the road next to a car park. The small number of houses at Bolton today stand clustered near the top of a hump in the landscape. An eighteenth-century cylindrical dovecote with a conical slated roof stands next to the road. Like many others across East Lothian, the adjoining stone farm buildings have been converted into homes.

COCKENZIE

This former fishing village stands immediately to the west of Port Seton, with which it has now merged; until the nineteenth century, they were two separate villages. Originally, Cockenzie was known as Cokeny Haven, a name derived from Cove of Kenneth or Covekenny. The powerful Seton family owned the harbour, which is recorded as being in existence in 1565. In 1591, James VI created the village 'Cowkainy', a free burgh of barony, in recognition of the work that Robert, Lord Seton, had done in constructing the harbour. It is thought that it was located at an inlet, which formed an ideal natural harbour at Boat Shore between Cockenzie and Port Seton.

Over the next century there was a brisk trade with Flanders to the extent that some local architecture mimicked Flemish styles. Fishing and salt-making were also important economic activities at Cockenzie. Around 1630, further improvements were made to the harbour but this work was later destroyed in a storm. At the beginning of the eighteenth century, the harbour was falling out of use because of the narrowness of its entrance. All this was about to change.

In 1715 the Seton family fell out of favour for supporting the Jacobites and the York Building Company took control of their extensive land holdings. It renovated Cockenzie harbour in 1722 and built a wooden wagonway from the coal mines at Tranent, a short distance to the south-west. It was one of the first harbours in the world to have been served by any form of railway. There are claims that the wagonway had been in existence since the late-sixteenth century. The present harbour dates from 1833, when it was constructed to a plan by engineers Robert Stevenson & Sons. The east and west breakwaters, comprised of red-sandstone blocks, enclosed the relatively small area of five acres. Shortly after it was completed, the harbour was handling 250 to 300 vessels a year, one-sixth of which were foreign.

There were also thirty fishing boats operating from the harbour. Many of the fishermen also crewed whaling vessels, which sailed from Leith and Newhaven. One of the men joined the search for Lord Franklin when he was reported missing while searching for the North-West Passage. By the 1880s, the number of vessels entering Cockenzie to fill their holds with coal was in serious decline. As the size of ships began to increase dramatically, the harbour became too small, but fishing boats continued to sail, catching cod, haddock and plaice. In winter, shoals of herring visited the Forth and were caught in nets.

Despite its small size, the harbour had a boatbuilding yard. During the Second World War it built motor launches and landing craft for the Admiralty and cabin cruisers for the War Office. After the war it specialised in fishing boats, although three minesweepers were built here from 1953–5. The last fishing boat, the *Sapphire*, was completed in 1969. In 1988 a replica of the *Charlotte Dundas*, reputed to have been the world's first steamship, was commissioned here. With the fishing industry in decline, the yard turned to working on small leisure craft, but it eventually closed. Flats have been put up on the site but as a tribute to the boatyard a stone carving has been installed on the harbour-facing side of the building.

Although the coal trade had long ceased by the second half of the twentieth century, the fossil fuel continued to play a major role in the

A colourful mural on the site of the former Cockenzie power station.

life of the village. In 1952, it was planned to replace Portobello power station; seven years later, construction started on a huge structure on ground immediately to the west of Cockenzie harbour. The new coal-fired power station began generating electricity in 1968. Until it was demolished in 2015, it was a major landmark, the two tall chimneys being visible from the Lammermuir hills. During the last decades of its operation it had the distinction of being one of only two coal-fired power stations operating in Scotland.

In contrast to this modern structure, the oldest building in the village is Cockenzie house, which fortunately is extant. It dates from the seventeenth century and was built by the Setons for their manager of the harbour and salt pans. William Caddell, who had set up a trading venture at Cockenzie with the Baltic ports, leased the house in 1732, along with the harbour and salt pans. The family eventually purchased the house and were associated with it for two hundred years; Bonnie Prince Charlie was entertained here shortly after the battle of Prestonpans. Francis Caddell, born at Cockenzie in 1822, travelled to Australia to set up the Murray Navigation Company. In 1867, he led an expedition to the Northern Territory to identify potential sites for settlements on behalf of the Australian government. He also became involved in whaling and pearl fishing, but met an untimely end when he was murdered by his crew in the Dutch East Indies in 1879.

Cockenzie house is now used by small businesses and local artists,

Cockenzie house, where none other than Bonnie Prince Charlie was entertained after the battle of Prestonpans.

but is also open to the public. In its gardens are a vaulted, gothic, grotto folly and two conical but ruinous gazebos. Cockenzie is centred on the village green, which stands next to the main road from Port Seton–Prestonpans. On its edge stand nineteenth century and later buildings.

DIRLETON

Sometimes described as the prettiest village in Scotland, Dirleton lies between Gullane and North Berwick in one of the most fertile parts of East Lothian. The origin of the name is uncertain. It could mean 'small town', originating from the Gaelic *direoil*, meaning small. A less likely explanation is that it is derived from 'Derili', a seventh-century Pictish king who is believed to have known St Baldred. Legend has it that around a mile to the east of Dirleton, at Kilmurdie, the Picts fought a minor battle with the Scots, who at that time controlled only the west of the country.

The village was once offered by John Ruthven as a bribe in the mysterious Gowrie conspiracy to tempt the assistance of Logan of Restalrig in what is believed to have been a plot to kill the king of Scotland. In one of his letters Logan states: 'I care not for all the other land of the Kingdom if I may get grip of Dirleton, for it is the pleasantest

Dirleton village green, with war memorial and parish church.

dwelling place in Scotland.' The plot failed and Sir Thomas Erskine slew two of the Ruthven brothers in defence of James VI. For this action he was rewarded with Dirleton castle and its lands, while Logan of Restalrig was lucky to escape with his life. By 1653, the castle had fallen into disrepair and was abandoned by its new owners, the Nisbets, who built Archerfield house as their residence.

Leaving aside the ruined castle, the oldest building in Dirleton is the parish church, which stands at the north tip of the village green. It is was constructed in 1612 when it was decided to move the parish church from Gullane, which was being overwhelmed with sand dunes. Permission was given to remove stone and timber from it to construct the new place of worship. Evidence was recently uncovered that prior to this there may have been a chapel next to the castle. Documents dating from the thirteenth century relate that there was a chapel of St Andrew, apparently founded by William de Vaux, as well as a further chapel dedicated to All Saints founded by his son. This was followed by a collegiate church established by Walter de Haliburton, 1st lord Haliburton of Dirleton. It was a far more modest establishment than the collegiate church of Seton. No trace of it remains.

The seventeenth-century church was built at the instigation of Thomas Erskine and Archerfield aisle was added in 1650, the first example of neoclassical design in Scotland. After the Reformation it was forbidden to bury people inside churches so the landed families often built aisles attached to churches or in some cases as standalones. More recent additions are the Gothic pinnacles on the tower, dating from 1836.

The churchyard has a number of notable memorials, some from the seventeenth century. There is a mural stone on the church wall to Revd James Glen, dating from 1749. A similar monument commemorates George and John Heriot, who lived at Castlemains in the seventeenth and eighteenth centuries, but the names are now illegible. One of the most ornamental examples belongs to Janet Seton, who died in 1749; on its front are mermaids and a grotesque face. By the nineteenth century, gravestones had become plainer with fewer decorations.

Located at the entrance to Dirleton parish church is the old school and schoolhouse. A short distance to the south, at the entrance to Archerfield estate, there is a nineteenth-century lodge house. It is named after the archers in the army of Edward I, said to have practised their skills here. The Castle inn – originally a nineteenth-century coaching inn – stands on the south-west corner of the village green. On the north side of the green is the Open Arms hotel, flanked on either side by cottages dating from the eighteenth and nineteenth centuries. Close to the main road, at the eastern edge of the village green, is the distinctive Vine cottage; it has gothic dormer windows and dates from the mid-nineteenth century.

A short distance to the south is the sixteenth-century gateway, which was formerly the entrance to Dirleton castle, but now leads to Castlemains farm, which has a long association with the village. In the 1820s, Mr Todd, its then owner, sent several men with carts to collect stones from the beach opposite Fidra island. They were caught unexpectedly by the rising tide, which engulfed the heavily loaded carts; two of the men and four horses were drowned. A less serious hazard was a troubled gentleman called Sandy Gibb who believed he was made of glass and often stood still in the middle of the road for fear of falling to pieces. When someone approached, he would ask them to give him a shove and he then continued on his way.

Along the south edge of Dirleton village green is an impressive wall with a two-storey tower at one end, built in the early-nineteenth century.

It encloses the gardens adjoining the castle, which date from the late-nineteenth and early-twentieth centuries. The formal Victorian west garden was reconstructed in 1993 and the north garden dates from the Art and Crafts movement of the 1920s. The castle gardens boast the longest herbaceous border in the world with a length of just over 700 feet.

In the early-twenty-first century, Dirleton's population was around five hundred. Surrounded by fertile agricultural land, the village primarily housed agricultural workers for most of its existence but now most residents work elsewhere.

DREM

The hamlet of Drem (population approximately one hundred) is located at the edge of the fertile northern plain. To the south are the slopes of the Garleton hills. Drem is said to be derived from *druim* (a ridge). It is shown as 'Dam' on at least one seventeenth-century map. In the Middle Ages the land belonged to the Knights Templar. Although there are the scant remains of St John's chapel (not accessible) the Templars probably did not have a significant presence here, as some sources suggest. Despite being granted the status of burgh of barony in 1616, and later being on a main road, the settlement failed to develop to any size.

Drem gave its name to an important wartime airfield, a mile to the north. Spitfires flew from here in defence of Edinburgh and Rosyth naval base. The main component of the hamlet is a row of single-storey 1830 pantiled cottages on the edge of a small green. The Edinburgh–London main line forms the southern boundary and, despite its size, Drem still has its own station. The junction with the branch line to North Berwick is a short distance east.

DUNBAR

Dunbar is the largest town on the North Sea coast in south-east Scotland. In 2020 its population was 9,400. The name comes from the Gaelic *dun-barr*, meaning the fort on the point. Since prehistoric times there has been a settlement here. The rocky outcrop, surrounded by the sea on three sides next to the harbour, made it an ideal defensive site.

The headland has been fortified since the Iron Age, when there were ditches and palisades. By the time of the Roman occupation the extent of the area enclosed by defences had increased, while the Middle Ages saw the construction of a formidable stone castle.

The history of the town revolves around its strategic defences, particularly the castle. It had an important role because of its position on one of the main routes used by invading English armies. Unfortunately, little survives either of the once-important castle or any other buildings from the town's early history. (The story of Dunbar castle is covered in the chapter entitled Castles.)

Although no trace of Belhaven harbour remains, its legacy lives on in these old houses, which were probably built with the wealth it created.

Dunbar's history has also closely revolved around its harbours. The first harbour was located at Belhaven bay, a short distance to the west of the town. Situated at the mouth of the Biel water, it offered a sheltered anchorage protected from the worst ravages of the North Sea. It is mentioned in twelfth-century records, when the earl of Dunbar controlled it. In the Middle Ages, it exported wool and hides, but ships called here infrequently. There is now little evidence that there was ever a harbour on this attractive part of the coast. Belhaven bay, like many other river mouths, silted up over the centuries. There is a small group of old houses dating from the eighteenth and nineteenth centuries, by which time Belhaven harbour was little used.

The present site of Dunbar harbour dates back to medieval times, when it was little more than a tidal anchorage sheltered by the castle rock. During times of siege, the castle was supplied by sea to thwart attempts at starving the garrison into submission. The harbour was also an important base for supplying the Scottish navy. The first steps were taken to construct man-made breakwaters at the beginning of the seventeenth century.

In 1655, the harbour was damaged by stormy seas. The Parliament, then under the control of Cromwell, granted funds for the east pier of what is now known as the old harbour or Cromwell's harbour. During 1785 the west pier was built but the following year the French traveller, Alexandre de la Rochefoucauld, remarked that it would be very dangerous to enter in stormy weather, as the boats would have to be towed in. The harbour was entered through a narrow gap in the rock. Once inside there was a wall on the seaward side providing protection from rough water. The space inside the harbour was described as being very limited, enough for only seven or eight small ships. Despite this, Dunbar's merchants traded successfully: wood, iron and flax were all unloaded on the quays while agriculture produce was exported. A customs house was built in 1710, but smugglers continued to land contraband goods such as tobacco on remote stretches of the coast.

In the mid-eighteenth century, the East Lothian and Merse Whale Fishing Co, founded in 1752, had five vessels based here that voyaged as far as Greenland. From 1785, Dunbar High Street was lit by whale oil. Whaling became unprofitable not long after and the company ceased its activities. The original whalebones forming the arch on North Berwick Law came from the jaws of a whale caught by a vessel based at Dunbar.

At the end of the eighteenth century, a dry dock was constructed and there was a customs house employing seven men. Smuggling was rife. There were eight ships employed in the coastal trade and a further eight in foreign trade. In addition, a further twelve fishing boats were based at the harbour. Just over forty years later, in 1835, there were fifteen small cargo ships involved in the coastal trade, but only three cargo ships employed in foreign trade. Imports to Dunbar harbour included wheat and barley, which was also exported from here. Coal was also imported. Just over twenty foreign ships called at the port in 1834. The New, or Victoria, harbour, now the main harbour, was built immediately to the west of the old one in 1842. It involved the construction of a new entrance, which required cutting a passage through the rock on which the ruins of the castle stand, inflicting further damage.

Dunbar old (or Cromwell's) harbour, which dates from the seventeenth century.

Fishing for herring in late summer was important; in 1855, five hundred Dunbar boats were involved. There is a stone statue commemorating the creel loaders a short distance from the harbour in Victoria Street. In the early-twenty-first century, fishing boats still operate from here, but most of the masts in the harbour belong to leisure craft. Several original eighteenth-century warehouses have been converted into flats and still stand today in the narrow streets adjoining the harbours; a former grain warehouse, now renovated, stands at the east end of Victoria harbour. At the edge of the old seventeenth-century harbour (also known as Cromwell's harbour) stands the fishermen barometer, erected in 1856: a 15-foot, ashlar-stone monument put up as a memorial to the town's fishermen, it houses a mercury barometer. Fishermen storm barometers were introduced to Scotland by vice-admiral Robert Fitzroy to prevent lives being lost at sea from unexpected storms and were placed at a number of harbours along the coast. The example at Dunbar was funded by public subscription.

Little remains of the medieval religious buildings. Dunbar parish church is located at the far south end of the town. Standing on top of gently rising ground and built of red sandstone, this attractive building can be seen from several miles away. In the past it acted as a landmark for sailors. The church is rectangular, with a tower over 100 feet tall. It was built 1818–21 in the Gothic style, incorporating battlements. The building was gutted by fire in 1987 and had to be extensively rebuilt. Although the interior is modern it contains an impressive statue of the last earl of Dunbar, George Home (1605–11).

The parish churchyard is protected by a watch house erected to deter body snatchers. Some of the gravestones date from the seventeenth century. As with many other East Lothian parish churches, the present church stands on an ancient site of religious worship. There has been a parish church in Dunbar since at least 1176, when it was dedicated to the semi-mythical St Bees, whose cult centred on the Cumbrian coast. In 1342, it became a collegiate church, but, after the Reformation in 1560, it reverted to parish church. In 1739, a spire was added but by the early-nineteenth century the building was deemed unsuitable and torn down, replaced by the present church.

It is thought that a medieval hospital occupied a site a short distance west of the parish church near Abbey Road, but there is no trace today. It was probably staffed by the monastery of Red, or Trinity, friars, and founded around 1240. Only the monastery's modest church tower survives, to the south of Delisle Street, a short distance from High Street. Recent excavations have uncovered a patterned tile floor from the Netherlands and part of a graveyard. Pilgrims on their way to St Andrews would likely have stayed at the monastery.

Like many other Scottish towns, Dunbar rapidly expanded from the nineteenth century onwards. Before this it would have consisted of little more than a high street, with buildings clustered around it. In 1768, its limits were defined by three gates or ports – one at the West Port, one at the south end of

Dunbar tolbooth, said to be Scotland's oldest council building still in use.

High Street and one at its east entry. High Street retains much of its late-eighteenth-century character. The oldest building is the distinctive town house (or tolbooth), a white-painted building dating from the sixteenth century, renaissance in style. The wood-framed spire, a rarity in Scotland, and the crow-stepped gable on the south wall are due to Dutch influence. The tolbooth served as the local prison and today is known as the Dunbar town house museum and gallery. It is run by East Lothian Council's museum service, incorporating a small museum of local history, and it hosts many exhibitions and events. It is reputed to be the oldest local-authority building still in use in Scotland.

Lauderdale house, of 1734, sits in High Street, Dunbar.

Standing on the right side of the tolbooth is an old mercat cross, which has been altered from its original form and is not its original position. On the opposite side of the road, in the West Port, are several early-eighteenth-century houses, some with pantiled roofs. A quarter of a mile long, High Street is dominated by Lauderdale house at its northern end. This large building of red sandstone was built around 1734 by Captain James Fall. It is rather an unusual location for a property that in many ways aspires to be a country house. Local tradition has it that the remains of a church were discovered when its foundations were being dug. In 1788, Robert Fall was obliged to sell due to financial problems and it was purchased by the earl of Lauderdale, who added two wings. In 1859, it was sold to the government and over the next century was used as a barracks. A large statue of a sphinx sits on the roof, watching over High Street.

John Muir, the pioneer conservationist, was born in Dunbar in 1838 and is among the best-known citizens of East Lothian. There is a statue of him as a boy standing in front of the old town house in High Street. The family home where he spent his childhood is a short distance away on the opposite side of the street; the building has been restored and turned into a small museum commemorating his life and legacy. Its exterior has a distinctive whitewash finish.

John Muir's father, Daniel, a religious zealot and former army-recruiting sergeant, ruled the family with a rod of iron. The boy began to develop an interest in the great outdoors when his grandfather took him for walks in Lord Lauderdale's gardens and the coast of East Lothian was also a great attraction. When Muir was eleven his family emigrated to America, settling in Winconsin, where they had a farm in the backwoods. Between 1859 and 1863, he attended the University of Wisconsin, initially reading medicine, which held little interest. He studied a number of other subjects but left without graduating.

During the American Civil War of 1861–5, Muir lived in Canada, and, on his return to the United States he took up work as a machinist in Indianapolis. He lost the sight of his right eye in an accident and for a time was blind in both eyes. However, the vision in his left eye returned, a development he may have ascribed to divine intervention because it was at this time that he developed strong religious beliefs. During this period, he went on many walking trips through the Midwest and into Canada; one was a thousand-mile trek from Indianapolis to the Gulf of Mexico.

In 1868, Muir travelled to California and worked on a sheep ranch and from 1869–73 he lived in the largely uncharted Yosemite valley, which he explored on foot, researching the complex geology and producing highly influential fieldwork. Muir was also a keen botanist and did much to help with the scientific classification of plants and trees, a particular favourite being the giant redwoods in Yosemite, some more than two thousand years old. He found time to indulge another passion, mountaineering, and some were of the opinion that he was the best climber in America. He climbed alone, with minimal food and equipment, scaling one Sierra Nevada peak after another, including Mount Whitney, the highest at 14,500 feet.

The journals and other writings produced by Muir on geology and botany became increasingly influential. Many distinguished academics and writers visited him in the Sierra Nevada, including poet and essayist

Ralph Waldo Emerson, one of the most influential thinkers in America. Muir argued that the still-pristine landscapes of the West should be carefully preserved and, thanks largely to his efforts, national parks such as Yosemite, Grand Canyon and Petrified Forest were established.

After marrying in 1880, Muir moved to Martinez, near San Francisco, where he managed a large fruit ranch owned by his new wife. It was here that he wrote his major books, works such as *The Yosemite*, *A Thousand-Mile Walk to the Gulf* and *Our National Parks*. He also continued to campaign on environmental matters and in 1892 founded the Sierra Club, an important conservation organisation. Muir was by now the leading voice in America for national parks and the environment. In 1903 he camped out in Yosemite with President Theodore Roosevelt. Muir received honorary degrees from the universities of Harvard, Yale, California and Wisconsin. He died in 1914, having returned once to Dunbar, where he visited many of the locations that had inspired his love of nature.

Appropriately, some of East Lothian's most attractive coastline is now included in the John Muir country park. It extends westwards from Dunbar to the mouth of the Tyne then north along golden beaches towards the river Peffer. There is also the John Muir long-distance footpath. Initially, it was confined to East Lothian, but to commemorate the centenary of his death, was extended west as far as the Firth of Clyde. The 134-mile route starts, appropriately, at Dunbar. In 2019, a 16-foot sculpture of a bear was erected on the south side of Dunbar, close to the A1, as a tribute to Muir. It has been christened the 'Dunbear'.

At the south-west corner of Victoria harbour, close to the ruins of the castle, there is a ship's propeller weighing four tons, painted black. It serves as a monument to another of Dunbar's notable residents, **Robert Wilson**. He was born in 1803 at The Shore, Dunbar, the son of Benjamin Wilson, a sailor and cooper. At the age of seven he lost his father when disaster struck the Dunbar lifeboat during a rescue attempt. His mother then moved to the countryside to make a living. Young Robert was close enough to return to Dunbar to study the journals held in the library of the Mechanic's Institute. While rowing boats in the harbour, Robert had pondered on methods of ship propulsion. Later in life, while working in Edinburgh as an engineer, he continued to experiment. With the backing of James Maitland, earl of Lauderdale, and the Highland Society he gave a demonstration of a working model in 1828. Further successful experiments were carried out in 1832 using an 18-

foot boat, which was propelled from the stern. The Admiralty was not impressed, persisting with paddle wheels for their steam-driven vessels.

Robert Wilson was not the only inventor working on ways of improving ship propulsion. Francis Pettit Smith approached Isambard Kingdom Brunel with a similar idea, which Brunel adopted for his ship the *Great Britain*. Soon after, in 1840, the Admiralty also decided to adopt screw propellers. It is not clear where Smith got his inspiration, but it appears that he, Wilson and several other engineers reached similar conclusions at about the same time. Robert Wilson moved to England and became manager of Bridgewater foundry, owned by Edinburgh-born James Nasmyth, inventor of the steam hammer. Wilson went on to improve the steam engine, as well as taking out patents for valves, pistons and other hydraulic machinery. Perhaps somewhat bitter that he did not get the credit he felt he deserved for the invention dearest to his heart, he published a pamphlet in 1860 entitled *The Screw Propeller – Who Invented It?* Two years later, the War department somewhat belatedly paid him £500 (£30,000 in 2020) for the use of his double-action screw propeller in what was then called the 'fish torpedo', later to be known simply as the torpedo. Robert Wilson died in England in 1882. A memorial to him at Dunbar was proposed as early as 1936, but it was not until 2003 that the ship's propeller was unveiled as a tribute to this innovative engineer.

EAST LINTON AND PRESTONKIRK

East Linton from the south.

East Linton stands on the lower reaches of the Tyne, at a rocky outcrop in the river. This creates a small waterfall, or linn, from which the village takes its name. It is referred to as East Linton, distinguishing it from West Linton in the Scottish Borders. The rapidly flowing water once powered mills, but in medieval times it was also an obstacle to travel. The main route from Edinburgh–England originally crossed the Tyne at a ford upstream near Hailes castle. This changed in the early-sixteenth century when a bridge, still in use today, was constructed at East Linton. For the next five centuries the village remained a fixture on the Great North Road.

Situated on a hillock above the Tyne at the east end of the village is Prestonkirk parish church. The village was originally known as Linton, then Haugh, with 'Prestonkirk' being adopted after the Reformation. It is one of three places in which St Baldred's body is said to be buried and a church that may have already been in existence at that time was dedicated to him. Jocelyn of Furness, who in 1185 wrote the hagiography of St Mungo (or St Kentigern), mentions that his mother, Princess Theneva, worshipped here. Furthermore, she relates that Mungo gave the charge of the churches of Prestonkirk, Tyninghame and Whitekirk to Baldred in the late-sixth century. The first documented evidence dates from 1127. Blahan was the priest at Prestonkirk, but nothing remains of the early Norman church in which he preached. The chancel housing the altar was added to the nave in the early-thirteenth century and dedicated by the Bishop Davide de Bernham in 1240. Fortunately, it survives today. Around that time, the Red Friars established a mission at Berwick, followed by a number of others, including one at Houston that stood a short distance from Prestonkirk parish church.

Alexander III confirmed the endowment of the friary in a charter of 1271–2 and may have visited the site. Being on the route of invading English armies, the buildings in the vicinity of East Linton would have suffered the ravages of both English and Scottish armies. In 1322, as Edward II marched north at the head of a large army, Robert the Bruce laid waste to much of countryside and its castles to deprive the English of supplies and shelter. When Henry Hotspur invaded Scotland in 1401, the villages of Hailes, Traprain and Markle and their granges were destroyed with the assistance of the earl of Dunbar. The English camped in the vicinity of Prestonkirk, but the following morning were taken by surprise by a Scottish army that had marched from Edinburgh castle. The English army upped stakes and fled towards Berwick-upon-Tweed.

Southern Scotland again suffered the ravages of English armies in 1544 and 1545 during the Rough Wooing. The village of Markle, on the edge of what is now East Linton, was destroyed once more. Two years later, the English army returned and on its way to Edinburgh passed through the area. It delivered a decisive defeat to the Scottish force at Pinkie in 1547 and then proceeded to erect a series of forts to consolidate its gains. The supply line to the large garrison at Haddington extended from Berwick through East Linton. The bridge across the Tyne was strongly contested, but it was only in the latter stages of the siege of Haddington that the structure was made unusable by French forces who were supporting the Scots.

During the sixteenth century a very distinguished priest lived in Prestonkirk. Born at Tantallon castle around 1474, **Gavin Douglas** was the third son of 5th earl Douglas, known as 'Bell the Cat'. He was educated for the priesthood at St Andrews and then attended the University of Paris. After ordination, he was first a clergyman at Monymusk in Aberdeenshire and then at Prestonkirk. In 1503, he left the parish to become provost of St Giles, Edinburgh. Gavin Douglas later became bishop of Dunkeld, but not before spending a year in prison on a trumped-up charge under an old statute for receiving Papal bulls. He was best known for his poems, many of which have been lost, and for his translation of Virgil's *Aeneid*, the first version of the Latin poem published in English. His life was brought to an abrupt end when he died in 1522 from the bubonic plague while in London.

The medieval church at Prestonkirk was demolished in 1770 and rebuilt, except for its square bell tower, which dates from 1631 and is extant. Further modifications were made to the building in 1881 and 1882, and new windows were added. There is another more recent church in the centre of East Linton; it was built in 1879 and is the most prominent building in the main street. Most of the buildings in the vicinity date from the nineteenth century and are constructed from red whinstone or grey, pink or yellow sandstones. A century earlier, East Linton consisted of little more than a single street with a few houses and cottages. At the end of the eighteenth century, expansion began in earnest when land was feued and houses were built at Brown's Place on what was then the northern edge of the village. Some of these buildings survive.

Over the next century it grew rapidly as a market centre surrounded by some of the most productive arable farmland in Scotland. By 1827 it was described as 'the handsome and populous village of Linton'. At one time there were no less than five watermills next to the waters flowing over the Linn. Although these have long ceased functioning, a number of the buildings in Mill Wynd have been converted into houses. There were busy weekly corn and cattle markets held in the main square. Towards the end of the nineteenth century it had fifty shops, an inn and twelve pubs. Labourers from as far away as Ireland often gathered in the village hoping to be hired for work on the surrounding farms.

In the second half of the nineteenth century, the picturesque village of East Linton and surrounding landscapes inspired **John Pettie** to become an artist. His parents bought a grocery shop in the village when he was thirteen and he spent much of his spare time painting. In 1859, at the age of twenty, he had one of his works displayed at the Scottish Academy, soon followed by another being hung at the Royal Academy in London. Many of his paintings were inspired by the novels of Sir Walter Scott or historical events. They include *The Flag of Truce*, *The Jacobites* and *An Arrest for Witchcraft*. In 1862, John Pettie moved to London and worked from a studio in Pimlico. He also took time to help other young Scottish painters who arrived in the city at the start of their careers.

Charles Martin Hardie was born in East Linton in 1858. At the age of seventeen he became a student at the Royal Scottish Academy. John Pettie, a relative, had encouraged him to paint. Unlike his mentor, he remained in Scotland, living in North Queensferry. Many of his pictures were also of historical scenes but others included portraits of Lord Balfour of Burleigh and the Very Reverend John Gillespie, now in the Scottish National Portrait Gallery. Charles Martin Hardie died suddenly in 1916 and is buried in Prestonkirk churchyard.

Like John Pettie, **Arthur Melville** moved to East Linton with his parents when he was a child. He initially worked in a grocer's shop there but later moved to Edinburgh to study art and in 1878 went to the *Académie Julian* in Paris. There he painted in watercolour and soon became one of Scotland's leading artists in this medium. His works were not unlike those of the Impressionists. He spent two years travelling in the Middle East, North Africa and Spain. Melville died in 1904, at the age of forty-nine, from typhoid.

In contrast, **Robert Noble** moved to East Lothian from Edinburgh and spent thirty years painting pictures of the river Tyne and East Lothian landscapes. He had studied art at the Trustees school in Edinburgh, and then, like many other young artists, visited Paris where he had several exhibitions of his landscapes. By 1900, East Linton had become a popular summer destination for other artists, who could be seen with their easels sitting next to the Tyne.

East Lothian's notable residents are not confined to artists. **Andrew Meikle** was born in 1719 and spent his childhood in the vicinity of Saltoun. His father had installed a mill there, which he had copied after visiting Holland, for the stripping of husks from barley. Meikle moved to Houston mill on the Phantassie estate, close to East Linton. Encouraged by the local landowner, George Rennie, he invented a threshing machine that could separate corn from straw. Sheaves of corn were fed into fluted rollers and onto a revolving drum, equipped with a beater to remove the grain. Initially it was powered by horse but soon it was harnessed to windmills. Andrew Meikle had also devised ways of making windmills work more efficiently by installing fantails, which kept the mill sails rotating at right angles to the direction of the wind. Later his threshing machine was adapted to be powered by steam. Although Meikle lived to the age of ninety-two, his revolutionary inventions made him little money. He was buried in the churchyard at Prestonkirk.

By 2011, East Linton's population had risen to around 1,700, although it had lost much of its importance as a market centre. The sixteenth-century bridge is still in use today but the former Great North Road, now the A1, bypasses the village a short distance to the south.

EAST SALTOUN AND WEST SALTOUN

Unlike some other East Lothian villages hidden away on low-lying ground, East Saltoun occupies a prominent position near the top of a gently sloping ridge, 460 feet above sea level. The origin of the name is uncertain. It could be derived from Nicolas de Soulis, or Soules, a contender for the Scottish crown in 1291. The village is said to have been originally known as Soulistoun, and, by abbreviation, Soultoun, which eventually became corrupted to Saltoun or Salton. Incidentally, the suffix 'toun' or 'ton' did not refer to a town but to a farm or farm settlement. East Saltoun was also known as Kirkton at one time. West Saltoun, a mile to the west, is a much smaller settlement than its counterpart, consisting of a few houses on either side of a minor road.

The first reference to Saltoun occurs during the twelfth century, when it was owned by the affluent and powerful Anglo-Norman family of De Morvilles, which held the hereditary title of Lord High Constable of Scotland down through a number of generations. Hugh de Morville was famed for his patronage of religious establishments, founding Dryburgh abbey in Roxburghshire around 1150. The lands of Herdmanston lay within the manor of Saltoun and were granted by Richard de Morville to his sheriff, Henry de St Clair, in 1162. One of Henry's descendants was Sir William St Clair, a staunch supporter of Robert the Bruce, who was awarded an engraved sword for his part in the battle of Bannockburn. It remained in the family until it was stolen in the early-nineteenth century. The St Clairs built a castle at Herdmanston, located on the banks of the Tyne, 1.5 miles north of East Saltoun; later, parts of it were incorporated into Herdmanston house. During the Second World War it was used to billet Polish soldiers, but, shortly thereafter, it was abandoned and left derelict. By the late 1960s it had become a ruin, and, despite the fact that parts of it were eight hundred years old, was demolished with explosives.

During the reign of Alexander III (about 1280) the greater part of the manor of Saltoun appears to have been owned by William de Abernethy. In 1445, his descendants acquired the title of lords of Saltoun of Abernethy. Saltoun hall, a massive gothic-style country house dating mainly from 1817, stands on what would have been the site of their castle (no public access). The family continued to live here until 1643, when the estate was sold by Alexander, 9th lord of Saltoun, to Sir Andrew Fletcher, a judge in the Court of Session.

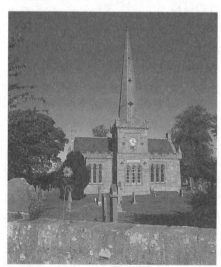

East Saltoun parish church of 1805.

Although the current parish church of East Saltoun dates from only 1805, it occupies a site near the heart of the village where there has been a place of religious worship since at least 1246. The present building was commissioned by John Fletcher Campbell 'as a monument to the virtues of his ancestors'. It is a small church, but has a very tall, thin spire.

In the cemetery are some gravestones that predate the present church. At the road junction in front of the church there is another monument to a member of the Fletcher family – a fountain carved in granite and Portland stone, topped by a group of angels. Dating from 1903, it commemorates John Fletcher. Most of the residences of East Saltoun are on a road that descends towards Pencaitland. They consist of the school house at the northern extremity and a house known as the 'Old Castle'. There is also a row of pantiled cottages, close to the church, dating from the early-nineteenth century. The manse, of 1802, stands near the top of the street on its east side. In 2000, the population of East Saltoun was around four hundred.

Of all the Fletchers associated with Saltoun, **Andrew Fletcher** is by far the best known; indeed, to many Scots he is a national hero. He was born at Saltoun hall in 1655, heir to Sir Robert Fletcher. His father died when he was 10 and parish minister Gilbert Burnet became responsible for his education. Later, he went on to describe his pupil as 'a Scotch gentleman of great parts and many virtues, but a most violent republican and extremely passionate'. In 1678, Fletcher was elected to represent Haddingtonshire in the Scottish Parliament and here his patriotic sentiments came to the surface. He was soon in conflict with the King's representative in Scotland, the duke of Lauderdale, whom he berated for the harsh treatment of the Covenanters.

It was only a matter of time before Fletcher was charged with treason and forced to flee. While on board a Dutch vessel bound for Holland, he is reputed to have thrown the captain overboard because he was smoking his pipe, an activity Andrew Fletcher disapproved of. While in Holland, he plotted with fellow exiles to overthrow the newly crowned James in the Monmouth rebellion. Back in England, he argued with the mayor of Taunton, a loyal Monmouth supporter, and shot him dead. He then fled to Spain.

In the meantime, the rebellion led by the duke of Monmouth was crushed. Agents of James II tracked down Fletcher and arrested him. He managed to escape their clutches and this time fled to Hungary, where he fought as a mercenary against the Turks. While he was abroad, his estate at Saltoun was confiscated and he was sentenced to death for treason *in absentia*. In 1688 he returned to Britain with William of Orange's invading army. It successfully overthrew James II, who was forced to flee abroad in what became known as the Glorious Revolution. Fletcher had his lands restored.

Fletcher believed the power of the monarch should now be limited. Furthermore, he set about creating a Scottish home-rule party. At the same time, the push for union between Scotland and England was gaining momentum. Fletcher backed the Darien scheme as he saw it as a means of asserting Scotland's independence. However, this ill-conceived attempt to establish a Scottish colony in Panama ended in disaster and had the effect of making Scotland more financially dependent on England. Fletcher drafted a bill that would have granted home rule to Scotland after the death of Queen Anne. It included measures to establish a Scottish army and to curb the powers of the monarch; not surprisingly, it was thrown out by the Scottish parliament. Fletcher was so annoyed with a number of the Scottish lords for favouring Scotland's union with England that he unsuccessfully challenged them to duels.

Social reform was another of his interests, but his ideas were so extreme that they were never adopted. One was that the 100,000 beggars and vagrants in Scotland should be taken into government service and put to work, effectively as slaves. Criminals were to be deported and employed as galley slaves to fight the Turks. At the last meeting of the Scottish Parliament, before it was abolished and the politicians moved to London, he declared that: 'It [Scotland] is only fit for the slaves who sold it.' His vocal opposition to the Act of Union, 1707, earned him the sobriquet, the Patriot.

After the Union of Scotland with England, Fletcher turned his back on public life and devoted his final years to improving his estate at Saltoun. He died in London in 1716 on his way home to Saltoun and was buried in the family vault in Saltoun parish church. A bronze plaque on the building commemorates his life: 'In memory of Andrew Fletcher of Saltoun. 1655–1716. Commissioner in the last Scottish Parliament. A Patriot who stood fearlessly for the interests of his Country.'

While living in Holland, Andrew Fletcher had become interested in mills that separated the husks from barley, a job performed manually in Scotland. In 1710, he returned to that country with James Meikle, a local millwright, to obtain the necessary ironwork for a similar mill at Saltoun. James Meikle's son Andrew is better known than his father for devising improvements to agricultural machinery and improving the operation of windmills.

East Saltoun was also the birthplace of **Alexander Muirhead**. In the 1850s, he moved with his parents to London. Here he struggled to have his broad Scots accent understood and was educated privately. He then studied at University College, London, where he is credited with recording the first electro-cardiogram of a human heart. On graduating, he worked for his father's firm, which specialised in cable telegraphy. Alexander patented an invention for 'duplexing' telegraph signals transmitted by submarine cables. This enabled messages to be transmitted and received at the same time.

Not content with sending messages down cables, Muirhead collaborated with Sir Oliver Lodge to build a simple radio that in 1894 transmitted messages between two Oxford buildings. Further experiments were made in which information was sent over the air using Morse code, now regarded as the first radio transmissions in the world. Although Marconi is generally given the credit for this, his invention was patented after that of Lodge and Muirhead. The Italian had heard of the work of these two men, but unlike them received the backing of the Admiralty and the Post Office for his experiments. There then followed a protracted legal dispute between the two parties concerning the patents. Only when Marconi agreed to buy the patent of Lodge and Muirhead, was he free to develop his business and make the 'wireless' a commercial success. The two original inventors faded into the background. Alexander Muirhead died in 1920.

ELPHINSTONE

Elphinstone is a village located two miles south of Tranent, on the southern slopes of the Tranent–Garleton ridge. At a height of four hundred feet, it has commanding views over the surrounding countryside. The name 'Elphinstone' is said to be derived from 'town on the hill'.

By 2020, the village's population was 430. There are few buildings of any age, as many of the old houses have been replaced in recent times. Two large coal mines – Limeylands and Fleets – once stood within a mile of the village, but they had closed by the 1960s, as had the railways that served them. A short distance to the west of the village there was once an early chapel. Beyond it stood Elphinstone tower, constructed in the fifteenth century or possibly earlier; standing nearly 60 feet on the top of a hill, it was a local landmark. It had a crack that extended its full length, and, according to local belief, this appeared the night Protestant preacher George Wishart was detained therein. Here he encountered Cardinal Beaton, who would have him burnt at the stake. In fact, the crack was probably caused by subsidence from old mine workings. In the mid-twentieth century, it was decided to demolish one of Scotland's best surviving examples of a tower house because it was thought to be in a dangerous state.

GARVALD

Garvald, tucked away at the foot of the Lammermuir hills. The last snows of winter blanket the hills, but summer is not far away.

This small village is hidden away in a narrow valley at the northern edge of the Lammermuir hills, 450 feet above sea level. Garvald means 'rough burn'. The settlement is five miles south of East Linton and six miles south-east of Haddington. It is little more than a single, narrow street. The older houses are constructed out of attractive red-sandstone rock and have pantiled roofs. This type of stone was formed when the region was a desert with sand, hundreds of million years ago.

The stream with an unusual name, Papana water, runs along the southern edge of the village before flowing into a number of other watercourses, then reaching the sea at Belhaven bay. Immediately to its south, the land rises steeply. In 1755, the Papana water overflowed its banks and flooded the village to a depth of 3 feet. At the end of the eighteenth century the population of the village was around two hundred. There were numerous sandstone quarries being worked at that time, one only six hundred feet from the village. There were also no less than four inns, as Garvald was on a well-used route across the Lammermuir hills. Goods that had been smuggled ashore at such places as Aberlady were sometimes hidden in the countryside around the village.

When the railway to Gifford opened in the early-twentieth century, families, many from Leith, made the short journey from the railhead to Garvald for summer holidays. The last of its sandstone quarries – which had supplied building stone to many of East Lothian's landmark buildings, including St Mary's church, Haddington – closed at this time. There are around sixty-five houses in the village, some of the cottages dating from the eighteenth century. At the west end there is the former Free church of 1845, its short tower crowned by a slated spire. The building now serves as the village hall. In 1703, Garvald was united with the adjacent parish of Baro. The church at the latter was demolished and no trace of it remains.

The current parish church is hidden away at the east end of Garvald. Some of the stonework in the north-west corner of the building dates from the twelfth century. At that time, the church and lands in the area belonged to the convent at Haddington. Nunraw lies a short distance to the south, but there is little evidence that nuns had any significance presence in the area. The north aisle of Garvald church dates from 1677 and there is a sundial from the same century on the south wall. In 1829, the building was extensively rebuilt with Gothic windows being added giving it its present appearance.

GIFFORD

Gifford is the largest and most important of the villages on the northern edge of the Lammermuir hills. It is 340 feet above sea level, four miles south-east of Haddington. The present village is relatively recent in origin, dating from the early-eighteenth century, and was one of the first planned villages in Scotland.

The original settlement was a short distance further up the valley of the Gifford water. Like the rest of East Lothian, it was once under the control of Northumbria. Evidence of this remains in the names of the nearby hills such as Law, Hope and Lammer, which are of Anglo-Saxon origin. Around 1020, the territory was ceded by the English to Malcolm II. In the reign of David I, Anglo-Norman lord Hugh de Giffard settled in Scotland, acquiring extensive estates in East Lothian. He was born in Wiltshire in 1156 but became a close associate of the Scottish kings, witnessing the signing of several important charters. The lands of Yester (*Yestrith*) in the parish of Bothans were conferred on him by Malcolm IV. *Ystrad* or *ystred* is an old British word for a strath or vale. Its church is recorded as being consecrated by David de Bernham in 1241 and was dedicated to St Cuthbert.

Bothans parish was later known as Yester, or unofficially as Gifford. A stone castle was constructed a short distance further up the valley, on a promontory between the Hopes water and a tributary, the Gamuelston burn. The grandson of Hugo de Giffard, or Gifford, one of the guardians of Alexander III, is credited with its construction in the thirteenth century although there was probably a timber motte and bailey castle here before the stone example. Only a few fragmentary ruins of this important stronghold survive, enclosed by woodland. Underneath is a vaulted chamber, which has given the castle notoriety.

It was alleged that Hugo de Gifford was a wizard and had used magical forces to complete 'Hobgoblin hall'. In c.1270, his daughter, Marion, was married to Sir David Broun, laird of Colstoun. As the wedding party walked towards Bothans church, Hugo de Gifford picked a pear from a nearby tree and handed it to his daughter. She was told her father could not afford a wedding dowry but as long as the pear was looked after the owners of Coulston would flourish. For several centuries the fruit was well cared for. In 1692, Lady Elizabeth, who had recently married George Broun, the 2nd baronet Coulston, took a bite of the pear. After that all kinds of misfortune befell the family. Her husband ran up large gambling debts and the estate was saved only when it was bought by his brother Robert Broun. The curse then fell on him. In 1703 he was returning from Edinburgh with his wife and four children when his carriage attempted to cross the Coulston water, which was in flood. The carriage was swept away and Robert Broun and his two sons were drowned. His wife and two daughters were saved. George Broun died in destitution in 1718.

Despite the Gifford family having at least one member with super-natural powers, it did not prevent the lands passing out of their possession in 1397. Janet, or Johanna, Gifford married Sir William Hay and the lands of her family then passed into the Hay family, as there was no male heir. Yester castle was abandoned in the mid-sixteenth century, after being attacked by the English, who captured it. In 1548, it was held by fifty soldiers but was recaptured not long after by Scottish forces; it was then garrisoned briefly by Spanish soldiers, who were fighting on their side. It was soon retaken by English soldiers. Towards the end of the sixteenth century, the Hay family embarked on the construction of a new tower house, situated a few hundred yards to the north-west. This was later extended, but, at the end of the seventeenth century, it was demolished. In its place Yester house was constructed.

The Hays wished to landscape the grounds around their new residence. As early as 1676, they began to move the entire village of Bothans 'peasants houses or bothies', which stood next to the tower house, half a mile from today's Gifford. It was laid out in an L-plan, with the main street and village green placed at a right angle to it at its western end.

Despite the neat streets, some new residents had difficulty adapting. Hen houses, byres and pigsties were built on the village green. The residents had the right to graze their sheep on Gifford common but often preferred to let them run around the streets. In 1755, measures were taken to improve conditions with geese and ducks confined to the owner's property. The situation still left much to be desired, as in 1773 Lord Tweeddale complained about pigsties being built in the street. In the following decade, further improvements were made to Gifford, with thatched roofs replaced by slate and pantiles.

Gifford was not solely dependent on agriculture; three mills were established, one of which produced paper for Bank of Scotland notes. It was a major employer, but closed in the 1770s. The other two mills produced textiles and linen. There was a bleach field near the village green where the linen was laid out.

By the early-nineteenth century, Gifford was not unlike how it looks today. Main Street is dominated by Yester church, its white painted tower crowned with a spire. It replaced the medieval church of Bothans, which still stands a hundred yards from Yester house (no public access to either). In 1420, Sir William Hay elevated the parish church to collegiate status and, after the Reformation, the Hays continued their patronage. Once the new church was built Bothans became the burial vault for the Hays of Tweeddale. The present parish church was completed in 1710 but incorporated some elements from the church of Bothans, including the medieval church bell of 1492 and the seventeenth-century pulpit. It is also influenced by Dutch design. There are many good examples of eighteenth-century gravestones in the churchyard.

Gifford town hall, of 1887, flanked by two houses of the early-eighteenth century.

At the opposite end of Main Street, there is the 1887 town hall, with its small spire replacing an earlier clock tower. It was originally the village school but converted to a hall to celebrate Queen Victoria's golden jubilee; on either side stands a house dating from the early-eighteenth century. A short distance in front of them, next to the road, is the market cross. In bygone centuries several routes across the Lammermuir hills converged on Gifford. Grain used to be transported from the Tweed valley to Haddington market on horseback, in single sacks. On the opposite side of the road, facing the village green, is the Tweeddale Arms hotel; it is one of the oldest buildings in the village, dating from 1685, painted in the traditional colour scheme of black and white. The Goblin Ha' hotel, named after the underground chamber at Yester castle, stands close by in the main street. On the west edge of the village green is an avenue of large lime trees leading to Yester house. Other large deciduous trees are located a short distance away next to

316

Gifford water. Many of these trees date from the late-seventeenth century or early-eighteenth century.

When the village was moved, around 1676, work on improving the estate grounds began with the planting of thousands of trees and the enclosure of a large area of parkland by a wall. By the early-eighteenth century, Yester house, still under construction, was surrounded by one of the most ornate formal gardens and the largest areas of parkland in Scotland. The formal garden had disappeared by 1760 when the architect Robert Adam, who was still working on extending and improving Yester house, had other ideas for the grounds.

Two prominent men with connections to Gifford are remembered by memorial plaques on a wall next to the Haddington road, opposite the church. The first commemorates **John Witherspoon**, son of James Witherspoon, the minister of Yester parish, who claimed descent from John Knox. John Witherspoon (1723–94) was not only a prominent minister in the Church of Scotland but also became one of the most influential figures in the movement for American independence, the only clergyman, in fact, to sign the Declaration of Independence. No less a personage than John Adams, second president of the United States, called him 'as high a son of liberty as any man in America'.

Witherspoon was educated at the grammar school in Haddington and went up to Edinburgh university in 1739, where he graduated MA in 1739, continuing there until 1743 to study theology. Appointed minister at Beith in 1745, he took time out to support the Hanoverians against the Jacobite armies of Bonnie Prince Charlie. However, he was captured at the battle of Falkirk and imprisoned in Doune castle; while a number of his fellow prisoners tried to escape Witherspoon, observing that many of the captives were suffering from severe injuries, opted to stay, a decision that would lead some to portray him as a coward.

If his physical courage was debatable his reformist zeal was not. He was a staunch opponent of patronage in the Church of Scotland, and campaigned for the rights of ordinary members to appoint ministers of their choice. He published *Ecclesiastical Characteristics* in 1753, a satirical attack on patronage, and several works on religious doctrine. Despite the opposition of influential factions in the clergy he was appointed minister in the Laigh parish of Paisley in 1756, a considerably more lucrative living than Beith.

Witherspoon's growing celebrity resulted in offers of a pulpit from influential churches at home and abroad, including Dundee, Dublin and Rotterdam, all of which he declined. However, in 1768, he accepted the post of president of the Presbyterian College of New Jersey at Princeton University. Under Witherspoon's energetic leadership the college's reputation and popularity grew rapidly. He also gave the college a strong political voice, and, unlike conservative elements in the Church of Scotland, he came out in support of American independence, outlining the reasoning in his *Thoughts on American Liberty*.

In 1776, he was selected for the crucial second Continental Congress in Philadelphia, which resulted in the Declaration of Independence, signed by Witherspoon and fifty-five other delegates. After this he continued vigorously to campaign for independence, inspiring his students at Princeton, most prominent among them James Madison, who became fourth president of the United States. Many more of Witherspoon's students became prominent in public life as judges, congressmen and cabinet members. Witherspoon also promoted Scottish emigration to America, a policy that led to him being roundly criticised by the press in Scotland.

Next to Witherspoon's memorial plaque is one to a renowned academic and politician, **John Mackintosh**. He was not born in Gifford but in later life became MP for East Lothian and Berwick. In fact, he was born in India, his family moving back to Britain when he was ten. He was educated at Melville college and later attended Edinburgh and Oxford universities. After spending a period as a lecturer at Glasgow and Edinburgh universities, Mackintosh taught in Nigeria. On returning to Britain, he was appointed professor of politics at Strathclyde University. In 1966, he was elected MP for East Lothian, and, not long after, resigned his professorial post to devote more time to his constituents. He was elected a further two times as an MP. Due to a clash with the prime minister, Harold Wilson, over devolution for Scotland (he was very much in favour) a cabinet post was never offered to him. In later life he resumed his academic career on a part-time basis, but died not long afterwards at the age of 48. Mackintosh wrote a number of acclaimed books on politics including *The British Cabinet* and *The Government and Politics of Britain*, as well as numerous articles for *The Scotsman* and *The Times*. He is buried in Gifford churchyard.

At the beginning of the twenty-first century the population of Gifford was around seven hundred.

GLADSMUIR

This small village crowns a ridge between Haddington and Tranent, with panoramic views of the Firth of Forth and the Lothians. It is 355 feet above sea level. The name is derived from *gled*, an old Scots word for a hawk or kite, once found in these parts. Until the end of the last century it was on the main Edinburgh–Berwick-upon-Tweed road. The settlement is now surrounded by large arable fields and woodland plantations.

In bygone centuries, much of the land to the south resembled a marshy fen. The ridge itself was better drained, with open moorland. In medieval times, the moor was part of the common lands of Haddington. The main building in the village is the parish church, on the north side of the main road. It is built in the Romanesque style and dates from 1839. It was seriously damaged by fire in 1886 and had to be rebuilt. The ruins of an earlier church are a short distance away in the churchyard.

Gladsmuir parish was created in the seventeenth century and its first church was a mile south of the present one. It occupied a site on the edge of Butterdean wood in what is now farmland; no trace remains. After being in use for around forty-five years, it fell into a ruinous state

The ruins of Gladsmuir's old parish church.

and was replaced by what is now the ruined example at Gladsmuir. Much of its south wall is now missing, but it still has its bellcote (a structure to house bells) on the west gable. There is a semi-circular arch on its north side that could have been the aisle of the Baillies of Lamington, who built the church and owned 'Hoprig', a short distance to the north. A number of burial monuments are on its external walls, the most striking a life-sized relief of Colonel James Ainslie in the uniform of the dragoons. Gladsmuir had a reputation for lightning strikes, probably because of its exposed position.

One of Gladsmuir's better-known residents was **William Robertson**. He studied at Edinburgh University and in 1743 at the age of twenty-two became minister at Gladsmuir. During his stay, he wrote his highly praised *History of Scotland 1542–1603*, published shortly after he left the parish to become a minister at Greyfriars, Edinburgh. In 1762, he was appointed principal of Edinburgh University and made an outstanding contribution to the intellectual life of that institution. This was the era of the renowned Scottish Enlightenment, in which Robertson was a leading light.

Later in the 1760s, Robertson's book on Charles V was published to wide acclaim. He began work on a history of the Americas, but abandoned this with the outbreak of the American Revolution. During the anti-Catholic riots of 1779, his house was seriously damaged because of his defence of the Roman Catholic vicar, General Hay. William Robertson died in 1793. A less scholarly work was written by another of Gladsmuir's ministers in 1705. It was entitled *Ingenious and Scientific Discourse of Witchcraft, a monument of superstition and credulity*.

Born on a farm at Bathgate in 1872, **Catherine Blair**, a more-enlightened individual, became a suffragette and an advocate for women. She married Thomas Blair in 1894 at Tranent. The couple worked Hoprig farm, half a mile north of Gladsmuir village. It also became a refuge for suffragettes, many of whom had undergone harsh treatment in prison. On one occasion, Catherine was reading a newspaper about the escape of a suffragette to France who happened to be staying with her at Hoprig farm! She was also responsible for establishing the first branch of the Scottish Women's Rural Institute; by 1931, the number of branches had grown to 850. The Mak' Merry Pottery was also her creation. It specialised in painting pottery blanks in a colourful style to a very high standard. Catherine Blair spent her final years in North Berwick, dying in 1946.

GULLANE

Gullane has been described as 'one of Scotland's most English-looking villages'. It had a population of 3,783 in 2011 and is situated near the coast, extending eastwards down the gentle slopes of Gullane hill, highest point 220 feet. Unlike much of the local landscape, which is intensively farmed, the village is surrounded by large areas of grass. This is because Gullane stands on extensive tracts of sand, blown inland from the coast. Being unsuitable for arable farming they have been put to use as links golf courses. This in turn has been responsible for the growth of Gullane, which until the end of the nineteenth century was an insignificant settlement. Its original name was *Golyn* – an old word for 'small lake' – sometimes spelt Golan or Gullan. There was once an adjoining sheet of water, which by the nineteenth century had been drained.

Its oldest building is the ruin of the former parish church of St Andrew, at the western entrance to the village. There may have been a church at Gullane from the ninth century, but the present ruins date from the second half of the twelfth century with alterations being made in the thirteenth and fifteenth centuries. It is oblong in plan and had a long narrow nave without aisles. In the churchyard there is one of the earliest gravestones in the Lothians. It is very small with a disk head, on which is carved a cross, perhaps dating from the twelfth century. The church of St Andrew at 'Golyn' was in existence before 1170, when its patronage was granted to the convent of Dryburgh on behalf of the church on Fidra island. It was the mother church of a chapel at Congleton, three miles to the south-east. This had been founded in the twelfth century by the Congleton family for their use and those who dwelt nearby. David de Bernham formally dedicated 'Golyn' church in 1242, but this bishop reduced the status of the church from a rectory to a vicarage. It was now served by one of the canons of Dryburgh with the assistance of a secular priest. The vicar was to receive twelve marks annually, the balance of the income going to the general revenues of the abbey, which at that time had large debts. Up until the Reformation its history was closely bound to Dryburgh abbey.

At the end of the sixteenth century, the vicar of Gullane church was removed from his post by James VI for smoking tobacco. The monarch, who had a hatred of witches, also disapproved of this habit. Not long after, Gullane church became smothered in drifting sand and was abandoned. It was thought this was caused by the marram grass being pulled up by locals for use in thatched roofs. In 1612, the Scottish parliament granted permission to move the parish church from Gullane, 'a decaying place', to Dirleton, 'a flourishing town'. Its stones and timber, if necessary, could be used in the construction of the new church. The extensive areas of sand dunes had what was one of the largest rabbit-warren complexes in Scotland and fetched a large rent, as rabbit meat was much in demand. Drifting sand continued to be a problem. In the early-nineteenth century, it had overwhelmed the manse, its residents forced to escape through the roof.

With the outbreak of war with France in 1793, regiments were formed for home defence. One of them, Grants Fencibles, was at Gullane in July 1795 when four of its soldiers were to be executed for mutiny. Two were pardoned but the other two were shot in the presence of a large crowd on the west side of Gullane Links. As late as the 1830s the village remained relatively small, with just fifty-nine families. The breeding and training of racehorses had become an important activity. By the late-nineteenth century, this activity was in decline and was dealt a final blow in 1892 when Lord Low prohibited the training of horses on Gullane hill following complaints from golfers.

The real growth came in the last decades of the nineteenth century after an eighteen-hole golf course was laid out in 1884 although there

Autumnal view over Gullane.

had been a seven-hole course since 1840. In 1891 the Honourable Company of Golfers moved from Musselburgh to the new Muirfield course on Gullane Links. The later Gullane courses, nos. 2 and 3, date from 1898 and 1910. A children's golf course was built in 1910 with six holes, perhaps the oldest of its kind in the world. The newly built railway brought increasing numbers of visitors to spend their holidays here. At that time there were six hundred inhabitants.

Most of the large villas on the slope of Gullane hill belong to the late-nineteenth or early-twentieth centuries. A new church was built in 1888 to cater for the increasing number of summer visitors, the first since St Andrews was abandoned in the seventeenth century. Appropriately, the modest structure was in a simple Norman style and would be not unlike the original church. It was followed by the episcopal church of St Adrian, of 1926. Local stone from Rattlebags quarry, which glows with crystals because of its volcanic origin, was used; it too is in the neo-Norman style. A tower was added in 1935, crowned by a small spire.

Next to Muirfield golf course at the east end of Gullane is Greywalls hotel, constructed in 1901 from Rattlebags stone. It was built for Alfred Lyttelton, a politician and outstanding sportsman. He wanted a residence as close as possible to the eighteenth green of the golf course. Edwin Lutyens, a leading architect, was responsible for the design. Greywalls was sold four years after it was completed to William James, a wealthy American, whose wife was allegedly the illegitimate daughter of Edward VII. Up until his death in 1910, the King was a frequent visitor to Greywalls. In 1948, the house became an upmarket hotel. The late comedian Ronnie Corbett had a second home next to the hotel; he was born in Edinburgh but later lived in London, often returning to holiday in Gullane.

Not long after Greywalls became a hotel, the Marine hotel situated at the eastern entrance to Gullane closed and became the Scottish Fire Services college. It continued in this role until 2015 when firefighters ceased to be trained here due to the merger of Scottish fire services and has now been converted to flats.

Half a mile north of Main Street is Gullane bay, with one of the most attractive beaches in East Lothian. It was requisitioned from 1941–6 for war use and fortified with anti-tank blocks, some of which still can be seen at either end of the beach. The dunes were later used to train personnel in the techniques of heavy-vehicle recovery in preparation for the Normandy landings.

HADDINGTON

Situated in the heart of East Lothian, Haddington has been the county town since the Middle Ages. It was built on a gravel terrace on the banks of the Tyne. On three sides it is surrounded by fertile, undulating, low-lying ground, but a short distance to the north are the slopes of the Garleton hills, which rise to a height of just over 600 feet. Roads converge on Haddington from the surrounding countryside. The town developed as a crossing point on the Tyne, which at this point flows fairly slowly. There has been a stone bridge here since at least the early-sixteenth century, but centuries before a timber bridge spanned the Tyne. Before this there was probably a ford in the vicinity used by travellers heading north towards the port of Aberlady after crossing the Lammer-muir hills. The name Haddington is said to be derived from the Gaelic *hofdingia-tun*, or in more modern form *heuedinge-town* meaning 'prince's' town. An older explanation is that is comes from a Saxon chief bearing the name Haden, who settled in the area.

The first written reference to Haddington occurs in the twelfth century. In 1128, David I made Haddington a burgh, one of the first towns in Scotland to have this status. Most burghs were under the protection of a castle, but Haddington was an exception as there was no castle here. It did have a royal palace in the twelfth century, which in those days would have been a modest structure, consisting of a hall and a few other buildings. When, in 1165, William the Lion became king, he approved its construction. A relatively short distance from Edinburgh, William spent much time here.

Alexander II was born in the palace in 1198. He ruled Scotland from 1214–49. By early the next century, visits by royalty become infrequent, possibly due to invading English armies; Haddington was destroyed in 1216 in one such raid. The palace survived until 1242, when it was set on fire in an effort to hide the murder of Padraig, 6th earl Atholl, following a tournament held in the town. Parts of the ruins were extant until recent times and were described as, 'several elegant and well-proportioned Saxon pillars and arches, a vault and some arched passages'; unfortunately, they were demolished to make way for the present county buildings in Court Street. The only reminder of the royal palace is a large plaque on the entrance to the offices.

In 1244, Haddington was destroyed by fire and it suffered yet again in 1297, when it was torched by the retreating Scottish army. On a more positive note, a grammar school was established towards the end of the thirteenth century. It is claimed that one of its pupils was John Duns Scotus, one of the most important medieval theologians. During the Renaissance his followers were sometimes called Dunses because of their obstinacy and conservatism, giving rise to the word 'dunce'. There was further destruction in 1356 by the English under Edward III. The previous year, the Scots had launched an assault on Berwick and captured the town; in response the English army launched a counter-attack, recapturing it. After overwintering at Roxburgh, Edward marched into the Lothians, laying waste to the land. He spent ten days at Haddington where the chronicler Fordun relates:

> He burned the toun, the monastery and the sacred church of the Fratres minors of Haddington, a costly and splendid building of wonderful beauty, whose quire, from its elegance and clearness of light was commonly called the Lamp of Lothian and a church which was the singular solace of the pious in that part.

It was during this campaign that the shrine at Whitekirk was damaged. Two years later there was a serious flood. Despite these episodes of destruction, a decade later Haddington had recovered, its trade through the port of Aberlady in a very healthy state. In 1388, there was further strife on the Scottish Borders with a series of raids. Although the English were defeated at Otterburn, Henry IV invaded Scotland in 1400 at the head of a large army; unusually, the town escaped serious damage and the King was given accommodation in the nunnery. Only a few months had passed before Henry Percy 'Hotspur' was leading two thousand men across the Lammermuir hills with the earl of Dunbar at his side. They laid siege to Hailes castle without success and instead turned their attention to Haddington, which they burnt along with the villages of Traprain and Markle. Not long after, Percy was forced to withdraw to Northumberland with the arrival of a Scottish army.

In 1421, it was nature's turn to deal a blow to the fortunes of Haddington, a large flood sweeping away many houses. Despite these setbacks, Haddington was now manufacturing cloth and its merchants were trading as far afield as Danzig. Glimmers mills on the Tyne also began operation around this time. A Dominican friary was founded in 1471 but did not thrive. At this time, Haddington was the fourth largest town in Scotland after Edinburgh, Aberdeen and Roxburgh. After a century of peace, Haddington was again at the mercy of invading English armies during the 'Rough Wooing', the last major conflict between

England and Scotland. Unlike previous conflicts when the English burnt Haddington and departed, this time, 1548, they built large earthwork fortifications around town. After one of the longest sieges in British history, the English garrison withdrew.

The Reformation of 1560 brought further disruption to Haddington. Its religious houses, including the important convent and Franciscan friary, were abolished. At the end of the century the traveller, Fynes Moryson, described Haddington as merely 'a pleasant village'. In 1598, a fire caused great damage in the town, destroying one side of High Street; it was caused by a maid carelessly placing a screen covered with clothes too near the fireplace. After that the town council instructed that the town crier should walk through the streets warning residents to guard against accidental fires.

Although gypsies were often persecuted, the measures taken against a group of them imprisoned in the tollbooth, in November 1636, were extreme. They may have been locked up for committing a crime but, even so, the men were hanged and the women drowned. Those with children escaped this fate, merely having their cheeks burnt before being driven out of the burgh.

A few years later, the town, like the rest of the country, was in the grip of plague. The sick who were likely to recover were sent to live in tents near Gladsmuir, the most westerly point of the parish. The movement of people was restricted and watchmen were placed at the town gates. Strangers were only allowed to enter if they could produce a certificate signed by a responsible person stating that they were disease-free. Foodstuffs were prohibited from areas suffering from the plague. Six years after the first deaths, the epidemic faded away.

The Union of Crowns in 1603 enhanced Haddington's importance, given its proximity to the main route south. One of the first post offices in Scotland was established here in the early-seventeenth century. Edinburgh merchants set up a weaving and fulling (cloth cleansing) works, which had mixed fortunes, but broadcloth was still being made in Haddington at the beginning of the following century. In the 1720s, Daniel Defoe described it as . . . 'an old half ruined town, formerly large, handsome and well built, has some handsome streets and a good bridge over the River Tyne.'

In 1745, General Cope marched at the head of a government army of 600 cavalry and 1,500 infantry, from Dunbar to Haddington, to confront Bonnie Prince Charlie and his Jacobite supporters; the army camped west of the town. Two soldiers in a scouting party ventured as far as Musselburgh in search of the rebels. They decided to reconnoitre a local public house in which they asked two men if they knew of the location of the enemy. Unfortunately for the two soldiers, the persons they engaged in conversation were Jacobite officers. The unwitting men were taken prisoner but later released. General Cope's army did not stay long at Haddington, marching to Prestonpans, where they were defeated by the Jacobites.

During the Napoleonic Wars, a considerable force of soldiers was stationed at Haddington, most locally raised militia, the council subsiding their uniforms, which were often smarter than those worn by regular soldiers! There were over a hundred huts for the infantry on the north-east side of the town providing accommodation for a thousand soldiers. The structures were wooden, pitched over and covered with tiles, and could house twenty-four men. A barracks for the cavalry was situated between Lydgait and Black Palings. There were even thirty members of the artillery who occupied part of Amisfield farm, the origin of the name Artillery park. With around two thousand soldiers in the vicinity of Haddington, their spending power was a powerful stimulus for the local economy. There was at least notable incident involving soldiers based here: Captain Rutherford objected to Dr Cahill removing a newspaper from the reading room, who had taken it to his own quarters as he was not feeling well. This trivial incident erupted into the two men fighting a duel. Rutherford, a bully, was fatally wounded; Cahill, on the other hand, survived to old age working in a dispensary.

Although the soldiers had mostly left by 1815, the town continued to prosper. It was surrounded by highly productive farms, producing bumper crops. By 1825 there were no less than four breweries plus the Nungate and West Field distilleries; there were also several flour mills. A weekly grain market was one of the busiest in Scotland. There was also an early attempt to introduce inexpensive literature for the working classes to fire their enthusiasm for reading. The *Cheap Magazine* was first published in 1813 and had a circulation of twenty thousand copies a month. It was published by George Miller, who set up the first printing press in East Lothian in 1795, moving it to Haddington in 1804. His venture failed after a couple of years due to distribution problems.

The town was connected to the railway network in 1846, but ten years later business had not developed as predicted and the line was reduced from a double to a single track. Edinburgh also had overtaken

Haddington as the largest grain market in Scotland, but throughout the nineteenth century grain was important to the local economy. In the 1890s, one or two small woollen mills were still in operation, but this industry, established several centuries previously, never fulfilled expectations. There were also breweries, foundries, a coach works, corn mills, agricultural-implement factories, a tannery and skinner. During the twentieth century, most of these enterprises disappeared. Besides a grain market, Haddington was also noted for its farmworker hiring market. This practice continued until 1925, by which time agriculture was becoming increasingly mechanised and farms no longer needed a large workforce.

Plaque, six feet above street level, recalling the most disastrous Hadddington flood of recent times, in 1948.

In an echo of the past, Haddington suffered further destruction during the Second World War. Fortunately, this was confined to three deaths, the destruction of a Market Street shop and some other property, the culprit a lone German bomber. More devastation was wrought by the floods of 1948 when the Tyne again overflowed and waters up to 10-feet high rushed through the streets; some 450 houses and fifty-nine shops were damaged. A few years later, Haddington received a boost to its population when a thousand former inhabitants of Glasgow were rehoused in the town as part of an overspill project. The population of Haddington grew from 4,401 in 1931 to around 9,000 in 2016. Although it has lost its status as an important agricultural market along with many of its traditional industries, the town is still an important regional centre. It houses the main offices of East Lothian Council although the Sheriff Court was transferred to Edinburgh in 2015. Farmers still descend on it to spend money in local shops.

Despite being one of Scotland's most important medieval towns, none of Haddington's domestic buildings of the period survive. The oldest structure is the ruin of St Martin's church, of the twelfth century. Built of red stone, it stands on the eastern edge of Haddington in an open area of parkland, close to the road to Traprain Law. Only the nave survives, relatively complete except for its missing roof. Excavations revealed that there was a square chamber east of the nave. Between

1153 and 1178, Countess Ada, mother of William the Lion, gifted the land near Haddington to Alexander de St Martin but his connection with the church is not known. In 1178, she went on to found a convent a short distance east of Haddington. Alexander de St Martin then gave the lands and tenements of St Martinsgate, including its mills, to this new religious house. It also acquired the tithes to St Martins church, later used by the convent to hold its courts. After the abolition of the monasteries and convents, Protestant church services were held in the building. It was later abandoned and fell into ruin.

The impressive St Mary's, Haddington, begun in the fourteenth century and the longest parish church in Scotland at 206 feet from east to west.

On the opposite bank of the Tyne is St Mary's, a short distance to the south of the town centre and close to Nungate bridge. It is an impressive late-medieval church, the longest parish church in Scotland and almost the same size as some of its cathedrals. It is thought that St Mary's may have once have had a distinctive, crown-like spire, similar to St Giles in Edinburgh, or at least there were aspirations to construct something in this style.

The first mention of the parish church at Haddington is in 1139 when it was granted to St Andrews by David I. This church is thought to have been a small Norman building, which occupied the site of the choir of the present church. The current building was begun some time after the destruction of the parish church in 1356 by English soldiers under Edward III, during a campaign known as 'Burnt Candlemas'. St Mary's is cruciform in shape and built of grey and red sandstone; a large tower stands at its centre. The impressive size of the building is indicative of the wealth of Haddington. The church took around a hundred years to complete and was at first a collegiate church. By 1450, it had no less than eleven altars attended to by numerous priests – Our Lady, Holy Blude, St Blaise's, St John's, the Three Kings of Cologne, St Salvator's, St Catherine's, St Mychael's, St Towbart's, Crispin and Crispianus and Trinity. The upkeep of the structure of the choir fell upon the priory of St Andrews, but the maintenance for at least part of the service was met by the town council. The status of a full collegiate church was not granted until the time of archbishop David Beaton (1539–46).

A decade or so later, during the siege of Haddington (1548–9), it narrowly escaped complete destruction by the garrisoned English army. The church suffered serious damage and was left completely roofless. John Knox – born just across the Tyne at Giffordgate – persuaded the council to repair the building so it could be used as the parish church. There was only enough money to restore and reroof the nave. As the population of Haddington grew the church underwent many transformations. It was not until the 1970s, four hundred years after the siege of Haddington, that the rest of the church was re-roofed and restored. The church bells, looted by English soldiers, were finally replaced in 1999. Within the church there is a burial aisle to the Maitlands of Lethington – the earls of Lauderdale. They had strong links with Haddington, occupying Lennoxlove tower a short distance to the south. In it lies the body of John Maitland, in his early life a strong supporter of the Covenanters. When King Charles came to the throne, Maitland wished to prove his loyalty and implemented a policy of persecution of the Covenanters. So disliked was Lauderdale that the Covenanters put a curse on him: 'may you never rest in peace'. Legend has it that his body moved position in the vault of St Mary's without human intervention; it was later found that from time to time flood water from the Tyne entered the vault and floated the airtight coffin into a different position! The large churchyard contains a number of old gravestones some of which date from the eighteenth century.

In medieval times, on the west bank of the Tyne, stood a Franciscan friary first mentioned in records in 1242. Associated with it was a magnificent church, which, due to its splendour, was given the name 'Lamp of the Lothian'. Unfortunately, it was burnt by the English, first in 1356 and again in 1547. After the Reformation the church was secularised but did not survive for much longer, being dismantled in 1572. Between 1769–70 the present Episcopal church was constructed on the site, with Gothic-style additions in 1843. St Mary's church stands a short distance to the south and close by there is a more recent place of worship in the form of a Roman Catholic church of yellow sandstone, built 1862.

Heading in the opposite direction along Sidegate Street towards the town centre is the white-harled (harling is a protective external plastering process using a slurry of pebbles or chips of stone) Haddington house, dating from 1648. Standing next to it is St Mary's Pleasance, a private garden open to the public. Appropriately, it recreates a Scottish seventeenth-century garden, including raised herb beds, a boxed hornbeam walk and an orchard.

The Goats of Haddington statue, located in Hardgate.

Haddington house is the oldest domestic building in the town. Until the 1950s, there was an even older building, a town house known as Bothwell castle. It was demolished around that time. In the same street are a number of Georgian residences, including Summerfield house with its Doric entrance. At the head of High Street, standing on a small area of grass next to the road junction, is the medieval custom stone. Close by there is a statue of two goats, their horns locked in combat. The sculpture dates from 1978, but this animal has a long association with Haddington, possibly dating back to the thirteenth century when it first appeared on the town's coat of arms.

Sidegate continues as Hardgate on which stands the white-harled, eighteenth-century, Kinloch house. At the centre of the town is High Street, of no great length, and, immediately north, running parallel, Market Street.

Although the timber medieval buildings are long gone, the layout of the streets remains much the same. The buildings in High Street today

331

are mainly Georgian, some with Victorian shop fronts added. The market cross stands close to the east end, but has been moved from its original position. Close by is a distinct building with a circular tower. It is the former Castle hotel, which at one time was a coaching inn dating from the eighteenth century. It had stabling for twenty-three horses and four carriages.

Sunrise over Haddington town house and High Street.

At the opposite end is the town house, which dominates the heart of Haddington. The first reference to the town house, or tolbooth, occurs in 1426. It is believed to have been situated in Market Street, some four hundred feet to the east of the present site. During the sixteenth century it was fortified with both a tower and a drawbridge. It was in such a ruinous state by the early-eighteenth century that council meetings were held in the library, and, by 1740, it was described as 'in danger of falling'. It was resolved that it should be partially demolished and the clock and bells were removed from the steeple and placed in storage. In 1742, a contract was placed to 'build and erect in good and sufficient work a town house and tolbooth' to a design by William Adam. The masonry from the previous tolbooth was to be used in its construction and it had a steeple in 'the old Dutch' style. The prison accommodation was soon found to be inadequate and the number of cells were increased by building more walls. An extension was built in 1823 to increase the capacity.

There were further problems in 1830 when the council considered 'the great disrepair of the town clock and the dilapidated appearance of the steeple'. The old steeple was dismantled to its foundations, replaced by the present long, slender example. Many of the buildings in Market Street date from the Georgian period. Numbers seven and eight, with their Palladian facades, were constructed in the 1760s. There are also two closes on the north side of the street, one of which leads to the eighteenth-century manse of John Brown and the site of his Burgher church, now occupied by a nineteenth-century chapel converted into flats. In Mitchell's Close there is a stair tower of the early-eighteenth century. Immediately to the west of the town house, Market Street and High Street merge into Court Street, a broad, open thoroughfare. In medieval times it was an open space but as the town expanded westwards, Georgian villas were built along the road. It was more than just a residential area as it also contains the county buildings. Close by is the Corn Exchange, of 1853, a single-storey building of classical appearance. It no longer functions in that role and is now used as a music venue. Haddington's former industries were concentrated along the banks of the Tyne. Although many of the buildings have been demolished, a few have been preserved. One of the best examples is Poldrate mill, which stands on the site of the medieval Kirk mill, a short distance south of St Mary's church. Dating mainly from the eighteenth century, it includes a granary, maltings and workers houses.

Haddington has had more distinguished citizens than any other East Lothian town, but only a small number are commemorated by memorials or statues in the town. The most famous is religious reformer **John Knox** and although Gifford and Morham have both claimed to have been his birthplace it is now generally accepted that it was Haddington.

There is no doubt that Knox (1514–72) is one of the most influential figures in the history of Scotland and certainly its most significant clergyman. His writings and sermons were the inspiration for the Protestant Reformation that swept away Roman Catholicism in the 1550s. He was an important social reformer, insisting that every kirk in the land should have a teacher to instruct children and that the church had a duty to care for the poor. Knox was also a brilliant historian whose writings provide telling insights into a crucial period. Yet there is still a degree of controversy about his legacy: he was seen, even by some allies, as too uncompromising, while his fulminations against women alienated many, including, for a time at least, Queen Elizabeth I of England.

John Knox was educated at Haddington grammar school and after attending St Andrews University he was ordained as a Catholic priest in the late 1530s. However, it was while working as an advocate in Haddington from 1540–3 that he was attracted to the fledgling Protestant movement, a particular influence being George Wishart, a fiery speaker who did much to spread the new religion and whom Knox heard preaching at St Mary's church. When Wishart was hanged and burnt at the stake in 1546 it set off a chain of events that led to the worst two years of Knox's life. The man who had ordered the execution of Wishart, Cardinal Beaton, was himself assassinated, throwing Scotland into turmoil and prompting Mary de Guise – regent on behalf of her 5-year-old daughter, Mary, Queen of Scots – to turn to her native France for help. In 1547, a French fleet duly arrived in St Andrews and took many Protestants into custody. Knox was one of those captured and he was sentenced to serve as a galley slave on one of the ships. It would be nineteen long months of unspeakable hardship before Knox was released.

Much of the next decade was spent in first, England, and latterly, in Geneva, where he was much influenced by Calvin, the great Protestant philosopher. Knox loved Geneva, which he described as the 'maist perfyt schoole of Chryst', and it gave time to think and write. It was during this period that his infamous tract, *The First Blast of the Trumpet Against the Monstrous Regiment of Women*, was published, in which he argues that for a woman to exercise sovereign power goes against the laws of nature. While his main target was the Catholic queen of England, Mary Tudor, it also offended her Protestant successor, Elizabeth I, who ascended to the throne in 1558.

The exile of John Knox ended in 1559. With the Lords of the Congregation (Protestant nobles) now in open revolt against Mary de Guise he came home to support them. He started by preaching a provocative sermon against Catholicism and 'idolatry' in Perth, causing a riot, and then travelled widely, rousing both the common people and the Protestant armies with his fire-and-brimstone speeches. Before long the insurgents were in the ascendancy and when Mary de Guise died in June 1560, the last obstacle to the creation of a Protestant state was removed. By August of that year, the Reformation Parliament abolished papal jurisdiction over Scotland and enshrined the new religion. Knox's dream had come true.

There was, however, a cloud on the horizon. In August 1561, Mary, Queen of Scots, the daughter of James V and Mary de Guise, and the rightful heir, arrived in Edinburgh to claim the throne. Although a staunch Roman Catholic, Mary gave official recognition to the reformed religion, the quid pro quo being that she could attend mass and practise her religion, as long as her observance was private. This was too much for Knox. In his eyes, 'one mass was more dangerous than ten thousand armed enemies'; he would brook no compromise of any kind with Roman Catholicism, even if his sovereign was an adherent.

As minister of St Giles in Edinburgh, Knox had the most influential pulpit in the land and from 1561–5 he used his sermons to rail against Mary and her faith, describing her as 'that wretched woman, the mother of all misery'. This did not go down well with those Protestant aristocrats who had accepted positions in the Queen's government, but Knox was unmoved. He also met Mary four times, and, while the interviews ended amicably, Knox stuck firmly to his view that all Catholic queens were Jezebels intent on persecuting God's people. He even turned down the opportunity to be Mary's spiritual adviser, fearing it was a ploy to encourage him to water down his sermons.

However, it would be Mary's own poor judgement and not Knox's preaching that would lead to her removal from the throne in 1567 and the subsequent exile to England. The reason was that just three months after the murder of her first husband, Lord Darnley, she married the main suspect, the earl of Bothwell, turning the nobles and most of the country against her.

Even with Mary gone Edinburgh was a dangerous place. Her supporters fought on, occupying Edinburgh castle during the 'lang' siege of 1571–3. For most of this time Knox found it safer to be in St Andrews, where he found an adoring audience among the many students in that most academic of towns. With the capital now safe, he returned to Edinburgh in the summer of 1572, preaching once again at St Giles despite his rapidly deteriorating health. His last sermon was given on 9 November and he died two weeks later.

The legacy of John Knox lives on to this day and he continues to be an inspiration to Presbyterians in Scotland and in many other countries. Almost all Protestant groups have at one time or another laid claim to his memory, the most heated debate taking place during the Disruption of 1843, when dissenters in the Church of Scotland left to form the Free Church of Scotland, claiming they were following Knox's principles. His writings have also proved to be highly influential, in particular his great work, *History of the Reformation in Scotland*, which was first published in 1587 and provides invaluable source material for this most crucial period in the nation's past.

There is a statue of Haddington's most famous citizen in the town, tucked away in the niche of the tower of a Gothic building that was once a school. It is in the eponymous Knox Place and can be viewed from the nearby street as the former place of learning has been converted into private flats. *The Builder* magazine commented not long after the erection of the statue that is was, '. . . hardly appropriate for a memorial to the great leveller of Medieval Observances'.

There is also a stone memorial to John Knox at Giffordgate, his birthplace. Its inscription, difficult to read, states: 'Near this spot stood the house in which was born John Knox in A.D. 1505. In commemoration an oak tree was here planted 29th March 1881, after the wish of the late Thomas Carlyle.'

John Gray was another preacher. Born in Haddington in 1646 he was best known as a scholar and book collector, who assembled an important library of early printed books, now in the National Library of Scotland. Appropriately, the local-history museum in Lodge Street in the town centre is named after him. It also contains archives and books for anyone undertaking research on East Lothian.

Overlooking a road junction at the west end of Court Street, which marks the entrance to the old part of the town, is a monument to **Sir Robert Ferguson**, MP for Raith. His statue stands on top of a forty-five-foot Doric column and is dated 1843. Despite this grandiose monument, Ferguson had rather tenuous links to Haddington. He was a native of Kirkcaldy who joined the Whig party and narrowly won Haddington from the Tories in 1835. At that time, the Whigs represented progressive causes such as the abolition of slavery and Catholic emancipation. When he stood for re-election two years later he was defeated by Lord Ramsay. The Tories went to great lengths to take the seat, even kidnapping a Whig supporter and dumping him on Traprain Law. Robert Ferguson died in 1840 at the age of 73.

Further along Court Street, outside the county buildings, is a red-sandstone monument modelled on the well head at Pinkie. It was designed by the well-known sculptor David Rhind and erected in 1880 to commemorate the eighth marquess of Tweeddale, **George Hay**. There is a marble bust of him in the centre of the monument. At the age of seventeen, Hay joined the army and had a long and distinguished career. While serving under the Duke of Wellington in the Peninsular War, he was wounded on two occasions. After he had recovered, he was posted to Canada to fight the Americans in 1813. Here he was captured and released only when the war had ended. After this, he returned to the family home of Yester at Gifford where he took great interest in agricultural improvements, invented several implements and pioneered deep ploughing. All the time Hay was still in the army and in 1842 he took up service again, spending six years in India as commander-in-chief of the forces at Madras. When he returned, he devoted the rest of the life to farming on his estate at Yester.

There is a long list of other prominent Haddington citizens, but there is little or nothing to remember them by in the town. They include **Walter Bower**, or Bowmaker, who was born there in 1385. He is thought to have been among the first Bachelors of Arts at St Andrews University. Seven years later, he became abbot of Inchcolm in the Firth of Forth, where he wrote *The Scotichronicon*, the first comprehensive history of Scotland, incorporating the earlier work of John of Fordun. Bower did not confine his activities to writing, often undertaking government assignments. In 1424, he collected ransom money for James I, who had been held captive by the English for eighteen years.

John Major, or Mair, born near Tantallon castle in 1467, was educated at the Franciscan friary in Haddington and is sometimes known as Haddingtonus Scotus. He went on to study at the universities of Oxford, Cambridge and Paris. He wrote books on logic and also *A History of Greater Britain which included accounts of both England and Scotland*. He discussed moral and legal questions arising from the Spanish discovery of America, arguing that the natives had political and property rights that could not be forfeited, at least not without compensation. Unlike Walter Bower, who had strong nationalist sentiments, he was in favour of the Union of Crowns. Many of his works were written while he was a teacher in Navarre, France. In 1518, he was made professor of philosophy and divinity at Glasgow university. Here one of his pupils was John Knox, although John Major was opposed to religious reform and very much for retaining traditional practices. However, he did believe in putting forward the truth as the means of destroying mythology. His last years were spent teaching theology at St Andrews.

A theologian of a later date who has associations with Haddington was **John Brown**. He was born near Abernethy, Perthshire in 1722. After a limited education, he spent time as a shepherd boy, but studied Latin and Hebrew with the assistance of a local minister. The local community became suspicious of his great knowledge and Brown was forced to undergo an inquisition. Not long after this, he left the area and became a pedlar. In 1747, he took up teaching and established his own school. Four years later he had qualified as a minister and accepted a post at the Burgher church at Haddington; a staunch Calvinist, he remained there for the rest of his life. Despite spending much time looking after his congregation, John Brown become best known for writing *The Self Interpreting Bible* for use by families. Other works include *A Dictionary of the Holy Bible* and *A History of the Churches of Scotland and England*. He also taught students, having accepted the Burgher chair of divinity at Glasgow university in 1768. His grave lies within St Mary's churchyard. There is also a plaque on his manse, located in the small John Brown Court on the north side of Market Street. The church where he preached for thirty-seven years was demolished not long after his death and replaced by a new building in 1806, since converted into flats.

Born in 1812 at Haddington, **Samuel Smiles** was a pioneer of self-help books. After burgh school, he attended Edinburgh university, studying medicine. Samuel Smiles then returned to Haddington, becoming town doctor. In 1837, his first book, *Physical Education or the Nurture and Management of Children*, was published; it was still in print sixty-eight years later. Not long after, Smiles moved to Leeds where he practised as a surgeon but then decided to devote his time to journalism. From 1838–45, he was the editor of the *Leeds Times*. Having a strong interest in railways, he met George Stephenson and wrote his biography. He also became secretary of the South-Eastern Railway but found time to write his best-known book, *Self Help; with Illustrations of Character and Conduct*. It promoted the philosophy of hard work and learning, citing the lives of famous engineers and encouraging the reader to follow in their footsteps. He wrote many other improving books, including *Character*, 1871, and *Thrift*, 1875, although his philosophy of making the best of one's circumstances came in for some criticism. Samuel Smiles died in London in 1904. He is remembered in his home town by a plaque on 62 High Street, marking his birthplace.

Haddington was the home town of the wife of another famous

nineteenth-century writer: **Jane Baillie Welsh**, the only daughter of a Haddington doctor, who lived in Lodge Street. In 1826, she married Thomas Carlyle and they lived in Edinburgh before moving to south-west Scotland. Here Carlyle wrote *The French Revolution – A History*, the inspiration for the Charles Dickens novel, *A Tale of Two Cities*. Another of his well-known works was *On Heroes, Hero Worship and the Heroics in History*. As Carlyle became more famous, the couple moved to London. Jane was encouraged to become a writer by her husband but she rebuffed his efforts. By 1866, Thomas Carlyle was regarded as one of the leading writers of the age. His wife supported him, despite both suffering from ill health and nervous disorders, which led to frequent arguments. Carlyle was appointed rector of Edinburgh University. A few weeks later Jane was out for a ride in London in her carriage, accompanied by her pet dog, when it was struck by a passing carriage. Shortly after, she suffered a fatal heart attack; the dog survived with only minor injuries. After the death of his wife at the age of sixty-five, Thomas Carlyle wrote little more. Jane Carlyle was buried in the choir of St Mary's church and a bronze tablet with a moving inscription written by her husband stands next to her grave.

Also born at Haddington in the early-nineteenth century was **George Harley**. He spent his early years at the family home in the grounds of Old Abbey Lodge. At the age of seventeen, he was studying medicine at Edinburgh University. While still a student, he performed a successful Caesarean operation on a woman who had died of a heart attack, and delivered a living child, despite little experience in this field. After graduating in 1850, Harley went to Europe to further his studies. While in France, he worked under Claude Bernard, whose monograph on the influence of the liver in diabetes led him to undertake further research on this subject. George Harley returned to England in 1855 to become curator of the anatomical museum at University College, London where he also lectured.

For his work proving that oxygen formed a chemical combination with a blood constituent (haemoglobin) Harley was elected Fellow of the Royal Society. He developed an interest in poisons after William Palmer was convicted of killing his friend John Parsons Cook with strychnine. A few years later, he wrote a paper 'The Poisoned Arrows of Savage Man', which proved that the Americas were populated by peoples from Asia. Harley met with little success as a practitioner, having only two patients in the course of a year. His career picked up when the president of the Pathological Society began using him as a consultant for patients with liver disease and kidney problems. In 1883, his book *Diseases of the Liver* was published and was widely read by doctors, in Britain and abroad. By now George Harley was suffering from eye problems due to the constant use of microscopes and in an effort to improve his vision, he spent nine months in darkness. He died in 1896 and is buried in the churchyard of St Mary's, marked by a gravestone. His daughter wrote his biography, assisted by Samuel Smiles, also from Haddington.

More recent residents of note include the rugby players **Jim and Finlay Calder**, born in Haddington. The twin brothers attended Stewart's Melville College school, where rugby became their main sport. Finlay Calder first played for Scotland in 1986: in the next five years he won thirty-four caps and captained the British and Irish Lions tour of Australia in 1989. Jim Calder won twenty-seven caps, playing his first international in 1981: three years later, he scored the try against France that won the grand slam for Scotland. Strangely, despite being the same age, the Calder brothers were never selected together in the same international team for Scotland.

Although the musician **Derek Dick** was born in Dalkeith, he has spent much of the latter part of his life in Haddington, where he has a recording studio. He rose to fame in the early 1980s as the lead singer in the rock band, Marillion, with 'Kayleigh' their best-known song. In 1988, he embarked on a solo career as 'Fish', a nickname given to him because of the amount of time he spent in his bath tub. His lyrics, sung with his distinctive voice, have been praised as poetic prose. He was voted number thirty-seven by *Planet Rock* listeners in 2009 in 'The greatest voices of rock' poll. In addition to his music, Dick's television acting credits include *The Bill* and *Rebus*.

Haddington has a population in the region of 9,000 in 2020.

HUMBIE

Situated in the south-western extremity of the county, Humbie is more hamlet than village. It is little more than a scattered group of houses and cottages that stand close to a bend on the road to Soutra. Until 1953, it could be said that there was no village in the parish. In the following decades a number of houses, a school and a community hall were constructed, and are now referred to as Humbie village. A short distance to the south there is another group of buildings, once the children's village, founded in 1886 by Mrs Stirling Boyd to give deprived children from urban areas a holiday in the countryside. The children resided in a number of small houses and cottages dispersed across an eleven-acre site. They were built in the attractive Arts and Crafts style, supporting a white finish capped with red roofs. The children's village underwent a change of use in 1967 and by the end of the century the site had closed. A few of the buildings have been retained in a residential development, which now occupies the ground.

Humbie parish church, which is some distance from the village.

Humbie parish church is isolated from the hamlet, half a mile to the north. It is hidden away at the foot of a narrow valley through which the Humbie water flows. The current building dates from 1800 and is in the Gothic style. It stands on the site of a pre-Reformation church. There are old gravestones – some dating back to the late-seventeenth century – associated with the earlier church. Deciduous trees totally surround the site; this is one of East Lothian's oldest woods.

In the seventeenth century, the parishes of Keith Marischal and Keith Hundeby were amalgamated with that of Humbie. These parishes owe their name to the powerful Norman-Scots families who once controlled these lands. Robert de Keith became an ally of Malcolm II and was made marischal of the kingdom and custodian of the royal regalia for killing the Danish general, Camus, at the battle of Barry in 1010. The origin of the name Humbie is unclear. In some old records it appears as Humby, Hundeby and Hundeley. The suffix *bie* appears in a number of local names and is thought to be old Norse for byre (a cowshed) or farmstead.

William Nicol, a well-known scientist, was born in Humbie around 1770. At fifteen he became assistant to his uncle, Dr Henry Moyes, helping the blind scientist with experiments and lecture tours. When Moyes died suddenly, Nicol continued his work by giving science lectures. He made Edinburgh his home and there he undertook experiments in fluid inclusions and studied fossil wood. He devised a method of producing rock sections so thin that light could pass through the structure, allowing its constituent minerals to be analysed under a microscope. His best-known invention is named after him – the Nicol prism, the first colourless plane polariser. For almost a century, these devices were the backbone of optical science and gave new insights into astronomy, crystallography and the nature of light itself. William Nicol died in Edinburgh in 1851.

INNERWICK

This small village is situated at the foot of the north-eastern edge of the Lammermuir hills. Its situation is unusual, occupying two low, adjacent ridges separated by a small stream. The settlement overlooks the narrow coastal plain along which the main road and rail routes link Scotland and England. The North Sea is just two miles to the east. 'Innerwick' is thought to be derived from 'village at the mouth of the river'. *Wick* is an old name for village and *inver* is a Celtic prefix for the mouth of a river. Another explanation of the origin of Innerwick is that it simply means 'inland village'.

Walter Stewart, to whom David I granted the manor of Innerwick, presented the church to the monks of Paisley, who retained it until the Reformation. William Wallace fought a fierce battle in the fields close to Innerwick, defeating the earl of Dunbar, a supporter of Edward I.

In 1670, Sir Peter Wedderburn obtained a grant of the rectory and vicarage tithes. The present church dates from only 1784 and is a modest

Innerwick parish church, which dates from 1784.

structure with a bell tower on the western gable. There are several good examples of eighteenth-century gravestones in the cemetery. The village is mainly constructed of pink-coloured stone, with few modern buildings. At its western edge, the red-pantile-roofed farm buildings of Temple Mains, dating from the early-nineteenth century, have been converted into an attractive residential complex and even the red chimney of the threshing mill has been preserved. Another building of note is the old post office, with its curved corner wall located next to the road junction. It has a sundial on its side, under which there is the following inscription:

> O'er every hour that's brightest, a shadow creeps,
> And he whose laugh is lightest full often weeps,
> Oh look we for the morrow, which hath no night,
> Where lost is every sorrow, in God's own light.

Although in the past Innerwick mainly housed agricultural workers, it is now populated by people who work further afield.

INVERESK

'The beautiful village of Inveresk, which, from its situation, houses and salubrity of air is justly reckoned the finest village and most healthy place in Scotland.' This is how author William Maitland described Inveresk in the eighteenth century. Consisting of little more than a single street, it retains its historic character with modern buildings notable by their absence. It is now virtually part of Musselburgh, which over the last century has advanced south to its boundaries.

'Inver', from the Gaelic *inbhir*, refers to river mouth, in this case where the Esk flows into the Firth of Forth. The village can lay claim to be one of the longest continually inhabited settlements in Scotland. There was once a major Roman fort occupying a small hill overlooking the Esk. Although it stood on ground just under a hundred feet high, it had a commanding view over the coast and surrounding countryside, and could be easily resupplied by sea, only a short distance away. The Romans never built any towns in Scotland, but there is evidence that there was a small settlement close to the fort, which probably housed craftsmen and merchants.

When the Romans abandoned Britain, the Inveresk fort site did not remain unoccupied for long. According to legend, a church was built here by the Irish missionary nun, Modwenna, who died in 519. It would probably have been constructed out of wood and wattle. Modwenna was said to have built her churches on the sites of King Arthur's forts. In the following centuries, at least one stone medieval church, dedicated to St Michael, stood on the same site. In the eleventh century, the parish was granted by Malcolm Canmore to the monks of Dunfermline abbey and by the thirteenth century St Michael's had become an important ecclesiastical centre. In 1242, it was chosen as the location for the first diocesan synod in Scotland and the clerics passed twenty-six decrees during their meeting here. Decrees included the sacred duty to keep church buildings in a good state of repair, that the clergy must wear distinguishing clothing and refrain from visiting taverns while travelling.

In the sixteenth century, John Wishart preached here, accompanied by John Knox. Around that time, the Roman fort was rediscovered. The remains included a cave with an altar and a *hippocaustum* (central heating). Mary, Queen of Scots instructed that these monuments of great antiquity should not be harmed. Unfortunately, at the end of the sixteenth century the altar was totally destroyed along with numerous other religious monuments across the country. The medieval church at Inveresk was still in use at the end of the eighteenth century as the parish church but was deterring worshippers because of its poor condition. It was demolished and replaced in 1805 by the present church, which has a distinctive tall steeple influenced by Wren. The temple of Apollo is said to have once stood on its site.

Rows of gravestones next to Inveresk parish church. Two thousand years ago, this was the site of a Roman fort.

The minister, **Alexander Carlyle**, was the driving force behind the new building. Born at Cummertrees, Dumfriesshire in 1722, he was known as 'Jupiter' Carlyle because of his imposing demeanour. He was minister at Inveresk from 1748–1805 and counted many leading intellectuals as his friends, among them Adam Smith and David Hume. The large cemetery occupies much of the area where there was once the Roman cavalry fort; it was extended in Victorian times and in the twentieth century. It includes a large monument to the Hope baronets against the eastern wall, a sarcophagus-style monument to the lords of Elphinstone and a white-painted, cast-iron sculpture of a coffin draped in military regalia to the south of the church marking the grave of William Norman Ramsay, an army major who fought at Waterloo.

Extending eastwards from the church for nearly a mile is a narrow road, lined with large impressive mansion houses. While nearby

Musselburgh developed as a commercial centre, Inveresk remained a retreat for the wealthy. A number of the more notable residences include Inveresk house, a short distance to the east of the church, which dates from the sixteenth century. On the opposite side of the road is Inveresk Gate, built in 1742; it was occupied from 1799–1938 by three generations of the Milne family – Sir David, Sir Alexander and Sir Archibald – all of them admirals.

Oak lodge was constructed around 1700, but extended in the following century. Catherine lodge, which has three storeys, takes its name from Catherine Fergusson of Ayrshire. Designed by Thomas Mylne, the manor house, built in 1748, is the most imposing of all the mansion houses in Inveresk: a seven-bay, classical villa with the nineteenth-century addition of a stair tower. The cartographer and geographer John Bartholomew, who owned Bartholomew maps, lived here from 1928–65. Halkerston was built in 1637, is square in plan and has a pyramidal roof resembling those found on farmhouses in the Netherlands at that time. It stands on a site that was once owned by the monks of Dunfermline, who probably had a residence in its vicinity. Close by is the White house, dating from 1700, which has been home to several famous Scottish military and legal personalities.

At the east end of Inveresk, the large mansions give way to cottages and two-storey houses. The National Trust for Scotland has a walled garden at Inveresk lodge, open to the public. It is on a south-facing slope with lawns and colourful borders at the top leading downhill to woodland with ponds; there is a seventeenth-century sundial along with a Victorian greenhouse and Edwardian conservatory. Inveresk lodge, like the other houses mentioned above, is not open to the public. It dates from 1683, but may incorporate parts of an older building. For much of its existence it was owned by the Wedderburn family, one of whom, John Wedderburn, supported the Jacobite rising of 1745, a decision that cost him his life. Around two centuries earlier, the battle of Pinkie was fought on the southern edge of Inveresk.

LONGNIDDRY

Longniddry had a population of 2,600 in 2011. Like many other East Lothian villages, it has become a dormitory town for Edinburgh, thirteen miles to the west. Situated on the main Prestonpans–Musselburgh road, it is close to the Edinburgh–London railway line. A short distance to the north of Longniddry is the Firth of Forth, but the sea has had little influence on the development of the village. There is no harbour here. The name Longniddry comes from *niddry*, the stream on the slope of the hill.

There is evidence that the area has been inhabited from an early date and many Bronze Age graves have been discovered around the village. A stone circle stood just to the west of the foot of Longniddry Dean until around a couple of centuries ago, when it was removed as part of an agricultural-improvement scheme. Unfortunately, little evidence remains of Longniddry's medieval history. Its castle stood next to the main road at the east end of the village between John Knox Road and the west end of Kitchener Crescent. Robert Bruce awarded the lands of Langnodryf to Thomas Sympil, on condition that he and his heirs provided one bowman for service in the army. In the later Middle Ages, the notorious Douglas family was in possession of the castle.

John Knox was engaged by Hugh Douglas to educate his two sons. During his time at Longniddry, Knox took the opportunity to preach to the local inhabitants in the village chapel, for which there are references as far back as the early-thirteenth century. In the grounds of Longniddry house, near 27 Gassel Park Road, there is a ruined wall with a window, known as 'John Knox's kirk'. Until 1840 the vaulted cellars of the castle could still be seen, but they were later removed and ploughed over. It was believed that at one time the castle had a tunnel that linked it with the sea. Longniddry was on the route of armies advancing up the coast and was prone to suffer from their depredations. In 1547, the English army under the duke of Somerset camped at Longniddry and devoured all the food they could find. The havoc wrought on the village would probably have been greater had not Hugh Douglas sided with the English. A consequence of his support for the enemy was the demolition of Longniddry castle a few years later.

During Oliver Cromwell's campaign in Scotland, his army spent a night here in torrential rain. The following day, as the soldiers made their way towards Musselburgh, Scottish cavalry mounted an attack on the rear of the column still at Longniddry. Major Lambert had his horse shot from underneath him and was briefly taken prisoner. The English cavalry drove off their assailants and succeeded in freeing Lambert.

Nearly a hundred years later, the battle of Prestonpans was fought a short distance to the west of Longniddry. The Jacobite army was victorious and shortly afterwards Prince Charles issued an edict that the lands of Seton-Winton, which included Longniddry, would be forfeited to him. The villagers were forced to thresh and deliver their wheat crop to Edinburgh, where the Jacobite army was camped. There was also a large rabbit warren owned by James Sibbald on the Links. In those days, rabbits provided a source of meat in the same way that dovecotes did. The soldiers shot most of the rabbits for entertainment, leaving so few that there were not enough to breed. Longniddry's troubles were not over yet: as the Jacobite army was about to march to England, a party of the Prince's regiment of Lifeguards arrived in Longniddry and appropriated all the horses and carts, which were taken to Dalkeith. It was intended to use them to transport Charles's baggage on the campaign.

Over the next two centuries, the village suffered mixed fortunes. Towards the end of the eighteenth century, it was a thriving agricultural settlement that extended south of the present railway line. That all changed when John Glassell purchased the barony of Longniddry. Glassell had made his fortune in the American colonies, but had to flee after independence. Initially suffering from a fever contracted abroad, he was confined to his residence, Longniddry house. The Agricultural Revolution was at its height and Glassell decided to maximise his investment. At first, he considered moving the whole village of Longniddry a short distance to the north, close to the seashore, as it was sitting on fertile land. In the end, he opted for demolishing more than seventy houses without bothering to provide alterative accommodation for the inhabitants. In the process, many of Longniddry's older buildings were swept away. By 1836 Longniddry's population had dwindled to around two hundred.

In the next century it underwent considerable expansion with the construction of many new houses. A small church was built in 1925. Up until that time, worshippers had to go to the church at Gladsmuir, two miles away. The village's oldest buildings are Longniddry house (private property), dating from the seventeenth century; its grounds, which once had orchards and woodlands, are now occupied by housing. The others are the pantile-roofed cottages which stand on the north side of the main road.

The author **Maureen Mcllwraith** (1922–2012), better known as Molly Hunter, was born and raised in Longniddry. She wrote books for both children and adults, many of which were inspired by events in Scottish history. James Bond actor **Pierce Brosnan** lived here for a short time in 1964 with his mother and stepfather, before moving to London.

MACMERRY

Situated to the east of Tranent, this village once stood on the Great North Road, now the A1, but was bypassed by a dual carriageway in 1996. The name 'Macmerry' means level high ground, from the word *magh*, a plain and *murean*, a hill.

Almost all the houses date from the twentieth century. The coalmines have long since closed and a small industrial estate is now the main source of work. At one time it had Scotland's most easterly iron-smelting works. Macmerry is probably best known for its Second World War airfield, located a short distance to the north, although little trace is left. Before the outbreak of war, there was a small aerodrome here with a number of private aircraft. It also briefly served as Edinburgh's civil airport. The population of Macmerry in 2017 was 1,800.

MUSSELBURGH

With a population of twenty thousand in 2017, Musselburgh is the largest town in East Lothian, with close to 20 per cent of the county's population living here. It is also the most recent, having spent most of its existence within Midlothian, becoming part of East Lothian only in 1975 after a change in local-government boundaries. It takes its name from the once-rich mussel beds found at the mouth of the Esk, now destroyed by erosion and pollution.

Musselburgh has also long been known as the 'Honest Town'. Its residents cared for Thomas Randolph, 1st earl Moray and regent of Scotland, during a long illness and when he died in 1332, Donald Mar, his successor, offered to reward the residents of Musselburgh for their devotion. This was declined as they said they were only doing what was expected of them, for which gesture it became known as the 'Honest Town'.

In recent centuries Musselburgh has incorporated what were once several dispersed villages, among them Fisherrow and Inveresk; the latter is the oldest and gave its name to the parish. Its church stands on a small hill overlooking the river Esk. A sixteenth-century stone bridge crosses the river a short distance away and tradition has it that the Romans had a similar structure on the site. The Edinburgh–London road has passed through Musselburgh making use of this crossing for many hundreds of years.

For most of its existence, the town was a short distance to the east of the Esk and did not occupy its banks until recent times. Musselburgh is an Anglo-Saxon place name, and, like many others in East Lothian, dates from the Dark Age occupation of the area by the kingdom of Northumbria. The suffix *burgh* signifies a town. The original name appears to have been Eskmouthe, or Eskmouth, as mentioned by Simeon of Durham as early as the seventh century. When the Lothians became part of Scotland in 1020, the Ecclesia de Muskilburgh passed under the jurisdiction of St Andrews. In the twelfth century, David I granted the manor of Inveresk or Musselburghshire, which included Musselburgh, Fisherrow and Inveresk church, to the monks of Dunfermline. In 1201, the barons of Scotland assembled at Musselburgh to swear their loyalty to the infant son of William the Lion, who later became Alexander II.

Being on the main route of invading armies, it suffered severely on a number of occasions. In 1544, part of the town, including the chapel of Loretto and the tolbooth, were burnt by an English army. Three years later, the battle of Pinkie was fought in the vicinity of the town. In 1548, Musselburgh and Dalkeith were burned by Lord Grey, who had commanded the English cavalry at Pinkie. On this occasion the town's records were destroyed. In 1638, the Marquis of Hamilton, ordered by Charles I to crush the Covenanters, was confronted on Musselburgh links by a gathering of several thousand people prepared to defend their religion.

Cromwell's army spent two months camped here in 1650, with the cavalry billeted in the town. From 1792 until the end of the Napoleonic Wars there was a large wooden barracks that could house more than two thousand militia and volunteer cavalry ready to repel a landing by the French. For a time, Sir Walter Scott was quartermaster of the Edinburgh Light Horse, which was based here. There was considerable dismay when the last soldiers left as they were a considerable source of revenue for local businesses, and, on one wall, the words 'A town to let' appeared. Long before this, Musselburgh had a growing number of industries, which offered an alternative source of income: large woollen manufac-turers existed well before 1703, but declined towards the end of the century; hides were also brought the short distance from Dalkeith to be tanned at Musselburgh.

The nineteenth century saw a great expansion in industrial activity. Bruntons rope makers were founded in 1876 and papermaking also provided employment. A large maltings and chemical works were built just to the west of Fisherrow. The long-established tanning industry also flourished at that time.

By 1960, Brunton's works occupied a 22-acre site a short distance to the south of High Street. At that time, it was Musselburgh's largest employer with over a thousand workers, supplying wire cables for suspension bridges across the world. By the end of the twentieth century there had been a change of fortune and the works had closed along with many other of town's industries. The old net-making factory on the banks of the Esk has been converted into offices while many others, including Brunton's, have since been torn down.

The oldest surviving buildings in Musselburgh are concentrated around High Street and its east end is very broad to accommodate markets. The tolbooth or town house is the most prominent building in the street with a tower crowned by an octagonal spire; the original building was more or less destroyed during the English invasion of 1544, with only the clock tower surviving. In the 1570s the council began work on a new tolbooth to house its chambers and a two-storey wing was added to the original structure from 1731–3; it has served as a court, jail and police station. Standing close to the tolbooth is the market cross and nearby is Musselburgh museum, which has local-history exhibits.

The tolbooth, Musselburgh, which dates from the 1570s, although the clock tower is considerably older.

A short distance along High Street to the east is the Parsonage, an early-nineteenth-century house once owned by Sir Walter Scott, who wrote some of the *The Lay of the Last Minstrel* here. Further along is an attractive group of buildings that includes the pantiled and yellow-harled French ambassador's residence; the ambassador apparently lived here in the early 1600s. Next to it is a white-painted tenement with a Tuscan pillar porch built around 1760 (these are private residences and there is no access to them). On the opposite side of High Street is the Episcopalian church of St Peter, with its tall, slender spire. Close by, a stone pillar stands on either side of the road. They were erected in 1770 and once stood closer together, marking the eastern entrance to the town.

In close proximity is Loretto house, dating from the eighteenth century. It now belongs to Loretto private school. In its grounds (no public access) stands a mound with an old stone doorway. It is all that remains of Loretto chapel, which once attracted visitors from all over Scotland; Thomas Duthie, a local hermit, was responsible for its foundation in 1534. Taking its name from the church of Loretto in Italy, it had a similar reputation as a place for miracles. James V performed a pilgrimage by walking to it from Stirling in 1536, before going on to France. After his death, Mary of Guise, his second wife, prayed here for twenty years. Disaster struck in 1544 when it was destroyed by English soldiers, but a few years later it was rebuilt. In an attempt to revive its fortunes, the chapel clerics faked a miracle in which a local youth, who was known for pretending to be blind, recovered his sight. The truth about his remarkable recovery eventually became known to the residents of Musselburgh. So enraged were they about being tricked that they demolished the chapel. When word of this reached the Pope, he excommunicated the entire population of Musselburgh – a situation that lasted 250 years!

On the opposite side of the road is Pinkie house, now part of Lorettto school. It can be seen at a distance from the school entrance or from the footpath that crosses the playing fields to the east. The name Pinkie is first recorded in the twelfth century as 'Pontekyn', which may be derived from the Welsh words *pant*, valley, and *cyn*, a wedge, referring to its situation in the valley of the Esk. The abbots of Dunfermline built a massive square tower house on the site in the early-sixteenth century, controlling the important road to England.

After the Reformation, Pinkie became the property of James VI's chancellor, Alexander Seton. Charles I (born 1600) spent much time here until the age of four. In 1613, the tower house was incorporated into a new building, creating one of the most impressive mansion houses in Scotland. Following Bonnie Prince Charlie's victory at Prestonpans, he stayed here as a guest. Other parts of the building were used as a make-shift hospital for his injured soldiers. In 1951, Pinkie house was acquired by Loretto school.

Mill Hill, situated to the north of High Street, represents the medieval back lane to the burgage plots (town rental properties) that once extended north from High Street. These plots were long, narrow strips of land running at right angles to the main streets of medieval towns. The houses stood at one end facing the street; behind them there would often be gardens or yards. A former church resembling a castle stands guard at the eastern end of the John Rennie Bridge, main route across the Esk. It was constructed in 1843, being extensively altered in 1889 when a tower and pinnacles were added.

It is thought that when the Romans had their garrison at the fort at Inveresk, their galleys may have been able to row their way up the Esk to supply it. There is also some evidence that in medieval times the river was navigable, as a David I charter refers to ships in the port of Inveresk. As late as 1712, an attempt was made to construct a new harbour close to the mouth of the Esk but this was soon abandoned in favour of Fisherrow. Today, the mouth of the river is unnavigable, as a tidal bank of sand and shingle stretches out from the land for more than a thousand yards. Fisherrow harbour, located in a shallow pocket surrounded by tidal rock, stands a mile to west of the mouth of the river. There is reference to a harbour at Fisherrow in 1592, but like many others at that time it may have relied on natural features alone. By the following century, it had a wooden pier infilled with stones.

Fisherrow harbour, which once had a large fishing fleet, but is now the preserve of leisure craft.

Oliver Cromwell considered using Fisherrow as a port to supply his troops, but rejected it in favour of Dunbar as he considered it too shallow. In 1712 it was treated as a quarry for the new harbour under construction at the mouth of the Esk, with boats from Fisherrow used to transport the stone. Work on it was abandoned as quickly as it had begun due to it silting up. A petition for a new harbour was presented in 1740 and work commenced on a new harbour at Fisherrow three years later; it was a small tidal basin enclosed by two stone breakwaters. White haddock were caught by the fishing vessels and the catches were transported on the backs of fisherwomen, who walked the five miles to Edinburgh to sell them; some could make the journey in under an hour! There is a 12-foot-high stainless-steel sculpture of a giant mussel, next to the seashore on Murdoch Green and a few hundred yards to the west of Fisherrow harbour. It depicts aspects of Musselburgh's history with images of agriculture, people, connections with the sea, the river and the Romans.

At the end of the eighteenth century, there were seven fishing boats based at Fisherrow employing forty-nine men. By 1839, it had risen to twenty-eight vessels crewed by 140 men. An experiment to clear the silt from the harbour was undertaken in 1835, when an opening was made in the east pier to allow tidal currents to wash the silt away. It proved unsuccessful; three years later it was again blocked. In 1847, this pier was repaired and extended after being damaged by a storm. It is built out of red-sandstone blocks and is 755-feet long. The west pier is more recent, having been totally reconstructed on old foundations in 1843–4 by engineers Robert Stevenson & Sons. Somewhat shorter than the east pier, it is 460 feet long. Rails were laid to the west pier in the hope that coal would be exported from here. In 1814 a waggon-way was built to connect the harbour with Pinkie Hill colliery. By the late-nineteenth century, only a few cargo vessels were called here, importing salt from Northern Ireland and pipe clay and tanners bark from England. The following century also saw a dwindling number of fishing boats sailing from here as herring and white fish stocks in the Firth of Forth declined in the 1930s. There was also increased competition after the introduction of large ocean trawlers in the 1950s. The number of fishing boats declined from twenty in the 1960s to just two by the end of the century and today the harbour is crowded with leisure craft. The small building that stands in front of it is the former customs house. A promenade extends eastwards from it with good views of the Firth of Forth.

Despite its size, Musselburgh has relatively few statues and memorials. There is a statue to **Dr David Moir**, *Delta*, which stands on a tall pedestal, overlooking the road junction at the west end of High Street close to the main bridge over the Esk. He was born in the town in 1798 and studied medicine at Edinburgh University. After graduating he returned to his home town, where he practised as a doctor from 1817–51. Moir was also a writer, contributing articles to magazines under the pen name of Delta. An outbreak of cholera in Musselburgh prevented him from having time to complete his history of medicine. David Moir is buried in St Michael's churchyard.

On the opposite side of the road, overlooking the Esk, is a yellow-sandstone fountain. Designed in the French style, it features carved fish, shells and shields and the coats of arms of Musselburgh, St Michael, Lord Randolph Murray and David Wright, who gifted it to the town in the 1890s. Further upstream on the banks of the Esk and close to the old 'Roman Bridge' is a statue of an archer. It was erected in 2018 and was created to represent various aspects of local history including the battle of Pinkie Cleugh in 1547 and the Musselburgh Silver Arrow competition, which dates back to 1603.

Notable residents of the town have included **John Grieve**, awarded the Victoria Cross during the Crimean war. He saved the life of an officer who was surrounded by Russian cavalry during the heavy-cavalry charge at Balaklava, decapitating one horseman and fighting off the others. He is buried in St Michael's churchyard, Inveresk.

Athlete **Yvonne Murray** was born in Musselburgh in 1964. She won many medals, including a bronze at the 1988 Olympic Games in the 3,000 metres and a gold medal in the 10,000 metres at the 1994 Commonwealth Games. The former middle distance and long-distance track and road-running athlete was inducted into the Scottish Sports Hall of Fame in 2007.

NEW WINTON

This attractive village on the east side of the Pencaitland–Tranent road owes its existence to Lady Ruthven, who lived in Winton house for the greater part of the nineteenth century. She was interested in the welfare of the area's inhabitants, particularly the farmers and miners who lived around Pencaitland. New Winton was built at her expense to provide accommodation for miners. During construction, Lady Ruthven would frequently visit the site and suggest improvements. The village consists of nineteenth-century cottages built around three sides of a large village green.

Although some additional houses have been added in the twentieth century, the hamlet retains its character with rows of terraced cottages surrounding a large village green on three sides.

NORTH BERWICK

The small town of North Berwick stands on the coast at the mouth of the Firth of Forth, and is one of the closest points to Fife. This factor was responsible for the establishment of a settlement here in medieval times when it became an important destination for those who wished to cross the Forth. There had been people living in the area from prehistoric times, as evidenced by the remains of a hill fort on North Berwick Law, the 613-foot hill that looms over the town. According to some sources, its original inhabitants came from the Elbe region on the opposite side of the North Sea and settled on the coast as there was an abundant supply of shellfish. The name 'North Berwick' is derived from 'barley farmstead' – *bere* in Old English means barley and *wic*, a farmstead. The prefix north was added to distinguish it from Berwick-upon-Tweed, which in medieval charters was referred to as South Berwick.

Although the town is now largely bypassed by the main routes heading south from Edinburgh via Dunbar, this was not always the case. In the eighth century, the Pictish king, Oengus I, established a monastery on the opposite side of the Forth at St Andrews, which housed relics of the saint who bore that name. From that time, it became the destination of pilgrims from all over Scotland and beyond. Those coming from the south made their way up the coast to catch the ferry at North Berwick. It is thought that it may have initially sailed from a point further along the coast at Broadsands, near Dirleton, but North Berwick developed into the main crossing point.

A small length of rock thrusting out into the sea formed the backbone of the early harbour. It consisted of a stone breakwater with North Berwick bay on the west side and Milsey bay on the east. In the mid-twelfth century, David, earl of Fife, established a ferry service between this point and Earlsferry. To provide accommodation for pilgrims, he had a hospital built next to the harbour, and, in 1413, more than fifteen thousand people made the crossing. There were also guest houses next to the current harbour on the site of the former granaries. No trace of a hospital remains today and only a fragment of the original parish church is extant. These buildings originally stood on what was an island until the eighteenth century, accessed first by a timber bridge and later by a causeway. The meagre ruins of the parish church of St Andrew's stands a short distance from the Scottish Seabird Centre. All that is left is a one-storey, rubble-built structure that was once its porch. The church was built in the twelfth century, but may stand on the site of an earlier timber example.

The small rectangular church was enlarged by the addition of a chapel in the thirteenth century and a tower was added in the following century; inside was an altar to the Virgin Mary. In 1312, its vicar is recorded as William, who pledged himself and his bay horse to the service of Edward II. The church's main claim to fame is that it was where two hundred witches allegedly gathered at Halloween in 1590 to conspire, by whipping up a storm, to sink James VI's ship, which was returning from Denmark.

The fragmentary remains of the twelfth-century St Andrew's church, North Berwick. It is located a short distance from the Scottish Seabird Centre.

Ironically, it was a storm in 1656 that severely damaged the church and swept away much of the surrounding graveyard. Its exposed location had been made vulnerable by the quarrying of the nearby volcanic rock. A new parish church was constructed a few years later, well away from the seashore, immediately to the south of High Street in Law Road. While it was being built, religious services were held in a long-vanished tenement. The second St Andrew's church was opened for religious services in 1664; it was furnished with pew boxes and was typical of an early post-Reformation church. The tower was not added for another century and it remained the sole place of worship in North Berwick until 1843. It is now an attractive ruin, its congregation abandoning it in the late-nineteenth century for a new building in High Street because it had become too small.

In the Middle Ages there was a convent of some importance situated on sloping ground half-a-mile west of the harbour. Its ruins stand next to Old Abbey Road on private ground but the tops of the buildings can be seen from the street. Today it is surrounded by houses, but when it was in use it stood in open countryside. What remains of the convent consists of a late-medieval range that included the kitchen and refectory; no trace of its church has ever been located. The convent was founded sometime between 1147–53 and dedicated to the Virgin Mary. It may have originally been a Benedictine house, only later claiming to be Cistercian in order to claim the privileges of that order. In 1199, Malcolm, earl of Fife, bestowed St Andrews church, the hospice and the harbour of North Berwick to the Cistercians. From that time, the nuns had control over the town's trade and agriculture.

In 1362, David II was sailing between North Berwick and Earlsferry when his vessel was almost shipwrecked. A chapel was constructed to the seventh-century saint, Monan, close to a point where he made landfall in Fife, an expression of his gratitude to God for the narrow escape. The shrine was initially cared for by the Cistercian convent at North Berwick. The nuns were responsible for operating the ferry and made trinkets for the pilgrims and the convent was a powerful influence on North Berwick until the Reformation.

To the east of the harbour, standing between houses on the seafront, there is a small, grassy mound that backs onto the East Links. It is the site of North Berwick castle. Like most medieval buildings of the town, little trace remains. A timber motte-and-bailey castle stood on the site in the thirteenth century, the property of the thanes of Fife. At the time of Bannockburn, it was held by an English garrison. As Edward II retreated after his defeat, his soldiers deserted the castle and fled to Dunbar. At the end of the fourteenth century the Lauders, who now controlled North Berwick castle, built a stone tower with a barmkin (defensive enclosure) on the mound. A few decades later, it had been abandoned, possibly in favour of the castle on Bass Rock, which was also held by the Lauder family. In 1435, the site of North Berwick castle and the surrounding land was gifted to the church.

When the Protestant religion displaced Catholicism, pilgrimages came to an end and North Berwick lost this lucrative business. The harbour, which had a long history as a minor trading centre, continued to be used by cargo ships and fishing vessels. In 1380, a ship heading from North Berwick to Flanders was captured and taken to Newcastle, its cargo sold off. That was not the end of the matter, as the mayor of Newcastle ordered those responsible to reimburse its owner, William Fawsyde, for his loss.

Robert II confirmed the earl of Douglas's right to have a port here and to erect a custom-house and tron (weighing beam). When North Berwick was granted its barony charter in 1381, the harbour was exporting small quantities of wool. In 1406, Robert III watched his young son James – later to become James I – depart on security grounds, on a vessel bound for France. James never reached his destination; he was captured by pirates off Flamborough Head and handed over to the English, who incarcerated him in the Tower of London for eighteen years before he was allowed to return to Scotland.

Foreign trade peaked early in the fifteenth century, but, even then, no more than ten tons a year was being exported. In 1425, the town was upgraded to a royal burgh, but, by 1500, the harbour's trade had shrunk to negligible levels. It fared little better over the following two centuries, although fishing gained importance with a herring works established in 1642. Even so, only two fishing boats and no cargo ships were based at North Berwick in 1700. When Bishop Pococke visited in September 1760 he found it 'a small ill-built town situated on a strand'. The harbour was located, as now, on the west side of the rocky peninsula; it could receive vessels of up to two hundred tons at spring tides, but more usually around a hundred tons.

The harbour was damaged by storms in 1788, 1802, and in 1811, when the outer end of the breakwater was almost completely washed away. The tower of St Andrew's church was still standing, having being retained as an aid to navigation, but was demolished around the same time.

The harbour of today dates from the nineteenth century, when it was rebuilt and repaired after the storms. No trace of the earlier medieval works remains. The renowned family of engineers, the Stevensons, drew up a plan proposing the complete rebuilding of the harbour, with facilities to restore the Forth crossing to Elie, but this plan was left on the drawing board.

The harbour continued to handle occasional cargoes of guano, potatoes and grain until the early-twentieth century, but the coming of the railway brought an end to much of the coastal trade. Herring fishing declined in the 1860s with the disappearance of the large shoals. There were still around thirty fishing boats based at North Berwick two decades later but numbers declined and by the 1980s only a handful of

A sea of sails next to North Berwick harbour. In bygone centuries the sails would have belonged to fishing boats or cargo vessels.

small lobster and crab boats were left. Although no longer reliant on handling cargo or fish, the harbour, now filled with leisure craft, remains at the heart of North Berwick. History has come full circle, with frequent sailings of boats packed with passengers, not on pilgrimages, but to view Bass Rock and May island.

The red-rubble, nineteenth-century warehouses have been converted into flats. An old hand crane still stands on the end of the northern breakwater. A short distance away is the Scottish Seabird Centre, one of East Lothian's leading tourist attractions. Close to the ruined fragment of St Andrew's church is an impressive red-granite Celtic cross, erected as a memorial to **Catherine Watson**, who drowned in 1889 at the age of nineteen. She had just finished bathing when she caught sight of three children, two boys and a girl, being swept out to sea. Fully clothed, she rushed into the water in an attempt to rescue them, but died in the attempt. The children were eventually rescued by the coastguard. Inscribed below the monument are the words: 'A loving tribute from her fellow students of the Glasgow School of Art, the work of one of their number.'

In the mid-eighteenth century, North Berwick was little more than a single street with houses and cottages on either side of High Street. The population was around seven hundred in the 1790s, with only two fair days being held a year. There was a major change in its fortunes in the following century when visiting the seaside became an important recreational activity. Among the visitors was Robert Louis Stevenson, who holidayed here, finding inspiration for his novels.

The increasing popularity of golf resulted in the North Berwick golf club being formed in 1832. The opening of the railway brought even more visitors to the town. By 1874, a further two golf courses were being played on. North Berwick attracted visitors for seaside holidays from large towns such as Edinburgh. It was ideal for this purpose, having two large sandy bays, one on either side of the harbour. Paddle-steamers ferried day-trippers down the Forth to spend a few hours ashore here.

The town was advertised on railway posters as 'The Biarritz of the North'. From 1831–1931 the population rose from 1,824 to 4,083, and, by 2016, this figure had risen to 5,880. Like many other seaside resorts, its popularity as a holiday destination declined with the advent of cheap overseas holidays. In the early 1950s, there were thirty-four hotels but by the end of the century only six. Despite this, High Street is often packed with summer visitors.

North Berwick is twenty-two miles from Edinburgh and many commuters now reside here; it is also a popular place to retire. The history of the town has been kept alive in the Coastal Communities museum in School Road. Most of the older buildings in North Berwick date from the nineteenth century or later. This is particularly true of High Street. St Andrew's parish church stands in this narrow street, enclosed by other buildings; it was built 1882–3 in the Gothic style, its tall tower a local landmark. Dating from around the same time is the Roman Catholic church, Our Lady Star of the Sea, in Law Road. There is also St Baldred's church towards the west end of the town, constructed in the Neo-Norman style in 1861.

Numerous large mansion houses and villas dating from the late-Victorian and early-Edwardian era can be found on the west side. An earlier impressive town house, The Lodge, of the eighteenth century, stands a short distance to the south of High Street. It originally belonged to the Dalrymple family, which was closely associated with this part of East Lothian. They owned another house, also built in the eighteenth century, which still stands on the opposite side of the road in Quality Street. At this time, the family was well represented in legal circles.

In an incident obscured by the mists of time, a warrior in the Dalrymple family threw large rocks at enemy soldiers attacking Bass Rock. The king yelled encouragement to him with the words, 'Hew, Dalrymple,

Gardens, Quality Street, North Berwick.

Hew' until the enemy withdrew. The grateful monarch stated that he should be known as 'Hew', and from that time on Hew was a common name in the Dalrymple family. Although The Lodge has been converted to flats, its grounds were purchased in 1939 and now form a split-level park. The lower park is a formal garden with an aviary; there is also a square eighteenth-century dovecot. The upper park has large open spaces with mature trees and views over the Forth.

OLDHAMSTOCKS

This village is probably the most remote settlement in East Lothian. In 2020 the population is around two hundred, compared to seven hundred in the 1830s. It is situated on the eastern edge of the Lammermuir hills, only a short distance from Berwickshire. The name is Saxon and derives from *aldham*, the old village, and *stoc*, a place. The first recorded evidence of Oldhamstocks occurs in a charter in favour of the monks of Coldingham, dated 1127, and witnessed by Adulf, minister of Aldehamstoc.

Today, it is little more than a single street of stone-built cottages and houses, stretched out along the northern slope of a valley at the foot of which the Oldhamstocks burn flows towards the North Sea. Located at a height of 470 feet, there are commanding views across the nearby landscape; a fault extending north to Innerwick and Broxmouth runs close by.

Cromwell's cottages stand at its eastern end. There was once an inn at Oldhamstocks, in which Oliver Cromwell spent a night on his way north. On being asked how he slept, he answered, 'As sweetly as though I had lain in Abraham's bosom.' At that time, the main road between Edinburgh and England, unlike today, headed inland up the valley and passed close by, but its inns had disappeared by the late 1800s as the railway and main road bypassed Oldhamstocks.

A single row of attractive cottages lines the road leading towards the church and village green; a market cross stands in the centre of the latter. It has been moved from its original position at the east end of the village, close to the crossroads. A law of 1672 gave Oldhamstocks the right to hold two village fairs a year. An eighteenth-century pyramidal pump/drinking well stands close by. A miniature steading from the same period

This drinking well, with pyramidal stone on top, is located on Oldhamstocks village green.

and the walled garden of the manse are found on the south edge of the village green. The former school, dating from the nineteenth century, is on the opposite side. Blackcastle manor house, home of the Hepburn family, once stood on a slope a short distance to the north of the church. It would have dominated the village, but was abandoned by the end of the seventeenth century and no trace remains.

The small parish church is now the main focus. It is an attractive, whitewashed building situated at the village's western edge. The date '1701' is inscribed above the old entrance to the church, which is somewhat misleading as it incorporates fragments of a fourteenth-century building; these include a portion of the east gable and some masonry courses at ground level. There is evidence that the earlier church was oblong in plan and had a square tower, somewhat broader than at present. The first church on the site dated back to the early-twelfth century, but was rebuilt a number of times. It was dedicated to St Michael and consecrated in 1242 by David de Bernham, the bishop of St Andrews, like many other East Lothian churches. Thomas de Hunsingoure was 'parson of the church of Aldhamstoke' in 1296. The Hepburn family aisle, built in 1581, stands on the east side; it is a solidly built structure with heraldic carvings on the walls. In the church-yard there are gravestones that date as far back as 1637. Several display the tools of the trade of the deceased.

There is a gravestone to James Broadwood, father of **John Broadwood**, who became a famous piano maker; he was born a short distance away at Cockburnspath in 1732 but grew up in Oldhamstocks. At the age of 29, John Broadwood left for London, where he made pianos, greatly improving their design by adding pedals and increasing the range of the keyboard. His legacy lives on in John Broadwood & Sons, one of the oldest and most-prestigious piano companies in the world and still in business today. Guarding the churchyard is a small watch tower built into the southern boundary wall; it dates from 1824, when fear of bodysnatching was at its height.

For over a hundred years from the mid-sixteenth century, the Hepburn family dominated the parish ministry. One became involved with Mary, Queen of Scots and the earl of Bothwell. Shortly after the murder of Darnley (the Queen's second husband), Bothwell wished to marry the Queen, but he had just married Lady Jane Gordon. While staying at his stronghold of Dunbar castle with Mary, he enlisted the the local clergy to overcome the problem. Revd Thomas Hepburn, a relation, agreed to cooperate and he published the royal banns at the sixteenth general assembly. Not long after, the couple were married at Holyrood palace. The union was opposed by most Scottish nobles and the couple were forced to flee to Dunbar castle. While Hepburn was making his way there with vital letters from Edinburgh castle, he was waylaid and the communications seized. After Mary had surrendered to her nobles at Carberry hill and Bothwell had fled abroad, Revd Hepburn held Dunbar castle in their name.

The stronghold was eventually taken and destroyed, but this was not the end of Hepburn's support of Mary. He helped her escape from captivity in Loch Leven castle and then he tried to retake Dunbar, but his small force of twenty men was easily defeated. For his actions, Hepburn was removed as minister of Oldhamstocks parish.

ORMISTON

Ormiston stands on the north bank of the Tyne on top of gently rising ground, at a height of 280 feet. At this point in its journey to the sea, the Tyne is little more than a stream flowing through arable fields. In the early-twenty-first century it had a population of two thousand. The original settlement stood some distance to the west by a river crossing. The name Ormiston originates from the Ormres family, who owned the land in the twelfth and thirteenth centuries. Ormr was a semi-mythical Anglo-Saxon settler, whose name meant serpent.

Their lands then passed to the Lindsays and from them by marriage in 1368 to John de Cockburn. He married Joneta, the only daughter of Alexander Lindsay, lord of Ormiston. The Cockburns built a castle on the south bank of the Tyne between 1450 and 1530. Members of the Cockburn family also held lands at Clerkington and had a great deal of influence over Haddingtonshire, serving as constables and sheriffs.

In the sixteenth century, the Cockburns sided with the Protestant cause. When the preacher George Wishart, a close friend of John Knox, was staying at Ormiston castle in 1546, soldiers under the command of the earl of Bothwell surrounded it and demanded that the preacher be handed over. After being assured of his safety, Wishart agreed to leave the castle; he was taken first to Elphinstone tower and then Hailes castle. Cardinal Beaton pressured Bothwell to hand Wishart over to him and he reluctantly complied. Not long after, George Wishart was tried by an ecclesiastical court at St Andrews, where he was hung and then burnt at the stake.

The Cockburns were at the forefront of the agricultural revolution. Adam Cockburn was the first landowner to enclose his fields and was also the first to practise fallowing. In 1690 he ploughed land that hitherto had been suitable only for poor grazing. It was then left before sowing and was in time able to produce a good crop. Another practice he introduced to Scotland was ploughing in the autumn and the sowing of winter wheat. Up until then, no ploughing had taken place before February. But it was his son, **John Cockburn**, who achieved fame. He attempted to abolish the traditional short-term leases for land and to replace them with leases lasting several decades, arguing this would encourage investment. At that time there were ten tenant farmers in Ormiston village. In the 1720s, John Cockburn also established a maltings, a brewery and a distillery, which produced 'pale malt, high flavoured ale and an excellent whisky'.

A more ambitious enterprise was to move the old village of Ormiston to its present site. Lord Gordon, a London civil engineer, was commissioned to lay out the new settlement; construction began in 1735 and was completed by 1746. Lord Gordon built himself a house here. John Cockburn intended that the new Ormiston would be a centre of enterprise; he introduced a bleach works, the second in Scotland, and a linen mill. Ormiston hall was built in 1745, two hundred yards from the castle. Unfortunately, Cockburn experienced financial problems and in 1747 was forced to sell everything, including Ormiston hall.

The country house was used to accommodate Polish troops during the Second World War. In early 1944, fire totally gutted the building. Its ruins were demolished in 1973, although some of the older walls were left. Close by, only the foundations remain of the earlier Cockburn residence, Ormiston castle. Not much is left of the medieval church of St Giles either, three hundred yards south of the mansion site. All that remains is a roofless aisle with walls standing to a height of ten feet.

Early in the thirteenth century, the church of St Giles was conferred by the bishop of St Andrew on the hospital at Soutra. A charter conferred on Soutra hospital by 'Radulph lord of Cranystoun' bears among its witnesses the name of 'Giles, lord of Ormystoun'. In 1462, it was transferred to Trinity College, Edinburgh along with all other churches belonging to Soutra hospital. After it was replaced by a new church a short distance away at Bryes, it was partially demolished in 1730.

Therefore, little remains of early Ormiston, whose castle, church and country house lay about a mile south of the present village. They occupied the top of a slope on the south bank of the Tyne, now heavily wooded. Many are the legacy of James Cockburn who planted large numbers of trees on his estate; pre-dating them is the famous Ormiston yew tree, said to be over a thousand years old. It stands close to the scant remains of Ormiston hall. Some of its outbuildings survive and have been converted to private residences, with new houses constructed in the vicinity.

Coal had been worked in the area for centuries. The most accessible seam was in the vicinity of Ormiston hall, which by the mid-nineteenth century had become so undermined by workings that it had to be propped up from underneath. At that time, there was little mining in the vicinity of Ormiston village itself, as the coal deposits were far underground. All this changed when John Clark founded the Ormiston Coal Company. Several large pits were sunk, served by the railway that skirted the northern edge of the village.

The character of the village underwent a change, with new houses being constructed to house the miners, while a church was built in 1936. Prior to that residents had a long walk on Sundays for religious observance; the nearest church was close to Byres farm on the Humbie road. It was built in 1696 by Adam Cockburn close to the ruined St Giles medieval church, which once served the village. It was reconstructed in 1856, but today the only evidence that there was a church here is the old cemetery.

By the early 1960s, the last pit had closed and in years to come the railway went the same way, converted to a footpath. Despite these changes, Main Street has retained its Victorian character. When John Cockburn laid out the new village of Ormiston, he instructed that the houses on it should be two-storey. Most of houses on Main Street date from the Victorian era, but Hillview at the east end is probably mid-eighteenth century. The house on the corner of Cross Loan is even older, perhaps dating from John Cockburn's time. Where Main Street narrows, there is another eighteenth-century house.

The oldest structure in the village is the fifteenth-century market cross. It is puzzling that it occupies a place in the principal street as it is thought there was no settlement here until the building of the new Ormiston village here in the eighteenth century. A chapel did exist in the vicinity. The character of Main Street is further preserved in the fact that deciduous trees still stand on either side as in previous centuries. At one time, there were market gardens around Ormiston, noted for growing strawberries. As they did not keep well, the punnets were delivered to the station in the early morning for transport to Edinburgh. When the royal family was in residence, strawberries from Ormiston were dispatched to Holyrood palace.

An obelisk in Peterhead granite, twenty-feet tall, stands at the eastern extremity of Main Street. It was erected in 1884 to commemorate **Dr Robert Moffat**, born in Ormiston in 1795. To find employment, he moved south to Cheshire where he worked as a gardener. Friction arose with his employer due to Moffat's Methodist sympathies and so he decided to become a missionary.

At the age of twenty-one Moffat travelled to South Africa, where he undertook a number of strenuous treks, the Royal Geographic Society receiving accounts of his journeys. In 1817, he set out for the kraal of the Namaquas, said to be a bloodthirsty tribe; they were successfully converted to Christianity. On that journey he encountered the Bechuanas, who give their name to Bechuanaland, and it was here that Robert Moffat spent most of his life as a missionary. The Bible was translated into the Bechuana tongue by him; he also wrote two books, including *River of Waters in a Dry Place*. His work was not confined to spiritual matters. When the Bechuanas were threatened by the Zulus, Moffat procured rifles for them and in the conflict that followed the hostile tribe was defeated. While on a return visit to Britain, he met David Livingstone and persuaded him to undertake his missionary work in Africa and not China as he had intended. One of his daughters later married Livingstone. In later life, when his health began to fail, he returned to England and died in 1883.

Charles MacLaren was born in Ormiston in 1782. Self-taught, he established *The Scotsman* newspaper with William Ritchie and John McDiarmid in 1817. He was also interested in science and geology and helped edit the sixth edition of *Encyclopaedia Britannica*. Between 1820 and 1846, MacLaren was the editor of *The Scotsman*. In his later years he was president of the Edinburgh Geological Society.

PENCAITLAND

This picturesque village is located on the banks of the Tyne, 270 feet above sea level; it had a population of 1,600 in 2017. A very old bridge is still in use today as the main crossing point of the river. It has a shield on the south side bearing the engrailed cross of the Sinclairs and the possible date of 1510. The village probably grew up as a Tyne crossing point on the Dalkeith–Haddington road. Today the oldest buildings are found on either side of this road, the Tyne dividing it into Easter and Wester Pencaitland. The name of the village is derived from the Cymric (or Welsh), *pen-caeth-Ilan'O* meaning 'the head of the narrow enclosure'.

In the late twelfth century, the manor of Pencaitland was owned by Everard de Pencaithland. The church and his manor, along with its tithes and other rights, were granted by him to the monks of Kelso for the salvation of his king, William. Bishop de Bernham consecrated the church in 1242 in what would have been an elaborate service lasting several hours. Some time before the 1306 accession of Robert the Bruce, Pencaitland church ceased to belong to Kelso abbey. Thomas de Pentkateland, who owned the lands at that time, made the mistake of allying with the English. He lost his lands when Robert the Bruce drove the English out of Scotland

and became king. Robert de Lawedir was rewarded with them for his services.

The lands passed to John de Maxwell after the succession wars that broke out with the death of Bruce. John de Maxwell granted an annuity of his lands to the monks of Dryburgh together with the patronage of the church at Pencaitland. The monastery collected tithes and in return provided a priest to perform services in the church at Pencaitland. In 1404, a castle was constructed by the Seton family a short distance north of the village; Winton house now stands on the site. Further downstream, Saltoun hall, on the banks of Birns water, occupies the site of another castle. Several other fortifications were once found in the vicinity, including Ormiston castle a short distance to the west. The monks of Dryburgh retained their interest in the church at Pencaitland until the Reformation.

The present parish church, near to the sixteenth-century bridge over the Tyne, stands on the site of an earlier medieval church. Most of the building dates from the sixteenth and seventeenth centuries. A stone tower stands at its west end, bearing the date 1631 and the initials 'I.O.' for John Oswald, a former minister. The tower is of irregularly coursed

Pencaitland church.

rubble up to the octagonal stage, which is built of ashlar and roofed with a small, slated spire surmounted by a weathercock. At one time there was a dovecote in the tower, with nesting boxes for pigeons. The church bell dates from 1636 and bears the inscription 'Pencaitland, fear ye the Lord'.

The walls of the present church are built on medieval foundations. Attached to the structure are two aisles, the oldest of which is the thirteenth-century Winton aisle. At one time it had a roof of stone slabs. It has been suggested this may either have been the original medieval church or perhaps served as the sacristy to the main building. On its corbels are the carved faces of devils, animals, men and angels. The Saltoun aisle stands next to the Winton aisle, which dates from the late-seventeenth century.

David Calderwood was one of its notable ministers. He began as a minister in the Scottish Borders but fell foul of James VI when he protested against the drafting of new church laws. After a prison sentence, Calderwood was banished to Holland. On the King's death in 1625, he returned to Scotland and became minister of Pencaitland. Here he researched and wrote a comprehensive history of the Church of Scotland, which was published around 1683, long after his death. Robert Douglas became minister at Pencaitland in the later-seventeenth century. His early life was spent as chaplain to Scottish soldiers fighting on the Continent under the Swedish king, Gustavus Adolphus. He later became a minister in Edinburgh and preached before the Scottish Parliament during the Civil War.

The churchyard has many interesting gravestones, although many older ones have unfortunately been removed. Some display the tools of trade of the deceased, including miners and quarrymens' tools. There are no less than three sundials, as well as many interesting inscriptions on the external church walls. On the west side there is a Renaissance tablet to 'Katherine Forbes, Daughter to Mr John Forbes Minister to the English Merchants Adventurers at Delf 1639'. She was the wife of the minister, John Oswald. Another inscription on the south wall remembers three people who died of violent fever in 1736. There are two small pantiled buildings, one at each end of the churchyard, dating from the eighteenth century. Known as offering houses, their purpose was to provide shelter from inclement weather for the church elders collecting on Sundays for the poor.

The nearby manse dates from the early-nineteenth century. Pencaitland house stood close to the church at the east end of the bridge. It was built in the seventeenth century, although parts may date from the fourteenth century. It burnt down in 1876 but two of its wings survived and are now houses. There were other old buildings, including a public house, near the church known as the 'college'. The name, the college, refers to a Roman Catholic place of instruction.

Just beyond the eastern edge of the village, next to the road junction, stands a war memorial in the shape of a cross. It was designed by Sir Robert Lorimer to the memory of the twenty-six men of the parish who were killed in the First World War.

On the opposite bank of the Tyne, an old stone market cross stands next to the road junction in Wester Pencaitland. It marks the site of the old market, where, in the eighteenth-century, fairs for 'horse and colt, sheep and all sorts of linen and woollen cloth' were held twice yearly, in June and October. Opposite is Belfry cottages, probably converted from an early-nineteenth-century school, which has a bellcote and a stone statue of a pupil perched over one of the doors. There is also a row of pantiled cottages dating from around 1800.

Many of the later cottages were built in the Victorian era by the Trevelyans, who lived in Tyneholm house. The village hall was commissioned by Arthur Trevelyan, an eccentric. He proposed that the inhabitants of Pencaitland should wear Turkish national costume to make it more colourful. He believed in social equality and did not like aristocrats, whom he referred to as 'the antichrist'. Among his other hates were soldiers – whom he called 'man butchers and moral lunatics' – horse racing, and, for reasons unknown, ploughs. At one stage, he wrote to Prince Albert complaining that he spent too much time shooting and that Queen Victoria wore too much jewellery.

After the end of the First World War, the council built new houses in Wester Pencaitland. Many of them were occupied by miners and manual workers, but, by the following century, Pencaitland had become home to many commuters. One well-known business is Castle Sound Studios, established in the 1970s in the former Pencaitland primary school. Many famous bands have recorded here, including Simple Minds, Runrig, REM and the Blue Nile.

PORT SETON

Port Seton is the last of a chain of continuous settlements that include Musselburgh and Prestonpans, extending eastwards from Edinburgh along the south shore of the Firth of Forth. It began as a small fishing village like Cockenzie. From 1655–65, George, 10th lord Seton, built the first harbour at Port Seton; it was called Port Seton to distinguish it from Cockenzie harbour, a short distance to the west. Incidentally, the name Seton is derived from 'sea town' but not a Scottish one. In the eleventh century the family held lands on the Yorkshire coast, from whence the name.

The construction of the harbour involved cutting through very hard rock, and explosives may have been used. There were twelve vessels based at the harbour in 1760, with a capacity of 590 tons. At that time, locally mined coal was a major export, much of it destined for Edinburgh. Salt was shipped to Hamburg, Bremen, Norway and the Baltic. Fishing boats also operated from the harbour, their catch consumed locally and as far away as Spain. By the early-nineteenth century, there had been a dramatic change in fortune; trade had declined during the Napoleonic Wars and frequent storms had destroyed much of the harbour. By 1810 it was described as almost inoperable. Ten years later, further hardships were inflicted on the fishing community when fish became scarce and catches very poor. The situation improved when the new Cockenzie harbour opened in 1835. Not all fishermen required the use of a harbour, as some dragged their boats over the cobbles to the sea.

Port Seton harbour.

The impetus for a new Port Seton harbour gained momentum when fees for fishermen were introduced at Cockenzie harbour. In addition, during the herring boom of the late-nineteenth century, Cockenzie harbour became too small to accommodate the large boats used for drift-net fishing. The construction of the new harbour was funded by subscription from the fishing community, as well as a gift of land from Lord Wemyss; the work was done from 1879–80. It is an early example of mass-concrete construction, at a time when most structures were stone. The middle pier was added five years later.

Throughout the twentieth century, Port Seton was an important fishing centre. In the 1970s, there were as many as fifty boats, the largest around 70 feet in length. They caught fish all over the North Sea and sometimes hauled up wartime mines. In 1995, one caught a torpedo containing 1,500 lbs of TNT, which was brought back to Port Seton to be detonated; it was one of the largest ever made by the Germans. By 2000, the number of fishing boats had declined to ten, employing forty men, and most of Port Seton harbour is now occupied with leisure craft. In the 1920s and 1930s the town was busy with holidaymakers and although it has declined in popularity, many people still come to Seton Sands holiday village, a short distance to the east.

Until the nineteenth century the villages of Cockenzie and Port Seton had so few inhabitants that they did not have their own parish church and worshippers had to travel to Tranent. The first church was constructed in High Street in the early 1830s. In 1904, building began on Chalmers Memorial church in Gosford Road, the main route through the town. The design is highly original, influenced by the Arts and Crafts movement, the saddleback tower crowned with a short, Swiss-style spire and the slated and dormered roof rising from very low eaves. It is the most prominent building in the town, standing on the main Edinburgh–North Berwick road. Unusually, High Street is now little more than a side street standing a short distance to the north but it has the Thorntree inn, one of the oldest inns in East Lothian. Opposite is Gardeners' Close cottage, which dates from around 1790. There is also Port Seton house opposite Elcho Place, which dates from 1709, when it was built as a summer house for the Seton family. Most of the other buildings in Port Seton date from the nineteenth and twentieth centuries.

The internationally respected artist, **John Bellany**, was born at Port Seton in 1942. His father and grandfather were both fishermen. The first few years of his life were spent in Eyemouth before returning to Port Seton. After school, he attended the Edinburgh College of Art. Bellany won a number of scholarships, enabling him to travel widely and to study European art. After graduating, he lectured at Brighton College of Art and then at a similar facility in Croydon. His work became widely known after some forty of his paintings – depicting himself and family while he was recovering from a liver transplant – were exhibited at the Scottish Gallery of Modern Art. This was followed by a documentary on BBC television. Exhibitions of his paintings took place across the world, including London, New York, Berlin and Melbourne and there are now few art galleries where his work is not represented. Despite his success he never forgot his place of birth, frequently returning to Port Seton to visit family and friends. He died in 2013.

The combined population of Port Seton and Cockenzie in 2016 was 5,293.

PRESTONPANS

At first sight, Prestonpans appears to be a small town consisting mainly of mid-twentieth-century municipal housing. However, it has a long and interesting history, which its residents have done much to preserve in the form of festivals, publications and wall murals. In 2016, it had a population of ten thousand. The town extends from the seashore up a slight slope, the Edinburgh–London railway forming the boundary on its southern edge. Originally, it consisted of a number of villages, which have since merged, including Prestonpans, Preston and Morrison's Haven. Its original name was Aldhamer. According to legend, 'Aldhamer', or 'Althamer', was an eleventh-century pirate who terrorised North Sea shipping. One day, his vessel was caught in a hurricane and swept into the Firth of Forth. It was dashed to pieces on the rocks and the ship-wrecked crew decided to give up their life of plunder and establish a settlement on the seashore.

Around 1184, the monks of Newbattle were given lands around Prestonpans and Tranent. They established salt pans at an early date on the coast and Aldhamer became known as Salt Prieststown, later becoming abbreviated to Salt Preston. Salt was produced by evaporation – fires were lit underneath iron pans containing sea water. It took around eight tons of locally mined coal to produce a ton of salt. Much of it was then transported overland to the Borders. During the Middle Ages, there was constant rivalry between Prestonpans and Preston, a short distance to the south. The latter was under the influence of the Hamiltons and other wealthy families and was on the main Edinburgh–London road, but Prestonpans remained the centre of economic activity. By the beginning of the fifteenth century, it had ten salt works producing 800–900 bushels per week and two centuries later, half of Scotland's salt was being made here.

At a time when most of the economy was reliant on farming, Prestonpans was a bustling industrial centre. By the eighteenth century, activities had diversified to include chemicals, pottery and brewing. The numerous breweries may have been inspired by monks, experts in this field. One of the oldest breweries was founded in 1720 and later came into the hands of the Fowler family, their ales becoming well-known across Scotland. In the mid-eighteenth century, there were no less than sixteen breweries in the town, but, by the early-twentieth century, only Fowler's remained in business. It too had gone by the

374

early 1960s. Whisky was distilled in Prestonpans, as far back as the reign of James II. Pottery was also responsible for putting Prestonpans on the map. There were tidal mills, which ground flint for its production. The first potteries were turning out their wares in the late-seventeenth century. Fifty years later, it had become the centre of the Scottish pottery industry. The products ranged from household pottery to the finest figures and porcelain. In Victorian times the potteries concentrated on basic wares; 'Broon Coo' teapots were turned out in enormous numbers. The brickworks at Morrison's Haven also made pottery, such as urns.

A soap works was established shortly after 1745, originally using ashes from seaweed and rough fat; it was still in business in the early-twentieth century, by which time the ingredients were refined animal and vegetable oils with snow-white alkali. It had a reputation for quality. There was also a sugar refinery, but, unlike the soap works, it was unsuccessful. In 1698, a glass works was established next to the harbour, with the assistance of skilled workers from abroad. It specialised in high-quality products, including glass for mirrors, watch glasses, window glasses and even spectacle glasses. Despite being granted a monopoly in Scotland, it lasted only a few years before ceasing business.

The sulphuric-acid works were founded by the chemist John Roebuck and Samuel Garbett in 1749. They selected Prestonpans because of the availability of coal. The vitriol works were the first in the world to use the lead-chamber process, which was a closely guarded secret. Sulphuric acid was used for linen bleaching and in other industries. In time, it became Britain's largest acid works, exporting much of its output. Salt manufacturing declined during the nineteenth century because of the availability of rock salt from Cheshire, but coal mining continued to flourish.

Prestonpans had an important harbour at Morrison's Haven, a short distance to the west. It was immediately to the north of the industrial museum and the main road that skirts its boundary; unfortunately, it has all but vanished. In the 1960s, it was filled-in with ash from the nearby Cockenzie power station, as part of a land-reclamation scheme. The harbour dated from 1526, when the monks wished to expand their market for salt and coal, and to provide a safe haven for fishing boats. James V granted permission for a harbour of one acre at Prestongrange and Alexander Atkinson was engaged to build it. By 1544, fish, hides and salt were being exported and lead imported. In the early-seventeenth century, ownership of the harbour passed to John Morrison and the harbour became known as Morrison's Haven rather than its previous name, Acheson's Haven.

In the 1680s, Morrison's Haven was exporting coal to the Netherlands, and, to a lesser extent, France. English boats, en route to Icelandic fishing grounds, would call in to take salt on board. Locally based boats caught herring and skate but Prestonpans was best known for its oysters. In 1691, an English ship is recorded as having been loaded with 12,000 oysters bound for Riga in Latvia; another vessel picked up a cargo of lobsters. Oyster fishing reached its peak from 1773–86, when there were numerous boats operating out of Morrison's Haven. The best oysters were known as pandoras and were found near the salt pans. London was an important market for the oysters, but they were also sold in Edinburgh and Glasgow. By the end of the eighteenth century, there was a drastic drop-off in catches due to over-exploitation.

Over time, improvements were undertaken to the harbour. English ships landed cargoes of tobacco, soap, bricks and paper; a few decades later, many of these products would be manufactured in Prestonpans. In 1705, there was also the arrival of apples and onions from Holland and a cargo of luxury goods that included English hats and gloves. During 1719, forty-one cargoes arrived at the harbour, including one of tobacco from Maryland, America. Duties imposed after the Union of England and Scotland, as well as the loss of several of Prestonpans ships at sea, led to a decline in foreign trade and the fortunes of the port. Smuggling was rife and there is a widely held belief that some of the older seafront houses have secret passages running down to the shore, once used by smugglers.

By the late-eighteenth century, foreign trade at Morrison's Haven included its much-in-demand pottery. Clay was imported from Devon and flint from Gravesend for its manufacture. Brownware was a popular export to many European countries and North America. The chemical works, established to produce sulphuric acid, now produced a wide range of products, which were also exported.

Prestongrange coal mine, immediately to the south of the harbour, was modernised in the later nineteenth century, as was the harbour itself to enable coal to be exported. Despite the additional works, the basin could accommodate only one vessel of no more than six hundred tons. By the 1930s, traffic had all but vanished and only one fishing boat and some leisure craft used Morrison's Haven. The basin was filled in and the area has been grassed over. Some upright timbers and the curving sandstone blocks of the coal jetty are still visible. The concrete back wall of the harbour dates from the twentieth century. A concrete base at the west end of the harbour walls would have supported the starboard harbour light.

Immediately behind the former site of the harbour, and centred around the old colliery, is Prestonpans industrial museum. Like the harbour, little remains of the salt-panning industry or many of the other industries that flourished here. On the seashore there is a large volcanic rock called 'Johnny Moat'. Tradition had it that if it ever fell over, the prosperity of Prestonpans would come to an end. This happened in 1952 and in the decades that followed most of the town's industries closed, including its colliery, brickworks, potteries and breweries. After a period of forty years the rock was put back on its perch. It is thought to be a blue whinstone boulder, transported by glaciers during the last Ice Age. There are however, more fanciful theories, including that it was a meteor or that it was blasted out of Arthur's Seat when that protuberance was a volcano.

Prestonpans is famed for its extensive collection of wall murals This one depicts the great environmentalist, John Muir.

For much of its existence Prestonpans consisted of little more than a single street: High Street, next to the seashore. Most of its buildings are relatively recent with a few exceptions, including the Boat Stone house, which has a relief of a fisherman's farewell and is dated 1630. There are a small number of old houses in Harlawhill and Kirk Street. What it lacks in historic buildings is made up by the large number of wall murals depicting scenes from the town's history. Prestonpans is sometimes known as Scotland's mural town. There are around thirty-five, most of which are on, or near, High Street with others in Cuthill park and Prestonpans railway station. They feature a diverse range of subjects – the battle of Prestonpans, witches, John Knox, John Muir, industrial scenes and even a drunken bar brawl.

The mural trail starts at Prestoungrange Gothenburg, a building with a mock Tudor frontage built in 1908. In the nineteenth century, Sweden attempted to curb the consumption of alcohol. The town of Gothenburg allowed alcohol to be sold only by a trust and most of the profits were to be used for projects to help the community. The idea was introduced to Britain, although it proved controversial even among Scottish temperance campaigners. 'Gothenburg' public houses were often established in mining areas: they had a contradictory role, selling beer but not spirits. No games or amusements were allowed, making the premises less attractive for drinkers.

Situated at the east end of the town is Prestongrange parish church. There was a fourteenth-century chapel administered by Newbattle abbey, which was destroyed during the English invasion of 1544. It stood in the south-east corner of Preston West churchyard in the centre of Prestonpans. Although no trace remains of the chapel, there are many interesting seventeenth- and eighteenth-century gravestones. Construction of the current parish church was undertaken in 1596; it had the distinction of being one of the first churches built after the Reformation. The building actually stands on the site of a vicarage that once belonged to Holyrood abbey, which was also destroyed in 1544; John Davidson, its first minister, paid for the construction. Not afraid to criticise bishops or even the king, he found himself in prison in 1601; on his release, he was restricted to the parish. In 1745, another minister watched the battle of Prestonpans from the church tower. There are graves of several Jacobite soldiers in the churchyard. In 1774, the church was rebuilt, leaving the tower the only remnant of the original structure. The churchyard has an interesting collection of old gravestones.

Immediately to the north is a small public garden overlooking the main road to Port Seton, with a statue of **Thomas Alexander**, looking out to sea. He was born in 1812 and went on to study medicine at Edinburgh University. Not long after, he joined the army, his first posting to the West Indies. Here he witnessed the deaths of many British soldiers from tropical diseases. Alexander requested medical supplies but received little response. After serving in Nova Scotia, where the cold was a major cause of death, he returned to Prestonpans and purchased a house, where his statue now stands. During the Crimean War he was principal medical officer of the Light Division and did everything in his power to alleviate the suffering caused by cholera and extreme cold.

Thomas Alexander did much to improve army sanitary conditions and to elevate the position of medical officers. Such was his reputation that he was appointed honorary surgeon to Queen Victoria in 1859. But, by the following year, he was dead at the age of 49. His body was returned to Prestonpans and he was buried where his statue now stands. It is not the only statue in Prestonpans. In the centre of town there is an impressive example in stone of a Scottish soldier of the Great War, part of the war memorial.

Prestonpans was once surrounded by market gardens that supplied Musselburgh and Edinburgh. The soils of the 100-foot raised beach, coupled with low rainfall, made it ideal for this purpose. Carrots were grown, along with cabbages. There were also orchards of apple, pear and plum with gooseberry and raspberry bushes and strawberry plants that stretched from the edge of Prestonpans village south to the railway station. By the mid-twentieth century this had all vanished, much of the land covered by housing.

While Prestonpans was the industrial centre, the seat of power lay a short distance to the south at Preston village, now the southern edge of the town. Here the Hamiltons, sometimes referred to as the 'Haughty Hamiltons', had a tower house, which, although now a ruin, is 90 feet high. It has no less than six storeys, the height of the original fifteenth-century building being enlarged upwards in the seventeenth century. The Preston estate came into the possession of the Hamilton family in the fifteenth century with the marriage of Sir John Hamilton to Jane Lyddell of Preston. The tower is all that remains of an extensive castle complex.

A short distance away from the tower, next to the road, is the mercat cross. It is one of the best-preserved examples in Scotland and is in its original position. Hamilton house, a two-storey, white-painted house constructed by John Hamilton in 1626, stands a short distance to the west in the main street and is owned by the National Trust for Scotland. The Hamiltons also constructed Preston house around the same time or possibly at the end of the sixteenth century; no trace remains, as it burnt down shortly after the battle of Dunbar in 1650. Standing opposite Hamilton house is the impressive Northfield house, built in the sixteenth century and at one time owned by the Hamiltons. It was acquired by Edinburgh merchant, Joseph Marjoribanks, who expanded and remodelled it in 1611. Today it is a private residence.

SAMUELSTON

Samuelston consists of little more than a single row of cottages on the north bank of the Tyne, three miles south-west of Haddington. It is best known for being infested with witches in the seventeenth century. Every trace of the church of St Nicholas, in which John Knox preached as a Roman Catholic priest, has long since disappeared.

SPOTT

The village of Spott sits on the northern edge of the Lammermuir hills, three miles south of Dunbar. It is overlooked by Doon hill, nearly six hundred feet in height, which played an important historical role. On its slopes, General Leslie and his troops prepared to combat Oliver Cromwell and his army on the plain below. The Spott burn flows along the northern edge of the village, its few houses standing on the narrow shelf between the burn and the rising ground of the rolling hills. This natural feature was the setting of an earlier clash of arms when the Scottish army attempted unsuccessfully to halt the advance of Edward I in 1296.

One theory about the origin of the Spott name is that it relates to its sheltered situation, another that it takes its name from a 'spot' on the ground west of the village where cattle were penned and guarded at night. The site where this took place is also known as 'Chesters', a prehistoric fort with a diameter of more than three hundred feet; it is surrounded by two earthen ramparts now only four or five feet tall.

Although an insignificant road runs through the village today, this was not always the case: it was once the 'Herring Road'. Fishwives often travelled on foot from Dunbar carrying their creels of salted herring, weighing up to a hundredweight, across the Lammermuir hills to the market at Lauder. The trade reached its height in the eighteenth and nineteenth centuries, when the herring fisheries grew rapidly. Spott's few houses and cottages are constructed out of deep-pink sandstone. Its church is a modest, T-plan, harled building with a bellcote at its south-west end. The structure dates from 1790 and was further remodelled in 1809. A place of worship has existed here since at least 1342 as Spott was listed as one of seven chapels under Dunbar collegiate church. It is possible the chapel was first established as a place of rest for pilgrims on their way to Iona who stopped to slake their thirst at St John's well, a holy well two-hundred yards north-west of the present church.

The witches stone stands a few hundred yards to the west of the village on the edge of the road, allegedly the site where Spott's witches were put to death.

STENTON

Like Garvald and Spott, Stenton, another of the Hillfoot villages (that is, villages at the northern foot of the Lammermuir hills), is located on the edge of the uplands, five miles south-west of Dunbar. It is three hundred feet above sea level. Deuchrie Dod, a detached 1,000-foot hill formed from silurian rocks with steep valleys on either side, lies immediately to the south of the settlement with the main mass of the Lammermuir hills a short distance beyond it. A small stream, the Sauchet water, flows down from the uplands and along the western edge of the village.

Stenton's name is Anglo-Saxon. It was originally Stanton, or, in Scots, 'Stanetoun' (Stonetown), so called because of the large number of small stones scattered on the land. Another theory suggests it may have been due to the number of red-sandstone quarries in the vicinity; most of the village is constructed of this attractive rock. Stenton was the superiority of the Lauder of the Bass family from the thirteenth century until the mid-seventeenth century. Henry the Minstrel mentions in his poem, 'The Wallace', that William Wallace rewarded Sir Robert de Lawedre with the lands of Stenton in 1297. Half the lands were forfeited by his family to Edward III from 1335–7. The Lauders finally relinquished their interest in Stenton in 1644.

The oldest structure in the village is the tower of the sixteenth-century parish church, later converted to a dovecote. The place of worship was rectangular, 60 feet in length and nearly 20 feet in breadth, and made of local rubble. The original parish church was not located in Stenton but in the hamlet of Pitcox, or 'Pitcokis', a mile to the north-east; it was under the collegiate church of Dunbar. Today Pitcox is an attractive hamlet consisting of a handful of houses, but any trace of the church has long since vanished.

The current parish church stands next to its ruined predecessor. It dates from 1829 and, compared to some village churches, is an impressive building with a magnificent tower and stained-glass windows. William Burn was responsible for its Gothic design. Mrs Ferguson donated a considerable sum for its construction, enabling the provision of a lavish building. The churchyard contains several interesting monuments dating from the seventeenth and eighteenth centuries. Standing on the other side of the road is the old manse, reconstructed after a fire in 1820.

The village consists of little more than a single street, with attractive houses and cottages constructed of deep-pink stone, and, in many cases, roofed with orange or red pantiles. The market tron stands close to the road, near the church. It was a public weigh-post and beam, used for bulk measurement, in Stenton's case generally wool and hides. In 1681, the Hamiltons of Pressmennan and Biel secured the legal right to

hold a weekly market and a twice-yearly fair at Stenton. Markets were held on the site of the tron until the mid-nineteenth century. Because of its relatively isolated position, the character of the village has not been spoilt by modern developments.

A little to the east of Stenton, next to the road, stands the 'rude' (rood) well, said to have been built by the monks of Melrose or

The medieval rood well at Stenton.

Jedburgh abbeys; it has a finely carved cover, sometimes referred to as the cardinal's hat. A mile or so to the south of the village is Pressmennan lake, an artificial creation occupying a narrow valley at the foot of Deuchrie Dod hill (*see plate section*).

TRANENT

With a population of 10,600 in 2016, Tranent is the second-largest town in East Lothian. It stands on top of a slope overlooking the Firth of Forth, two miles distant. The landform is part of the Tranent–Garleton ridge, which has a flat or gently undulating surface sloping steeply away to the west of the town. Tranent was originally known as Travernant, meaning 'the hamlet in the vale', from the Welsh *tref*, a homestead or village and *nant*, a valley. A less-believable explanation is that a party of Vikings landed on the Fife coast, but were repulsed by the locals, who shouted 'Tranent, Tranent!' meaning 'let them swim over' (to the shore of East Lothian). Since the Middle Ages it has been a centre of coal mining. The original settlement stood on the east side of a narrow north–south ravine, the only feature of its type in the Tranent–Garleton ridge.

The first reference to Tranent occurs in twelfth-century charters of Holyrood abbey, in which it is recorded that Thorald was the owner of the lands of Tranent. Thorald was the last of his line and his lands passed into the possession of Malcolm, the monarch. The next proprietor of these lands was Robert de Quincy, an English baron who acquired them from William the Lion in 1165. It is recorded that c.1184 he granted to the monks of Newbattle the lands of Preston. There they established a farm, which was called Prestongrange, with common pasture in the manor of Tranent for ten sheep and for oxen to cultivate their grange. Robert de Quincy also gave them six acres of meadows at his manor of Tranent and twenty cartloads of peat.

Robert's son, Seyer de Quincy, set out for Palestine in 1218 to join the Crusades and was killed the following year. The lands he held in and around Tranent then passed to his brother, Roger de Quincy, who was earl of Winchester and became lord of Tranent as well. When he died in 1264, his three daughters inherited his estate. The family sided with John Balliol against Robert the Bruce, losing their lands when Bruce became king. The lands of Tranent were given to the King's relative, Alexander de Seton, who already owned a neighbouring estate.

Unfortunately, few buildings of any antiquity remain. One exception is a ruined, L-plan tower house to the north of the town. It once would have had commanding views over the surrounding countryside, but is now hemmed-in by houses. The building is private property but can be seen at the end of a small lane off Church Street, just beyond its junction with Sanderson Wynd. Built of sandstone rubble, the tower house dates from the sixteenth century. Little is known of its history although it stands on lands that belonged to the Setons. There may have been a previous fortification here dating back to the thirteenth century. The Vallance family acquired the current tower house in the seventeenth century and it later served as a barracks and stables. Legend has it that it is linked by tunnel to Falside castle, two miles away.

Being on the main invasion route, Tranent was sacked many times. In 1547, the English army got to Tranent a few days before the battle of Pinkie but found it deserted; every man, women and child had fled with their possessions to the safety of the coal workings burrowed into the hillsides. Only a worn-out ox stood in the centre of the road, unable to move out of the soldiers' way. The troops, being short of food, took charge of it. Not long after, the ox's owner, described as a 'witless Jock, the village fool', appeared. He claimed it was a gift from his mother when she died and demanded its return. The soldiers had by this time already eaten the wretched animal. They took its alleged owner prisoner and pressed their spear points into him to reveal the whereabouts of the rest of the inhabitants; eventually, he agreed to lead them to the pit mouths. The soldiers then attempted to drive the people out of the old workings by lighting fires at the entrances and blocking up others. No one emerged. The soldiers were reluctant to go underground. There were so many subterranean workings linked together that the fugitives and their animals remained unscathed.

In 1745, Tranent was on the periphery of the battle of Prestonpans, fought a short distance to the north-east on lower ground. The day before the battle, a party of Highlanders entered Tranent at the west end and made their way down the Heugh to the churchyard, within five hundred yards of the enemy. The government forces responded by dispatching cavalry, armed with carbines, forcing the rebels to make a rapid retreat. That night, the Highlanders pitched their tents a short distance to the west of Tranent. Bonnie Prince Charlie, when passing the house of Windygoul, a short distance to the south of the town, was greeted by a number of women. One asked to kiss his hand; he not only granted the favour but also took the girl in his arms and gave her a kiss on the lips, calling her 'a bonnie lass'.

At the end of the eighteenth century, there was more strife in the vicinity of Tranent in the form of civil disorder. In 1797, with the French Revolution in its infancy, and Britain at war with that country, the Scots Militia Act was passed. It was intended to raise a force of six thousand, but there was much opposition to this. On 28 August 1797, **Joan 'Jackie' Crookston** organised a protest march towards Tranent

Jackie Crookston statue, Main Street, Tranent.

from Gladsmuir, where she lived. She used her drum to orchestrate continual chants of 'no militia', intimidating local justices and land-owners. The following day, a riot broke out, when delegates met in Glen's inn. Trouble had been anticipated, with the cavalry deployed to keep the peace. The soldiers came under attack from protestors throwing stones from the roof and some of them opened fire with empty cartridges. It did not deter the unrest. The Riot Act was read, with order briefly restored. The situation then deteriorated further when live amm-unition was used: Jackie Crookston was shot dead, alongside George Elder; Mary Allan, aged 17, was hit as she fled down a lane, but survived.

The violence was not confined to the streets of Tranent. The cavalry attacked suspects in the surrounding countryside, many having no connection to the protests. Peter Ness was chased until he fell and was shot while on the ground; he had been going to Tranent to collect his pay. Stephen Brotherstone and James Crichton were walking towards the town when they were shot at; having missed the target, one of the cavalrymen attacked the men with his sabre, killing one and severely wounding the other. Peter Lawson was on his way to Tranent with a pile of wood when he was shot in the side; one of the soldiers then put his unloaded pistol against the victim's face and pulled the trigger several times to intimidate him. Lawson later died from his injuries.

Senior cavalry offices eventually restored order. By this time, twelve people were dead and many more injured, including women and children. The Cinque Light Dragoons, responsible for most of the atrocities, were never held to account. Their commanding officer was Colonel Viscount Hawkesbury, a future prime minister, who was not present. It was reported that: 'His lordship was blamed for remaining at Haddington as his presence might have prevented the outrages of the soldiery.' Jackie Crookston is remembered by a statue that stands in the civic square in the centre of the town. It was unveiled in 1995.

In 1830, Tranent experienced a serious water shortage. Its inhabitants were driven to drink from stagnant pools and horse ponds. Some drew water from the Great Day Level (a drainage dyke for mine workings) while others fought over the few drops from the main village well. Hundreds of people became sick as a consequence, many with ailments unknown in the locality. The lack of water from the traditional wells was eventually attributed to a mineshaft being driven into the great sand bed; water had previously flowed through this geological formation.

Three years went by, but nothing had been done to rectify the situation. It was necessary to take legal action before the mine owner returned the water to its original course. Even when work was taken to block the shaft, it was many months before the water returned to its former level and the epidemic began to abate. In 1837, another shaft was driven into the great sand level and the water disappeared again. Tranent had to wait until 1883 before it received a satisfactory supply of water, when it was piped from a reservoir at Crichton some eight miles away.

The oldest buildings, which generally date from the nineteenth century, are strung out along the Edinburgh–London road from east to west. Before the coming of the railway, six stagecoaches passed through Tranent every day, except on Sundays when only the mail coach ran. The Haddington and Dunbar coaches changed horses at an inn located towards its eastern extremity. Passengers could also get food and drink. The town is no longer on the main route south, having being bypassed by a dual carriageway in the late-twentieth century.

Tranent parish church is situated on the north edge of the town, on ground sloping towards Cockenzie and the Firth of Forth. It is attractively located with views over the Firth of Forth. Legend suggests that monks associated with the monastery on Holy Island established a chapel here in the eighth century. It was dedicated to St Martin of Tours, who founded the monastic system in western Europe and was the patron saint of beggars. The present building dates from 1800, has a tower, and, like many other East Lothian churches, stands on the site of a much older building, of which some fragments are incorporated in the structure.

There has been a church here since at least 1145, when it was granted to Holyrood abbey by Thorald, son of Swain. The Augustinian monks received feudal dues that were owed to the church and in return a priest would be provided to say mass. In addition, Tranent had the role of providing clothing for Holyrood abbey. Later, the lord of the manor gifted a considerable portion of the lands at Tranent to Newbattle monastery, which housed the Cistercian order.

Tradition has it that the stones used to build the first church came from the ravine known as the Heugh. It was from this exposure that coal was mined at an early date. This feature still exists and can be found close to the town centre; a footpath runs along its bottom. There is a variation to this story, which relates that the stones came from the shore at Cockenzie and were passed along a human chain to the church site. During the English invasions of 1544 and 1547, the building was plundered and badly damaged; for many years it was left without a roof. By the end of the eighteenth century the church was again becoming unsuitable for worship, being damp and dangerous. It was decided to build a new structure.

The churchyard is surrounded by deciduous trees and is unusually rich in monuments and gravestones. A recumbent slab, lying to the south of the church, is a memorial to Alexander Crauford, a former priest of Tranent, who died c.1489. From the 1700s there are numerous pedimented tabernacle monuments as well as headstones, many featuring the skull and crossbones. There is also a table stone monument for the Seton family. On the south side of the churchyard there is a double-lectern-style dovecote.

One of the town's best-known residents was **Peter Hume Brown**, born here in 1850. He came from a poor home but managed to get a place at Edinburgh University. He had intended becoming a minister, but decided to concentrate on Scottish history. After graduating, Brown taught at a private school in Edinburgh, resigning seven years later to write. His works included a biography of John Knox and *Early Travellers in Scotland*. Among his most widely read works was *A Short History of Scotland*, extensively used as a school textbook. There was also a more scholarly work in three volumes on Scottish history. In 1901, Brown was appointed professor of ancient Scottish history at Edinburgh. Seven years later, he became historiographer royal for Scotland. He died in 1918.

A number of well-known footballers were born in Tranent, including Neil Martin, who won three caps for Scotland in the 1960s.

TYNINGHAME

The village stands at the foot of Lawhead hill, which rises to a height of 180 feet. To the south, the Tyne winds its way to the sea through flat, intensively farmed fields. Like several other villages in East Lothian, Tyninghame has been moved from its original site, which lay some distance to the east and close to where Tyninghame house stands today. It was an ancient settlement dating back to the Dark Ages when the area was part of the kingdom of Northumbria. The name is Anglo-Saxon, meaning the hamlet on the Tyne from the word *ham*, village, and *ing*, meadow. By 756, there was a monastery here. It has been suggested that long before this there was a Roman settlement here although there is no evidence for this. The village and its monastery were burnt by the Vikings in 941. The next mention of the settlement occurs in a charter that King Duncan granted to the church of Durham in 1094. It also names five other places in East Lothian, including Auldhame and Scoughall. The church at Tyninghame enjoyed the privilege of sanctuary.

Patrick de Leuchars was its rector during the reign of David II. He eventually became bishop of Brechin and chancellor of Scotland. George Brown, rector in the reign of James III, rose to the post of bishop of Dunkeld. Later he became involved in the murder of the king at Sauchieburn. The manor of Tyninghame and its church belonged to the bishops of St Andrews; it was held for a time for the archbishop by the earl of Haddington, but in 1628 full ownership of the property was obtained by the earl. In the succeeding centuries the manor was reconstructed as Tyninghame house and major landscape improvements undertaken by planting hundreds of acres of trees. The original village, which lay close to the residence, was moved about half a mile to the west. The ancient church of Tyninghame became a private chapel to the earls of Hamilton. It survives today in a ruinous state, consisting of little more than a few arches. There is neither access to it nor to Tyninghame house.

The new village of Tyninghame was constructed in the 1760s to house estate workers. It stands next to the North Berwick–Dunbar road. The main street has pink-sandstone houses and cottages on both sides of the main street. Almost all the buildings date from the nineteenth

Picturesque cottages in Tyninghame.

century and the village has not been spoilt by modern developments. The village hall, remodelled in 1842, is among the oldest buildings. Unusually, the new village of Tyninghame does not have its own church, as the parish was merged with that of Whitekirk in the eighteenth century and the place of worship is located there.

WALLYFORD

Wallyford, like Whitecraig, is a former mining community. It is situated immediately to the east of Musselburgh at the foot of the ridge that extends towards Tranent. It is about a mile from the Firth of Forth. Although Wallyford is close to the Great North Road and on the medieval Salters Road, its origin is fairly recent, as it is not shown on early maps. When the battle of Pinkie was fought in 1547, there was probably nothing more than one or two farms here.

In 1786, the important St Clements Wells distillery was opened and remained in operation until 1833. A colliery was sunk in the late-nineteenth century not far from the site of the distillery. At that time,

Wallyford was described as a collier village in Inveresk parish with a population of 341; by 2017 its population had grown to three thousand. Today Wallyford has been almost completely absorbed by Musselburgh, their boundaries blurred by new housing estates and many people now commute to Edinburgh.

Wemyss Gardens and Inchview stand on the site of Wallyford country house, thought to have been built in 1672. By the nineteenth century, it appears to have been abandoned and by 1876 it was inhabited by up to twenty-seven families of miners. Not long after, it burned down, although its ruins were not finally demolished until the 1980s.

Writer **Margaret Oliphant** was born in Wallyford in 1828, but spent her childhood at Lasswade until her family moved to England ten years later. At the age of sixteen she wrote her first novel and then achieved success in 1849 with *Passages in the Life of Mrs Margaret Maitland*, her first published work. Two years later, she had her novel serialised in *Blackwood's Magazine*, the start of a long relationship with this leading literary publication. Margaret Oliphant suffered several tragedies in her life, including the death of her husband, when she was left in considerable debt only a few years after their marriage, and later the death of her daughter. Writing usually under the name 'Mrs Oliphant', her books were very popular. Her output was prolific and included a number of novels on Scottish life, the most important being *The Minister's Wife* and *Kirsteen*. At her death in 1897, Margaret Oliphant had written over a hundred novels plus thirty works of non-fiction on a range of subjects, among them history and travel.

WHITECRAIG

This village is two miles south of Musselburgh and only six miles from Edinburgh. Although it is on Salters Road, a route that has linked Prestonpans with Newbattle since medieval times, this settlement is the most recent of all East Lothian villages. It dates from the early-twentieth century when houses were built on agricultural land to house miners working in nearby coal mines. Prior to this, many lived in the hamlet of Deantown, west of Carberry, but with the opening of new collieries, including Smeaton, it was unable to cope with the influx of miners. By the early 1950s, the construction of its council housing had come to an end. St John's church was built in 1953. The name of Whitecraig is derived from one of two rocky outcrops between here and Musselburgh; the other was known as Redcraig. Both were sources of sandstone used in the construction of buildings in Musselburgh and its vicinity. There is a footpath from Whitecraig to Penicuik, Midlothian.

WHITEKIRK

Whitekirk church, which dates from the twelfth century, but was largely reconstructed, beginning in 1439.

The village is situated on the south facing slope of Whitekirk hill, which rises to 250 feet. The Peffer burn, an insignificant stream, flows nearby and enters the North Sea just over a mile away. The lands of Hamer, along with the parish church, were gifted to the canons of Holyrood by David I.

Today, Whitekirk is little more than a hamlet with an attractive church, rich in history. Located 4.5 miles south-east of North Berwick, it was once an important destination for pilgrims, some 15,653 from many countries visiting in 1413, many attracted by the reputed healing properties of its holy well. In fact, so many people were visiting that hostels had to be built to provide them with shelter. Whitekirk was originally known by the name 'Hamer', which signifies 'the larger village', distinguishing it from the now vanished Aldhame, a short distance east. At one time it may have been known as 'Fairknowe'.

The present name is derived from 'white church' as the church here, St Mary's, once had lime-washed walls. It dates back to the twelfth century, with a major reconstruction beginning in 1439, when Adam Hepburn of Hailes built the vaulted stone choir. The main layout and structure of the church have survived largely intact since then, although everything but the stone walls was destroyed by a fire in 1914. The restoration of the interior commenced in 1917, with the assistance of the renowned Scottish architect, Sir Robert Lorimer. Today, its walls are no longer white, but of natural stone with a red hue. St Mary's provides us with a vital link to our past: it is one of very few medieval churches still in active use in Scotland in 2020.

Medieval chroniclers mention two significant events involving Whitekirk church. In the first, it received the unwelcome attention of an invading English army during the burnt Candlemas in 1356; ships with supplies anchored in the Firth of Forth and some of their sailors came ashore to plunder Whitekirk church, which was full of treasures. One of the sailors stood on the high altar and snatched a ring from a statue of the Virgin Mary; in doing so, the finger broke off. He then proceeded to commit further sacrilege by climbing on the head of the statue to gain access to a room above, in which the clergy had hidden their possessions. On finding them, he threw them down to his colleagues. As the sailor was leaving the chancel a crucifix, two feet tall, fell from above and dashed his brains out. Once back aboard their ships there was a violent storm; they foundered, and, along with the ill-gotten gains, went to the bottom of the sea. With the English soldiers losing their supplies they were forced to retire and Scotland is said to have been saved because of the insult to the Virgin Mary in the Whitekirk shrine.

The second event involved Enea Piccolomini, an Italian diplomat, who was sent to Scotland by the Pope to urge James I to go to war with England. His ship encountered a winter storm in the North Sea and Enea pledged that, if he got to land safely, he would make a pilgrimage to the nearest shrine of the Blessed Virgin; almost immediately, the weather improved and his ship was able to anchor at Dunbar. To give thanks to God for his survival, he walked ten miles barefoot over frozen ground to the shrine at Whitekirk. He had to make the return journey in a litter, as he got a chill and later developed rheumatism, which bothered him for the rest of his life. Only when he arrived at Newcastle did he feel that he had returned to 'a civilised part of the world', in contrast to Scotland and the far north of England, which he thought 'wild, bare and never visited by the sun in winter'. In 1458, he was elected Pope Pius II.

The shrine at Whitekirk was later visited on a regular basis by James IV but became much less significant after the Reformation. In 1633, Whitekirk was made part of the bishopric of Edinburgh but when this was abolished it reverted to a parish church.

When the persecution of the Covenanters was at its height, a large open-air service was conducted on Whitekirk hill on 5 May 1678, where a thousand people gathered to hear preacher John Blackadder. Word reached the authorities and sixty soldiers, under Charles Maitland, were dispatched from Bass Rock to break up the meeting. The crowd, encouraged by James Learmont, refused to disperse. Some of the soldiers were surrounded and disarmed by the Covenanters and in the scuffle one of the soldiers was shot dead. Not long after, five men were arrested – James and George Learmont, Robert Hepburn of East Fenton, William Temple and Bryson from Dunbar. They were tried in Edinburgh and James Learmont and William Temple were found guilty and sentenced to death; Learmont was executed at the Grassmarket on 27 September 1678. Years later, a man on his deathbed confessed he had killed the soldier in self-defence and James Learmont was not in the immediate vicinity at the time. There is a large pile of stones on the summit of Whitekirk hill on which the triangulation point is fixed. It is believed to mark the burial place of two Covenanters who were killed by soldiers from the garrison on Bass Rock between 1670–80.

Whitekirk church was set on fire in May 1914. This act of destruction was long attributed to the suffragettes but recent research indicates the cause was probably an electrical fault. Fortunately, its red-stone walls sustained little damage and the structure was restored by Robert Lorimer. The present church dates mainly from the fifteenth century and is cruciform in plan, with a squat central tower crowned by a slated roof. Surrounding it is a churchyard with many interesting tombstones. There is now no trace of the historic Our Lady's well; according to one source it was located 220 yards east of the church. It was believed to possess remarkable healing powers and was frequented by childless women. Its waters dried up in the early-nineteenth century, possibly due to improvements in agricultural drainage.

The other building of significance at Whitekirk is the tithe barn, which stands a hundred yards north of the church. It incorporates the base of a tower, part of the castle or house built by Oliver Sinclair in 1540 from the demolished pilgrim houses. Four years later it was set on fire by English soldiers. They returned in 1548 during their occupation of Haddington and again set fire to Oliver Sinclair's property, along with the village of Whitekirk.

WHITTINGEHAME

Although there has been a village at Whittingehame for many centuries, today it is almost non-existent. The name, like Tyninghame, is Anglo-Saxon and means 'the settlement of Hwita'. Another explanation is that it is derived from 'the village of the white meadow'. The oldest surviving building is Whittingehame tower house, which stands on the wooded bank of Whittinghame water and dates from the late-fifteenth century. It was built by one of the Douglas family, who became earls of Morton.

The lands of Whittingehame were owned by the earls of March until 1372, when George of Dunbar conferred them on James Douglas of Dalkeith, who had married his sister Agnes. His son became first Lord Dalkeith and his grandson – on marrying a daughter of James I – first earl Morton. It was at Whittingehame tower in 1567 that the fourth earl plotted the assassination of Lord Darnley. On his execution his title and lands ceded to the Crown but were later returned to a family representative. By the eighteenth century, the land had passed into the possession of the Hays of Tweeddale.

In 1817 the land was sold to James Balfour, from another ancient Scottish family. He constructed Whittingehame house, a few hundred yards from the tower house. It was described as 'a splendid mansion of Grecian Architecture'. Sir Robert Smirke, responsible for designing the British Museum, was its architect. Like many other landowners of his time, Balfour relocated the original village. It stood a short distance north of the present church in fields just beyond the minor road. No visible traces of the village, which dates back to medieval times, remain today.

At first the new settlement was called Whittingeham as opposed to Whittingehame, although it is now known as Luggate, the name of the stream that flows close by. Today it consists of nothing more than the old school house and a row of cottages, all in red sandstone. The original Whittingehame village, in contrast, was once a thriving settlement with a school, brewery, inn and small hall. The farmworkers lived alongside bakers, dressmakers, millers, tailors, shoemakers and weavers. By 1792, however, it was in decline with only 141 inhabitants and many of its houses in the process of being torn down.

The first church in the area was established as far back as 664, when St Cuthbert brought Christianity from England. It was located near Luggate, half-a-mile north-east of the present church, in a field that is still known as Kirklands. In 1225, a new stone church was built and dedicated in 1245 by the bishop of St Andrews. Until 1372, it only had the status of a prebendary chapel of the collegiate church of Dunbar. In that year, however, it became a parish church in its own right, dedicated to St Oswald.

By the early-eighteenth century, the church was in a ruinous state, so a new site was selected a short distance away, close to Whittingehame tower. Construction of the new church began in 1722. Much of the wood for the new building was brought by sea to Cockenzie, then transported inland on servants' carts; for every yoking they were rewarded with a pint of ale. The attractive red sandstone was carried from the quarry in the same manner. A century later, it was extensively remodelled in the Gothic style on the initiative of James Balfour. A tower with spiky battlements was added at its western end. There are a number of eighteenth-century gravestones as well as a burial enclosure of the Buchan Syderfs of Rucklaw. More than two hundred burial cists were unearthed in the vicinity of the site of the medieval parish church. Unfortunately, they were all destroyed, some of them being used in the construction of local roads.

Several members of the Balfour family raised at Whittingehame house went on to become eminent citizens. Francis, son of James Balfour, developed a love of natural history from an early age. He studied natural sciences at Cambridge, where he became interested in animal embryology, becoming a pioneer in this field. In 1878, he was elected a fellow of the Royal Society. Four years later, Balfour was appointed the first professor of animal morphology at Cambridge, after publishing his ground-breaking work, A Treatise on Comparative Embryology. His career was cut short when he died in a climbing accident on Mont Blanc and his body was returned to Britain and buried at Whittingehame.

Arthur James Balfour, born in Whittingehame, was British prime minister from 1902–5. He is seen here in 1905 with another prime minister, David Lloyd George (*Balfour is on the right*).

Francis's brother, **Arthur James Balfour**, became prime minister. Born at Whittingehame house in 1848, he attended Eton and Trinity College, Cambridge and after graduating he looked around for a seat in Parliament. It was not a difficult process, thanks largely to his family connections: his father had been a Tory MP while his mother's brother was Robert Cecil, later Lord Salisbury, secretary of state for India and a future prime minister. In 1874, at the age of just twenty-six Balfour became Conservative MP for Hertford (a pocket borough in the gift of the Cecils). It is questionable if he was cut out for a life in politics; although a gifted intellectual who produced an original book on philosophy, he was a solitary figure who did not relish mixing with the electorate and was a poor public speaker.

His uncle had other ideas. Salisbury appointed him to a string of important ministerial jobs, most notably as chief secretary for Ireland in the period from 1887–91 when nationalist agitation was at its most troublesome. Balfour had little sympathy for the Home Rule movement, earning the sobriquet 'Bloody Balfour' for his ruthless suppression of rural unrest. Despite his less than glittering reputation as a cabinet minister, Salisbury was determined that his nephew would succeed him as prime minister and twice placed him in the key post of leader of the House of Commons, the second period in that office running from 1895–1902. When 'Bob' Salisbury stood down due to ill-health in 1902, he recommended that his nephew should be his successor. So it was that A. J. Balfour became prime minister, an act of nepotism that gave birth to the phrase that means 'without any difficulty at all': that is, 'Bob's your uncle'.

Balfour's three years in 10 Downing Street have largely been forgotten and were marred by serious disagreements with a faction in his own party, led by Joseph Chamberlain, that wished to impose tariffs. He did manage to pass an important Education Act and also engineered the Anglo-French entente cordiale, but the 1906 election produced a Liberal landslide (with another Scot, Henry Campbell-Bannerman, becoming prime minister), a result that both protectionists and free traders in the Tory party blamed on Balfour's weak leadership on the tariff issue.

Despite this devastating loss, Balfour continued to play a pivotal role in public life. He stayed on as leader of the Conservative party until 1911 and was appointed First Lord of the Admiralty in the war cabinet of 1915, and then foreign secretary in 1916. It was while in this latter position that he produced the famous Balfour Declaration of 1917, a document that pledged the support of the British government for a national home in Palestine for the Jewish people. After the end of the First World War, Balfour served as a government minister from 1919–22 and then from 1925–9.

He became Earl Balfour in 1922 and was honoured by many universities for his intellectual achievements, but, despite such a glittering career, he always came home to East Lothian for the summer holidays. He loved his home county, which he considered 'the paradise of golfers and Whittingehame lies at its centre'. He died in 1930 and, like his brother, was interred at the family's private burial ground at Whittingehame. Not long after, the Balfour family gave up Whittingehame house and moved to the much smaller Whittingehame tower. At the beginning of the Second World War the house was used to house Jewish refugee children arriving in Britain through the *kindertransport*. In the 1980s, the house was converted into private flats. There is no public access to Whittingehame house and the tower. Both are also well concealed by deciduous woodland from the nearby public roads.

PLACES TO VISIT

Listed below are brief details of many of East Lothian's attractions and old buildings. An Ordnance Survey map reference is included for most of them. The 1/50,000 maps, no. 66 Edinburgh and no. 67 Duns, Dunbar and Eyemouth, cover all of East Lothian. Perhaps the best map is the 1/25,000 explorer map no. 351, Dunbar and Haddington. Explorer map no. 345, the Lammermuir hills, covers the south of the county. There is an excellent network of footpaths by which the county can be explored and information boards can be found in many places. It should be noted that some of the buildings listed below are private and should be viewed from a distance. Also, cultivated fields should never be walked across. Finally, the Lammermuir hills is also a working landscape and access to some sites is not available at certain times, including the shooting season.

AERODROMES

DREM AERODROME – NT508813. Many of the buildings of this Second World War airfield survive and can be seen from the Drem–Dirleton road. Some of the accommodation blocks have been converted into shops at Fenton Barnes retail park (NT512816), where there is an information board about the aerodrome.

EAST FORTUNE AERODROME – NT552783. Established during the First World War, East Fortune also played an important role in the Second World War. It is now home to the Museum of Flight, Scotland's main aircraft collection, which includes an iconic Concorde aeroplane. The west end of the runway is home to numerous microlight aircraft.

East Fortune was one of the most important aerodromes established in Scotland in the First World War and also became an important base for airships. This memorial commemorates the 1919 crossing of the Atlantic by the R.34 airship, stationed in East Lothian, and is located at the Museum of Flight.

MACMERRY AERODROME – NT444734. The A1 now runs across the site of this Second World War airfield. Mustard gas was stored in underground tanks here! Most buildings have been demolished but some of the accommodation quarters can still be seen next to the road at Penston.

PENSTON AERODROME – NT451716. There was a First World War airfield in fields on the east side of the B6363, near Macmerry. No trace remains.

BATTLEFIELDS

There have been several major battles in East Lothian. Most are commemorated with modest memorials.

BATTLE OF ATHELSTANEFORD (832) – NT534774. Flag heritage centre in the grounds of the village church on Main Street. Battle thought to have been fought a short distance to the north of the village in the vicinity NT535 784

BATTLE OF CARBERRY HILL (1567) – NT374696. Small memorial to Mary, Queen of Scots in woods on top of hill. Car park in woods to the south of Carberry lodge house. Monument some distance from the car park.

FIRST BATTLE OF DUNBAR (1296) – NT676761. Fought in vicinity of Wester Broomhouse farm and Doon Bridge on the road to Spott. There is no memorial for this battle.

View from Doon hill of the site of the second Battle of Dunbar, 1650. It was fought on low-lying ground at the bottom of the slope.

SECOND BATTLE OF DUNBAR (1650) – NT698768. Monument next to road at Broxmouth, near Oxwellmains cement plant. Battle fought a short distance south-west of the monument.

BATTLE OF PINKIE (1547) – NT362713. Small memorial south of Wallyford. Close to the road, near the junction with A1. Accessed from minor side road.

BATTLE OF PRESTONPANS (1745) – NT403 741. Stone monument on eastern edge of Prestonpans near main road to Longniddry. Site of battle was actually further east, near roundabout.

BEACHES

East Lothian has forty miles of coastline, including steep cliffs and pebble seashores. There are also long stretches of golden sands, particularly along the northern edge of the county. A small charge is made by most of the car parks. The map references are for the nearest car park for the beaches.

BELHAVEN BAY, at the mouth of the river Biel. A short distance west of Dunbar. Small car park on east side of bay at Belhaven, NT663787 but the main one is in the John Muir country park on the west side of Belhaven bay at NT652787.

GULLANE BAY – NT476831. A short distance to the north of Gullane and fringed with sand dunes. Good views of the coastline from the car park.

NORTH BERWICK – NT557844. To the east of the harbour there is a long stretch of sand at Misley bay. Melbourne Road and Marine Parade form the boundary to the beach. Large man-made pool at its west end, where children can paddle and sail boats. On the opposite side of the harbour there is West bay with roadside parking along Beach Road.

SEACLIFF – NT606845. Situated to the south of Tantallon castle and accessed by a private road off the A198 at Auldhame. Coin-operated barrier at top of track leading to beach.

SETON SANDS – NT431782 and NT436766. A long stretch of sand that extends from Port Seton to Longniddry. Easily accessible from the B1348 road, which runs close to its southern edge.

THORNTONLOCH – NT752744. One of East Lothian's smaller beaches, edged by impressive sand dunes.

TYNINGHAME – NT627809. At the end of a minor road off the A198 known as Limetree Walk, which terminates at a small car park. From here the seashore can be reached by a half-mile walk through woodland. There is a rocky outcrop at the mouth of the Tyne but to the north we find one of the most impressive beaches in East Lothian. Ravensheugh sands and Peffer sands form a broad beach two miles in length.

YELLOWCRAIG – NT517855. This is one of East Lothian's most popular beaches. There are good views of Fidra island and its lighthouse. The broad beaches extend almost all the way to North Berwick.

BRIDGES

ABBEY BRIDGE – NT533745. A sixteenth-century, stone-arch bridge a mile east of Haddington. Small car park near north end.

BEGBIE BRIDGE (Samuelston) – NT491710. Single-arch bridge, two miles south-west of Haddington.

Dunglass bridges:
OLD BRIDGE – NT772723,
NEW BRIDGE – NT769720,
DUNGLASS BRIDGE – NT771721,
DUNGLASS RAILWAY VIADUCT – NT772721. The Dunglass bridges stand on the boundary between East Lothian and Berwickshire. The New Bridge is accessed from the roundabout on the A1, taking the minor road to Dunglass and the railway viaduct can be viewed from here. The old bridge can be accessed by footpath to the seashore.

LINN BRIDGE (Old Tyne Bridge) – NT592771. The sixteenth-century, stone-arch bridge is in the south of East Linton, on the road to Dunbar.

NUNGATE BRIDGE – NT519737. Sixteenth-century bridge on the east side of Haddington, near St Mary's church.

OLD BRIDGE (Roman Bridge), Musselburgh – NT340725. Three-arched, sixteenth-century bridge. There may have been a crossing here when the Romans were in occupation of the fort at Inveresk.

NEW BRIDGE, Musselburgh – NT342726. An attractive, five-arch, stone bridge dating from early-nineteenth century, downstream from the Old Bridge.

SALTOUN BRIDGE – NT458674. Single-arch, stone bridge on the West Saltoun–Pencaitland road.

VICTORIA BRIDGE – NT518739. Modern cast-iron bridge dating from 1900 on the east side of Haddington.

CASTLES

BARNES CASTLE – NT528766. The ruins can be seen from the road to the west to Athelstaneford. A footpath also runs next to the castle but there is no access to the ruins.

DIRLETON CASTLE – NT516839. An Historic Scotland property on the south side of Dirleton village.

DUNBAR CASTLE – NT678793. On the cliff top at the west tip of Dunbar harbour. Good view of the ruins but there is no access to them.

FALSIDE CASTLE – NT378710. Restored tower house, two miles south-west of Tranent. It is a private house and there is no access

The fragmentary remains of Dunbar castle. In the Middle Ages it was one of the most important fortresses in Scotland.

to the building, but it can be seen from the minor road which runs close to it.

FENTON TOWER – NT543822. A restored tower house stands prominently on high ground at Kingston. Private property, but there are good views of it from the road that runs close by.

GAMELSHIEL CASTLE – NT649648. Fragmentary remains on lower slopes of Sparleton hill near north tip of Whiteadder reservoir.

GARLETON CASTLE – NT509767. On the north side of the Garleton hills. No access to the ruin but good views of it can be obtained from the Haddington to Drem or Athelstaneford roads that pass close by.

HAILES CASTLE – NT575758. Historic Scotland property open most times. It stands close to a minor road between Haddington and East Linton. Access road is narrow and, in places, single track.

INNERWICK CASTLE – NT735737. Ruined castle overlooking a deep valley. Can be accessed via Thornton Glen nature reserve by a narrow path along a steep-sided valley. The ruins are visible from the Innerwick–Oldhamstocks road when there is not too much undergrowth. The ruins are private property and should not be entered, as they are in a dangerous condition.

NORTH BERWICK CASTLE – NT561852. A grass mound on the seafront on the eastern edge of North Berwick. It was a motte-and-bailey castle, a rarity in south-east Scotland.

PRESTON TOWER – NT391741. Stands in a small public park on the road to Prestonpans. No access to interior.

REDHOUSE TOWER – NT463771. Stands next to the Longniddry–Ballencrieff road. No access to the ruin itself but it can be viewed from the adjacent garden centre.

SALTCOATS CASTLE – NT486819. Can be seen at a distance from the main road approaching Gullane from the west or from nearby footpath.

SEACLIFF TOWER – NT612842. Minor ruins overlooking the coast, to the south of the car park for Seacliff beach.

STONEYPATH TOWER – NT596714. East of Garvald. An impressive restored tower house. A private residence but it can be viewed at a distance from footpath or local road.

TANTALLON CASTLE – NT596851. Historic Scotland property, two miles east of North Berwick. Parking off the North Berwick–Dunbar road.

WAUGHTON CASTLE – NT567809. Little is left of this once important castle. The scant remains can be seen from minor roads that run close by. No access to ruins.

YESTER CASTLE – NT 556666. Located half-a-mile south-east of Gifford. Only fragmentary ruins of this once-important castle, now concealed by woodland and not easily accessible, still stand. The subterranean chamber still exists.

CHURCHES

There are a number of interesting ruined churches in East Lothian. They include the following.

DUNGLASS COLLEGIATE CHURCH – NT767719. In the care of Historic Scotland. Access up driveway by lodge house at entrance to Dunglass estate. Visitors must keep to the ground around the church.

GLADSMUIR OLD PARISH CHURCH – NT458733. Behind the present parish church. Next to the Haddington–Macmerry road.

GULLANE OLD PARISH CHURCH – NT482827. Stands near the west end of town on the main road.

NORTH BERWICK OLD PARISH CHURCH – NT553852. In the town centre on Law Road, close to High Street.

STENTON OLD PARISH CHURCH – NT622742. Stands in the grounds of the present impressive parish church. In the centre of the village next to the main road.

The following are three significant churches in East Lothian:

SETON COLLEGIATE CHURCH – NT417752. Historic Scotland property. On the main road, a mile west of Longniddry.

ST MARY'S CHURCH – NT518736. A very large historic church situated on south-east edge of Haddington, on the road to Gifford.

WHITEKIRK PARISH CHURCH – NT595815. Stands next to the North Berwick–Dunbar road.

Many towns and villages have small, picturesque churches. They include the following examples.

ABERLADY PARISH CHURCH – NT462798. In the west of Aberlady, next to main road.

DIRLETON PARISH CHURCH –
NT513842. On the north edge of
the village green.

DUNBAR PARISH CHURCH –
NT682787. An impressive,
nineteenth-century structure in red
sandstone, on the site of a
medieval church. A recent project
is due to be completed here in
2020, which will involve a
permanent exhibition.

GARVALD PARISH CHURCH –
NT591709. A small church at the
extreme east edge of the village.

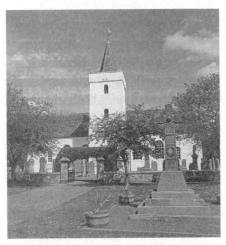

The white-harled parish church of Gifford
is one of the county's most attractive
places of worship. It dates from 1710.

GIFFORD (YESTER) PARISH
CHURCH – NT535681. Distinctive
whitewashed building stands at the
east end of Main Street.

HUMBIE PARISH CHURCH –
NT461637. Hidden away in
woodland, half-a-mile north of the
village.

INNERWICK PARISH CHURCH
– NT721739. Stands on a ridge in
the centre of the village.

OLDHAMSTOCKS PARISH
CHURCH – NT737706. A
whitewashed church in the west of
the village.

PENCAITLAND PARISH CHURCH
– NT443690. Stands between
Wester and Easter Pencaitland, next
to the main road.

PRESTONPANS PARISH CHURCH
– NT388746. In Kirk Street, a short
distance south of High Street.

SPOTT PARISH CHURCH –
NT674756. A small church next to
the road to the east of the village.

TRANENT PARISH CHURCH –
NT403734. In the north of the
town, next to the Prestonpans
road. Has many old tombstones in
its grounds.

WHITTINGEHAME PARISH
CHURCH – NT603737. Hidden
away up a track off a minor road.
There are few other buildings in
the vicinity.

COAL MINING

PRESTONGRANGE MUSEUM –
NT373735. Stands on the site of
the former Prestongrange colliery,
immediately west of Prestonpans,
and incorporates several of its
buildings. They can be viewed
externally at most times from the
surrounding footpaths.
Unfortunately, little other evidence

of this once extensive industry survives in East Lothian. Almost all of the buildings have been demolished and the spoil heaps landscaped. The large mound at Meadowmill sports centre at Prestonpans (NT402740) has been created from the spoil heap of an old coal mine. A flag commemorating the battle of Prestonpans flies on it and good views can be had from here. The large coal-fired Cockenzie power station (NT393753), a major landmark in East Lothian, closed in March 2013 and was demolished. There are several monuments to commemorate the men that once worked the mines. The first is a seven-ton carved sandstone block flanked on either side by small coal wagons, which stands in the centre of Wallyford, NT366719, on the south side of Salters Road. On the southern edge of Wallyford, NT371715, next to the A1, there was once a spoil heap, the site of which has been landscaped. In its vicinity are ten carved stones illustrating the history of coal mining in the vicinity. A sculpture of two miners working underground, NT397740, located close to Gardiner Terrace and its junction with Schaw Road in the south of Prestonpans.

COUNTRY HOUSES

There are several ruins of early country houses:

AULDHAME HOUSE – NT602846. Next to the track to Seacliff beach. Admission charge to the beach.

LOCHEND HOUSE – NT678780. The fragments of a once important seventeenth-century laird's house in the south of Dunbar, now surrounded by modern developments. The ruins stand in woods on the north side of Kellie Road, close to a minor road junction leading to Baillie Court.

SEACLIFF HOUSE – NT608844. Ruins of a large Victorian country house surrounded by trees overlooking the beach. No access to ruins.

MARKLE MAINS – NT579775. Immediately west of East Linton. Ruins in the grounds of Markle fisheries, described as a laird's house of the seventeenth century. The fisheries may charge a parking fee. Trout fishing available in the nearby loch.

There are many impressive country houses and large town houses in East Lothian, but most are private residences and not open to the public. Several can be observed from local roads.

BANKTON HOUSE – NT395736, Prestonpans. A private house but it can be seen from the A1.

COCKENZIE HOUSE – NT401756, Cockenzie. House and grounds open to the public. Next to the main road on the western edge of Cockenzie/Prestonpans.

GOSFORD HOUSE – NT452785. Near Longniddry. One of Scotland's most impressive country houses. Tours of the house on certain days. Grounds open on payment of a small fee. They contain all the trappings appropriate for a large country house including a large pond with a stone-arched boathouse, NT459747, a curling pond, NT455787, and mausoleum, NT456789.

LAUDERDALE HOUSE – NT678790. Dunbar. A very large house, not in the countryside, but rather located at the north end of High Street. Not open to the public.

LENNOXLOVE HOUSE – NT515721. Near Haddington. Guided tours on certain days. Can be seen from a minor road that runs along the southern boundary of its grounds.

LUFFNESS HOUSE – NT475804. Not open to the public, but can be viewed through the trees from the main road on the east side of Aberlady.

NEWBYTH HOUSE – NT586800. Near Whitekirk, can be seen at a distance from footpaths in the vicinity.

NEWHAILES HOUSE – NT326725. Musselburgh. A property of the National Trust for Scotland. Tours of house and access to the grounds at most times. Its grounds have many of the features associated with an important country house including stables, NT326724, ruined teahouse, NT325729, icehouse, NT327726, and a small grotto, NT325727.

PRESTONGRANGE HOUSE – NT378737. Prestonpans is the clubhouse of Royal Musselburgh golf club. There is no general public access but the course is open to visitors who wish to play a round.

SETON HOUSE – NT417750. On the site of Seton palace. Not open to the public but visible from the grounds of Seton collegiate church.

TYNINGHAME HOUSE – NT619798. Near East Linton. Can be seen in the distance across the mouth of the Tyne from the John Muir Way.

WINTON HOUSE – NT438694. At Pencaitland. Its grounds except those in the immediate vicinity of the house can be reached by footpaths from the village and are open to the public.

A number of large country houses have been converted into hotels, including Archerfield house, NT505841, near Dirleton, Carberry tower, NT363696, two miles south of Musselburgh, Greywalls, NT490835, on the east edge of Gullane, next to Muirfield golf course and St Germains (bed and breakfast), NT427 747. Information correct at time of publication but liable to change).

DOVECOTES

A large number of dovecotes survive, although many are in the grounds of country houses and farms and therefore not accessible. Examples that can be viewed from the outside include the following.

ATHELSTANEFORD VILLAGE – NT533774. In the grounds of Athestaneford parish church. Now a small museum.

BOLTON VILLAGE – NT506701. Next to the road through the village. No access to the dovecote.

DIRLETON CASTLE – NT516840. In the north-east corner of the castle grounds.

DRYLAW HILL – NT585780. East Linton. Can be seen on top of Drylaw hill from a distance.

HADDINGTON – NT518737. Lady Kitty's garden near Nungate Bridge.

NORTH BERWICK LAW – NT563842. A dovecote stands in a field on the east side of North Berwick Law. Visible from the nearby minor road.

ORMISTON HALL. Although little remains of Ormiston hall its unusual, circular dovecote stands in a field, NT412673, and can be seen through the trees on the east side of the B6371.

PENCAITLAND VILLAGE – NT441689. Dovecote in the centre of the village on the north side, close to the main road.

PHANTASSIE – NT596774. In a field next to the footpath close to East Linton.

PINKIE – NT350729. Musselburgh. In playing fields near High Street.

PRESTON TOWER – NT390742, Prestonpans. Dovecote in the gardens next to Preston tower. Another dovecote, NT386738, stands next to Mid Road on the south edge of Prestonpans and is associated with the seventeenth-century Northfield house, a private residence that can be seen in the distance.

TANTALLON CASTLE – NT595850. The dovecote stands in front of the castle.

TRANENT – NT402734. Close to the parish church on the north side of the town.

FARM BUILDINGS

There are numerous examples of farms with substantial outbuildings, many around East Linton. The best examples are where the soil is most productive. They can be seen from the nearby roads, but note they are private property.

BEGBIE – NT492708. Red-pantile farm buildings next to the road.

INNERWICK – NT718739. Farm buildings with chimney converted into homes.

PAPPLE FARM – NT591724. Impressive, Gothic-style, farm buildings that can be seen from a minor road north of Garvald.

PHANTASSIE FARM – NT595772. East Linton, close to road to Dunbar.

SALTOUN HOME FARM – NT465688. South of Pencaitland on the road to Saltoun.

SAMUELSTON – NT486710. A good example of a farm chimney on buildings next to road.

SUNNYSIDE FARM – NT595754 and Traprain farms – NT592759 on the road between East Linton and Traprain Law.

Tithe barn – NT596816. Whitekirk. Private residence. Can be seen from Whitekirk church.

FORTS AND FORTIFICATIONS

In the first half of the sixteenth century, Scotland suffered several incursions by the English. Castles were by this time were an ineffective form of fortification and had been replaced by forts with earthen embankment walls. Unfortunately, few traces remain of the several built in East Lothian.

BASS ROCK FORT AND PRISON – NT602872. Ruins next to lighthouse, south side of island.

DUNBAR BATTERY – NT681793. Dunbar harbour. Small stone fort located on Lamer island. It offers sculpture, interpretation and an amphitheatre, in which events are held.

This tithe barn at Whitekirk, now converted to a house, is perhaps the oldest surviving farm building in East Lothian. Some parts date from the sixteenth century.

FRENCH CAMP – NT763717. Dunglass. Earthwork ramparts survive from a large, sixteenth-century fort. Footpath to the top of the hill. Walkers should keep to footpaths when in Dunglass estate.

HADDINGTON – NT515743. A large fort with earth and timber walls was built around the town of Haddington in 1548. Unfortunately, almost nothing survives.

LUFFNESS – NT474803. The French built a fort in the grounds of Luffness house in the late 1540s. Its northern perimeter was probably close to the Aberlady–Gullane road. There is no access to the grounds of Luffness house.

NAPOLEONIC SIGNAL STATION – NT557843. Near the summit of North Berwick Law.

A number of fortifications used to protect the coast against the possibility of invasion during the Second World War survive. Most common are concrete anti-tank blocks. They are concentrated on the coast facing the North Sea and can be found on the south side of Belhaven bay (NT650789, NT643788), and anti-glider posts further west at Hedderwick sands, NT636790. On the coast at Tyninghame there are numerous examples, including at NT632806, NT636811, NT630813, NT626818, NT620823 and a pillbox at NT620828. Further examples can be found at Gosford, NT442778.

GARDENS

One of the features associated with large houses was the walled garden. Several have been revived in recent years and are open to the public.

AMISFIELD WALLED GARDEN – NT534742. A mile east of Haddington. On the minor road, entrance through the former gateway of the estate, a short distance south of Abbey Bridge. Admission fee.

ARCHERFIELD WALLED GARDEN – NT501837. In Archerfield estate, off the Gullane–Dirleton road.

INVERESK LODGE GARDEN – NT348717. On the main street at the south end of Inveresk. Administered by the National Trust for Scotland. Admission fee.

REDHOUSE GARDEN CENTRE – NT464771. Located next to Redhouse castle. On Longniddry–Drem road.

ST MARY'S PLEASANCE (Lady Kitty's garden) – NT518736. Next to Haddington house and St Mary's church. Administered by Haddington Garden Trust. On Gifford Road, south Haddington.

SMEATON NURSERY GARDENS – NT594786. Centred on an old walled garden, although the mansion house has long since disappeared. Near East Linton, on the road to Tyninghame.

LODGE HOUSES

There are numerous surviving examples of lodge houses, but many are no more than small cottages, as at the entrance to Newhailes house, Musselburgh. They can be seen from the road on which they stand but most are private residences. There is no access to the adjoining country house unless stated.

AMISFIELD HOUSE, WEST GATE – NT524738. Two twin-storey lodge houses at the entrance. The house has long since been demolished but many of the ancillary buildings survive on its former grounds, now a golf course. They include the stables, NT529742, an ice house, NT528744, and an eighteenth-century temple, NT531744, next to the river Tyne. These can be seen from a footpath that runs through the grounds, but access to the golf course is not permitted. There is also a Gothic folly on rising ground, NT534738.

BROXMOUTH PARK LODGE HOUSE – NT698770. On the road to the A1, east of Dunbar. There is also a folly (tower), NT700778, for Broxmouth Park house. It is in the caravan site but can be seen from the road that passes close by.

CARBERRY TOWER LODGE HOUSE – NT359697. Access to hotel. South of Whitecraig.

GOSFORD HOUSE, WEST LODGE OR RAILWAY LODGE – NT445766. East side of Longniddry on the main road. There is no access to the house and grounds

Broxmouth Park lodge house, near Dunbar. It dates from the early-eighteenth century.

through this entrance. Entry to grounds is from the east side.

NORTH LODGE, NUNRAW HOUSE – NT591705. On a minor road to the south of Garvald.

NORTH LODGE FOR SALTOUN HALL – NT459689. Next to Spilmersford Bridge, near Pencaitland. This is a large lodge house.

NORTH LODGE, WINTON HOUSE – NT434700. Impressive Gothic lodge house stands next to the Pencaitland–Tranent road.

TYNINGHAME LODGE HOUSE – NT611792. Next to North Berwick–Dunbar road, at Tyninghame village.

YESTER HOUSE: LODGE AND GATE – NT535677. On south edge of Gifford. Impressive entrance to Yester house.

LOST DOMAINS

COTTYBURN – NT468758. Some overgrown ruins next to a minor road is all that remains of this hamlet. Abandoned in nineteenth century.

DOLPHINGSTONE HOUSE – NT382727. Close to the A1, near Tranent. No access to the site but a footpath runs close by.

HEDDERWICK HOUSE WALLED GARDEN – NT637778. The red-brick walled garden of the demolished house can be seen on the slope to the north of the Dunbar–East Linton road.

KILSPINDIE CASTLE – NT462801. Aberlady. On the north side of the church. A few stones mark the site of the castle.

The remains of Kilspindie castle (*right*).

MORHAM CHURCH – NT557726. A small church tucked away in a hollow off a minor road. Only a handful of houses keep the church company where there was once a village and in medieval times a castle.

ST PATRICK'S CHAPEL – NT483844. Located almost on the seashore, to the north of Gullane

HARBOURS

East Lothian harbours are modestly sized but attractive. All are easily accessible, except for Seacliff.

COCKENZIE HARBOUR – NT397756. West of Port Seton.

DUNBAR OLD AND NEW HARBOURS – NT680793 and NT682793. North-east side of town.

FISHERROW – NT334730. Musselburgh. On the west of town, close to main road.

NORTH BERWICK HARBOUR – NT553856. At the eastern end of the town.

PORT SETON HARBOUR – NT405760. A short distance north of the main road through town.

SEACLIFF HARBOUR – NT603848. At the Gegan. Said to be the smallest harbour in Scotland. Can be reached by walking from car park.

Disused harbours and anchorages include the following examples.

ABERLADY BAY – NT465802. The old harbour was located on the west side of the bay at Kilspindie. The rotting wooden hulks of several small vessels can be seen in the mud. Tradition says that the Earl of Wemyss wanted to enhance the view of the seashore and purchased several vessels from local fishermen, which he placed on the beach.

BELHAVEN BAY – NT662790. It was located close to Dunbar on the east side of Belhaven bay. No traces of this medieval harbour remain. Car parking on east side of the bay.

MORRISON'S HAVEN – NT373738. It was on the north side of the road to Musselburgh, next to Prestongrange museum, and immediately west of Prestonpans. Now reclaimed land.

INDUSTRY

BELHAVEN BREWERY – NT665784. Located on the western edge of Dunbar, close to the main road. Tours available by prior arrangement.

ESK NET MILLS – NT339723. Next to river Esk at Musselburgh. Good views of the outside of the building from footpaths. No access to interior.

GLENKINCHIE DISTILLERY – NT443668. Located amid farmland, a mile south of Wester Pencaitland. Tours of distillery available. Car park next to road.

PENCAITLAND MALTINGS – NT435687. Close to Pencaitland village. Its tall silos tower over the landscape. There is no access to the plant but the Pentcaitland railway footpath skirts the southern perimeter.

PRESTONPANS SALT WORKS – NT385746. Prestonpans. A tower marks the site of the last saltpan in Scotland. Next to seashore, off High Street.

TORNESS NUCLEAR POWER STATION – NT746751. South of Dunbar next to the A1. Visitor centre. Also, good views of power station from Skateraw.

IRON AGE

There are numerous sites of Iron Age forts and settlements.

The largest was on TRAPRAIN LAW – NT582748. It can be reached by the minor road which runs along the north side of the hill. Car parking on side of road.

NORTH BERWICK LAW – NT556842. There is a car park at the end of the track on the west side of the hill, accessed from Haddington Road. Outstanding views from the top of the Law.

CHESTERS FORT – NT508783. Off Drem–Haddington road. Small car park. In care of Historic Scotland.

There is further fort on a ridge on the east side of the Garleton hills at KAE HEUGHS, NT518763, which can be accessed by a footpath that runs close by.

Kidlaw, Lammermuir hills. Gorse bushes cover the site of the former Iron Age fort.

One of the best-preserved examples is the misleadingly named WHITE CASTLE at NT612686. It stands next to a minor road between Garvald and Whiteadder reservoir. Car park on edge of road. There are several other forts on the northern edge of the Lammermuir hills, including KIDLAW, NT512642 (*see photo opposite*). It can be seen from the footpath that runs close to its west side. To the south of it is WITCHES KNOWE at NT518634. There is another fort, STOBSHIEL MAINS, NT498638, close to the road from Kidlaw. Further east and higher up near the summit of HARESTONE HILL there is another example, NT570635. Three miles south-east of Gifford, there are several forts. They include BLACK CASTLE at NT580661 and GREEN CASTLE, NT582657, not far from the Gifford–Duns road. A further example is found further to the west on sloping ground, NT572652.

LIGHTHOUSES

BARNS NESS LIGHTHOUSE – NT723772. Located three miles south-east of Dunbar. There is a small road to it that runs along the shore from Broxmouth. No access to the lighthouse or immediate grounds.

BASS ROCK LIGHTHOUSE – NT602872. Can be seen in the distance from the shore. Also, good views of it from boat trips to the island.

The sun rising behind Barns Ness lighthouse.

FIDRA ISLAND LIGHTHOUSE –
NT512869. Best vantage point is
the beach at Yellow Craig.

LIMESTONE BURNING AND QUARRYING

CATCRAIG LIME KILNS –
NT715772. Near Barns Ness
lighthouse, it can be accessed by a
minor road along the shore from
Broxmouth.

OXWELLMAINS CEMENT PLANT
– NT706763. The plant dominates
the landscape to the south of
Dunbar. Good views from lay-bys
close to the plant on the A1. The
huge quarry and large machinery
can be seen from the small road on
the seashore that goes from
Broxmouth to Barns Ness
lighthouse. Nineteenth-century
lime kilns survive at a number of
locations and the best examples are
as follows.

SKATERAW LIME KILNS –
NT737753. Close to Torness power
station. Reached by a minor road
off the A1, through the hamlet of
Skateraw.

Other small kilns can be found at:

KIDLAW – NT508643. Lime kiln in
the centre of a field. No access but
visible from the road.

PHANTASSIE – NT602768. South-
east of East Linton, next to the
Stenton road.

SPILMERSFORD – NT455688. East
side of Pencaitland, near the road
to Saltoun. Car-park access.

There is a large disused quarry on
the north-east side of Traprain Law,
NT584748. The igneous rock was
used to build and repair roads in
East Lothian. Visible from the road
that runs next to Traprain Law.

MARKET CROSSES

East Lothian has several good
examples of market crosses (mercat
crosses). Most are conspicuously
placed.

ABERLADY – NT464799. East end
of High Street.

DUNBAR – NT679789. In front of
town-house museum, High Street.

GIFFORD – NT533688. The
Square, Main Street.

HADDINGTON – NT516738. East
end of High Street.

MUSSELBURGH – NT346727.
On the east side of the tolbooth in
High Street.

OLDHAMSTOCKS – NT739706.
On the village green, west end of
village.

PENCAITLAND – NT441688. On
the main street in the centre of the
village.

PRESTON – NT391740. Next to the
road, south edge of Prestonpans.

STENTON – NT621742. A
reconstructed tron (weight-beam)
on the main street, close to the
church.

MONUMENTS AND MEMORIALS

The most impressive is Hopetoun monument – NT501764. On top of the Garleton hills. Car park off minor road that runs around the northern side of hills. There are also woodland walks on Garleton hills. Good views of surrounding countryside.

There are a number of obelisks, a popular form of monument in the nineteenth century. There is a good example in the grounds of Newhailes house, Musselburgh, NT325726, which is open to the public.

BANKTON HOUSE, COLONEL GARDINER'S MONUMENT (an obelisk) – NT394738. Accessible via a pathway running eastwards from the south platform of Prestonpans railway station. No access to the house or grounds.

BALFOUR MONUMENT – NT575729. Obelisk commemorating James Balfour, which stands next to a minor road to the south of Traprain Law. It is close to the top of a hill and there are good views of the surrounding countryside.

ORMISTON – NT416693. An obelisk commemorating the missionary, east Main Street.

TYNINGHAME HOUSE – NT615798. This obelisk stands at the edge of a field and can be seen in the distance from the main road to North Berwick.

Other monuments and memorials.

CATHERINE WATSON MEMORIAL – NT554855. A large Celtic cross near North Berwick harbour.

JOHN RENNIE MEMORIAL – NT597771. Just outside East Linton located on a boundary wall, next to the Dunbar road.

R.34 AIRSHIP MEMORIAL PLAQUE – NT552782. Next to the road, near entrance to the Museum of Flight, East Fortune.

RAF COASTAL COMMAND MEMORIAL PLAQUE – NT554856. North Berwick harbour, next to Scottish Seabird Centre.

REVEREND R. W. V. S. SELBY WRIGHT – NT739758. A cross mounted on a stone plinth on the seashore at Chapel Point, Torness.

WHALE ARCH (replica) – NT556842. Top of North Berwick Law.

MUSEUMS AND VISITOR ATTRACTIONS

Coastal Communities museum – NT556853, School Road, North Berwick. A small museum in a nineteenth-century schoolhouse, dedicated to the history and prehistory of the area.

DUNBAR TOWN-HOUSE MUSEUM AND GALLERY – NT679789, Dunbar town house, Dunbar. Changing historical exhibitions as well as a local-history display area.

EAST LINKS FAMILY PARK – NT648786. West Barns, near Dunbar. A farm-themed activity park with live farm animals and activities for children.

JOHN GRAY CENTRE MUSEUM – NT515738, Lodge Street, Haddington. Interactive museum on the history of East Lothian. Building also contains East Lothian archives.

JOHN MUIR'S BIRTHPLACE – NT678790, High Street, Dunbar. A small museum dedicated to the life of pioneering conservationist John Muir.

MUSEUM OF FLIGHT – NT552783, East Fortune airfield, near Haddington. Scotland's main aviation museum and one of the main collections of historical aircraft in Britain.

MUSSELBURGH MUSEUM – NT344728 close to tolbooth, High Street, Musselburgh. History of Musselburgh from earliest times.

MYRETON MOTOR MUSEUM – NT486794, in countryside to east of Aberlady. Collection of antique vehicles, motorcycles and auto memorabilia.

PRESTONGRANGE MUSEUM – NT373856, Morrison's Haven, Prestonpans. Situated on the site of a former coal mine, the museum is devoted to the industrial history of Prestonpans dating back four hundred years.

SCOTTISH SEABIRD CENTRE – NT554856. The harbour, North Berwick. Interactive cameras zoom in on wildlife on the nearby islands, including Bass Rock and Craigleith.

RAILWAYS

There are no preserved railway lines in East Lothian. Prestongrange museum has some preserved rolling stock and a short length of track. Good views of trains using the east-coast line can be had in the vicinity of the road junction at Ballencrieff, NT481779. The former branch line between Longniddry, NT449763, and Haddington, NT499738, is now a footpath. A section of the former railway to Gifford has been converted into a railway walk; it runs from near Cousland, NT370689 to NT454665, south of Pencaitland. There is a footpath along the Cockenzie waggon-way, forerunner to the railway, NT398757 to NT403734, which starts at the eastern edge of Prestonpans although the route commenced at Tranent.

RELIGIOUS HOUSES

CARMELITE FRIARY RUINS – NT472802. In woodland at Luffness, next to the footpath a short distance east of Aberlady.

CISTERCIAN CONVENT AT NORTH BERWICK – NT545850. At North Berwick next to Old Abbey Road. Some of the ruins of

The Tyne at Abbey Bridge, east of Haddington. In the Middle Ages, an important Cistercian convent was located here.

the taller structures overlook the road. No access to the ruins, which are on private property.

CISTERCIAN CONVENT AT HADDINGTON – NT521739. St Martin's church is now a ruin on the east edge of Haddington. It stands in open ground, next to the road to Whittinghame. In its early history it belonged to the convent located immediately east of Abbey Bridge on the north bank of the Tyne, NT536747 (*see photo above*). There is no trace of any building of this once important religious community.

NUNRAW ABBEY – NT593700. Can be seen from the minor road to the south of Gavald. No access to the abbey.

PENSHIEL GRANGE FARM – NT641632. On slopes on the south side of Whiteadder, Lammermuir hills. It is close to the track known as the Herring Road, from where it can be viewed.

TRINITARIAN MONASTERY – NT679788. Dunbar. Remains of the church tower close to West Port off High Street.

ROADS AND PATHS

Great North Road was the original name for the Edinburgh–London road, the most important thoroughfare in East Lothian. It is now best known as the A1. Its route has altered greatly over the last century, originally passing through Haddington and East Linton, now bypassed. Another old route is Salters Road, which ran from Prestonpans–Dalkeith. In bygone centuries most people travelled on foot out of necessity. In recent years long-distance walking has become popular again, although primarily for recreational purposes. Dunbar is now at the beginning of the John Muir Way, which traverses central Scotland and terminates at Helensburgh on the Firth of Clyde. There is also a link that runs south from Dunbar along the coast, allowing walkers to connect with the Berwickshire coastal path and the Southern Upland Way at Cockburnspath. A useful internet site is East Lothian Council's core paths, which shows the routes of the two hundred miles of official footpaths in the county on sections of Ordnance Survey maps.

ROMANS AND THE DARK AGES

There are no visible remains of the Roman occupation of East Lothian. The Romans had a large fort at Inveresk, NT343720, now site of the cemetery for Inveresk parish church.

ABERLADY ANGLO-SAXON CROSS (reconstruction) – NT462798. Close to Aberlady parish church, next to the main road.

LOTH STONE – NT578741. South-west side of Traprain Law, next to the field boundary. Can be seen from the footpath that runs along west side of Traprain Law.

ST BALDRED

PRESTONKIRK PARISH CHURCH – NT593778. On the eastern side of East Linton, next to the Tyninghame road. St Baldred's Well is marked by a plaque and stands on the opposite side of the road, next to the river Tyne. A number of places are named after Baldred, but may have had little connection with him.

ST BALDRED'S BOAT – NT609852. A reef off Seacliff, marked by St Baldred's beacon.

ST BALDRED'S CAVE – NT605845. Seashore next to Seacliff beach, reached by taking a minor road at Auldhame. Payment at the barrier to access the beach, which is part of Seafield estate.

ST BALDRED'S CRADLE – NT637813. A hollow in a rock formation on the coast at Tyninghame. Limetree Walk, off the main road to the north of Tyninghame, has a car park that gives access to the mouth of the Tyne and Ravensheugh sands.

STATUES AND SCULPTURES

There is a growing number of statues and sculptures in East Lothian.

BEN SAYERS, GOLFER – NT548854. On the side of Beach Road next to the golf course at North Berwick.

Statue of creel loaders, Victoria Street, Dunbar.

CREEL LOADERS – NT679791. Stone carving of a group of figures located in Victoria Street, a short distance from Dunbar harbour.

JACKIE CROOKSTON – NT405727. Civic Square, High Street, Tranent.

JOHN MUIR STATUE – NT679789. High Street, Dunbar, next to the tolbooth.

SEABIRD STATUE – NT554856. An Arctic tern next to the Scottish Seabird Centre, North Berwick, one of East Lothian's top tourist attractions. Boat trips are available to visit Bass Road. There are also several other statues in the vicinity including a bird watcher looking out to sea.

STATUE OF AN ARCHER – NT344725, close to the Old Bridge over the Esk, Musselburgh.

THOMAS ALEXANDER STATUE – NT387746. In memorial garden next to High Street, Prestonpans.

WAR MEMORIAL – NT386745. Statue of Scottish First World War soldier on seafront, High Street, Prestonpans.

Statues on tall stone columns:

DR DAVID MOIR – NT343725. West end of High Street, Musselburgh, near bridge over the Esk.

ROBERT FERGUSON MP – NT512738. End of Court Street, Haddington, next to road junction.

GIANT GOLF-BALL SCULPTURE ON ROUNDABOUT – NT360728. Levenhall, Musselburgh.

GIANT-MUSSEL SCULPTURE – NT331730. A 12-foot-high stainless-steel sculpture of a mussel shell at Murdoch Green, off the Edinburgh Road, Musselburgh.

HORSE-RACING SCULPTURE – NT326723. On the roundabout at the entrance to Newhailes house, Musselburgh.

STONE AGE AND BRONZE AGE

East Lothian has several good examples of standing stones. Unfortunately, they generally stand in cultivated fields and can only be viewed at a distance.

BRONZE AGE HUT CIRCLES, NORTH BERWICK LAW – NT555839. There are traces of Bronze Age huts on its slopes.

DOON HILL TIMBER HALL (site of) – NT685757. Historic Scotland property. Access off A1, south of Dunbar. Minor road to top of Doon Hill.

EASTER BROOMHOUSE STANDING STONE – NT680766. In fields with no access. Can be seen on the horizon from the road to Spott, a short distance from the roundabout on A1.

KIRKLANDHILL – NT616776. Next to East Linton–Dunbar road in a field. No access to the stone.

PENCRAIG STANDING STONE – NT581768. Stands on Pencraig hill in a field near the road a short distance from East Linton. There is a footpath in its vicinity.

There are several other megalithic monuments on the Lammermuir hills, including stone circles, although these are only a foot or so in height. They include 'Nine Stones' at Nine Stone Rig, NT626650, a short distance north of the Gifford–Duns road near Whiteadder reservoir. A footpath runs close to site. It was probably a cremation cemetery. Close by are the Crow Stones, NT618651.

There are also burial cairns on the summits of Spartleton hill, NT653656, and Priestlaw hill,

Winter's sunrise behind the standing stone on Pencraig hill, near East Linton.

NT652624, overlooking Whiteadder reservoir.

TOWNS AND VILLAGES

DUNBAR – NT675790. High Street is well-preserved and includes an old tolbooth. It has a picturesque harbour that is overlooked by the fragmentary remains of Dunbar castle.

GULLANE – NT485830. An attractive town surrounded by world-famous golf courses.

This plaque on Haddington's council buildings records that there was a royal palace on this site during the Middle Ages. It burnt down in 1242.

HADDINGTON – NT518739. In the Middle Ages this was one of the most important towns in Scotland; there was even a royal palace here. Its centre has fortunately escaped modern development. In the vicinity of High Street there are several good examples of old Scottish houses.

NORTH BERWICK – NT550850. An attractive coastal town. Its tourist attractions are centred around the harbour and include the Scottish Seabird Centre.

On the lowlands of East Lothian, the following are attractive villages with numerous cottages.

ATHELSTANEFORD – NT535774, DIRLETON, NT515840, TYNINGHAME, NT610791.

There are several picturesque villages on the north edge of the Lammermuir hills: GIFFORD NT534680, GARVALD, NT587708, and STENTON, NT622742. Further east is OLDHAMSTOCKS, NT741706.

WALL MURALS

PRESTONPANS – NT386746 (approximate). Renowned for its imaginative wall murals depicting the town's history. Many of them are on, or close to, High Street, which runs close to the seashore. There is also a tall, wooden, totem pole next to High Street erected in 2006, NT383744.

WELLS

BURNS'S MOTHER'S WELL – NT508723. Near Bolton on the roadside from Haddington. It commemorates Agnes Burns, mother of national bard Robert Burns. Car-park close by.

Ornamental fountain of 1882 in the square, East Linton.

EAST LINTON ORNAMENTAL FOUNTAIN – NT592772. On the site of a drinking well. In the square in centre of village, erected 1882.

JUBILEE HORSE TROUGH – NT714738. Stands next to a minor road in woodland, a short distance west of Innerwick.

ROOD WELL – NT623745. At the side of the road at the eastern edge of Stenton.

ST JOHN'S WELL – NT672756. North-west side of Spott church.

WINDMILLS AND WATERMILLS

BALGONE WINDMILL – NT553828. In a field near the North Berwick–Haddington road. There is no access to the site but it is visible from nearby roads. Another windmill tower stands on the south-west of Oxwellmains cement plant, which at one time could be seen from the A1, NT702763, but is now obscured by trees. No access.

Bermaline mill, Haddington.

BERMALINE MILL – NT518742. A relatively modern mill in east Haddington. Older mills close by have been converted to housing. Can be seen from Victoria Bridge.

MILLS OF KINTREATH – NT562849. Ruins of old mills in The Glen, a woodland area on the east side of North Berwick.

POLDRATE WATER MILL – NT518734. A preserved watermill on southern edge of Haddington, close to St Mary's church.

PRESTON WATER MILL – NT595779. National Trust for Scotland property. Stands close to the road to Tyninghame at East Linton.

WITCHES

NORTH BERWICK, ST ANDREW'S CHURCH – NT554856. A large number of witches were alleged to have held their covens on the Old Kirk Green, which is now in the vicinity of the modern-day harbour. They were accused of meeting the Devil here and plotting the death of James VI in a notorious witch trial.

SALTOUN FOREST (Saltoun big wood) – NT465665. In 1629 Alexander Hamilton, a reputed wizard of East Lothian, confessed to meeting the Devil in Saltoun wood at his trial and bewitching to death Lady Ormiston and her daughter.

SAMUELSTON HAMLET –
NT484708. Two miles south-west
of Haddington. Many witches
came from here.

WITCHES STONE – NT669752.
On the roadside a short distance
west of Spott.

WOODLANDS

There are woodland walks at the
following locations.

BINNING WOOD, NEAR
WHITEKIRK – NT600805. Parking
next to the North Berwick–Dunbar
road.

BROCK WOOD – NT662748.
Three miles south of Dunbar.
Managed by Scottish Wildlife Trust.

BUTTERDEAN WOOD –
NT460730. Owned by the
Woodland Trust. Car park at north
end of wood, near Gladsmuir.

LOCHEND WOOD – NT676778.
Managed by Dunbar community
woodland group. South Dunbar,
extends to 75 acres.

ORMISTON, YEW TREE SAID TO
BE ONE OF THE LARGEST OF ITS
KIND IN SCOTLAND – NT412676.
It can be reached by footpath from
the A6093. Ormiston castle and
Ormiston hall were located close
by but little remains of either.

PRESSMENNAN LAKE –
NT621725. Woodland Trust wood
half-a-mile south of Stenton. Walks
around lake. Car park at west end,
off minor road.

SALTOUN BIG WOOD –
NT465665. Near East Saltoun. One
of the largest areas of woodland in
East Lothian. Accessed from minor
road that runs between East
Saltoun and West Saltoun.

THORNTON GLEN – NT735740.
Near Innerwick and accessed at
Crowhill. Managed by Scottish
Wildlife Trust.

WOODHALL DEAN – NT685734.
Managed by Scottish Wildlife Trust,
four miles south of Dunbar. Car
park at the north end near where
minor road crosses Woodhall burn.

YELLOW CRAIG WOOD –
NT519856. A broadleaved wood
next to the shore at Yellow Craig
beach.

Bibliography

BOOKS

Baker, Sonia, *The Country Houses – Castles and Mansions of East Lothian*, Stenlake Publishing, 2009

Baker, Sonia, (editor), *East Lothian Fourth Statistical Account, The County, Vol. 1, 1945–2000*, East Lothian Council library service, 2003.

Baldwin, John R., *Exploring Scotland's Heritage – Lothian and The Borders*, RCAHMS, 1989.

Breeze, David J., *Roman Scotland*. Batsford, B. T., Historic Scotland, 1996.

Butt, John, *Industrial Archaeology of Scotland*, David & Charles, 1967.

Cameron, Charles W., *Scottish Witches*, Jarrold Publishing, 1990.

Crone, Anne & Hindmarch, Erlend, with Woolf, Alex, *Living and Dying at Auldhame*, Society of Antiquaries of Scotland, 2016.

Dennison, Patricia E., Stronach, Simon, and Coleman, Russel, *Historic Dunbar – Archaeology and Development*, Historic Scotland, 2006.

Dick, David, *A Millennium of Fame in East Lothian*, Clerkington Publishing Co. Ltd, 2000.

Dickson, F. S. A., and Scot, John, *Emeralds Chased in Gold or The Islands of the Forth – Their Story, Ancient and Modern*, Oliphant, Anderson and Ferrier,1899.

Easson, D. E., *Medieval Religious Houses – Scotland*, Longmans, Green and Co., 1957.

East Linton Local History Society, *By the Linn Rocks – The Story of East Linton and the Parish of Prestonkirk*, East Linton Local History Society, 1999.

East Lothian Council, *Heritage Explorer – A Guide to over 100 Archaeological Sites*, East Lothian Council, 2013.

East Lothian Tourist Board, *A Walk Around Historic Dunbar*, East Lothian Tourist Board, 1991.

Edwards, Kevin J., and Ralston, B. M., (editors), *Scotland After the Ice Age*, Edinburgh University Press, 2003.

Ferrier, Walter, M., *The North Berwick Story*, Royal Burgh of North Berwick Community Council, 1980.

Glendinning, Miles and Martins, Susanna, *Buildings of the Land*, RCAHMS, 2008.

Gray, Forbes, and Jamieson, James, *A Short History of Haddington*, SPA Books Limited, 1995

Green, Charles, *East Lothian*, William Green & Sons, 1907.

Groome, Francis, *Ordnance Gazetteer of Scotland – A Survey of Scottish Topography, Volumes 1–5*, William Mackenzie, 1896.

Hume, John, *The Industrial Archaeology of Scotland*, volume 1, *The Lowlands and Borders*, B. T. Batsford Ltd, 1976.

Johnston, Arran Paul, *Blood Stain'd Fields – The Battles of East Lothian*, Prestoungrange and Cuthill Press, 2013.

Lang, T. D., Lang, B. D. and Marshall, B., *The Seven Ages of an East Lothian Parish being the Story of Whittinghame from Earliest Times*, Robert Grant and Son, 1929.

Lelong, Olivia and MacGregor, Gavin, *The Lands of Ancient Lothian*, Society of Antiquaries of Scotland, 2007.

Lenman, Bruce, *From Esk to Tweed – Harbours, Ships and Men of The East Coast of Scotland*, Blackie, 1975.

Louden, D & Rev. Whitefield, W., *East Lothian Studies*, John Hutchinson, 1891.

McAdam, A. D., & Clarkson, E. N. K., *Lothian Geology – An Excursion Guide*, Scottish Academic Press, 1986.

McIntosh, I. G. and Marshall, *The Face of Scotland*, Pergamon Press, 1970.

McNeill, P., *Prestonpans and Vicinity: Historical, Ecclesiastical and Traditional*, John Menzies & Co., 1902.

McNeill, Peter, *Tranent and its Surroundings – Historical, Ecclesiastical*, Facsimile Publisher, 2016 (facsimile of 1884 book).

McWilliam, Colin, *The Buildings of Scotland – Lothian except Edinburgh*, Penguin Books, 1978.

Martine, John, *Reminiscences and Notices of the Parishes of the County of Haddington, 1890*, reprinted by East Lothian Council library service, 1999.

Martine, Roddy, *This Too Shall Pass – Reflections on East Lothian*, Birlinn, 2009.

Miller, James, *The Lamp of Lothian, or the History of Haddington*, Lightning Source UK Ltd., 2017 (facsimile of 1844 book).

Miller, Joyce, *Myth and Magic – Scotland's Ancient Beliefs and Sacred Places*, Goblinshead, 2000.

Moffat, Alistair, *East Lothian in Photographs*, Deerpark Press, 2006.

Muir, M. A., *East Lothian – Cambridge County Geographies*, Cambridge University Press, 1915.

Phillimore, R. P., *The Bass Rock: Its History and Romance*, Facsimile Publisher, first published 1911, reprinted 2016.

Pugh, R. J. M., *Swords, Loaves & Fishes – A History of Dunbar*, Harlaw Heritage, 2003.

Ritchie, Anna, *Scotland BC*, Historic Buildings and Monuments, 1988.

Robertson, D. M., *Longniddry*, East Lothian district library, 1993.

Roland, Paxton and Shipway, Jim, *Scotland Lowlands and Borders, Civil Engineering Heritage*, Institution of Civil Engineers, 2008.

Scottish Natural Heritage, *East Lothian and the Borders – A Landscape Fashioned by Geology*, British Geological Survey, 1997.

Sommerville, Robert, *General View of the Agriculture of East Lothian*, G. and W. Nicol, booksellers to His Majesty,1805.

The Best of East Lothian's Wildlife, East Lothian Council, 2011.

The Royal Commission on Ancient and Historical Monuments and Construction, Eighth Report with Inventory of Monuments in the County of East Lothian, RCAHMS, 1924.

Skinner, B. C., *The Lime Industry in the Lothians*, Studies in Local History, University of Edinburgh, 1969.

Smith, Robin, *The Making of Scotland – A Comprehensive Guide to The Growth of Scotland's Cities, Towns and Villages*, Canongate, 2001.

Smith, Sally, *Cockburnspath – A History of a People and Place*, Dunglass Mill Press, 1999.

Snodgrass, Catherine P., *The County of East Lothian – The Third Statistical Account of Scotland*, Oliver and Boyd, 1953.

Statham, Craig, *Lost East Lothian*, Birlinn, 2011.

The First (1789–1799) and New (1841) Statistical Accounts of Scotland, Haddington, Volumes 1, 2, and 3, The Grimsay Press, 2008.

Towill, Edwin Sprott, *Saints of Scotland*, Saint Andrew Press, 1978.

Tuckwell Press, *Haddington Royal Burgh – A History and Guide*, Tuckwell Press, 1997.

Urwin, Gerald, *Feat of Arms or The Siege of Haddington*, Calder Wood Press, 2006.

Westwood, Jennifer and Kingshill, Sophia, *The Lore of Scotland – A Guide to Scottish Legends*, Random House, 2009.

Whyte, Ian and Whyte, Kathleen, *Discovering East Lothian*, John Donald Publishers, 1988.

Yeoman, Peter, *Pilgrimage in Medieval Scotland*, B. T. Batsford, Historic Scotland, 1999.

MAGAZINES

East Lothian Life, issues 3–95, PJ Design.

WEBSITES

British Newspaper archive – britishnewspaperarchive.co.uk

Canmore – canmore.org.uk – online catalogue to Scotland's archaeology, buildings, industrial and maritime heritage.

East Lothian Council – www.eastlothian.gov.uk (see under sections: archaeology, history, tourism, museums and visitor attractions. This has an excellent set of maps of East Lothian footpaths, which can be downloaded.)

Scotland.forestry.gov.uk/images (East Lothian section). Native woodland survey of Scotland, East Lothian.

Acknowledgements

Thanks to Ross Dimsey for editing, formatting and assisting with the text. Thanks also to Gordon Patterson, Peter Ramage and David Elder (Haddington Local History Society), and, Pauline Smeed (Dunbar and District History Society).